PUBLICATIONS OF THE McMASTER UNIVERSITY
ASSOCIATION FOR 18TH-CENTURY STUDIES
VOLUME ONE

The Varied Pattern: Studies in the 18th Century

EDITORS

PETER HUGHES · DAVID WILLIAMS

A. M. HAKKERT, LTD.
TORONTO
1971

Copyright © 1971 by A. M. Hakkert Ltd.
All rights reserved

Set in Aldine Roman and Caslon Antique
by A. M. Hakkert Ltd.
Toronto, Canada
Printed in the Netherlands

Design by Hilary Norman

Standard Book Number
88866-505-9
Library of Congress Catalogue Card Number
70-159260

A. M. Hakkert Ltd.
76 Charles Street West
Toronto 5, Ontario
Canada

Preface

This volume is the first in a series that will explore the range and diversity of eighteenth-century culture. The articles that follow were first presented and discussed at seminars and symposia sponsored by the Association for Eighteenth Century Studies of McMaster University. The reader will note differences of field and approach, but he will also recognize, we believe, shared cultural traditions that justify such interdisciplinary studies. This common understanding, which in the period itself permitted dialogue between enemies and friends, opponents and allies, should now encourage a similar dialogue among modern scholars.

The links that join the articles that follow account for the way in which we have grouped and edited them. We have placed together articles whose subjects reflect the major themes of our year's work: Imaginary Voyages, for example, Art History, and Political Economy. We have also presented articles whose affinities with one another have become clear in retrospect: literary genres, religious history, education and social development in Spain, France and Russia. Although we have maintained a consistent form of reference, we have allowed each author to adopt the style and scholarly form most appropriate to his subject.

We gratefully acknowledge the support and encouragement that we have received from McMaster University, in particular from Vice-President William F. Hellmuth and Dean Alexander G. McKay. It would be impossible to thank singly each of those members of the Association who have given help and advice. We should like, however, to express our thanks to Dr. Paul Walton who undertook the preparation of the photographic plates that appear in this volume. We should like finally to thank Joan Murray, Anya Humphrey and Katharine Peacock of A. M. Hakkert Ltd. for the efficiency and understanding that they have shown in the preparation of this book for publication.

P.H.
Toronto, 1971   *D.W.*

List of Contributors

John Browning, Department of Romance Languages, McMaster University

Roger Clark, Department of Romance Languages, Memorial University, Newfoundland

Goldwin French, Department of History, McMaster University

Nigel Glendinning, Department of Spanish, Trinity College, University of Dublin

Donald Greene, Department of English, University of Southern California

Henry Guerlac, Society for the Humanities, Cornell University

Harold Guite, Department of Classics, McMaster University

Samuel Hollander, Department of Political Economy, University of Toronto

Peter Hughes, Department of English, McMaster University

Robert Johnston, Department of History, McMaster University

Samuel Macey, Department of English, University of Victoria

James Noxon, Department of Philosophy, McMaster University

Ronald Paulson, Department of English, The Johns Hopkins University

Ronald Rosbottom, Department of Romance Languages, University of Pennsylvania

Aubrey Rosenberg, Department of French, Victoria College, University of Toronto

Robert Rosenblum, Institute of Fine Arts, New York University

Peter Swann, Royal Ontario Museum, Toronto

Gordon Vichert, Department of English, McMaster University

David Williams, Department of Romance Languages, McMaster University

Contents

ix

●

●

Plate 1. Raphael, *Paul Preaching at Athens.* London, Victoria and Albert Museum.

Plate 2. Hogarth, *Paul before Felix.*

Plate 3. Hogarth, *Paul before Felix Burlesqued.*

Plate 4. Hogarth, *A Harlot's Progress,* Plate 6.

Plate 5. Hogarth, *A Laughing Audience.*

Plate 6. J. Wright of Derby, *A Philosopher giving a Lecture on the Orrery.* Coll. of Mr. and Mrs. Paul Mellon.

Plate 7. J. Wright of Derby, *An Experiment on a Bird in an Airpump.* London, Tate Gallery.

Plate 8. J. Wright of Derby, *An Academy by Lamplight.* Coll. of Mr. and Mrs. Paul Mellon.

Plate 9. B. West, *Death of General Wolfe.* R.A., 1771. Ottawa, National Gallery of Canada.

Plate 10. J. Reynolds, *Lady Charlotte Spencer.* c. 1775. Coll. Edouard de Rothschild.

Plate 11. J. Barry, *Portrait of Edmund Burke and the Artist in the Character of Ulysses and his Companions escaping from the Cave of Polyphemus.* R.A., 1776. Cork, Museum and Art Gallery.

Plate 12. R. Wilson, *Cader Idris: Llyn-y-Cau.* c. 1774. London, National Gallery.

Plate 13. G. Barret, *Powerscourt Waterfall.* c. 1764. Liverpool, Walker Art Gallery (Roscoe Collection).

Plate 14. G. Barret (and S. Gilpin), *Llanberis Lake, North Wales.* R.A., 1777. Nottingham, Castle Museum and Art Gallery.

Plate 15. J. Wright of Derby, *Vesuvius in Eruption.* 1774. Derby, Museum and Art Gallery.

Plate 16. W. Marlowe, *Lake Geneva.* c. 1765-68. London, Art Market.

Plate 17. W. Hodges, *A Crater in the Pacific.* c. 1772-75. Brighton, Art Gallery.

Plate 18. W. Hodges, *The Monuments of Easter Island.* c. 1772-75. Greenwich, National Maritime Museum.

Plate 19. J. Webber, *Poedooa.* c. 1777. Greenwich, National Maritime Museum.

The Varied Pattern:
Studies in the 18th Century

The Education of Lemuel Gulliver

The sum total of this epistle is this: it is to tear down, and
to pull out, and to destroy all wisdom and righteousness as
man understands them. This is to happen whatever regard
they may have in men's judgment, even in our own
convictions, and no matter with what deep sincerity they
are practiced. After that its purpose is to set and establish,
even to magnify, sin, no matter if we used to think that it
was not there and could not be there. It was on this
account that St. Augustine said . . . 'This investigation is
almost its sole concern, fought for so bravely and in so
many ways as almost to wear out the reader. But at the
same time it is a fatigue that is profitable and health-
giving.'   —Martin Luther,
        Commentary on the Epistle to the Romans

Can we not see that this voyage is not what we need to be
cured of, but that it is itself a natural way of healing our
own appalling state of alienation called normality?
        —R.D. Laing, *The Politics of Experience*

Lemuel Gulliver is a decent, sober, solid Englishman, a
representative of the best that western European civilization
(English brand) has produced up to the time of his adventures.
He is in every sense a normal, middle-of-the-road human being.
He is of the middle class, the son of a small landowner with
enough ready capital to give his children a fairly good start in
life; a moderately successful practitioner of a respectable
profession; middle-brow — a hard-working student at a respectable but not outstanding Cambridge college, later a conscientious reader, in his spare time, of "the best authors, ancient and
modern." He is even the middle one of five brothers. In his late
twenties and established in his profession, he marries, for
prudential reasons — "being advised to alter my condition" —

the second daughter of a respectable tradesman, who brings him a respectable dowry, and he settles down to practice his profession and raise a family of faceless but no doubt respectable children.

He is a "man of good will," fulfilling his role in society responsibly, trying to treat those around him decently and keep on friendly terms with them. He is extremely sensitive to the mores of his society and to the opinion of those around him: his deep concern, in the predicaments he finds himself in when he arrives in Lilliput and Brobdingnag, to perform his excretory acts in privacy is amusing; less amusing — frightening, indeed — is the way in which, when the Lilliputian authorities unjustly impeach him of high treason and threaten his life, he seems more than half convinced of their rightness and unwilling to put up any but the feeblest defense of himself — a phenomenon noted in some modern political trials and sometimes attributed to "brainwashing."

His naive honesty comes out in his narrative, filled with closely observed, indeed often irrelevant, detail, and in his straightforward, masculine prose — colloquial and unpretentious, though "educated"; sometimes a little clumsy, but all the more appealing for that. Indeed, when we have been in his company for a short time, our hearts warm to him, we "identify" with him. He is "our sort" — the average man, *l'homme moyen sensuel*, the man-on-the-street, the salt of the earth, one of those (we say complacently to ourselves) who have made modern Britain and America what they are — and what Swift wants to happen is that we identify with him so completely that we live through the same experiences he does and undergo the same painful process of re-education that he does.

For he is one of us — one of those whose epitaph was written by T.S. Eliot, "There lived decent, godless people, / Their only monument an asphalt road / And a thousand lost golf balls." Swift significantly bestows on him the name "*Gulliver*." He knows of no values beyond those he has absorbed from his own cultural environment, one of the chief being a profound complacency that his own modern white

Anglo-Saxon Protestant culture is the acme of human achievement, and that any mode of thinking and behaving that differs strikingly from it is *a priori* inferior. It is to him — to us — that Swift and Eliot and a thousand other prophets and preachers, from Job and Jeremiah and Ezekiel, through Paul and Augustine and Francis of Assisi and Savonarola and the author of *Everyman* and Donne and Wesley, down to certain "radical" novelists and poets of today, address their message: "decency," respectability, conformity, unquestioning acceptance of the norms of the "civilized" society around us is not enough.

For Gulliver is dangerous. The proof of this is the history of the vaunted "western civilization" which he and his fellows constitute — which we constitute — a history which, as the King of Brobdingnag tells him, has hitherto consisted of "a heap of conspiracies, rebellions, murders, massacres, revolutions, banishments, the very worst effects that avarice, faction, hypocrisy, perfidiousness, cruelty, rage, madness, hatred, envy, lust, malice, and ambition could produce." If the history of the seventeenth century could be so described — and it can — what would Swift have written of the history of the twentieth, when the "small pittance of *reason*" bestowed on the Gullivers has been used "to aggravate our *natural* corruptions," and, where the seventeenth century produced its hundreds of thousands of victims of gunpowder and primitive instruments of torture, to escalate the figure into tens of millions with the help of megaton bombs and nuclear warheads and napalm and gas chambers? Let us not be taken in by Gulliver's agreeable surface. Heinrich Himmler, too, was just such a "man of good will," a suburban Sunday School teacher in appearance and personality, in the most conscientious and unselfish way dedicating his very capable mind and administrative talents to the fulfillment of Hitler's "final solution," perfectly assured that he was acting for the good of his country and "civilization" in general. And then let us ask ourselves in what way our own fundamental values differ from those of Gulliver and Himmler, and what guarantee we have that in similar circumstances our own minds would not work in the same way.

Is this too harsh a comparison for the likable and

"inoffensive" Lemuel Gulliver? To be sure, much of the time we see him to good advantage. This is particularly so during the First Voyage where he is allowed to look down on a swarm of miniaturized Gullivers acting out, *en masse*, the political events of his own day. Though Gulliver of course is not yet able to make the connection, what he sees is a fairly accurate reproduction of the history of Britain in the reigns of Anne and George I – and of other countries and later times as well. The Lilliputians and Blefuscans refuse to believe that the universe contains "any other regions than the two great empires of Lilliput and Blefuscu"; nothing is more important to each of them than that it maintain its military superiority over the other, and, when opportunity offers, that it attempt to obtain complete domination over the other. The idea that both might learn to live on terms of equality, amicably sharing their tiny universe between them, strikes them as absurd and abhorrent. The power struggle has acquired an ideological basis in the great debate over the morality or immorality of breaking eggs at the big or the little end, which has so far produced eleven thousand martyrs for their respective beliefs; and the shallowness of a mere literal interpretation of the great text in their Bible, *"All true believers shall break their eggs at the convenient end,"* is rejected with contempt by both devout Big-Endians and Little-Endians.

Conformity to accepted ideology is always preferred to what is pragmatically successful: Gulliver's use of unconventional means to save the Empress from being incinerated in her palace results in her becoming his bitter enemy, and prepares the way for his being sentenced to blindness or death for his treason in refusing to use methods of "overkill" to reduce the Blefuscans to complete subjection. Individuals achieve political power not because of their qualifications for it but because of their ability to entertain and flatter those who confer political power. Swift's satire against Marlborough and the Whigs, who wished to use Britain's military might to crush France permanently and refused to consider a peace that would allow France to coexist with Britain, is obvious; so is the satire against methods of selection of high political figures in the days of

Walpole and the Duke of Newcastle. But the modern reader will
have no difficulty in recognizing the equal applicability of the
satire to the twentieth century. Gulliver is the Lilliputians'
atomic bomb, and there were those who, when the West
acquired it, urged that it be used exactly as the Lilliputians
wished to use Gulliver. The importance of the television
"image" in modern elections is not very different from the
importance of dexterous rope dancing in the choice of
Lilliputian statesmen.

In the First Voyage, Gulliver's greater physical size seems to
give him temporarily a wider mental perspective than that of
the Lilliputians, and enables him to see the folly and immorality
of their values (though he is still far from the crucial recognition
that at home they are his own values). In the Second Voyage,
however, a revelation takes place — to the reader, if not yet to
Gulliver. Gulliver is himself viewed as a Lilliputian through the
eyes of the giants; what the King of Brobdingnag sees, as he
holds the arrogant little Englishman on the palm of his hand, is
precisely what the Gulliver of Part I saw in the Lilliputians. And
what the King, and we, see is not pleasant. Although it is
generally said that the Fourth Voyage is the crucial and most
shocking part of Swift's work (and it is indeed important), it
can be argued that the physical filth and petty malice of the
Yahoos are small matters, when judged by the criterion of their
total harmful effect, compared with the horrifying passage
where Gulliver, the representative of "western civilization,"
describes with the utmost relish the virtues of gunpowder
(today, it would be nuclear weapons):

> The largest balls thus discharged would not only destroy
> whole ranks of an army at once, but batter the strongest
> walls to the ground, sink down ships with a thousand men
> in each to the bottom of the sea; and when linked together
> by a chain, would cut through masts and rigging, divide
> hundreds of bodies in the middle . . . would rip up the
> pavements, tear the houses to pieces, burst and throw
> splinters on every side, dashing out the brains of all who
> came near.

Even more shocking — more nauseating than any piece of Yahoo behavior — is the devastatingly superior sneer by the "enlightened," the "civilized" Gulliver at the King's appalled refusal of his offer of this simple means to absolute power: "The miserable effects of a confined education . . . A strange effect of narrow principles and short views! . . . a nice, unnecessary scruple, whereof we in Europe can have no conception." And Gulliver magnanimously forgives the King's short-sightedness on the grounds that he is after all only a backwoods prince, without access to the sources of enlightenment that have given Gulliver his superior education. This, let it be repeated, is what we get when we scratch the pleasant surface of the decent, considerate, "civilized" Gulliver — the man who is responsible for the history of the modern western world, which in the twentieth century has produced atrocities, Passchendaele, Auschwitz, Buchenwald, Hiroshima, Biafra, that would have been beyond Swift's darkest imagination.

What is wrong with Gulliver? The King of Brobdingnag states it clearly: "He was amazed how so impotent and grovelling an insect as I . . . could entertain such inhuman ideas, and in so familiar a manner as to appear *wholly unmoved* at all the scenes of blood and desolation which I had painted." The trouble is an inadequacy of emotional response toward his fellow creatures, a lack of feeling, a callous heart. Gulliver is later to proclaim in words which are devastatingly ironic when juxtaposed with this passage, "There were few greater lovers of mankind, at that time, than myself." Gulliver's love for the abstraction "mankind" may be great, but clearly his love for the individual John, Peter, Thomas who are maimed and slaughtered by his cannon balls is minimal. Rather than such a "philanthropist," the reader is forced to conclude, it is preferable to be such a "misanthropist" as Swift proclaimed himself, who has nothing but detestation for the Gulliverian brand of "love of mankind" and its consequences.

We may pass quickly here over Part III, the voyage to Laputa and its contiguous regions. This is not because the Struldbruggs, and the "scientists," isolated from any reality outside their own crackpot minds, have no bearing on the issues at hand. They have a great deal. It is wrong to say, as many have said, that Part III demonstrates Swift's reactionary distrust of modern science. A hater of modern science and technology could not have put such words as the following into the mouth of the King of Brobdingnag, who is obviously Swift's spokesman: "Few things delighted him so much as new discoveries in art or in nature" (though gunpowder, as Gulliver describes its use, is not one of them), and "he gave it as his opinion that whoever could make two ears of corn or two blades of grass to grow upon a spot of ground where only one grew before would deserve better of mankind, and do more essential service to his country than the whole race of politicians put together." What is wrong with the academicians of Lagado is that they are not scientific enough. The scientist as Bacon conceived him, and as the King of Brobdingnag conceives him, is like the bee in *The Battle of the Books*, distrusting, with scientific humility, the ability of his own unaided mind to arrive at useful knowledge, but industriously seeking out, through observation and experiment, that knowledge which the external world, God's creation, affords him. The Lagadoans are like the spider who boasts "of being obliged to no other creature, but of drawing, and spinning out all" from his ingenious mind.

But in Part III, Gulliver, for whatever reason, virtually disappears as a character, as the protagonist of the book, for the time being, and is replaced by a featureless observer. We resume the education of Gulliver in Part IV. Here the breakthrough is made, the shell is penetrated, the defenses collapse. How is this achieved? We have no right, of course, to expect Swift to provide us with a realistic explanation; he is not writing a tragic drama but an allegory, and it would be perfectly legitimate for him merely to indicate arbitrarily that, for the purposes of his exposition, a change of heart takes place in Gulliver, never mind how. But in fact something rather like a credibly motivated dramatic crisis does occur. At the beginning of the Part, Gulliver has been marooned by his mutinous crew and left to starve on a presumably deserted island. Seeking food and shelter, he is attacked by the nauseous herd of Yahoos. For the first time in his life he becomes fully conscious of the meaning of evil: the world seems to hold nothing for him but rejection, hostility, alienation. Then, to his astonishment and joy, he is rescued from his terror and loneliness by the kind Houyhnhnms, who are in no way alarmed or made hostile by his strangeness ("I was a stranger, and ye took me in"). One of the most moving, and significant, passages in the work is Gulliver's speech humbly pleading with the horses for help; every shred of his worldly-wise complacency is gone — this is unaccommodated man speaking, a poor, bare, forked animal:

> Gentlemen, if you be conjurers, as I have good cause to believe, you can understand any language; therefore I make bold to let your worships know that I am a poor distressed Englishman, driven by his misfortunes upon your coast, and I entreat one of you to let me ride upon his back, as if he were a real horse, to some house or village, where I can be relieved. In return of which favour I will make you a present of this knife and bracelet.

It is the first time in the whole work that we have heard Gulliver speak in a tone of such real emotion; there has been an entire change of idiom, as in Lear's "O, I have ta'en too little care of this!" With suffering, humility comes, and with it, in the end, wisdom.

When he gets to know the Houyhnhnms' language and their way of life, his admiration increases. Families are not rent by hostilities and jealous squabbles as in England. Possessiveness toward their children is unknown; they have as much affection for their neighbors' children as for "their own" (whatever "one's own" means, as applied to the children one has biologically produced). They believe that marriage should be undertaken in the most serious spirit, with a view to the future happiness of the couple, their children, and the community: neither monetary considerations nor "love" (that is, temporary infatuation) enters into the arrangements, and their marriages are uniformly happy. They do not make a great public fuss about the fact of death, but call it "retiring to their first mother." Business and government are conducted simply, quietly and efficiently. They have no words in their language for "lie" and "pride."

Gulliver wishes desperately to stay with the Houyhnhnms and continue to share their life of quiet, happy fulfillment. Able at last to see the life of Yahoodom from an external viewpoint, he is filled with horror at the thought of descending again into the hell of animosity, cruelty and misery from which he has been rescued. But it cannot be, for the Houyhnhnms do not exist on the face of this earth. Their name means, we are told, *"the perfection of nature"* — the full realization of the potential for good which God placed in his creation. But, according to orthodox Christian teaching, the perfection, and perfectibility, of nature came to an end simultaneously with the Fall in the Garden, when sin — the original sin of pride — entered the world. The Houyhnhnms, who have no pride, are in the state of innocence which has been unattainable by man since that time. So Gulliver (like Adam) must be ejected; and, like Adam, he at first falls into despair at the thought of what he has lost. He faints at the touch of his wife; and, at the sight of his children, "when I began to consider that by copulating with one of the Yahoo species I had become a parent of more, it struck me with the utmost shame, confusion, and horror."

Modern critics have raised their hands in shocked condemnation at Gulliver's repudiation of that great WASP middle-class virtue, family "togetherness," and have seen it as clear evidence of his "madness," contracted from too prolonged association with the Houyhnhnms, whose simple, quiet, affectionate way of life they believe Swift cannot possibly want us to admire. ("There is no need, I think, to suppress a feeling of amusement as we read of their placid, awkward domesticity," one of the most influential of such critics writes — we of the century of the nuclear bomb and the gas chamber need not suppress our amusement at them! The tone is irresistibly reminiscent of Gulliver's "The miserable effects of a confined education.") Yet let us imagine an analogy: a decent German, who during the whole of the Hitler régime has been marooned, let us say, on a remote South Sea island, knowing nothing of what has been going on, is suddenly returned to his family, and finds them living a complacent existence on the outskirts of Auschwitz or

Buchenwald, ignoring or tolerating the activities that take place there. He might well faint away at their touch. The sole difference with the Gulliver family is that the slaughterhouses of Blenheim and Malplaquet were somewhat farther removed in distance. Perhaps madness consists in *not* fainting at the realization that one is a member of a race which is capable of perpetrating such horrors. It is also well to remember the saying of Jesus, in Swift's Bible, "If any man come to me, and hate not his father, and mother, and wife, and children, and brethren, and sisters, yea, and his own life also, he cannot be my disciple," and the example of Christian, in *The Pilgrim's Progress*, a work recommended by Swift, who, when his wife and children cried after him to return to the City of Destruction, put his fingers in his ears and ran on, crying "Life! Life! Eternal life!" The modern reader may, if he wishes, condemn the point of view expressed by Jesus and Bunyan — possibly because he does not understand it — but he should not think that, because he does so, Swift did.

Gulliver's outburst of hysteria when he returns to the human world has analogies in other classic processes of re-education. In the orthodox Christian theory of religious conversion the necessary first step to eventual salvation is "conviction of sin": in psychotherapy it is the patient's recognition of his imperfection, the stripping from his eyes of the ego-bolstering delusions, the pleasing but erroneous "image" of himself that he cherishes but that continually causes trouble for him by its failure to correspond with reality. The first result of this step is despondency, self-hatred, "the dark night of the soul." Yet that despondency is only the beginning, not the end, of the process of conversion or of psychotherapy. The next step is to accept the truth about one's sinfulness, one's moral and characterological weakness, to learn to live with that truth, and having done so, nevertheless work to improve oneself, recognizing always that it will be a slow, painful process with many backslidings.

So it is with Gulliver. This reaction of despondency is, of course (as critics of *Gulliver* have pointed out), the result of pride, the shock to one's ego at the thought that essentially one is no less fallible than the rest of the sinful human race (the hypothetical German might well ask himself, "Had I been here, would I have resisted Hitlerism any more than my relations did?").

But Gulliver's outburst of horror and loathing when he is returned to the human world is not the end of the story, though an astonishing number of modern critics have treated it as if it were — in spite of Swift's attempt to guide them by inserting in his final chapter heading the statement *"The author ... proposeth his manner of living for the future."* We are allowed to see Gulliver five years after his return, in his "little garden at Redriff" (like *Candide, Gulliver's Travels* ends in a garden, as the book of Genesis begins in one), where he describes his present way of life to us. It consists of three occupations: "to apply those excellent lessons of virtue which I learned among the Houyhnhnms, to instruct the Yahoos of my own family [i.e., household] as far as I shall find them docible [teachable] animals, to behold my figure often in a glass," in order to remind himself that he is a Yahoo.

This is the perennial Christian program: in our own behavior to strive for "the imitation of Christ" (knowing that we, as sinful human beings, can never attain such perfection); to try to teach others around us to do the same; constantly to mortify our pride by reminding ourselves of our fallen, imperfect condition — "If we say that we have no sin, we deceive ourselves, and the truth is not in us," as Swift daily repeated out of his Prayer Book. Or, as a modern poet has skillfully summed up the doctrine of original sin and the Great Commandment, on both of which the teaching of Swift, a perfectly orthodox Protestant clergyman, rests, "You shall love your crooked neighbor/ With your crooked heart." It is not an ideal that will be attained overnight (or in six months, as the Letter to Richard Sympson, which Swift added to the work in 1735, ironically points out), and it can never be attained completely by even the greatest human saint, in whom some trace of the original sin of pride will always linger. Nevertheless, it is the ideal toward which the Christian is commanded to strive.

The point of the work, then, is the old fundamental one of the Christian (and not only Christian) ethic. As Christian in *The Pilgrim's Progress* realizes at the beginning of that story – he, too, is an ordinary, "decent," average citizen of the City of Destruction – worldly values are not enough. The "inoffensive," "harmless," ordinary member of society who uncritically accepts what he is told by those around him is, in history, responsible for an incredible, horrifying amount of harm; Eliot's "decent, godless people" are desperately in need of re-education, both for their own sake and the sake of those who come into contact with them. That process of re-education may be painful indeed (as Christian's was); but if one's soul is to be saved, if the world is to become less of a Yahooland, it must take place.

The foregoing is, of course, a simplified account of what goes on in the book. Very likely Swift did not sit down to begin writing it with any clear intention of composing a straightforward moral fable. Like *Huckleberry Finn* (which it resembles in a number of ways, not least in being a great moral fable) it is several other things as well. As Mark Twain conceived his book, to begin with, merely as a sequel to the highly popular *Adventures of Tom Sawyer*, Swift may well have thought of *Gulliver* at first as a burlesque of popular, sensation-laden travel books – perhaps specifically of *Robinson Crusoe*, published only two years before Swift began writing – and a satire on the credulity of their readers. His use of minute corroborative detail, intended to give artistic verisimilitude to an otherwise bald and unconvincing narrative is almost indistinguishable from Defoe's.

But he soon becomes engrossed in Gulliver's experiences, as Mark Twain did in Huck's, and for long stretches of the narrative forgets all about the "tall tale" burlesque. At the end of the story, he seems to remember that purpose with a start (as Mark Twain suddenly remembers Tom Sawyer) and inserts some satiric thrusts about Gulliver's "truthfulness" which have helped to muddy the waters of interpretation of the moral fable. Like *Huckleberry Finn*, Swift's book is a cleverly composed narrative of adventure, competent enough in itself to make it attractive to children (and film producers). Furthermore (still like *Huckleberry Finn*) it is often humorous simply for the sake of humor; when Swift thinks of something to laugh at ("Vive la bagatelle!"), he doesn't hesitate to jot it down. No one could argue that the fun poked, for example, at Lilliputian handwriting ("neither from the left to the right, like the Europeans; nor from the right to the left, like the Arabians; nor from up to down, like the Chinese . . . but aslant from one corner of the paper to the other, like our ladies in England") is anything but pure fun, without relevance to the central moral purpose of the work.

Nevertheless, the reason for the greatness of *Gulliver's Travels* is that central moral purpose. Like *Huckleberry Finn* — but far more radically than even that fine work — it is a profoundly, devastatingly subversive book. It leaves intact none of the cherished values of modern western civilization — patriotic "love of country," pride in its history and its political, legal and educational institutions, its conventions of marriage and family life, its attitudes toward longevity and death, its aesthetics of female beauty, its confidence in the wonder-working powers of large scientific research foundations; these, and much more, are pitilessly deflated and shown as shams, disguises for short-sighted human greed, vindictiveness and ego-inflation. Above all, it relentlessly attacks, as the most formidable ancillary of those vices, the complacent assumption that the superior race of *Homo sapiens*, with its divine legacy of "reason," denied to the "lower animals," possesses qualities which must inevitably tend in the direction of virtue and happiness. In reply to shocked protest against such views, Swift has an impregnable argument: "Look at the record. Look at the ghastly toll which your vaunted western 'civilization,' which human nature guided by its own 'superior' instincts, has exacted over the centuries in the form of aggression, oppression, massacres, tortures, public and private misery." And had Swift been able to foresee how greatly human "reason," in the twentieth century, would be able to improve over the seventeenth and eighteenth in the technology of these matters, he would have seen no reason to soften his indictment.

Since that indictment is unanswerable, readers of the work, ever since its first publication, have desperately sought ways to avoid having to face it. The device chiefly used in the eighteenth and nineteenth centuries (though one finds critics as intelligent as Eliot, Leavis and Aldous Huxley still using it well into the twentieth) was an *ad hominem* argument, based on some highly distorted biography of Swift — the work was the product of a "diseased mind." Swift was a "misanthrope," he was insane, therefore what he wrote need not, indeed must not, be taken seriously. Victorian "liberals" like Macaulay and Thackeray become positively hysterical in their denunciation of this madman whose work presents so dangerous a threat to the Victorian pretense that all's right with the world, or, if small corners of imperfection remain in it, the built-in tendency to progress in the human race will soon inevitably eliminate them.

After the cataclysm of World War I, such facile optimism was no longer tenable. Nevertheless, those literary students in whose time the incredible Yahooisms of 1914 and beyond were inescapable realities have generally (with a few distinguished exceptions) been as determined as the Victorians to shut their eyes to what Swift is telling them. The host of ingenious misreadings of the work, of finding "ironies" where Swift is writing in the most deadly seriousness, that have been published in the last few decades passes belief. So multifarious and complex have the subtleties of recent explication of the work become that it is now a commonplace for a commentator to begin with a lamentation about its immense difficulty and sometimes a prediction that its full meaning will always elude the grasp of critics, however penetrating. One writer has even proposed that we should frankly acknowledge that Swift could have had *no* coherent intention in composing a work that so baffles all attempts to elucidate it. This is an odd fate for Swift, who so scathingly pilloried "dark authors" and "those numberless commentators, whose scholastic midwifery hath delivered them of meanings that the authors themselves perhaps never conceived."

A great deal of what has recently passed for criticism of

Gulliver's Travels is not literary criticism at all, for all that its writers make use of critical terms like "irony," *"persona"* and so on, but an attempt to explicate its moral teaching. It is an attempt doomed to failure from the start, since its authors begin by premising the truth of their own moral values – values which, like Gulliver's, they have absorbed from their own contemporary cultural environment and never dream of questioning, but which (like the early Gulliver's) are completely contradictory to Swift's. The result is the bafflement mentioned above: it is as though the Gulliver of the Second Voyage were trying to explicate the King of Brobdingnag's comments on gunpowder in terms of his own assumptions and reconcile them with his own views. Needless to say, Gulliver would have to resort to discovering a great deal of subtle irony in the King's pronouncements, irony that has escaped everyone but the shrewd Gulliver. Modern critics have had to attribute an equal amount of irony to the Reverend Jonathan Swift, Doctor of Sacred Theology, priest and dean, when they discover that he is really satirizing the Houyhnhnms for too careful an observance of the Ten Commandments: how (they ask) can we seriously suppose him to be recommending a way of life so dull, so "sterile," so absurd as that of a group of beings who do not lie, steal or commit adultery?

Swift, as usual, does his best to make his "message" clear. In his letters he gives his opinion of Gulliver – the early "sane," "normal" Gulliver as such critics see him, before he "goes mad" as a result of becoming too much enthralled with the "impossible" values of Houyhnhnms:

> I am not such a prostitute flatterer as Gulliver; whose chief study is to extenuate the vices, and magnify the virtues of mankind, and perpetually dins our ears with the praises of his country, in the midst of corruptions.

In his famous letter to Pope, on his completion of the book, he gives as lucid and unequivocal an explication of his purpose as any author has ever done of any work:

> The chief end I propose to myself in all my labors is to vex the world rather than divert it . . . I have ever hated all

nations, professions, and communities, and all my love is
towards individuals. For instance, I hate the tribe of
lawyers, but I love Counsellor such a one, Judge such a
one, for so with physicians (I will not speak of my own
trade), soldiers, English, Scotch, French, and the rest, but
principally I hate and detest that animal called man,
although I heartily love John, Peter, Thomas, and so
forth. . . . Upon this great foundation of misanthropy
(though not Timon's manner) the whole building of my
Travels is erected; and I never will have peace of mind till
all honest men are of my opinion.

Swift is proclaiming his very proper distrust of abstractions
like "Britain," "France," "America," "the legal profession,"
and above all *"Homo sapiens,"* words which people use to
bolster their egos and for which they are ready to commit
atrocities. But — and this is the point of Swift's remarks to Pope
— one cannot love an abstraction. One can, however, attribute
an inflated value to an abstraction, and then be filled with pride
at the thought of one's own association with it; and many
people have mistaken this cheap emotion of self-congratulation
for love. Pride in one's membership in the "superior" human
race — or a section of it possessing a certain color of skin — in a
nation, a profession, a community, even in a specially favored
"religious" group, is incompatible with love as understood in
the Great Commandment of the Gosepl, "Thou shalt love thy
neighbor as thyself"; and this is why Swift hates the concepts of
"man," "nation" and so on. One's neighbor is John, Peter,
Thomas, not "mankind," "England" (or "America"), "the legal
profession" and the like. It is well to put quotation marks
around such words, for they *are* only words, abstract concepts.
One cannot love a word, an abstraction; one can only love some
individual, concrete object. Man as individual is one thing;
mankind *en masse*, fighting for the "honour" of its "own"
country or profession or color or race, is another. Swift's
"misanthropy" (but "not Timon's manner") is directed, perfectly properly, against the latter, unlike Lemuel Gulliver,
whose proclaimed "love" of the vague concept "mankind" does
not extend to the individual Johns, Peters and Thomases whom

his cannon balls tear to pieces.

Nothing, it would seem, could be clearer. Swift's purpose in the work is not, as many modern students have tried to persuade themselves and others, to confirm us in our complacency about ourselves — to assure us that human life as it is now lived is an admirable compromise between the absurdities of the Houyhnhnms on the one hand and the Yahoos on the other, and that the comfortable, reassuring pre-Houyhnhnm Gulliver (who is so normal, so "sane," so like ourselves) is much preferable to the highly disturbing post-Houyhnhnm Gulliver. Its purpose, Swift says flatly, is *not* to give us comfort; it is to *vex* us — and how the now popular "compromise" interpretation could possibly vex anyone is hard to see.

The book then teaches a "hard," not a "soft" lesson, to use the terms which Professor James Clifford has applied to the two opposing lines of interpretation of the work in the twentieth century. But it would be wrong to push this "hardness" to the point of saying, as has been done, "The book ends in complete negation," "Swift preaches a gospel of entire despair for the human race," or the like. We are, and shall always be, imperfect Yahoos, not perfect Houyhnhnms. Nevertheless Swift clearly tells us that various degrees of Yahooism are possible. The Yahoos of Houyhnhnmland are the descendants of a (possibly English) couple, perhaps shipwrecked there. They have had, to guide them, neither the Houyhnhnms' infallible reason nor, as with some individuals, at least, in Europe, a moral tradition originating outside themselves, but only their corrupt natural instincts; and so, generation by generation, they have deteriorated, physically, intellectually and morally (William Golding's *Lord of the Flies* gives an interesting modern treatment of the same theme). They belong to a lower level of existence than even the Yahoos of England — the Houyhnhnms and Gulliver at first have difficulty in recognizing that they are the same species as Gulliver — though, ironically, as Swift points out, their intellectual degeneracy has preserved them from such atrocities as the greater "reason" of the Europeans enables them to commit.

At the other end of the scale are the Brobdingnagians. They

are still Yahoos, and have their faults and sillinesses, stemming from the sin of pride – they name their capital "Pride of the Universe," and their court ladies and their zoological scholars (who attempt to classify Gulliver) are less than paragons of rationality. Nevertheless, if the Houyhnhnm ideal of perfect virtue is unattainable – as, by definition, any ideal is – Europeans would do well to try to raise themselves at least to the Brobdingnagian level: "I shall say nothing of those remote nations where Yahoos preside, amongst which the least corrupted are the Brobdingnagians, whose wise maxims in morality and government it would be our happiness to observe." Improvement, then, Swift is telling us clearly, is possible; but it will not be suddenly and completely achieved in six months, as the "newly corrupted" Gulliver of the Letter to Sympson thought; nor, certainly, will it be assisted by our closing our eyes to the horrors of the history of "civilized" western man and dwelling on "the dignity of human nature" and the "good" that is inherent in it. It will be achieved only by the program which Swift's book is trying to persuade us to undertake – to make each of us take a long, hard look at things as they really are, to be sickened by them, to recognize the source of these horrors in our overweening concern for our own prestige and our own material welfare at whatever cost in misery to others – our sinful pride – and, continuing to recognize our intrinsic sinfulness (beholding our "figure often in a glass"), work honestly to try to rectify it, however slowly, however painfully, and at whatever cost to our foolish self-esteem. It is, however reluctant every generation has been to accept it, the lesson taught many centuries ago by St. Paul and St. Augustine, by orthodox Christian teachers of morality ever since, and by many wise teachers of morality and mental health outside the Christian tradition.

Donald Greene

Digressions in Imaginary Voyages

The problem of digressions in the novel has been much discussed in recent times, but in the type of novel known as the imaginary voyage, no such attention has been given to the matter. The purpose of this essay is to discuss ways in which digressions in a certain kind of imaginary voyage might be classified. I am not so naïve as to suppose I can provide some all-embracing definition as to what constitutes a digression, but I do hope to show that if the word is to have any real value as a critical term it is important to apply it according to fairly rigorous criteria.

Over the past few years, a reappraisal of the seventeenth- and eighteenth-century novel has been going on, and one of the consequences has been, that episodes that were once regarded as irrelevant digressions are now considered, not only relevant to the purpose of the novel, but sometimes, of the very essence of the work.

Scarron's *Le Roman comique*, published in 1651, contains certain digressions long considered to be *hors d'oeuvre* and inserted purely for purposes of entertainment. But one modern critic has described these episodes as "integral parts of the novel, functionally related to its purpose and structure,"[1] and another authority recently stated that the insertion of these digressions, "loin d'alourdir le roman . . . lui donne au contraire tout son sens."[2] Another example of this new approach to digressions is found in the reassessment of *La Princesse de Clèves*. This famous novel, published in 1678, has always been criticized as structurally unsound because of certain supposedly irrelevant sections. But now, the work is considered to be "a

1. E. Simon, "The Function of the Spanish Stories in Scarron's *Roman comique*," *L'Esprit créateur*, III, 1963, pp. 130-136.
2. R. Mortier, "La Fonction des nouvelles dans le *Roman comique*," *Association internationale des études françaises. Cahiers*, XVIII, 1966, pp. 41-51.

carefully constructed whole, in which not only is liaison in a general sense preserved between the elements of the plot, but the traditional device of the digression is used with such a sense of unified purpose that the integrated episodes cease to be digressions at all."[3]

Perhaps the most striking illustration of this change in attitude towards digressions is found in the treatment of Sterne's *Tristram Shandy*, published in 1759. Up to the twentieth century this novel was generally regarded as a series of disconnected anecdotes and irrelevant digressions that completely obscured whatever was supposed to be the author's principal intention, if indeed he had one. But several modern critics now subscribe to the view, originally propounded by Sterne himself in his novel,[4] that there are really no digressions at all in *Tristram Shandy* since there is "no forward-moving architectonic plot from which to digress."[5] And similar views are now held about the structure of Diderot's *Jacques le fataliste*.[6]

Certain types of novels lend themselves better than others to digressive techniques. One can think, for example, of the picaresque novel and its ramifications. And there is also the epistolary form. The imaginary voyage is another kind of novel that lends itself to the inclusion of digressions, but, as I have said, it has been excluded from the sort of critical reappraisal I have been talking about, so that there has been no real discussion as to how digressions in imaginary voyages should be treated. What I propose to do is examine the digressions in a certain type of imaginary voyage and suggest ways in which they might be classified. My remarks will concern, specifically, three French imaginary voyages but perhaps what I have to say will also have some relevance to similar works in other literatures.

3. J.W. Scott, "The 'Digressions' of the *Princesse de Clèves*," *French Studies*, XI, 1957, pp. 315-322.

4. See chapter XXII of the first volume.

5. J. Traugott, ed., *Laurence Sterne. A Collection of Critical Essays*, Englewood Cliffs, N.J., 1968, p. 9.

6. See J.R. Loy's introduction to *Jacques the Fatalist and his Master*, Collier Books, New York, 1962.

The three works to be discussed may be safely classed as utopian and they are generally regarded as most representative of their type. By this I mean that, although few people agree about how the imaginary voyage should be defined,[7] most of us recognize certain categories of imaginary voyages, and the three I shall be talking about are all of the type that embodies a utopian element. They are, first, Gabriel Foigny's La Terre australe connue, which first appeared in 1676 and was later published under the title of Les Avantures de Jacques Sadeur;[8] second, Denis Veiras' Histoire des Sévarambes, first published in 1677;[9] and, finally, Simon Tyssot de Patot's Voyages et avantures de Jaques Massé, which, despite the date 1710 on the title-page of four different editions, first appeared some time between 1714 and 1717.[10]

These three works are usually taken together in any discussion of imaginary voyages and, apart from the voyages of Cyrano de Bergerac, they are probably the best known in seventeenth- and eighteenth-century French literature. They all have a similar narrative technique and structure. They are told in the first person, by the hero, who begins his story with details of his childhood and family background in Europe. In the next section of the novel the hero goes to sea, is shipwrecked on an unknown coast, in the region of Australia, where he discovers an ideal community. Here he spends a number of years, during which time he learns the language, customs, laws, religion, history, and so on of the utopian society. Finally, he leaves the country and returns to Europe.

Now, as with other novels, the first essential when dealing with the digressions in imaginary voyages of this type, is to distinguish between what is a relevant digression and what, in

7. Most of us would agree with the view that "no final inclusive and exclusive definition of the imaginary voyage is possible." This was the conclusion of P.B. Gove, The Imaginary Voyage in Prose Fiction, New York, 1941, p. 175.

8. My references are to the reprint of the novel in F. Lachèvre, Les Successeurs de Cyrano de Bergerac, Paris, 1922, pp. 60-163.

9. My references are to the 1716 edition, published in Amsterdam by Etienne Roger.

10. See my article "The Voyages et avantures de Jacques Massé and the problem of the first edition," Australian Journal of French Studies, No. 3, 1970. I have retained the original form and spelling of all titles.

fact, is of the very essence of the novel. The failure to make this distinction is apparent in the thinking of one critic who stated that "the desire to picture Utopias . . . exercised a disintegrating influence upon all the important *voyages imaginaires*" with the result that they "are broken by digressions germane to the purpose of composition."[11] It seems to me, however, that if the purpose of an imaginary voyage is to depict a utopia, then any episode that is devoted mainly to enhancing our knowledge of that utopia should be regarded not as a digression "germane to the purpose of composition" but as of the very essence of the novel. So that all the discussions about religion, education, government etc., that are so common to this type of novel should be treated not as digressions from some fundamental purpose but as the very purpose itself. And it follows from this, that any episode that only partly contributes to our knowledge of the imaginary society should be treated as a relevant digression. And any episode that contains no information about the utopia should be termed irrelevant.

All this is fine so long as one can be reasonably sure that the author's main intention was to portray a utopia. In practice, however, it is not always possible to be sure of this. For, as one critic has shrewdly observed, there is, in imaginary voyages of this type, "une grosse part de jeu de l'esprit, et moins une courageuse entreprise de critique sociale que l'exploitation d'un genre romanesque."[12] As a general principle, however, if the major portion of the novel is taken up with the period spent by the hero in the utopian community, then we should proceed on the assumption that the author's purpose was to portray a utopia, and we should classify the digressions accordingly.

But what if this initial assumption proves, on closer inspection, to be invalid, or, for some other reason, it is not possible to feel sufficiently certain that the author's purpose was to describe a utopia? Suppose, for example, that an

11. A.J. Tieje, "The Expressed Aim of the Long Prose Fiction from 1579 to 1740," *Journal of English and Germanic Philology*, XI, July 1912, pp. 402-432.
12. See Henry Peyre's review of E. von der Mühll's *Denis Veiras et son "Histoire des Sévarambes" (1677-1679)*; Paris 1938, *The Romanic Review*, III, 1939, pp. 302-304.

imaginary voyage is largely devoted to the utopian element but that, on analysis, this element is found to be full of irrelevant digressions. Then it is no longer so clear what the author intended. Or take the case of an imaginary voyage in which the utopia does not occupy a major portion of the novel, but is simply one stage in the hero's travels and adventures. In situations such as these, our system of classifying the digressions according to their degree of relevance to the purpose of the novel, is inadequate, and we are obliged to look for some other way of dealing with the digressions.

One obvious alternative is to classify them according to their degree of relevance to the narrative. For we should not forget, whatever may have been the author's other intention, his aim was also, and perhaps primarily, to tell a story. The imaginary voyage is, as stated, a type of novel, and while it is true that the narrative is often simply a framework for other elements in the novel, this is not always the case. The hero is frequently an active participant in the affairs of the utopian society and the adventures he experiences prior to his discovery of the unknown country are often continued during his residence in that country. This means that an episode that is irrelevant to the portrait of a utopia may be an essential part of the narrative. So that it is not sufficient to classify the digressions in only one way, and at least two kinds of relevance must be taken into account.

These two approaches will, I think, enable one to handle most of the digressions that occur in imaginary voyages that embody a utopian element. But there will, sometimes, still be episodes that are not susceptible to either kind of classification — episodes that seem irrelevant both to the utopian element and to the narrative framework. In this case it is necessary to examine the other elements of the novel and study their relationship to the novel as a whole. These episodes, for example, may have something to do with the tone or mood of the novel or of a particular section. They may be inserted purely for entertainment or for a change of pace or subject matter. Their degree of relevance to the novel will perhaps best be determined by their quantity and by how much the novel is affected if they are removed. Let me try and clarify these general observations by applying them to the three specific imaginary voyages I have cited.

As already pointed out, the works of Foigny, Veiras and Tyssot de Patot are ostensibly similar from a narrative and structural viewpoint but, as we shall see, a closer examination of their methods of composition reveals important differences. What I hope to show is that Foigny's *La Terre australe connue* provides a simple illustration of an imaginary voyage in which the main purpose was clearly to portray a utopia, and I also hope to show that this novel is characterized by an absence of digressions; Veiras' *Histoire des Sévarambes* is a more complex affair in which the main purpose becomes less clear as the work progresses, and in which there is a variety of digressions; Tyssot de Patot's *Voyages et avantures de Jaques Massé* provides an example of an imaginary voyage in which the utopian element is of secondary significance, and in which there is an abundance of irrelevant digressions.

Foigny's imaginary voyage comprises one volume and is divided into fourteen chapters. The first three chapters, about one fifth of the novel, are taken up with biographical details and adventures that occur before the discovery of the unknown country. Jacques Sadeur, the hero, was born at sea. The ship was wrecked off the coast of Spain and his parents were drowned. The orphan, who, incidentally, was a hermaphrodite, was eventually adopted by a Portuguese countess who brought him up and gave him a good education. One day, as he was walking along the coast, he was seized by pirates who carried him off. The pirate vessel was destroyed in a storm and our hero was picked up by another ship bound for the East Indies. The ship stopped at the Cape of Good Hope where he took the opportunity of exploring the Congo. He described the appearance and way of life of the inhabitants, with comments on the flora and fauna. After this he rejoined the ship which was wrecked off the coast of Madagascar. He managed to reach a small island where he was attacked by various wild and unusual animals and birds. He took to the water again to escape these dangers and reached another island which turned out to be a whale. After further hair-raising adventures he was seized by a giant bird that carried him to the shores of an unknown Australian country. These first three chapters, then, contain a mixture of realistic and fantastic elements. The next nine chapters, that is, most of the rest of the book, are occupied with the hero's life among the Australians who, by a happy coincidence, were also hermaphrodites. Each of the chapters in this section is devoted to providing information about some aspect of the imaginary society, whether for satirical, didactic, or other purposes. One chapter deals with the geographical and topographical description of the land, another with the constitution and customs of the society, and another with the religion. Other chapters discuss the attitude of these people towards life and death, their sporting and other activities, the language they speak, the animals and birds native to the area, certain scientific and other curiosities, and the problem of war. The last two chapters, about one tenth of the novel, deal with the hero's escape from the Australian society on the back of a bird, his stay on the island of Madagascar with a description of the place, and his eventual return to Europe.

According to one authority, "the complete lack of any unified plan in La Terre australe connue precludes any attempt to generalize about the purpose of the book."[13] It is true that there are inconsistencies in Foigny's utopian community but, for the purpose of classifying the digressions, this is of no account. We are not concerned with why Foigny portrayed a utopia or what he intended it to represent, but simply whether or not his intention was to depict one. And since the major portion of the book is devoted to a description of this imaginary society we can assume, on the basis of quantity alone, that the author's purpose was to portray a utopia. If we classify the episodes in this section of the novel according to the amount of information they provide about the Australian society, we discover only two short passages that are not wholly devoted to enhancing our knowledge of this society. One of

13. G. Atkinson, *The Extraordinary Voyage in French Literature before 1700*, New York, 1920, p. 82.

them is an account of some scientific inventions which are all of a fantastic nature and in sharp contrast to the otherwise realistic portrayal of the society.[14] But although this episode contributes nothing to our knowledge of the society, it does contribute to the non-realistic element of the narrative. So we have here an example of a digression that is irrelevant to the purpose of portraying a utopia but relevant to the narrative. The other episode that, at first glance, seems out of place in the utopian section, involves the hero who, in the course of a battle, displays affection for a girl in the enemy camp.[15] This incident is clearly essential to the narrative since it is because of Sadeur's attachment to this girl, who is not a hermaphrodite, that he is condemned to death. And it is because of this sentence of death that he decides to leave the country. But the incident also enlarges our knowledge of the people in that it provides an example of their inhuman attitude towards their enemies and is an illustration of the inflexibility of their laws.

There are only two digressions in Foigny's novel, that, according to my system of classification, could be regarded as irrelevant both to the utopian element and to the narrative framework. Both these digressions occur outside the utopian section, one before the discovery of the country and one when the hero has left it. These two sections are the one describing the African Congo and the one dealing with Madagascar.[16] If they were removed from the novel the narrative would be unaffected. These episodes do, however, contribute to the attempt to provide a realistic tone to the narrative since they are concerned with real places, and the accounts of them are based on genuine travel reports. So that, although they are irrelevant to the narrative framework and to the main purpose of the novel they play an important role in the attempt at authenticity. Foigny's novel, therefore, provides a good example of an imaginary voyage in which digressions are conspicuously absent and in which the main purpose was to describe a utopia.

14. Lachèvre, *op. cit.*, pp. 127-128.
15. *Ibid.*, p. 146.
16. These sections occur in chapters two and fourteen.

Veiras' *Histoire des Sévarambes* is a much longer work than that of Foigny. It comprises two volumes which are divided into parts instead of chapters. The first volume is in three parts and the second in two. About the first eighth of the book is taken up with biographical details and with events that occur prior to the discovery of the utopian community. The hero, Captain Siden, like Foigny's hero, travelled on a ship bound for the East Indies which was wrecked off some unknown coast in the Austral region. Captain Siden organized the survivors who searched for food, built stockades etc., and became an established community. Since there were, among the survivors, four times as many men as women, Captain Siden decided, in order to avoid trouble, to set up a polyandrous society. We are first introduced to the Sevarambians when Siden sends out a party to explore the country, and the men return accompanied by an official of the utopian society. The rest of the first volume and all of the second volume, except for a few lines at the very end, are devoted to accounts of various aspects of the Sevarambian society — their origins, government, laws, education, religion, language, and the like. On the basis of quantity alone, therefore, we can assume that the author's intention was to portray a utopia.

There are, however, five episodes that appear to have no relevance to this purpose. They all occur in the second volume, they are all fairly lengthy and, together, they account for about one quarter of the second volume.[17] The first episode tells how two Sevarambians managed to sleep with their girl friends before they were married; the second concerns a dispute between a mathematician and a painter; the third is a fairly straightforward love story of the boy meets girl variety, the fourth is a dissertation on poetry and prose, and the last is another love story involving the struggle of three men to gain the hand of the Viceroy's daughter. One critic has argued that "the love episodes . . . have a more or less vital connection with the main thread of the narrative,"[18] but it seems to me that

17. Pages 20-34, 40-48, 80-98, 249-258, 267-276.
18. R.E. Tieje, *The Prose Voyage Imaginaire before 1800* (Unpublished dissertation), University of Illinois, 1917, p. 193.

since none of them involves the hero in any way, and since the narrative framework is based on the hero's personal experiences, these episodes are quite irrelevant to the narrative. There is a feeble attempt on the part of the author, to integrate two of these episodes into the narrative but the rest are presented quite unceremoniously. The simple love story, for example, is recounted, because the two lovers were the subject of one of the many oil paintings that hung in the Temple of the Sun. Veiras, himself, referred to the story as a digression. The story of the Viceroy's daughter is introduced with the remark that its unusual nature makes it worthy of the reader's attention.

The function of these digressions is clearly to provide entertainment and a change of pace from the largely factual and realistic account of the laws and customs of the Sevarambians. But they also serve another more practical purpose. Since it was, and still is, the general practice to publish volumes of equal length, it was necessary for Veiras to find some method of prolonging the utopian section. And the irrelevant episodes provide this necessary padding. The implication is, however, that by the second volume the author's preoccupation was as much with the length of his novel as with the account of a utopia. And this impression is strengthened when one realizes that most of the essential principles of the utopia are provided in the first volume, and that the second volume tends to elaborate and exemplify these principles rather than provide additional ones.

There are two other lengthy episodes in the second volume; one of these concerns a hypocritical priest and the other deals with the persecution and death of two martyrs.[19] Since both these episodes clearly form part of the religious satire and, furthermore, provide information about the state of the country before it was remodelled as a utopia, they are unquestionably relevant. The problem is to determine their degree of relevance. The episode concerning the priest seems to me to be not merely relevant but essential, since without it, the reader would know little of the pre-Sevarambian religion. The

19. Pages 129-165, 167-201.

story of the martyrs, on the other hand, is simply one illustration of the effects of the priest's hypocrisy, and should, therefore, be regarded as a relevant digression.

In the non-utopian section of the novel, there is an episode, already mentioned, that involves the setting up of a polyandrous society.[20] This episode has relevance not only to the exploits of Captain Siden, but also to that part of the utopian section in which the attitude of the Sevarambians towards women and marriage is discussed. We can sum up, then, by saying that Veiras' novel provides a good example of an imaginary voyage that involves a variety of relevant and irrelevant digressions. The author started out with the intention of describing a utopia but this intention became increasingly obscure as the work progressed.

Tyssot de Patot's *Voyages et avantures de Jaques Massé* comprises one volume which is divided into sixteen chapters. The first five chapters, about one fifth of the novel, are taken up with biographical details and events that occur prior to the discovery of the unknown country. Jacques Massé, like the heroes of Foigny and Veiras, had a good education but this was interrupted by the death of his father. At the age of eighteen he decided to study to be a ship's doctor so he could see the world. He studied first in Paris and then in Dieppe from where he signed on a ship bound for Martinique. We are not surprised to read that the ship was wrecked in a storm and our hero was picked up by a passing ship that took him to Lisbon. From Lisbon he boarded a ship bound for the East Indies. This ship finally went aground off an unknown coast somewhere in the Austral region. Jacques and the other survivors organized a makeshift community in this fertile area. Eventually Jacques and two of his friends decided to explore the interior and, after many days march and a series of hair-raising adventures, they discovered a utopian society. The next six chapters, that is, about two fifths of the book, are devoted to the period spent by Jacques and one of his friends, among the unknown people. Here we have the usual details about their language, customs,

20. Pages 63-69.

laws, religion, the geographical situation, the industries, and the like. The last five chapters, which occupy the remaining two fifths of the book, are concerned with Jacques' exploits after he has escaped from the ideal society. After another series of breathtaking adventures he rediscovered the other survivors still living in their makeshift colony. The men were eventually picked up by a passing ship and taken to Goa. Here Jacques got into trouble with the Inquisition and was thrown into prison. Finally, he was sentenced to the galleys for life and placed on a ship bound for Lisbon. This ship was attacked by pirates and Jacques was carried off to be sold as a slave in the region of Algiers. He was eventually reinstated through the good offices of the British consul in Algiers, and the book ends with his return to Europe.

The first striking difference between Tyssot's imaginary voyage and those of Foigny and Veiras is that, in Tyssot's novel, the utopian element clearly does not occupy the major portion of the book. Three fifths of the book are devoted to events that occurred before and after the discovery of the unknown country, and only two fifths of the novel are concerned with the country itself. And when we look more closely at the two hundred or so pages that deal with Jacques' period of residence in the unknown country we discover that a good deal of space is given up, not to a description of the laws, customs, etc. of the country, but to episodes that have little or nothing to do with enhancing our knowledge of the ideal society. The utopian section is, in fact, filled out with a number of short and entirely gratuitous anecdotes. There is a story about a kind of goat used for pulling barges along the canals. One of these animals was so obsessed with always taking the same route home that one day, when he was forced to go in another direction, he broke from his harness and escaped, only to turn up at home a few days later.[21] Another story concerns a nobleman who, in trying to help a damsel in distress, narrowly escaped being murdered by the girl's mother.[22] Another anecdote has to do with a dispute

21. Pages 141-144.
22. Pages 229-235.

between a son and his father in which the son tried to drown his father.[23] Apart from these short, irrelevant episodes there is a much longer digression that occupies some forty-four pages of the novel.[24] This concerns the love affair between Jacques' friend and one of the wives of the king of the utopian community. If we add to these episodes the number of scientific digressions that throw no light on any aspect of the unknown country we discover that of the two hundred pages devoted to Jacques' stay in the ideal society only about seventy or so pages are taken up with a description of it. Furthermore, when we examine this description in more detail, we discover that even here, Tyssot had no real interest in portraying a utopia. In the first place, his account of the grammar of the ideal language contains contradictions and was clearly not worked out;[25] some of his descriptions of other aspects of the society are taken straight from earlier writers of utopias such as More, Foigny and Veiras; but even more striking evidence of Tyssot's lack of interest in his utopia is provided by his failure to include or comment on the only feature about which he was competent to pass judgement, that is, the problem of education. Tyssot was a teacher himself and surely had ideas on the subject of education which had been a feature of nearly all the utopias from the time of Plato. This failure even to mention the topic seems to me to indicate a clear lack of interest in the problems of constructing a utopia.

If Tyssot's main purpose was not to describe a utopia what was it? It is my impression, from an examination of the structure of the novel, from a study of the digressions, and from what we know of Tyssot himself, that he used the imaginary voyage genre, not primarily for didactic or polemical ends but as a vehicle for the display of his scholarly and literary talents. Tyssot's novel, in fact, is much more a *jeu de l'esprit* than a

23. Pages 248-252.
24. Pages 274-317.
25. Both Foigny and Veiras had special interests in the problems of language but there is no evidence that Tyssot shared this interest. The ideal language in *Jaques Massé* was said to contain no imperative but the narrator then proceeded to give an example of one. He also confused the conditional with the subjunctive, and the pluperfect with the conditional perfect.

serious attempt at social reform. Just less than one third of the novel is devoted to discussions of and satires on religion. This element is distributed throughout the book. Similarly, almost another third of the book is taken up with Jacques' adventures. The rest of the novel, apart from the seventy odd pages describing the utopia, is filled with digressions, anecdotes, treatises, and the like. The result is that about equal space in the novel has been given to questions of religion, to adventures and to digressions.[26]

I have already noted the digressions that occur in the utopian section and it is now necessary to take a brief look at the digressions that occur in the two sections dealing with events before and after the discovery of the unknown country. In the first section there is an anecdote about a negro slave who hanged himself rather than face his master's wrath,[27] a story about a young man who swindled a Dutch merchant out of a large sum of money,[28] and a portrait of a brutal sea captain who broke his left arm and subsequently died of gangrene.[29] In the second section, there is a humorous account of a sailor whose moustache was shaved off while he slept,[30] a story of a ghost that turned out to be a dog,[31] a mad boy who broke out of his chains,[32] and a lengthy digression about the adventures of the young man after he had swindled the Dutch merchant out of his money.[33] In addition there are discussions about astronomy and time, there are dissections of cadavers described in detail, treatises on earthquakes and microscopes, and there is even a

26. There is much room for disputing my division of the novel into these three categories. On the question of the religious satire, for example, D.R. McKee, in his monograph *Simon Tyssot de Patot and the Seventeenth Century Background of Critical Deism*, Baltimore 1941, identified five sections dealing with the religious question — pages 22-46, 148-196, 380-396, 412-442, 455-477. The fact that I disagree with McKee's inclusion of pages 22-46 which incorporate material not concerned with the attack on religion, does not affect the number of pages devoted to this topic since I would include other pages that are not mentioned in his classification.

27. Pages 29-31.
28. Pages 49-53.
29. Pages 54-56.
30. Pages 402-403.
31. Pages 404-408.
32. Pages 446-453.
33. Pages 484-502.

short poem thrown in for good measure.[34] All these digressions are irrelevant to the narrative.

The religious element, as we have said, occupies no more space than any other element, and there are grounds for believing that had Tyssot excised all the satirical passages but one (entitled *The Fable of the Bees*), the novel would still have been considered offensive on that account.[35] Certainly one of the aims of the book was to satirize religion but what I am suggesting is that this aim was not more important, and was probably less important, than Tyssot's overwhelming desire to display his talents and versatility.

Here something should be said about Tyssot himself.[36] He was born in 1655 of Huguenot stock. When he was nine years old, his family fled from France to Holland. Tyssot had no formal education but he was energetic and ambitious. His main interest was mathematics. For a time he taught French in Holland as did many other French refugees but, eventually, despite fierce opposition from the authorities, he was appointed Professor of Mathematics at a college in Deventer in the province of Overijssel. At the same time he made a name for himself as a poet and wit in the local salons run by members of the Dutch landed gentry who imitated the manners of French aristocratic society. Tyssot was regarded by his salon friends as a sort of Voiture *cum* Fontenelle, who also combined the talents of Rabelais and Montaigne. His one ambition was to be famous and he seems not to have cared in what fields he made his name. His first publication, a mathematical treatise, was published in 1694 and was favourably reviewed. Tyssot thought, at that time, that he was destined to make his name in the academic world, but although he wrote other treatises and dissertations of a mathematical and scientific nature he was unable to get them published. It was not until some twenty years after his first

34. Pages 7-10, 32-39, 41-43, 83-97, 216-219, 256-264, 270-272, 375-394, 432-437.

• 35. According to the *Mémoires et journal inédit du marquis d'Argenson*, Paris, 1858, "La *fable des Abeilles* surtout est restée célèbre," p. 126.

36. A detailed biography of Tyssot is available in my forthcoming book entitled *Tyssot de Patot and His Work (1655-1738)* to be published in the *Archives internationales d'histoire des idées*.

publication that he finally managed to get into print again. This time it was with the imaginary voyage *Jaques Massé*. Unfortunately, this novel did little to enhance his reputation since, because of the religious satire, he was forced to publish it anonymously. In his correspondence Tyssot revealed how he would have liked the novel and its author to be regarded:

> Je suis bien aise de ce que vous êtes de mon sentiment par rapport à la beauté du voyage de M. Massé; il est en effet instructif, il est agréable, bien diversifié, rempli d'incidents rares et curieux, et son auteur y fait suffisamment connaître qu'il avait de l'érudition, du savoir, du génie, et qu'il pouvait, pour ainsi dire, passer pour universel dans les sciences.[37]

The point Tyssot wanted to emphasize was that while others before him may have written imaginary voyages and utopias and used them for satirizing the religions, laws and customs of European society, no French writer before Tyssot (in Tyssot's view that is) had ever before used this genre to reveal such erudition, tell such marvellous stories, keep the reader in a constant state of excitement and suspense, make him alternately laugh and weep, and all with such verve and style. And these effects were achieved primarily through the use of irrelevant digressions, to an extent that it would not be unfair to say that these digressions constituted for Tyssot the most important feature of his novel, for it was through the digressions that he could display his versatility in the arts and sciences.

What can we conclude from these remarks about the use of digressions in these three imaginary voyages? In the first place, I have shown that by focussing attention on the digressions it is possible to make certain distinctions that have previously escaped our attention. The works of Foigny, Veiras, and Tyssot de Patot are usually lumped together in any discussion of imaginary voyages, but I hope I have demonstrated that it is a mistake to treat them in this way. The novel of Foigny is a

---

37. *Lettres choisies*, II, p. 251.

compact fusion of the realistic and fantastic in the service of the author's main intention which was to portray a utopia. It is characterized by an absence of digressions. Veiras' novel is almost wholly realistic. The author started out with the purpose of depicting a utopia but found himself unable to sustain it and was obliged to fill out his novel with a number of irrelevant digressions. Tyssot de Patot never intended the portrayal of a utopia to be anything but a subsidiary element of his novel. His purpose was to display his talents as a scholar, writer, wit, in short, as the all-round *honnête homme*. As a consequence, his novel abounds in irrelevant digressions.

My second conclusion is that, if the study of digressions can be used, as I have suggested, to determine the purpose of one type of imaginary voyage, it might be worthwhile to look for a similar system of classification that will apply to imaginary voyages in general.

Aubrey Rosenberg

Voyages curieux d'un Philadelphe (1755): an Anonymous Utopia of the Mid-18th Century

In 1932 Nicolas van Wijngaarden, in his study of *Les Odyssées philosophiques* in seventeenth- and eighteenth-century French literature,[1] drew attention to a little-known novel that had appeared in France in 1755 and of which there is apparently only one existing copy. No other critic, before or after Wijngaarden, has had the opportunity, or maybe the inclination, to take a closer look at the anonymous *Voyages curieux d'un Philadelphe* (to be found in the Bibliothèque Méjanes, Aix-en-Provence).[2] This is a sad neglect for the book has a number of qualities to recommend it, not the least of which is its significance as a typical production of the utopian tradition in mid-eighteenth-century France. Wijngaarden is to some extent responsible for this neglect, for although he grants the work some value,[3] he describes it as a typical late seventeenth-century production and attacks it on the grounds of bad taste. Apart from misquoting the title, and making a number of other errors of fact,[4] Wijngaarden makes the curious claim that this is "une des premières oeuvres émanées de l'officine d'une loge de franc-maçonnerie."[5] He provides little

1. Nicolas van Wijngaarden, *Les Odyssées philosophiques en France entre 1616 et 1789,* Haarlem, 1932, pp. 189-197.
2. Anonyme, *Voyages curieux d'un Philadelphe dans des pays nouvellement découverts,* La Haye, Aux dépens de la Compagnie, 1755. Bibliothèque Méjanes (Aix-en-Provence), Fonds anciens: C.4395.
3. Wijngaarden, p. 197: "... le [sic] *Voyage curieux d'un Philadelphe* forme une oasis dans ce désert de relations sortant de l'esprit ancien-régime des Lesconvel et des Terrasson."
4. Wijngaarden, p. 189, describes the book as "1 vol., 490 pp. in-12." There is one volume but it contains two parts: the first numbered pp. 3-291, the second numbered pp. 3-327.
5. Wijngaarden, p. 189.

evidence or justification for this remark which, if true, would undoubtedly lend added importance to the book. It is not sufficient to argue that, because a book is full of optimism and faith in human reason, or because it contains a disguised attack on the Jesuits, it is therefore imbued with masonic doctrine. However, there is nothing to support Wijngaarden's view and the *Voyages curieux* is no more a concoction of the freemasons than are *Candide* or *La Nouvelle Héloïse*. That is not to say that these works do not contain expressions of opinion which any self-respecting freemason might be expected to share, but this is true of so much eighteenth-century literature that there seems to be little reason to single out this particular text in such a way. The *Voyages curieux*, in spite of Wijngaarden's remarks to the contrary, is very much a work of its time, and I would like to examine it from various points of view to show some of the progress achieved in utopian writing during the first part of the eighteenth century, as well as some of the reasons for this progress.

It is evident that by 1755 there had taken place in France a process of sophistication in utopian writing which in itself reflects a much wider movement of thought and criticism. At the same time it is as well to point out that all utopian literature belongs to the realm of human myth and, as such, will contain certain unchanging elements. Thus, although it is not difficult to show that, technically, a work such as Morelly's *Basiliade* (1753) is a remarkable advance on a work such as the anonymous *Antangil* (the so-called first true utopia written by a Frenchman,[6] published in 1616), these utopias of the middle and late eighteenth century also belong to a tradition, and consequently contain elements and techniques common to even the earliest writings of this nature (French or otherwise). It comes as no surprise, therefore, to find in the *Voyages curieux* some of the recurring themes of much utopian literature: common ownership of property, a deistic form of religion, an absence of currency, public granaries, and above all the

6. Wijngaarden, p. 17: "... la première utopie écrite par un Français en langue française ..."

brotherhood of love which is implicit in the name "Philadelphian." Nor is it with any sense of novelty that the reader discovers a strong satirical element, largely, but not entirely, introduced through discussions between the outsiders and the inhabitants of utopia. All these things are present in the *Voyages curieux* and it is not there that we must look for the real interest of the book. Before discussing some of the influences responsible for utopian writings such as the *Voyages curieux*, it will help to have a brief résumé of the book and its structure.

The first significant fact is that we are dealing with not one but four imaginary societies, only one of which is practical in human terms. There are three main protagonists: a Frenchman called the Chevalier de Richordie, an English sea-captain called Roswick, and a tame savage eventually baptized Richard. The early chapters of the book tell the story of Richordie's upbringing, his mis-spent youth and subsequent ruin. He is obliged to leave France and heads for England under his assumed name of Richordie, which, as he explains, reflects in English something of his intention to get "rich or die." His intention is in fact not simply financial, but rather to achieve those ideals of so many eighteenth-century heroes: virtue and happiness, all the more so after being the victim in London of a French Protestant confidence trickster. He sets sail with Roswick and, after the traditional storm and shipwreck, they are cast ashore somewhere in the East China Sea. They find themselves in the land of the Wayserdans, or, as Roswick is assumed to have written in his non-existent English version, the "Wiser-than-us." At first sight the Wayserdans are a savage people, wearing no clothes and jabbering an incomprehensible language. Richordie and Roswick are immediately adopted by two females who duly become their wives after appropriate ceremony and marriage vows sworn in public. After learning the language which, in its written form, is compared to Chinese, the two visitors are integrated into the society and discover that the Wayserdans have an admirable, if somewhat unsophisticated, system of government and religion, based, as is so often the case in utopia, on the "laws of nature."

Long discussions take place with the King who is not over-impressed by European customs, Richordie at times being hard pressed to put them in a good light. This type of critical dialogue occurs frequently in utopian writing, and appears prominently in the works of Foigny, Lahontan, and Stanislas Lesczinski.[7] Part of the description of the land of the Wayserdans is devoted to two animals found there and their strange characteristics: the Piacours and the Sottards. The Piacours are fat and lazy; they force the Sottards to work for them without reward, and spend most of their time lying in caves with as many female Sottards as they can get hold of. More Piacours are encountered when Richordie and Roswick go as ambassadors to a neighbouring island (the land of the Pingades) in an attempt worthy of Gulliver to head off a threat of war. Here the Piacours are venerated by the inhabitants and appear to represent some of the perversions of the Roman Catholic church. The Pingades themselves seem to represent the Papacy and the ultramontane threat to the church in France, and it was no doubt partly because of this that Wijngaarden describes the *Voyages curieux* as a work that might easily have appeared at the time of Bossuet. However, by concentrating on the limited religious satire, Wijngaarden has overlooked the much more relevant social satire of the book: the oppression of the poor by the socially privileged. Eventually Richordie and Roswick find an English ship which takes them back to London, along with a pair of Sottards and a Wayserdan, soon to be baptized Richard. The year is 1686.

There follows a visit to Paris which provides the occasion for Richard to make violent criticism of social and religious practices there. As a result the three companions are inspired to set up a new society, the Philadelphians, based to some extent on their experiences in the land of the Wayserdans, but further developing and codifying these ideals. The author (i.e. Richordie) claims that the new society quickly grew to one hundred and fifty-eight members, although this early success was not maintained (partly because of persecution by the authorities in

7. Stanislas Lesczinski, *Entretien d'un Européen avec un insulaire du Royaume de Dumocola*, n.p., 1752.

England) and their numbers at the time of writing (supposedly 1705) have dropped to fifty-two. Richordie marries a French girl living in London but is almost immediately sent by King William II to find out more concerning the Wayserdans. His ship and that of Roswick is wrecked before they arrive at their destination, but by fortunate coincidence the three comrades are the sole survivors. This time they find themselves on a strange island called Laïquehire, presumably intended as a reflection of the state of affairs in France ("Like-here"). This overly allegorical land is divided into two parts: upper and lower. The people of the lower part are poor and oppressed by the Divinities living in the superior regions who possess a wide range of magical talents. The ruler or "Golif" welcomes the Europeans, presenting them with gifts of a magic wand and medals to cure evil spells. However, after noting the wretchedness of the poor and particularly their oppression by birds of prey called "bloudsokres" (bloodsuckers?), the companions kill one of the birds and are obliged to flee to another island.

This is the land of Goudlas (Good-laws?) inhabited by a relatively backward people who have few laws or social structures. This is a perfect opportunity for putting into practice the lessons learnt in other places and the three travellers lose no time in establishing a complete system of government, reforming and reducing the power of the priests or "pronifers," and setting up trade relations with a neighbouring people on the island of Alboury. Richard marries a girl of French descent (and therefore of appropriate Christian upbringing) and is proclaimed "Spadogif" or King in time to prevent his departure with Richordie and Roswick. After a brief visit to another island nearby, and a rather obscure interview with the daughter of Divine Justice and Truth, they are picked up by a Dutch ship and return to Europe. Richordie finds his wife in France where she has fled to escape the clutches of the infamous Lord Brifork, while Roswick makes a name for himself by curing people with his magic medal. He is later persuaded by William Penn to settle in Pennsylvania as "Inspector of Public Health" and leaves England in 1704 (by which time Penn in fact had left America never to return).

Richordie consoles himself with the thought that all men are his brothers, and that the knowledge of Roswick's good deeds will bring him all the happiness he needs.

The ideal of the brotherhood of men and more particularly the secret society formed by Richordie, Roswick and Richard, as well as mention of a sign by which members of the society may recognize each other, were no doubt some of the reasons which led Wijngaarden to say that this work belongs to the freemasonry movement. It is true that from about 1725 masonic lodges had sprung up all over France and it is generally recognized that the ideals of freemasonry were close to those which provided much of the driving force behind the Revolution. It is also true that freemasonry as a movement had suffered excommunication in 1738 and again in 1752. From 1767 until 1771 all masonic meetings were banned in France. At the same time it is known that Montesquieu, Helvétius, Frederick II, and many other outstanding names in eighteenth-century French literary history were freemasons, with the name of Voltaire being added to the list in the nick of time on the 7th April 1778, less than two months before he died. Although the *Voyages curieux* cannot be linked directly to the literature of freemasonry, there are earlier works with masonic associations, as for example Ramsay's *Voyages de Cyrus* (1727) and Terrasson's *Sethos* (1731). There exists today in Lille a lodge of freemasons called the "Philadelphians" but there is no evidence of its existence in 1755. There did exist, however, in England toward the end of the seventeenth century a Philadelphian Society inspired principally by a mystic prophetess named Jean Lead. Their aim, based largely on a cabalistic interpretation of the holy scriptures, was to prepare the coming of the Philadelphian church, itself the herald of the New Jerusalem. This purification of the church was to take place, according to their interpretation of the prophet Daniel, after two thousand three hundred years, which (assuming Daniel wrote in the year 600 B.C.) works out conveniently at the year 1700. This is just one aspect of the chiliastic tradition which spread throughout Europe at this time and which plays a significant role in the wider tradition of utopian thinking, secular or otherwise.

It is worth pointing out that the events recounted in the *Voyages curieux* are supposed to have taken place between 1678 and 1704, and that the author describes a secret society which did in fact exist at that time. After the appearance of Prévost's novels in France, the writer of imaginary voyages and societies felt free to avail himself of a specific historical reality within which to set his work. In *Cleveland*, for example, this historical reality is very carefully integrated into the fictional mainstream, thus developing the air of authenticity and credibility which these authors considered essential to their novels. There is similar interplay between fiction and historical accuracy in works other than those of Prévost, and as late as 1759 the *Journal des Savants* lists Foigny's *Sadeur, Glantzby,* and *Leguat,* as well as Prévost's *Robert Lade,* as genuine travel narratives.[8] It is with Prévost, however, that this technique of interweaving the real and the imagined is most skilfully developed. This is only part of a wider process of refinement of the novelist's technique which takes place in eighteenth-century France, and which began with elements such as the "superfluous" digression found in Vairasse, Tyssot de Patot and others.

The influence of Swift, and *Gulliver's Travels* in particular, on French writers has frequently been examined,[9] and it is not surprising to find the anonymous author of the *Voyages curieux* duly paying his respects to the author of *Gulliver*. Assuming the role of editor of Richordie's work, the author goes so far as to compare Richordie's outstanding character with the simplicity and genius of Gulliver, adding that the two knew each other in London, developed a close friendship, and carried on a frequent correspondence during Gulliver's lifetime. Richordie himself claims Gulliver as an authority on the widespread distribution of *sottards* in many countries of the world.[10] These rather facile acknowledgements of a debt to Swift point to an influence which goes somewhat deeper. A number of works in France

8. *Table générale des matières contenues dans le Journal des Savants,* Paris, 1759, VIII, p. 708.
9. See for example: Sybil Goulding, *Swift en France,* Paris, 1924.
10. *Voyages curieux,* Part I, p. 3 and p. 140.

which appeared after 1726 have been variously associated with Swift's influence: specifically the anonymous *Voyages de Glantzby* (1729) and the Abbé Desfontaines' *Le Nouveau Gulliver* (the voyage of Jean Gulliver, son of Lemuel, 1730). Swift's influence on these books is at best a very general one, and his contribution to the development of the utopian novel in France is essentially in tone and technique. There is little evidence of irony (with the exception of Tyssot de Patot) in the French utopian novel until some time after 1726, but by 1755 and the *Voyages curieux*, irony had become an almost indispensable tool, not only of the utopian writer, but in a much wider field of literature and philosophical writing. This is evident not only in the work of Voltaire, for example, but also in most of the utopian writing from about 1740 onwards. The author of the *Voyages curieux* is thus able to write of genuine utopian ideals, while at the same time keeping his tongue very much in his cheek. Like Swift or like Ludvig Holberg in *Nicolas Klim* (1741) the author makes no serious attempt to convince his readers that Richordie or any of his companions really existed, and with great ease can develop a series of imaginary societies, all of which fall more or less within the utopian framework. The satirical element is thus maintained throughout, as much by implication as by direct reference to specific institutions. The technique is not new (it had received brilliant treatment at the hands of Cyrano de Bergerac one hundred years earlier), but it is to Swift that much of the credit must be given for its incorporation in the world of the novel. The Wayserdans, the Laïquehirois, and the Goudlasours (to say nothing of Piacours, Sottards, and Bloudsokres) reveal more of human weakness than they do of human achievement. In this respect they are second cousins of the Houyhnhnms. By 1740 the utopian novel in France has come of age and no longer needs to take itself quite as seriously as it did during its formative years at the end of the seventeenth century.

There is, however, one important aspect of satire in the *Voyages curieux* which owes little, if anything, to Swift, but belongs rather to a tradition in which the names of Lahontan and Montesquieu take pride of place. This is the criticism of

European institutions by the exotic traveller, and it is perhaps here that the *Voyages curieux* shows its greatest originality. Although Lahontan's Huron, Adario, had taken a similar path, Richard in the *Voyages curieux* is the first inhabitant of utopia to leave his country and visit Europe, the most interesting part being his stay in France. Like the Persians, Usbek and Rica, before him, Richard obtains immediate success by virtue of his exotic appearance and the peculiarities of his pidgin French. His success is greatest with the females and it is not long before he spends a night with one of the ladies he has met. When Richordie and Roswick arrive next day for dinner they find Richard acting as though he were master of the house, to the obvious embarrassment of the lady concerned. Having been told that after marriage the husband becomes master of all, he had assumed that marriage was the same in France as among the Wayserdans and had therefore merely accepted his rights. Upon learning that the lady in question already has a husband he is furious, mainly because she has broken a vow, a basic crime among his people. The situation and the misunderstanding are not unlike those between the *Ingénu* and Mademoiselle de St. Yves, and indeed the whole episode is astonishingly similar to that found in Voltaire's story thirteen years later. For Richard, however, there are more serious matters to be discovered: the absurdities of the law-courts, the irreverence of church-goers, the large numbers of poverty-stricken people, the deceits of the rich, and the hypocrisy of the clergy. In fact the only admirable institution in France in Richard's eyes is the monastic order of Chartreux, which he praises for its withdrawal from society and general virtue. Visits to other monasteries and abbeys elicit criticism for their lack of useful contribution to society and their excess wealth, and in despair Richard beseeches his friends to return to England. It is as a direct result of these various disappointments that the decision is made to found the society of Philadelphians. The criticisms in themselves are not particularly original, but they are typical of the stock-in-trade of the "philosophes" and mark an extreme development of the novel as propaganda. It is perhaps the final limit in the progress of the utopian novel before the individualistic utopia of Rousseau marks other, more exciting directions.

The ideal society of the *Voyages curieux* emerges as an amalgamation of the ideals of the Wayserdans, the Philadelphian constitution, and the institutions of Goudlas. It is a utopian vision not far removed from the communistic ideal which Morelly based on the "code of nature," and also the notion of social contract as Rousseau describes it. The enlightened despot or Lawgiver, even if disguised as the interpreter of the General Will, finds his parallel in the utopian literature of the eighteenth century, and the *Voyages curieux* illustrates a specific development of this tradition. Although the imposition of laws is practically inherent in all utopian doctrine (Utopus in More's *Utopia*, Sevarias in the *Histoire des Sévarambes*, for example) and a large number of utopian societies have retained their original legal code for thousands of years (as in *Antangil* and Lassay's *Royaume des Féliciens*), there is a new interpretation which emerges strongly in the eighteenth century: the description of the reform in progress, or the moment of utopian creation. Mentor in Fénelon's *Télémaque* (1699) is the most outstanding example of this, although similar episodes find their place in the works of Marivaux (Emander in the *Effets surprenants de la sympathie*, 1713-14), Prévost (Cleveland among the Abaquis and, in the same text, Mrs. Riding among the Nopandes, 1731-39), Le Sage (Marguerite du Clos with the Hurons in the *Aventures de Robert Chevalier*, 1732) and D'Argens (Meillcourt among the Troglocites in *Le Législateur moderne*, 1739). The utopian creation in Goudlas thus belongs to a mid-century pattern which reflects some of the admiration of the "philosophes" for the enlightened despots of Northern Europe at about the same time.

If these remarks demonstrate sufficiently the close links between the *Voyages curieux* and other utopian literature of the period, they do not illustrate the stylistic achievements of the book. Reference has been made to the process of sophistication which took place in French fiction during the first part of the eighteenth century. The *Voyages curieux*, with its light and ironic tone, its moments of semi- or pseudo-erotic description, and even its propagandist allegory, belongs to the literature of the 1750's. In this respect it is close to the writings of Coyer (*L'Ile frivole*, 1751) and Morelly (*Naufrage des Iles Flottantes*, 1753) and maybe even Voltaire (*Zadig* and *Candide*). Whether intended or not as a protection from the hand of censorship, there is a distinctly rococo frivolity ornamenting much of French fiction during the mid- and even late-eighteenth century. At the same time the utopian element maintains its force, fulfilling its essential function as a political science laboratory for those groping their way towards new social concepts. Perhaps it could also be described as a witches' kitchen for it was, at least in part, in the utopian literature of the eighteenth century that France concocted the magic brew of revolution.[11]

Roger Clark

11. Since this article was written two other copies of the *Voyages curieux* have come to light: one at the Bibliothèque Nationale in Paris, the other at the Princeton University Library. Further examination of the copy in Aix-en-Provence strongly suggests that the actual place of publication was Paris and not La Haye.

Structure in the Cartas Marruecas of Cadalso

This is the third time I have tried to collect my thoughts on paper about Cadalso's *Cartas marruecas*. According to a Spanish proverb I should be more successful than in the past: "A la tercera va la vencida." But an English proverb warns me success depends on luck: "Third time lucky." Luck is hardly something academics confess they look for; and critical victories are not something I believe in. What the third time really means so far as I am concerned is the opportunity to revise my earlier views in the light of the passage of time, changing critical approaches to literature (my own and those of others), and our state of knowledge about this particular work.

In 1956 my chief concern was with tension in the *Cartas marruecas*.[1] I avoided as far as possible the discussion of themes and topics in isolation, and tried rather to see how the way in which they were expressed by the three main characters — the two Moors Gazel and Ben-Beley, and the Christian Nuño — and how the order in which the topics arose contributed to the meaning of the whole. The aim was to find the resultant of the forces at play in the work, as is normal in fiction. Subsequently I felt the need to readjust the balance a little, and relate the topics themselves to the work of other eighteenth-century and earlier writers. Consequently in my contributions to the prologue of the edition of the *Cartas* which I prepared with Lucien Dupuis around 1964,[2] I wrote rather more about

1. My ideas were first of all worked out in Chapter 5 of my doctoral dissertation, *Joseph de Cadalso (1741-1782). His life and his works; and his thought in relation to the stoic tradition*, for the University of Cambridge (Vol. I, pp. 285-357). In a modified version these subsequently formed the basis of Chapter 5 of *Vida y obra de Cadalso*, Madrid, Gredos, 1962, pp. 86-101.

2. The edition — José de Cadalso, *Cartas marruecas*. Prólogo, edición y notas de Lucien Dupuis y Nigel Glendinning, London, Támesis, 1966 — was prepared two years before it was published. Dupuis and I modified one another's contributions and no section is wholly attributable to one of us only. In subsequent notes, the abbreviation *Cartas* refers to this edition.

subjects like "luxury" and approaches to history, to place the Cartas marruecas more clearly in the context of eighteenth-century thought. I also contributed some passages on rhetorical style, showing how Cadalso used the rhythmic and repeated pattern, "poetic" prose of the Ciceronian tradition, to create emotional climaxes where these were appropriate. Since then I have realised that it might have been more useful to hold up Cadalso's rhetoric against that of the theorists of the period (Luzán's *Poética,* Capmany's *Filosofía de la elocuencia,* or Madramany's rather later *Tratado de la elocución*); that I ought to have said more about non-rhythmic sound effects (internal assonance and so forth); and that on the whole more should have been done to relate stylistic devices to the underlying philosophy of the work, as I had found it easier to do when discussing similar passages in the more consistently poetic *Noches lúgubres.*[3]

Some six years on I naturally feel that what I ought to have done was to re-examine the whole structure of the work — deep structure, of course, and also the more superficial plot structure; structure of individual letters; sentence structure and language structure generally — to see whether anything of significance emerged that I had not adequately taken into account originally. It is therefore to these aspects of the *Cartas marruecas* that I wish to devote myself in the first instance in this essay before going on to see the relevance of the particular "travel literature" or other traditions in which his structure seems to place Cadalso, and to discuss briefly some of the pressures which produced such a structure.

Structural investigations tend to presuppose two things about a work of literature. Firstly, that the work is the end product of a *completed* organising process (conscious or unconscious); secondly, that linguistic structures and patterns reveal something about a particular work, as well as about the cultural and rhetorical conventions of its time and milieu. The first of these two presuppositions is very difficult to apply to the *Cartas marruecas,* the second less so.

---

3. Cf. José Cadalso, *Noches lúgubres,* edición, prólogo y notas de Nigel Glendinning, Madrid, 1961, especially pp. lxiv ff.

Normally, when a work is printed under an author's supervision it is reasonable to assume that he felt its organising process to be complete. In Cadalso's case, however, the *Cartas marruecas* (and the *Noches lúgubres* too for that matter) were posthumous publications; we do not have a manuscript or text which shows us the state of the work when he first submitted it for publication, and the organising process may not have been carried through to its conclusion. Some aspects of the structure therefore may have been provisional rather than definitive, and this raises obvious problems for the would-be interpreter.

We can argue that this is the case of the *Cartas marruecas* if we examine the manuscript index of the letters in the Biblioteca Nacional, which is different from the first printed index, and look at the headings of the letters themselves.[4] It seems clear from erasures and corrections to the MS index and from the discrepancies between it and the manuscript copies of the *Cartas*,[5] that Cadalso was not absolutely sure where to put the two letters about lawsuits between parents and children (Letters 18 and 19), nor the one on bull-fighting (72); that he originally left a gap between two letters on true friendship (Letters 46 and 47; in the Index, letters 46 and 48); and that he had letters 59 and 60 (on the methods of writing history and on the difficulties which arise as a result of false distinctions between use and abuse, right and wrong) in reverse order, suggesting that he first put a particular *after* a general, and then changed his mind. It is further evident that the grouping of letters and their serial arrangement was not definitive from letter headings. In the first published editions the letter headings are nearly always rationalised: if two or three letters in a row pass between the same correspondents, the first one states, say, "From Gazel to Nuño," the next two merely have "From the same to the same." Exceptions in the first edition are Letters 34 and 50, both of which say "De Gazel a Ben-Beley" when "Del mismo al mismo" would be sufficient. Eight more such discrepancies occur in the Osuna Manuscript which Dupuis and I used as the basis for our

4. Cf. *Cartas*, pp. 205-209.
5. Cf. *Cartas*, pp. 206-208 (Nos. 18, 19, 47, 48, 59, 60, 72).

edition and believe to be an early text.[6] A possible hypothesis would be that these letters were not written in sequence but merely as a series of "one-offs" from one of the main characters to another. When he placed them in a particular sequence and gave them a particular number Cadalso did not perhaps bother to rationalise the headings. Alternatively he placed them provisionally rather than permanently in position. The letters this hypothesis could apply to are 51, 54, 57, 58, 64, 74, 76, 77. We may also note that Letters 47 and 49 were joined, constituting one letter, in the Hispanic Society's MS,[7] and that Letter 27 had no heading at all in the Osuna MS.[8]

All of this suggests that some of the letters were conceived as independent entities rather than as part of a planned sequence or serial pattern. In most of the cases so far mentioned, the content of the letters would also support the "one-off" argument. Letter 34 is the only one about planners (*proyectistas*) and the wild scheme for canals to bisect the Iberian peninsula; Letter 50 is about translations, and unlike 34 does not even mention Nuño, Gazel or Ben-Beley, so could even have begun life as a totally independent piece of work. Letter 51 is a "dictionary" letter, which discusses politics and politicians, picking up the threads of a pattern first established in Letter 8 but not related to those which immediately precede or follow it. Letter 54 is another of the same group "on fortune and making a fortune." 57 and 58 deal with methods of writing history (a topic first touched on in Letters 5 and 9) and criticism respectively. 64 is about the various requests for fashion advice which Gazel received when he first arrived in Madrid; chronologically, therefore, it belongs earlier in the book. 74 is about foreign criticisms of Spain; 76 includes a letter from a lady to Gazel; and 77 is concerned with the persistence of seventeenth-century styles in eighteenth-century Spain, and contains the list of Baroque book titles which Cadalso probably noted down from the *Gaceta de Madrid*

6. Cf. *Cartas*, pp. xlviii-liv.
7. *Cartas*, p. 110. Cf. the bibliography (*Cartas*, p. lvi) for details of the Hispanic Society manuscript. The error also extended to the *Correo de Madrid* edition.
8. Cf. Biblioteca Nacional, Madrid, MS 10.688.

between 1757 and 1772.[9]

If these "one-off" letters seem to provide evidence of initial non-sequential or loose organisation, other facts about the work support the same conclusion. Certain letters are clearly linked by common fictional devices, and within the final sequence these form separate groups, not necessarily written at the same time, but clearly germinating from the same original seed. The scattering of them of course aids the sense of continuity and unity in the work. The most obvious groups are the "Dictionary" letters of Nuño, and the letters which derive from matter in Nuño's brief-case: the history of Spain in Letter 3; the "observaciones y reflexiones sueltas" of Letter 39; the book-titles of Letter 77; the Heroic History of Spain whose prologue fills most of Letter 16, and the letter from Nuño's sister in Letter 35.

Another obvious sub-group is constituted by other letters within letters, following the model of Montesquieu's Letters 28, 51, 78 (written by persons other than Nuño or Ben-Beley to Gazel): Letters 75 and 76 for instance, or Letter 33, which includes a copy of a letter from Nuño to Gazel in one from Gazel to Ben-Beley.

We could also see as a group those letters which explicitly contrast Morocco and Spain (Letter 7 on Education, for instance; 10 on Marriage; 12 on Nobility; 18 on the attitudes of sons to fathers; 41 on Luxury). Possibly we could put down as yet another separate group those letters which are overtly cast in epistolary form. In reality, it is surprising how few of these there are in a work supposedly made up of letters. To some extent Montesquieu's *Lettres persanes* set an obvious precedent here as in other fictional devices used by Cadalso: the form of anecdotal letters which start "Hier matin . . ." (45). "Etant l'autre jour dans ma chambre . . ." (49), "J'étais l'autre jour dans une société . . ." (52) and so forth. Montesquieu by no means ends all his letters formally with *Adieu* or some other appropriate rounding-off phrase. On the other hand he does date them all carefully, which Cadalso fails to do. The only letters with

9. *Cartas*, pp. 170-172.

formal endings in the *Cartas marruecas* are the first two and the last one (1, 2 and 90); also 17, 42, 44, 62 and 86; others, like 71, 84 and 85 make references to other letters and so give a sense of being a part of an exchange of correspondence.

Cadalso also makes surprisingly little use of plot sequence devices which sustain the reader's interest in characters in such an absorbing way in the *Lettres persanes*. Looking at the travel framework of *Cartas marruecas* we find it to be almost conspicuous by its absence. There is the explanation of Gazel's presence in Madrid in the train of the Moroccan ambassador at the beginning (Letter 1) and we assume that the subsequent letters are written in the capital. The first references to travel within Spain occur in Letter 25, and 26 is logically enough about the varying character of people in the Spanish provinces. 27 could have been written anywhere, but 29 is clearly written after a visit to the southern part of France, and concerns the French character. 33 refers to Gazel's journeys through the south of Spain (Granada and Cadiz), yet Gazel's reported conversations with Nuño in 34 seem to imply that the Moor is already back in Madrid, and reference to Nuño's house in 39 and walking in Madrid in 40 confirm this. 43 is written from a provincial city (and is internally dated 1768); 45 from Barcelona; but by 53 Gazel is with Nuño again and there is no sign of a further move until 67. To judge from letter 67, a lot of time has elapsed over the last twenty-four letters – six years, in fact: there is a reference to 1774. Gazel is in Bilbao, and letters that follow logically refer to life in provincial cities and in the country (69 and 70). But in Letter 72 Gazel appears to be with Nuño again – presumably in Madrid – and this is most clearly the case in Letter 74. 78 is about Spanish universities and contains specific matter about Salamanca, but we need not assume that Gazel is actually there at the time of writing, and he is undoubtedly in Madrid in Letter 80. Only in the last two letters does Gazel move on once more to the south, prior to taking ship for Africa.

The travel line in the *Cartas marruecas* is, then, extraordinarily vague. And as we have already hinted when talking about the lapse of time between Letter 43 (dated 1768) and 67 (dated 1774), the time sequence is not as designedly *vrai-semblable* or rational as that of Montesquieu's *Lettres persanes*. Indeed there are some gross discrepancies. The reference to Jorge Juan's death in Letter 7 puts it in or after 1774. Evidently the clock has to be put back by the reader to enable him to follow Gazel to the provincial city referred to in Letter 43 in 1768.

It is evident from these inconsistencies and absences that Cadalso is not interested in some of the most obvious characteristics and possibilities of travel literature. He takes the detached observer and the exotic eyes, but he does not really go into the nature of their exoticism except in limited ways, as I hope to show. We learn nothing of substance about the Moroccans' way of life, their society and attitudes, as we do from the *Lettres persanes* about the Persian way of life. Nor do we find here much sign of interest in travel for its own sake, and in the natural sequence of events. A carriage breaks its front axle and a shaft in Letter 69, but little else happens; journeys by sea, shipwrecks, the dangers of storm and pirates, travel by land and peril by bandits were exploited to a much greater extent in Spain by Cervantes in his novels than by Cadalso in the *Cartas marruecas*. Thinking of the "exotic traveller" possi-bilities, the Moors are not even such rare birds in Spain as Persians would have been in other parts of Europe.[10] Apart from the rich vein of Moorish and *Morisco* stories from the sixteenth and seventeenth centuries, Madrid readers of the *Cartas*, had the book come out in the mid-seventies as it was intended to, would have no doubt recalled the Moroccan ambassador's visit to the Spanish capital less than ten years previously, recorded in two prints of the period as well as in the Madrid Gazette.[11] The audience already had the picture and did not need it to be painted.

10. Cadalso points out the relative scarcity of foreign travellers in Spain in the Introduction (*Cartas*, p. 3, lines 14-16). In Spanish literature, however, the Moor is a frequent visitor. Cf. José Caso González, 'El comienzo de la reconquista en tres obras dramáticas,' *Cuadernos de la cátedra Feijoo*, 18 (*El Padre Feijoo y su siglo*, vol. III), p. 505.

11. Cf. *Cartas*, p. xiii.

Cadalso must have felt that these aspects of travel literature were not germain to his purpose. Even the coach breakdown is not a disaster in itself, but a useful way in to observation about life in the country as opposed to the towns. The imagination is given less rein in the *Cartas* than in other travel works (and in other works by Cadalso), and the vicissitudes of life which were so admirably reflected in travel for earlier Spanish writers were here reflected by much more every day experiences.

It seems clear then that we cannot consider plot or narrative sequence as fundamental elements in the structure of the *Cartas marruecas*. Their absence is more relevant than their presence. In retrospect it was wrong of me perhaps to assume consistent sequential development through the work when I first wrote about it in a doctoral thesis. Possibly, indeed, our modern ways of reading lead us to expect works to grow organically in a linear way, and perhaps prevent us, if we are not careful, from reading some eighteenth-century works in the way appropriate to them. Either we have been on rapid reading courses, or we have acquired the facility to read rapidly in order to keep up with the world's presses. To be a proper eighteenth-century reader you need to have plenty of leisure hours stretching in front of you to read slowly aloud, and not many of us have that. It is true that there were skippers in eighteenth-century Spain. A contemporary of Cadalso who translated the works of the Marqués Carraccioli even went so far as to print all the wise philosophical observations and morals in italics, so as to catch the rapid reader's eye.[12] On the other hand, since reading aloud was common, slow fragmentary reading of works was the norm which the writer assumed in his public. Cadalso's younger contemporary Jovellanos did not even read plays at a sitting.[13] And he was happiest with an evening's pot-pourri of reading from two or three different books — so much for *his* inevitable sense of a work's unity. Small wonder that readers even savoured the delights of single lines of poetry

12. Cf. F. M. Nipho, *Viaje de la razón por la Europa por el marqués Caracciolo*, Parte segunda, Madrid, 1799, f. 4 v.

13. Cf. entries in Jovellanos' diaries for 4-5 April 1797; 25-26 April 1806; 1-2 October 1806; and 22 and 28 November 1806.

at the time,[14] rather than the nowadays indivisible poem as a whole. The sound and rhythm of prose were important audially as well as being aids to sense.

It looks, then, as if Cadalso's *Cartas marruecas* may have been written so that they could be read in this fragmented way. Extracts were certainly read aloud at the *tertulia* Cadalso and his friends had at the Fonda de San Sabastián.[15] And it is interesting to note that the first sign of the *Cartas marruecas* in print was the publication of part of one letter (Letter 7 on Education)[16] and the whole of another (letter 45 on army cadets)[17] which preceded the serialisation of the whole work in a periodical, the *Correo de Madrid*.

This fragmentary view of the work does not mean that Cadalso did not structure it at all. It should be noted that in other works, Cadalso showed a very obvious concern with developing overall patterns. In the *Noches lúgubres* there is a clear evolution of attitude on the part of the main character Tediato, repeated and parallel fictional situations, and an attempt to impose rational and imaginative patterns on an irrational situation. Notably too Cadalso organises his collection of poems entitled *Ocios de mi juventud* in such a way that the poems not only have an individual meaning by themselves but, sometimes, an added significance as a result of their position in the volume: very uncommon in Spain. The collection starts with a group of poems on writing poetry and ends with poems which describe Cadalso's feeling that he must give up poetry after the death of his mistress. There are also significant changes of direction within the volume, or juxtapositions which seem to engender a new meaning or irony, rather than provide merely variety. The poem "Sobre ser la poesía un estudio frívolo y convenirme aplicarme a otros más serios" is logically and ironically followed by "Sonetos de una gravedad inaguantable,

14. Cf. J. Mor de Fuentes, *La Serafina*, Zaragoza, 1959, p. 157 ('de doce literatos o aficionados que lean de buena fe y con inteligencia a Virgilio o a Meléndez, cada uno se impresiona más o menos con sus rasgos, cada uno prefiere o pospone estos a aquellos versos').

15. Cf. E. Cotarelo y Mori, *Iriarte y su época*, Madrid, 1897, pp. 115 ff.

16. Cf. *Cartas*, p. lvii.

17. *Cartas*, p. lviii.

excepto los finales de cada uno"; similarly the rather Pindaric ode on the Count Ricla's birthday is followed immediately by an anti-Pindaric Anacreontic, "Vuelve, mi triste lira / Vuelve a tu estilo humilde." Later a long poem about Cadalso's own misfortunes, "Carta escrita desde una aldea de Aragón a Ortelio," is followed by two general illustrations of the changeability of fortune.

The organisation of *Ocios de mi juventud* in fact suggests an interest in thematic structures and developing attitudes, perhaps also an interest in relativity, particularly in the presentation of alternative stoic and anacreontic or epicurean solutions to problems of fortune and human misery. I shall certainly return to this last point again, but in the meantime another look at the *Cartas marruecas* shows in my view the same interest in thematic or topical rather than chronological or narrative coherence as the *Ocios*. Even allowing for an incomplete organisation process, the arrangement suggests that individual topics were more important than coherent ordering.[18] This does not mean that there is no ordering at all; but the *Cartas marruecas* are composed perhaps as a garden rather than a stream, with clumps of flowers echoing beds of roses.

It is obvious that some letters are designed to continue, amplify, correct or modify the views of others. The fact that three very different characters are involved makes this a natural as well as a meaningful process within an epistolary work. Consecutive letters with a thematic link are 12 and 13 on Nobility (first broached in 7 too); 18 and 19 on relations between fathers and sons; 20, 21 and 26 on the Spanish character; 43 and 44 on old Spain; 35 and 36 on linguistic change; 46 and 47 on Friendship; 49 and 50 on cultural contacts between France and Spain; 54 and 55 on Fortune; 27 and 28 and later 84 and 85 on posthumous fame; finally 69, 70 and 71 on country life, retirement and commitment to society. An example of a fairly characteristic treatment of the thematic links is to be found in 43 and 44. The first describes the

18. Cadalso himself states part of the problem in the *Introducción*: "no hay en el original serie alguna de fechas, y me pareció trabajo que dilataría mucho la publicación de esta obra el de coordinarlas" (*Cartas*, p. 4).

unchanging pattern of life in provincial Spanish cities and expresses Gazel's admiration for the Spaniard's respect for the memory of the dead; while the second adjusts the balance by pointing out the dangers of excessive devotion to the past "sin distinción de crítica."[19]

This process of getting a subject in perspective is fundamental to the work. The reader's attention is even drawn in a single instance to it by an explicit cross-reference. This comes at the beginning of Letter 4 which carries the note "See Letter 48" — one which modifies the view of the eighteenth century expressed in the earlier letter. The manuscript version of the index also explicitly points to modifications of the contents of one letter by another (or sometimes within the letter itself), although the earliest published table of contents normally fails to do so. For example, Letter 11 is "Advantages and drawbacks of various Spanish manners" ("Cumplimientos. Familiaridades; sus utilidades e inconvenientes"). Letter 16 is "Ingratitude of modern nations to their heroes; disadvantages of this ingratitude; beneficial effects of the virtue opposed to this vice"; and similar two-sided letters are 41 (on Luxury) and 43 and 44, which we have already discussed. Letters 69 and 70 on country life are also clearly contrasted. In the MS list they are "Descripción de la vida retirada" and "Crítica de la dicha vida" respectively.[20]

Clearly there is more than one possible way in which the modification process is used by Cadalso. From one point of view he uses it to correct a misconception of what, in his view, seems an error. From another standpoint, he uses it to suggest that there is more than one solution to a given question. The first position suggests an acceptance of certain absolutes; the second position is relativist.

This relativism extends into many aspects of the work, although Cadalso's clearest expression of his acceptance of a relativist viewpoint occurs in another work only recently discovered and printed: his *Defensa de la Nación española*

19. *Cartas*, p. 105, line 66.
20. *Cartas*, p. 208.

contra la Carta persiana LXXVIII de Montesquieu. There he writes "Everything is relative in this world; there is nothing which is positively what it is. A stone is heavy by comparison with wool and light by comparison with lead."[21]

The doctrine of relativism could clearly be one of Cadalso's most obvious reasons for looking to Montesquieu for a literary mould.[22] Yet perhaps Cadalso relies on it even more than the Frenchman for his organisation of the *Cartas.* It is explicit in Cadalso, more implicit in Montesquieu. The contrast of Moorish and Spanish patterns of behaviour and the sense that Mohammedanism and Christianity are as valid the one as the other, is clearly derived from the foreign letter form, though there is a tradition of noble Moors in sixteenth- and seventeenth-century Spanish literature.[23] But the modification of views from one letter to the next, and the re-opening of a subject in a later letter seems very much an extension of relativism by Cadalso. It is true that there is an example of it in Montesquieu's Lettre XVIII, but one cannot take Mehemet Ali as seriously as one takes Gazel, Nuño or Ben-Beley.

Fragmentary composition also perhaps invites readers to look for links or for relativity where Cadalso does not draw attention to it. Relativism can emerge in the different treatment of minor topics in various of the *Cartas marruecas* even when one letter is not directly modifying another. The question of the monarchy is an interesting case in point. Letter 73 is the only letter to deal ostensibly with this matter. The title in the MS version is non-committal: "Breve noticia de los reyes de la Casa de Borbón."[24] More eulogistic is the published title

21. Cadalso, *Defensa de la nación española contra la Carta persiana LXXVIII de Montesquieu,* edición, prólogo y notas de Guy Mercadier, Toulouse, 1970, p. 15. The assertion that 'todo es respectivo' obviously became a commonplace in Spain at this period, since the dramatist Leandro Fernández de Moratín puts it into the mouth of the pedant Don Hermógenes in *La comedia nueva.*

22. On Montesquieu's interest in relativism cf. R. Shackleton, *Montesquieu. A critical biography,* Oxford, 1961, p. 36. Montesquieu's interest in awakening his reader to contrasting points of view is also studied by John Falvey in his article "Aspects of fictional creation in the *Lettres persanes,* and of the aesthetic of the rationalist novel," *Romanic Review,* LVI, No. 4, December 1965, pp. 248-261.

23. Professor José Caso González draws attention to this in the article mentioned in note 10 above.

24. *Cartas,* p. 208.

(perhaps not Cadalso's but the editor's) "Varones insignes de la casa reinante en España."[25] The letter itself is of course flattering to the Bourbons and approves of their paternalistic approach to sovereign rule which benefits the King of Spain's subjects. Yet this eulogy is inevitably set by the reader against the condemnation of the Hapsburgs in Letter 3, and the two together provide a position of perspective on kingship. In Letter 3 the fatal consequences for Spain of the personal and political ambitions of Philip II, Philip III and Philip IV are attacked in terms which the censors could quite clearly not permit. If we had any doubts as to the authenticity of the critical views to be found in the manuscript copies of the work (which were completely altered in the printed versions), comparable passages in the recently published *Defensa de la nación española* now dispel them.[26]

Equally relativist apparently, but rarely explicitly, is Cadalso's view of religion. The whole work obviously reflects, as we have already said, a willingness to accept the equal validity of Moorish and Christian standards. Details confirm Cadalso's acceptance of this position. At the end of Letter 42 Nuño writes to Ben-Beley of the "ser supremo que nosotros llamamos Dios, y vosotros Alá."[27] In 87 Gazel speaks of the sense of unity between "dos hombres racionales de cualquier país o religión."[28] A relativist view of certain religious superstitions or miracles also emerges from the letter on the supposed appearance of St. James at the battle of Clavijo.[29] The philosopher may doubt the validity of the appearance and yet should he spread his doubt as if it were necessarily right? Belief may be wrong in this instance but it was useful in that it encouraged the ordinary soldier to win the battle.

A similar position occurs when posthumous fame is being considered. The philosopher can see that posthumous fame is an absurdity. Yet people should not be discouraged from believing

25. *Cartas*, p. 208.
26. *Op. cit.*, ed. Guy Mercadier, Toulouse, 1970, pp. 8-9.
27. *Cartas*, p. 101, line 44.
28. *Cartas*, p. 193, lines 14-15.
29. Letters 86 and 87.

in it if it is a spur to virtue and noble or heroic action while they are alive. (The position is similar to that of Marmontel in his article on *Gloire* for the *Encyclopédie*.)[30] About style too Cadalso is sometimes a relativist. In the Introduction he points out that what might seem an overdecorated, sublime style to a European is natural to a Moor. There is no readily perceptible right or wrong about it.[31]

If relativism and the search for impartiality seem therefore an essential element in the work and may be partly reflected in both the macrostructure and the microstructure of the *Cartas marruecas*, what about absolutes? Much of the work seems to take truth as an absolute. Gazel is clearly pursuing it in relation to Spain in the early letters and believes that it is ascertainable; elsewhere virtue and "Hombría de bien" seem absolutes, since "entre ser y no ser hombre de bien no hay medio."[32] However the major absolute in the work would appear to be reason, as is often apparent from the form of individual letters and even the interlinking of sentences, as well as from the topics. As I have pointed out elsewhere, many of the letters take the form of a demonstration:[33] a generalisation followed by supporting evidence; or a case-history or anecdote followed by a generalisation. The technique of turning from Gazel to Nuño for an impartial or more considered view of the matter, or to Ben-Beley, reflects a similar confidence in the value of experience to rational processes. It is no surprise that the work laments the lack of study of the experimental sciences in Spain and approves of professors who read Newton in their cells even when they are required to teach Aristotelian physics in their university classes.[34] A similar belief in reason lies behind the satire of scholastic disputations. The desire to define things and get them straight by rational thought is also, of course, behind Nuño's dictionary letters.

30. In Marmontel's view *gloire* is a dream, but a valuable dream. "Le désir d'éterniser sa gloire est un enthousiasme qui nous agrandit" (cf. *Bélisaire*, Maestricht, 1782, pp. 233-34).
31. Cf. *Cartas*, p. 4, lines 40-49.
32. Cf. manuscript title for Letter 52, *Cartas*, p. 207.
33. *Cartas*, p. xxiv.
34. Cf. Letters 6 and 78, *Cartas*, p. 173.

Although something very like this combination of absolutes and relativity exists in Montesquieu, the *Cartas marruecas* are not really all that close to the *Lettres persanes*. A comparison is instructive. Cadalso's letters are narrower in scope and in some ways more concentrated and dramatic as a result. The main characters are of one sex only and basically only of two types: the young and inexperienced (Gazel); and the older, maturer and more philosophical (Nuño and Ben-Beley). This balancing of the characters reflects perhaps a more obvious concern with didacticism. The older characters correct the young. The topics considered are also for the main part related to Spain. Or rather, there is far more about Spain in the *Cartas marruecas* proportionately, than there is about France in Montesquieu's *Lettres persanes*. When Cadalso leaves the analysis of Spanish society, its manners past and present, its strengths and its weaknesses, it is not usually to look at the patterns of behaviour of other countries. There is a little about Morocco (but infinitely less than there is about Persia in the *Lettres persanes*) and there is also a little about France, but no counterpart for Montesquieu's passages about Moscow, England, Italy, Tartary and so forth. There can be no doubt about it that the relativity of the *Cartas marruecas* if more obvious, is very much less quantitatively speaking than that of the *Lettres persanes*.

When Cadalso leaves Spanish problems it is rather to look at wider, human, supranational problems. Indeed, to return to the structure of the work, it looks as if there is a clear patterning of the *Cartas marruecas* which puts Spanish social and political *mores* in a wider moral and historical context. Cadalso's shuffling of Letters 59 and 60 is evidence of this. Throughout the work groups of letters concerned with Spain are interrupted by letters on universal moral questions. There is a constant move in fact from the particular to the general. Thus, if the first thirteen letters are about the Spanish character and the history of her development and decline, the fourteenth and fifteenth seem to move out on to a different level. The fourteenth is about victory celebrations and the irony of countries singing *Te Deums* almost regardless of whether they have won or lost; the topic is an illustration of false pride on a national level. Letter

15 seems to be about pride and conceit on an individual level: everyone despises people in different careers from their own. Letter 16 returns to the subject of Spain's history but Ben-Beley's first letter which follows is about the inevitability with which man grows tired of things which initially delight him, except virtue: an obviously general philosophical (indeed Stoic) theme. In this instance there is no thematic link between the Spanish topic Letter 16 and the moral topic 17 that I can see, unless virtue is being proposed as an alternative to the heroism of Cortes as a pattern to be followed.

After Letter 17 the pattern repeats itself. Letters 18 to 26 cover a variety of Spanish topics: family life, university education, social climbing in Spain. Then in Letters 27 and 28 the question of posthumous fame raises a wider human problem. Subsequently there seems to be an increase in the frequency of philosophical letters. 31 to 36 deal with mainly Spanish matters; but 37 with good and evil; 38 with Spanish pride; yet 39 with the disorder of the world. And this more rapid exchange in the two main types of letter according to my analysis is only broken by the long batch of Spanish letters from 56 to 64: a group which, as I noted at the beginning of this essay, contains no less than three of the "one-off" letters on Spanish topics which Cadalso may have been uncertain where exactly to place, and finally deposited there.

What does this alternation of Spanish and philosophical letters signify? Clearly on one level it reflects a belief in the interrelationship of economic and social problems with moral and philosophical ones. But I feel that it also perhaps reflects a certain pessimism about life and progress which makes the *Cartas marruecas* ultimately rather different from similar works in other countries.[35]

The satire of *moeurs* and institutions may reflect the personal miseries of a writer, but generally speaking it is

---

35. An exception among travel books is perhaps Johnson's *Rasselas*. Parallels between this work and Cadalso's *Cartas marruecas* which suggest that the former may have been a source for the latter have been discussed by Elizabeth May in her article "Dr. Johnson's *Rasselas* and the *Cartas marruecas* of Cadalso," which she kindly allowed me to read in typescript.

designed to provoke awareness of weaknesses and ultimately change. The structure of the *Cartas marruecas* has always seemed to me to reveal a paradoxical approach to satire on Cadalso's part. The mockery and the language are often utilitarian and look for reform. One sort of luxury is "útil," another "dañoso"; there are "inconvenientes" about certain patterns of behaviour; and "los malos proyectos y proyectistas perjudican al estable cimiento de las novedades utiles."[36] Furthermore, Cadalso makes some of his criticism very directly — more so than Montesquieu, for instance. If Gazel and Ben-Beley have a perspective on Spanish affairs which is distorted by their Moroccan background, that of Nuño is focussed directly on the problems of his country. There may be distortion in Nuño's view too, but the involvement is evident and even at times emotional. This implies a desire on Cadalso's part to seek remedies if they exist, and not merely draw attention with wit to the *status quo*. At the same time, the letters also express a certain lack of faith in man's ability to reform. He has difficulty in distinguishing right from wrong, useful ways from dangerous paths. In a passage in the Introduction he provides a clue to the apparent paradox behind the work in a statement which is closer to the author himself than those of the fictional characters Nuño, Gazel and Ben-Beley. Which style of writing is better — the Arabic or the European? he asks. "No lo sé. No me atrevo a decidirlo, ni creo que pueda hacerlo sino uno que ni sea africano ni eruopeo. La naturaleza es la única que pueda ser juez; pero su voz, ¿dónde suena? Tampoco lo sé. Es demasiada la confusión de otras voces para que se oiga la de la común madre en muchos asuntos de los que se presentan en el trato diario de los hombres."[37]

A similar pessimism about reason — so easily confused by the passions — is expressed by Nuño in Letter 21. "Sí, Ben-Beley, tan poca cosa es el entendimiento humano, que si quiere ser un poco eficaz muda la naturaleza de las cosas buenas en malas por buena que sea. La economía muy extremada es

36. Cf. MS title of Letter 34 (*Cartas*, p. 206).
37. *Cartas*, p. 4, lines 45-49.

avaricia. La prudencia sobrada, cobardía; y el valor precipitado, temeridad."[38] Later in the work Gazel too expresses a comparable disenchantment with human nature, and in Letter 43 maintains that it even vitiates virtue itself. Nuño, in his reply (Letter 44), makes precisely the same points which occurred in Letter 21 in remarkably similar language: "Confírmate en la idea de que la naturaleza del hombre es tan malvada que, para valerme de tu propia expresión, suele viciar hasta las virtudes mismas. La economía es, sin duda, una virtud moral, y el hombre que es extremado en ella la vuelve en el vicio llamado avaricia; la liberalidad se muda en prodigalidad, y así de las restantes."[39]

Although some later letters (notably Letters 47 and 48) argue for a balance between pessimism and optimism, the two views permeate even the language of the work. In Letter 24, for instance, irony points out the need to restrain ambition and status-seeking for the good of the state. Yet irony in Letter 15 reaches a far from positive conclusion: an awareness of the weakness inherent in human nature ("en todas las facultades humanas hay cosas ridículas"), is apparent, yet there is no sense that specific correction is possible or that the state could benefit by it.

Inevitably we must ask whether the paradox at the heart of the work is in any way resolved. It might be reasonable to seek an answer in the character of Nuño himself, who is equally paradoxical. Nuño sees all too plainly some of the defects of contemporary Spain; he also sees the inadequacies and inaccuracies of some of his country's critics. When he points out the strengths of Spain's character in the past he clearly implies that he is not a pessimist in his view of Spanish character. The virtues of the past need to be revived. At the same time, one may well ask what Nuño himself does to bring about the changes he seems to feel are necessary. At the beginning of the

---

38. *Cartas*, p. 62, lines 94-97.
39. *Cartas*, p. 103, lines 2-6. It is interesting to note that the pessimistic term used to describe human nature here — "tan malvada" — was deleted by censors or editors and replaced by the phrase "está corrompida" in late manuscripts and the printed editions. The substitution brings the passage into line with teaching about the Fall.

work he is described as "separado del mundo, y según su expresión, encarcelado dentro de sí mismo."[40] He seems essentially an inactive member of society: perhaps a victim. And yet when Gazel admires country retirement in Letter 69, Nuño criticises those who opt out from society. But his own tendency to opt out is further indicated by his refusal to publish his dictionary (Letter 6 and so forth). The problem for the reader becomes still more acute when he finds that "opting out" is not merely a possibility considered, objectively as it were, within the work: the option of a character, no more, no less. It is also a possibility clearly entertained by the writer himself, or editor if you prefer, when he decides not to publish the work but rather to burn it in the *Protesta literaria* at the end of the *Cartas* proper.

How is the paradox to be read and understood? Does it merely give a positive shock to the reader, rather as the *dénouement* of a tragedy might be said to give a shock – purging the emotions and causing the audience, through awareness of dangers, to alter the patterns of their own lives? This would be a fair interpretation if the paradox were just to be seen as a rhetorical device. The paradox would, as it were, make the reader more aware of the need for heroic virtue, and the encouragement of others less virtuous than himself.

But it could also be more than a rhetorical device. A sense of the real isolation of virtue in society and of the Spanish writer more particularly seems to be built into the central structure of the work in Nuño, and is heightened by the tragic sense of existence which Nuño expresses for instance in his *Observaciones y reflexiones sueltas*, which I once thought might be an explanation of the apparent lack of order in the *Cartas* as a whole.[41] Nuño there points out how he gave up organising his notes into categories when he saw the lack of rational order in man. "Cuando vi el ningún método que el mundo guarda en sus cosas, no me pareció digno de que estudiase mucho el de escribirlas. Así como vemos al mundo mezclar lo sagrado con lo

40. *Cartas*, p. 9, lines 14-15.
41. Cf. Nigel Glendinning, *Vida y obra de Cadalso*, Madrid, 1962, pp. 99-100.

profano, pasar de lo importante a lo frívolo, confundir lo malo con lo bueno, dejar un asunto para emprender otro, retroceder y adelantar a un tiempo, afanarse y descuidarse, mudar y afectar constancia, ser firme y aparentar ligereza, así también yo quiero escribir con igual desarreglo."[42]

Furthermore, the sense of isolation of the virtuous writer in a predominantly irrational world finds expression as a topic in several of the letters. It first emerges in Letter 6, in Nuño's dedication of his dictionary to the water-seller Domingo de Domingo, where he speaks of his difficulty in finding a protector for a serious work. At the end of the letter he explains the plight of philosophers. There are "unos hombres rectos y amantes de las ciencias que quisieron hacer a todos los hombres odiar las necedades, que tienen la lengua unísona con el corazón, y otras ridiculeces semejantes."[43] Since men despise them, they must simply withdraw to their garrets and let the world roll on. Another letter whose subject points in a similar direction is Letter 70 where Nuño discusses once again the harsh fate of the scientist or the man of learning in the society for whose benefit he works. The theme returns in Letter 83, which is concerned with the particular fate of men of letters in Spain.

Perhaps it is also the case that the topic of friendship is related to the sense of isolation of the man of virtue. Friendship between Nuño, Gazel and Ben-Beley is at the heart of the work. But according to Letter 46 "no puede haber amistad duradera sino entre hombres de bien."[44] Ben-Beley in that letter sees true friendship as a source of increased virtue in those who share it. Friendship could therefore be instrumental in improving the balance of good and evil in society as a whole. Yet it is seen as an exception rather than a norm: a source of solace to the virtuous which is out of the reach of those who are actively evil. The position is clearly different from that found in Cienfuegos' poetry and in Meléndez Valdes, for example, where friendship is seen as a good to be sought because it unites men in a sense of

42. *Cartas*, p. 93 (Letter 39), lines 14-26.
43. *Cartas*, p. 24, lines 85-87.
44. *Cartas*, p. 207.

equality in society.

It is possible that part of the meaning of the *Cartas marruecas* can be clarified by reference to the literary traditions and conventions which explain some of the structure of the work. The most immediately obvious tradition is that of Turkish, Persian and Chinese letters – evidently Montesquieu, perhaps also Goldsmith. From these Cadalso clearly takes the relativity of approach, and the use of comic contrasts between normal and exotic life styles for satirical ends. The anecdotal techniques he uses also derive in part from works of the same kind. Much then of his positive satire – satire aimed at producing a clearer understanding of the problems of reform – may be said to stem from this European tradition. It is also evident, however, that he is working in Spanish traditions too. Recently, John B. Hughes, following Dolores Franco and others, has devoted a chapter to contrasting Cadalso's *Cartas* with Quevedo's *La España defendida*.[45] The most obvious echoes in Cadalso's works of earlier Spanish writers are of those writing in the moralistic and economic traditions: Fray Luis de Granada, Quevedo in his *Sueños,* and Cervantes, on the one hand; Fernández de Navarrete, Miguel Antonio de la Gándara, Bernardo Ward and Campomanes on the other. From the Spanish economic tradition, of course, Cadalso merely takes details; explaining situations, pointing to certain dangers of policies and specifying remedies. From the moralists he takes patterns as well as detail.

The use of the man of experience – Ben-Beley or Nuño – to qualify the views of a younger man, for example, seems very palpably a reminiscence of Critilo and Andrenio's relationship in *El Criticón,* or the combination of Quevedo and Desengaño in *El mundo por de dentro.* The approach to the criticism of the old man who is commonly venerated yet has contributed nothing to society reminds one of – although in some matters

---

45. John B. Hughes, *José Cadalso y las Cartas marruecas,* Madrid, Tecnos, 1969, chapter 6, pp. 87-100. A more obvious parallel would have been between Quevedo's work and Cadalso's *Defensa de la nación española.* The latter work, like the *España defendida* whose title it seems to recall, is concerned to rebut certain specific criticisms of Spain rather than to examine dispassionately both the weaknesses and the strengths of Spain as is the case in the *Cartas marruecas.*

of detail it is significantly different from — similar passages in Quevedo. Above all the dictionary letters echo a strong tradition in Spanish literature of which there are examples in Antonio de Guevara, Lope de Vega and Quevedo in the sixteenth and seventeenth centuries, and Luis José Velázquez, the marqués de Valdeflores, in Cadalso's own time. The criticism of the life of retirement also found frequent expression in Spain before Cadalso: Pérez de Oliva in the sixteenth century and Nipho in the eighteenth are two examples, although the topic is a universal one and there is nothing about Cadalso's treatment of it to suggest he is writing in a specifically Spanish tradition as opposed to a Classical (Cicero) or a French one (Vattel).

The moralistic tradition is in its own way as positive in its belief in reason as the economic or Enlightenment rational one. For Gracián, travel through life is a source of lessons. Andrenio discovers the moral and physical dangers of the behaviour which in the first instance most appeals to him. He ought to behave more like Critilo, who is constantly applying critical faculties and showing him the right way. Cadalso in part uses the travel element in a similar manner to Gracián. Yet the *Cartas marruecas* also takes from the moralistic tradition a certain pessimism about human nature without apparently accepting the Christian faith which would qualify the pessimism and fit it into a larger optimistic frame: a benevolent deity and the promise of perfection in eternal life.

Cadalso's assimilation and use of Spanish and non-Spanish traditions does not really help us to *resolve* the paradoxical aspects of the *Cartas marruecas*. Frankly I do not now think that the opposites and inconsistencies in the work can necessarily be resolved, at least not by me. My theory that an active Ciceronian-type stoicism seemed to bring the positive and negative sides together was, as has been suggested, an oversimplification. I do not think that one need necessarily look for a Hegelian synthesis to the thesis and antitheses of the *Cartas marruecas*. The deep structure *is* a tension.

Cadalso has in part accepted new systems of his own times and yet has not wholly renounced more traditional systems.

Either he could not, or would not, reconcile some of the conflicts which his marriage of systems produced. Part perhaps of the fascination of the *Cartas marruecas* stems from the tension at its centre. Its attempts to find solutions which are workable while recognising the impossibility of achieving any wholly satisfactory answer to Spain's or man's problems is more sympathetic to us at this point in time than the more golden city approach of some eighteenth-century writers.

The main object of the present essay has been to show that conflicts and contrasts indeed exist; and that the deep as well as the surface structures of the work express conflicting views. This is the *quiddity* of the *Cartas marruecas*. Is it possible to say why it is as it is? There may certainly be psychological explanations for some of the dichotomies, but a major cause of the conflicts within Cadalso is almost certainly the society of which both he and the language he uses are in some sense an expression. He himself shows his awareness of some of the pressures when he makes Gazel define the various classes of writer in Europe in Letter 66, "Unos escriben cuanto les viene a la pluma; otros lo que les mandan escribir; otros todo lo contrario de lo que sienten; otros lo que agrada al público con lisonja; otros lo que le choca con represión."[46] Obviously Cadalso was not one of those in the first category, who could write "whatever came into his mind." Did he really intend to shock the society he wrote for? His expressed design was to reconcile extremes and avoid controversy. In the Introduction Cadalso asserts that he has published the letters "por cuanto de ellas no se trata de religión ni de gobierno."[47] and seems to welcome prudent restriction. In Letter 39 Nuño is reported as saying that nothing new can be said about monarchies, "que sea útil a los Estados, o seguro para los Autores."[48] It is one of the ironies of the intervention of censors before publication that the word "seguro" was deleted and "de beneficio" substituted in this passage.

Study of the variants in the text shows how Cadalso's

46. *Cartas*, p. 141, lines 1-4.
47. *Cartas*, p. 4, lines 34-35.
48. *Cartas*, p. 94, lines 26-27.

original ideas were modified in a large number of small but significant instances. It is evident that he would have had to restrain himself in a number of ways if he wished the work to pass the censors. Not only was heterodox material about government and religion inevitably cut, but also any words which could be held to reflect adversely on the national honour. I imagine that the paragraph about the failure of Spaniards to appreciate even Cervantes in his own time (in Letter 83) was omitted by censors or editors for precisely this reason.

The censorship and the continued existence of the Inquisition not only in fact explain ambiguities; they also explain some of the apparent dilutions of Montesquieu's recipe in Cadalso. It is obvious that Cadalso had to be guarded or indirect in his relativism, and not express overtly deist as opposed to orthodox Catholic positions. On sexual matters he had to be equally guarded. He could not have put the kind of material into his work which Montesquieu did. Although Cadalso's letters to Tomás de Iriarte show that he had a ready wit in that area, enjoyed using it and appears to have accepted man's sensual nature without criticism, the nearest we get to this position in the *Cartas marruecas* is the calculation about the number of copulations achieved by the boastful young Spaniard in Letter 10. Naturally I am not suggesting that sexual matter is a necessary concomitant of a work of this kind. But its absence leaves the positions of Nuño and Gazel (and by extension those of Cadalso) unclear in certain philosophical areas. It is certainly the case that Cadalso's friend Moratín's *Arte de putas* contains far more challenging statements about the nature of man and human society than any of those he expressed in works obviously intended for publication. His argument about the lack of social utility of some of the virtues is particularly revealing.

Some of the paradoxical elements in Cadalso's work must, then, be due to the author's necessity to suppress material in certain areas: exactly how much he and others suppressed is an insoluble problem for historians of ideas working on the literature of the Enlightenment in Spain. But other pressures existed which may also explain conflicting aspects of the *Cartas*. The obvious respect for the monarchical system and acceptance of a traditional hierarchical society, for instance — how far is this Cadalso's real position, as opposed to one he adopted in order that the work could be printed? Biographical information and the impression gained from his other works suggests that the ambivalent approach to hierarchies *was* Cadalso's own position, not merely the one he ascribes to fictional characters. An early satirical work attributed to him certainly attacked the *morals* of both Church and Court, and he may well have held anti-church and aristocracy views in the 1760's when he could afford independence. At the same time he subsequently lived by the hierarchy — applied for and was admitted to the Order of the Knights of St. James; and sought promotion in the Cavalry Regiment with which he served. If his views were really extreme he must have been forced to compromise them. Banishment from the Court by the Count of Aranda may have made him critical of the government, but his financial position was such that he could not afford to act independently. The circles in which he lived and moved both as an officer and as a writer were primarily those of the ruling classes, and it would have been surprising if he had not been forced to accept some of their values.

As a writer depending on others for money rather than publishing his works at his own expense he must also have had to accept — as nearly all writers do — the pressures of his likely readership. To judge from the subscription lists of the period which I have recently been examining for the years 1755 to 1820, any shift towards a more middle-class non-hierarchy reader was slight in the 1770's. Consequently anti-establishment work could only be of a very limited kind, asserting, for instance, the right of the *noble* to criticise the monarch (in itself a suggestive subject), as do a number of plays of the period, which also strongly oppose political tyranny in general.

The pattern of characters selected by Cadalso for his *Cartas marruecas* supports the view that he wrote the work with the establishment clearly in mind. Ben-Beley is a retired minister; Gazel a young diplomat; Nuño moves in circles which are obviously those of the upper class. The discussions in the work about the nature of nobility and the obsession of people with status and titles seem rather designed to show the need for nobles to be useful to society and deserving of honour than to question the value of the nobility altogether. Nuño's apparent willingness to treat everyone as equals – he raises his hat to everyone he passes in the street except a rich and useless old man – is surely out of line with the view that ordinary people ought to be kept in ignorance of some aspects of history in another letter. Reason is not for them, theirs not to reason why.

Despite these limitations, which stem once again from a conflict of systems, the *Cartas marruecas* is an important work in the context of eighteenth-century Spanish letters. It is not the first work in Spain to deal with moral and national problems in a largely relativistic way. Nor, incidentally, is it the first to imitate there the *Lettres persanes*. A particularly important precursor is Clavijo y Fajardo's periodical *El Pensador,* which not only discusses some of the Spanish problems like education, superstition and bull-fights which recur in the *Cartas marruecas,* but also discusses some things in an open-ended fashion. Clavijo's work also allows less room for compromise. Whereas the *Cartas marruecas* seeks impartiality by respecting the old as well as the new Cadalso's relativism and invitation to discussion is obviously on a broader scale and is more emphatically and coherently expressed. Its particular mixture of wit and pathos, and its attempts to modify systems in which its author had been brought up and under which he had to live, continue to command, and in my view will go on commanding, sympathy and readers.

Nigel Glendinning

Language, History & Vision: An Approach to 18th-Century Literature

When Coleridge looked back on the eighteenth century, he perceived in both its culture and its politics a civilized bridge between two Barbary shores of fanaticism. The first of these was the eruption of enthusiasm that marked the religious upheavals of the sixteenth and seventeenth centuries. The second, and the one that brought that culture to an end, was the visionary fanaticism of the French Revolution:

> The magic rod of fanaticism is preserved in the very adyta of human nature; and needs only the re-exciting warmth of a master hand to bud forth afresh and produce the old fruits. The horror of the peasants' war in Germany, and the direful effects of the Anabaptists' tenets (which differed only from those of Jacobinism by the substitution of theological for philosophical jargon), struck all Europe for a time with affright. Yet little more than a century was sufficient to obliterate all effective memory of these events. The same principles, with similar though less dreadful consequences, were again at work from the imprisonment of the first Charles to the restoration of his son. The fanatic maxim of extirpating fanaticism by persecution produced a civil war. The war ended in the victory of the insurgents; but the temper survived, and Milton had abundant grounds for asserting that 'Presbyter was but Old Priest writ large!' One good result, thank heaven! of this zealotry was the re-establishment of the Church. And now it might have been hoped that the mischievous spirit would have been bound for a season, 'and a seal set upon him that he might deceive the nation no more.' But no! The ball of persecution was taken up

with undiminished vigor by the persecuted. . . . The same principles dressed in the ostentatious garb of a fashionable philosophy once more rose triumphant and effected the French revolution.[1]

This passage from the *Biographia Literaria* both hints at and asserts evidence from which one might fashion a view of eighteenth-century culture and literature at once broader and more precise than those that prevail in our time. In what follows I shall offer an outline of such a view, a guide map for a new approach to eighteenth-century literature.

Some of Coleridge's opinions first bear repeating and expanding to bring out their implications. We should notice that he includes English fanaticism or enthusiasm among the theocratic, visionary, and revolutionary movements that transformed the cultures of Germany, the Netherlands, Bohemia, and France during the seventeenth and eighteenth centuries. Coleridge was not alone in believing that England was grievously and notoriously marked by its wars of religion. In the Bodleian Library there is a manuscript collection of poems by no less a witness than Marvell's Lord Fairfax, who reckoned in doggerel verse that

> When Italy is wthout Fish
> When France wthout Treason is
> In England longe noe war we see
> Then wthout Earth the World shall bee.[2]

And as Coleridge extends his comments through both space and time, we begin to notice the shaping of a theory of cultural history that explains why he was later so attracted to the first great work of cultural history in any language, Giambattista Vico's *Scienza Nuova*, published first in 1725 and, in its third and final form, in 1744.[3] Like Vico, Coleridge suggests that cultural history is a cyclic movement from barbarism to civility,

---

1. *Biographia Literaria*, ed. George Watson, London, 1956, pp. 109-110.
2. MS. Fairfax 40, p. 637.
3. For Coleridge's acquaintance with Vico and the *Scienza Nuova*, see George Whalley, "Coleridge and Vico," in *Giambattista Vico: An International Symposium*, ed. Giorgio Tagliacozzo and Hayden V. White, Baltimore, 1969, pp. 225-244.

and that the culture of civility or humanism is continually vitalized and destroyed by movements erupting out of the counter-culture of external barbarism or of internal and underground enthusiasm.[4]

This is not only the thesis of Coleridge in the nineteenth century and of Vico in the eighteenth. It is also the cultural premise of poets, dramatists, novelists, preachers, historians, statesmen, and readers in that long moment of English and French literature that lasted from the English Civil War to the French Revolution. Upholders of the mediated and hierarchic culture of humanism - Corneille, Bossuet, and Voltaire; Dryden, Swift, Pope, Gibbon, and Johnson - creatively opposed those who spoke for the unmediated and subjective culture of enthusiasm - Pascal, Racine, Fénelon and Rousseau; Wesley, Richardson, and Christopher Smart.

Each defined the other, and the two cultures combined to create the diversity of eighteenth-century literature. The great figures and works of the age achieve their complexity in part by poising within themselves both cultural impulses; through allusive satire, as in Dryden and Pope, through ventriloquism, as in Swift's *Tale of a Tub*, through introspection, as in Samuel Johnson. And in French literature, as Lucien Goldmann has shown in *Le Dieu Caché*.[5] Racine's tragic vision arises from social and cultural tensions within enthusiasm. His verse makes everything manifest except the truth. Racine's metaphors, like his Jansenist God, are at once concealed and domineering; and his characters, like Pope's Eloisa and Abelard, are finally and tragically "enthusiastic." They are "filled with a god" who will not speak to or through them, who turns away his face and abandons them to the articulate torment of their own voices and solitude. In a significant shift of enthusiasm from religion

---

4. A bold and provocative development of this general thesis appears in Friedrich Heer's *The Intellectual History of Europe*, London, 1966, to which I am greatly indebted. A more limited but parallel interpretation appears in Norman Cohn's *The Pursuit of the Millennium*, 2nd ed., New York, 1961. Cohn's sub-title, "Revolutionary messianism in medieval and Reformation Europe and its bearing on modern totalitarian movements," is a précis of the larger argument.

5. Paris, 1959, esp. ch. VII, "Jansénisme et Vision Tragique," pp. 157-182, and the final ch. XVII, "La Vision Tragique dans le Théâtre de Racine," pp. 347-446.

to primitivism, Diderot toward the end of the eighteenth century balances Racine's stylistic ambiguity toward the end of the seventeenth. In works such as his *Supplément au Voyage de Bougainville*, Diderot replaces spiritual vision by sexual ecstasy as the object of enthusiasm. Nature and desire are the new hidden god and inner voice. And yet typically, paradoxically, in the distinctive stylistic tension of the period, Diderot tells us that we must be utterly instinctive and primitive, all "a wonder and a wild desire," in a peroration that owes more to the tone, learning, and style of Bossuet than to the glad animal cries of Bougainville's noble savages:

> Combien nous sommes loin de la nature et du bonheur! L'empire de la nature ne peut être détruit: on aura beau le contrarier par des obstacles, il durera. Ecrivez tant qu'il vous plaira sur des tables d'airain, pour me servir des expressions du sage Marc-Aurèle, que le frottement voluptueux de deux intestins est un crime, le coeur de l'homme sera froissé entre la menace de votre inscription et la violence de ses penchants.[6]

When we approach the period's literature through its transformations of language, we begin to discover that its most characteristic late developments, primitivism, evangelical fervour, and revolutionary zeal, are displacements or analogies of early developments, heroic allusion, enthusiasm, and messianic vision. More than alliteration links Winstanley, Wesley, and Wordsworth; Racine, Rousseau, and Robespierre.

It is crucial to an understanding of the period's literature that we rediscover those other links that join language and vision through history. Specifically, we must recognize first that fanaticism and enthusiasm were in the eyes of contemporaries, especially of their contemporary opponents, as much matters of stylistic as of spiritual disorder. The evidence is everywhere. Dryden's backhanded slap at Elkanah Settle, that he was "a kind of fanatic in poetry" should prepare us for the critical as well as political significance of lines such as these:

6. In *Diderot: Oeuvres*, Pléiade, ed. André Billy, Paris, 1951, p. 998.

A numerous Host of dreaming Saints succeed;
Of the true old Enthusiastick Breed:
'Gainst Form and Order they their Pow'r imploy;
Nothing to Build, and all things to Destroy.
But far more numerous was the Herd of such,
Who think too little, and who talk too much.[7]

Swift in his turn sought to reform and "ascertain" the English language as a response to the damage it had suffered at the hands of fanaticism, and the *Letter to a Young Poet* doubtfully attributed to Swift would, in its guying parallels between poetic and religious inspiration, less doubtfully suggest his views.[8] The crazed energy of the poetasters and Grub Street hacks who assault Pope at Twickenham combines inspiration and madness, while their syncopated antics resemble the contemporary styles of Quakers and Shakers: "Fire in each eye, and Papers in each hand,/They rave, recite, and madden round the land."[9] And finally, we might recall to mind the link between poetry, prophecy, and "phrensy" implied by Samuel Johnson's sequence of definitions in his *Dictionary* for the term "enthusiasm" itself. The first definition is both the best known and the most hostile: "A vain belief of private revelation; a vain confidence of divine favour or communication." Johnson supports this meaning by quoting Locke's opinion that *"Enthusiasm* is founded neither on reason nor divine revelation, but rises from the conceits of a warmed or overweening Brain." But the second and more neutral definition raises the other sense of inspiration by offering "Heat of imagination; violence of passion; confidence of opinion." A third definition sounds even more assertive and much more complimentary. It calls enthu-

7. *Absalom and Achitophel,* ll. 529-534. J. R. Sutherland makes some excellent remarks about the links between these various threats to "Form and Order" in both their literary and social meanings in his *Preface to Eighteenth Century Poetry,* Oxford, 1948.

8. *The Prose Works of Jonathan Swift,* ed. Herbert Davis: *Irish Tracts 1720-1723 and Sermons,* with an Introductory Essay and Notes on the sermons by Louis Landa, Oxford, 1948, pp. 327-345. Landa presents his doubts concerning Swift's authorship in his introduction, pp. xxvi-xxvii.

9. *Epistle to Arbuthnot,* ll. 5-6.

siasm "Elevation of fancy; exaltation of ideas."[10]

The connection between enthusiasm in religion and exaltation in style becomes even stronger when we remind ourselves of the full meaning of the sublime in eighteenth-century culture. To us, perhaps because the academic mind finds the sublime less unsettling if and when it is treated merely as a rhetorical feature of style, the term evokes either vague references to an even vaguer figure called Longinus or knowing attempts to analyze we know not what, that *je ne sais quoi* that lies beyond the reach of both art and criticism. But when the early nineteenth-century art critic Martin Shee looked back on the eighteenth century he saw in the sublime a precise analogy to incoherent methodist and enthusiastic attempts to express and describe intense spiritual experience: "those who talk rationally on other subjects," he says "no sooner touch on this, than they go off in a literary delirium; fancy themselves, like Longinus, 'the great sublime they draw,' and rave like methodists, of inward lights, and enthusiastic emotions, which, if you cannot comprehend, you are set down as un-illumined by the grace of criticism, and excluded from the elect of Taste."[11] This suggests that the sublime was a secularized or camouflaged outburst of enthusiasm. One might go even further and suggest that the sublime was to aesthetics what the French Revolution was to politics. Before Edmund Burke detected the indwelling spirit of enthusiasm among the Jacobins and regicides of France, he discovered an indwelling power of the sublime in the noise of raging storms, thunder, cataracts, and artillery. A.W. Schlegel once made an interesting joke about Burke's distinction between the Beautiful and the Sublime. In Burke's eyes, said Schlegel, "the Beautiful is a tolerably pretty strumpet, and the Sublime is a grenadier with a big moustache."[12] This is interesting not because it is especially funny, but because it

10. See *Johnson's Dictionary, A Modern Selection,* ed. E. L. McAdam Jr. and George Milne, New York, 1963, p. 166.

11. From Shee's *Elements of Art,* 1809; quoted in Samuel H. Monk, *The Sublime,* Ann Arbor paperback edition, Ann Arbor, 1960, p. 3.

12. Quoted in William K. Wimsatt and Cleanth Brooks, *Literary Criticism: A Short History,* New York, 1964, p. 260.

points once again to the impression left by Burke that there is a connection between aesthetic sublimity and warlike conflict. They both express enthusiastic forces in nature and human nature directed against order and civility.

They are also however directed *toward* a mode of expression: toward the re-barbarizing of language. Enthusiasm in all its forms seeks to shape and distort language into the cry of ecstasy, the speaking in tongues, the barbarian war-cry, the slogans of the crowd, the godlike thunder that, as Vico pointed out, gave the first men and women their sense of power and guilt. In its most intense forms this re-barbarizing of language abandons altogether the language of men and takes up the language of gods - the gestures of manifest power and finally the silences of unmediated vision. If we listen closely to the voice of the Bard from Milton to Dryden to Pope we hear great changes in poetic tone and linguistic level. The speakers change, as it were, from gods to heroes to men. And if we listen from Pope to Blake to Wordsworth the dialects change again; the speakers change back from men to heroes to gods.

Readers of Vico's *Scienza Nuova* will recognize the reference here to his theory of the tripartite structure of language. I shall take up later this key to poetic style, but I should like to offer for now a neglected eighteenth-century perspective on the romantic notion of re-barbarizing language in order to achieve poetic expression.

The culture and literature of the eighteenth century show that they in that age remembered what we today too often forget: that the difference between barbarism and civilization is both originally and continually a difference in language. The barbarian is an aboriginal enthusiast; the enthusiast is a latter-day barbarian. The Greek etymology of the word suggests the imitative babbling, *bar-bar*, of the βάρβαροι, of those who do not speak Greek. Βαρβαρίζω means to speak in an outlandish way, i.e. in a foreign tongue. But this notion is closely connected to the linguistic excesses of enthusiastic religious frenzy. In his *Ecclesiastical History*, for example, Eusebius uses the term ξενοφωνέω to describe the ravings of a heretical trance. Now ξενοφωνέω likewise means to speak in an outlandish way, but it seems to mean more exactly "to speak in tongues," to speak out of the inspired power of glossolalia.[13]

The clash between social ideologies that accompanies this clash between languages can be heard in Erasmus' accusation that Luther lacked *civilitas*, by which he meant that Luther wrote in the inflammatory vernacular. "I converse with you in Latin," he observes in the *Hyperaspistes*, "you utter what you have to say against me in the German of peasants, mariners, artisans, and blacksmiths." In the same work Erasmus puts the matter even more simply: "You call for revolt, and you can see revolt arising everywhere because your books are written in German."

But this ancient contrast between barbarism and civilization also allows that a nation or society or class that attains and clings to a highly articulated and literary language remains civilized and memorable, no matter how greatly it is threatened by violence and incoherence. Gibbon expresses his age's and his culture's devotion to the word in describing the state of the Greek language at Constantinople in the fourteenth century: "In their lowest servitude and depression, the subjects of the Byzantine throne were still possessed of a golden key that could unlock the treasures of antiquity; of a musical and prolific language, that gives a soul to the objects of sense and a body to the abstractions of philosophy" (*Decline and Fall*, Ch. LXVI). And this remained true: Constantinople retained its saving remnant of civilized and learned citizens in the midst of barbarian assaults on Greek culture and language. Gibbon links these two assaults in his next sentence: "Since the barriers of the monarchy, and even of the capital, had been trampled under foot, the various barbarians had doubtless corrupted the form and substance of the national dialect. . . ."

It would require a great shift of taste for a modern reader to admit that Gibbon and his age were right to prefer civilization to barbarism. Shelley was right to say that "the savage is to ages what the child is to years" in his *Defence of Poetry*, but Samuel

---

13. Eusebius, *Ecclesiastical History*, v. 16. Quoted in R. A. Knox, *Enthusiasm: A Chapter in the History of Religion, with Special Reference to the XVII and XVIII Centuries*, Oxford, 1950, p. 30.

Johnson seized on an equal truth, and one neglected today, when he said that both children and savages are cruel, and implied that they are no fit source of example for civilized adults. It would require an even greater shift in style for our age to give up, in favour of more conscious and articulated forms of discourse, the ideal of artless sincerity. But if we are to appreciate eighteenth-century literature we must begin, however inwardly and tentatively, to make shifts such as these. We might first accept for the sake of argument, or in memory of the traditions that once called upon the educated to preserve and renew their culture, the possibility that civilization with all its discontents is better than barbarism with all its pleasures.

If we are to appropriate for ourselves the expressive values of eighteenth-century literature, we must recognize that those values rested on a creative defence of the word against two kinds of attack. One kind of attack came from those in Sprat's Royal Society or among the followers of Descartes and Locke who objected that language was too vague, too filled with echoes. The other came from the reviving enthusiasts, who objected that language was not vague and resounding enough. The first group objected to what the modern followers of Wittgenstein have sometimes called the magic of language. The second objected, as it were, that what was needed was more than the magic of language. Beyond spells and curses they demanded speaking in tongues and the voice that speaks in the whirlwind or out of the burning bush. The first wanted to reduce the language of men to the level of formulae and sense-data; the second wanted to raise that language beyond the level of heroic expression (for what has Christ to do with pagan heroes?) up to the level of the divine logos, the Word of God. Both attacks and both kinds of objections, insofar as they distorted the expressive powers of language, were looked upon by the makers of eighteenth-century literature as barbarian in their origin and tendency.

We need to remember what men of that age did not need reminding of; Pepys's account of Fifth Monarchy men with their murderous attacks and exalted cry, "The King Jesus, and their heads upon their gates!"; the sectarians of Saint Médard, given to convulsions and to threatening their opponents with knives (one of those being Voltaire's brother Arouet); the Gordon riots in London; the enragés of the French Revolution. We need to remember, if we are to understand the tensions within eighteenth-century culture, that in 1704, the year in which the Battle of Blenheim supposedly inaugurated an era of parade-ground warfare and rational politics, both of which were celebrated by Addison's confident verse in *The Campaign*, that in that same year, in the district of the Cévennes, the French prophets and their Catholic enemies slaughtered one another by the thousands in ferocious guerilla warfare. It is not coincidence that 1704 was also the year of Swift's *Tale of a Tub*, nor that Shaftesbury's *Letter Concerning Enthusiasm* of 1711 was provoked by the activities of these same French Prophets or Camisards in England. We know from the Book of Proverbs that where there is no vision the people perish. Those who shaped eighteenth-century culture knew from experience that where there is too much vision, both the culture and the people perish.

Their memories of both the wars of religion and scientific revolution of the preceding generations, however, had developed among contemporary writers a troubled sense that so much of what they accepted as civilized had once been barbaric or even barbarous. Barons had once been brigands or regicides, articles of religion had once been causes of bloodshed, commonplaces of science had once been scandalous heresies. And as antiquarians and historians began to re-examine the artifacts and records of their own Christian and Graeco-Roman civilization, they discovered that the Biblical and classical literature on which so much depended was neither static nor certain nor even unquestionably civilized. In defending tradition and high culture against the sceptics and fanatics, eighteenth-century writers and thinkers discovered in their own essential texts and sources grounds for scepticism and disturbing signs of fanaticism.

A great work of criticism by a French Oratorian, Richard Simon's *Histoire critique du vieux testament* (1679) founded higher criticism of the Bible. And as Dryden saw in colouring his *Religio Laici* with the implications of the *Histoire critique* . . . , Père Simon had called in question much more than the evidence of text-quoting Puritans. In Dryden's poem, in Pope's *Essay on Criticism*, in Simon's *Histoire critique* . . . , and in many similar works, criticism became the path to discovery in literature and theology. This critical spirit continued throughout the first half of the eighteenth century the intellectual attitudes of the Counter-Reformation, which everywhere encouraged the critical study of literature and the creative study of history. The study of literary texts guarded against a rigid or partial approach to scripture, while the study of history was intended to replace the study of the physical sciences. The high culture of the eighteenth century was in fact more the result of an *alliance* between Counter-Reformation and Enlightenment than the result of a struggle. Both the Church and its enemies spoke the same humanist idiom, the schools of the Oratorians taught a curriculum based on the literature and history advocated by the most enlightened authors such as d'Alembert, and when the Jesuits were expelled from France in 1764, leaving a hundred schools without teachers, both d'Alembert and Diderot saw this as a victory for Jansenist and Gallican enthusiasm – and as a defeat for the cause of enlightenment.[14] On the level of popular religion the Anglican Church paralleled the work of the Counter-Reformation,[15] and that parallel extends to the high culture of the age. One might define the essence of the Catholic (and Anglican) Counter-Reformation in ways that make those movements remarkably similar to both eighteenth-century literature and the Enlightenment. All of these cultural phenomena emphasized that uniformity of belief, aesthetic standards, and common sense were paradoxically necessary conditions of individual salvation, genius, and judgment. With one or two important exceptions, the major English authors were believing Christians whose faith took a sacramental, hierarchical and mediated form: Dryden, Swift, Pope and Johnson show how

14. Roland Mortier, "The 'Philosophes' and Public Education," *Yale French Studies,* 40, pp. 63-68.
15. "The Counter-Reformation and the People of Catholic Europe," *Past and Present* 47, May, 1970, pp. 51-70.

pervasive and parallel the Anglican, Catholic and "enlightened" influences were. They shared with their continental contemporaries such as Vico and Voltaire an obsession with history as a process made by man that also made the world of man what it was.

This notion of historical process was a genuine discovery of the time: it later became a mainspring of eighteenth-century culture and literature. Vico expressed this concept in a wonderful summary: "This world of nations has certainly been made by man, and its guise must therefore be found within the modifications of our own human mind." That idea dovetails the growth of culture, the process of history, and the myth-making powers of the literary imagination. And the great work in which it appears, the *Scienza Nuova* of 1744, is at once an attempt at cultural history, an identification of historical process with reality, and a major work of literary aesthetics.

The focus and origin of this "New Science," whose title boldly asserts Vico's attempt to replace the sciences of matter by the sciences of man, is an extended and brilliant study of Homer. In looking back on Homer, and more generally on what Bacon, one of the *Scienza Nuova's* heroes, called the "exemplar states" of Greece and Rome, Vico perceived what the Renaissance veneration for antiquity had concealed for so long. He perceived that the classical cultures had grown up from barbarism and that their literatures are the record of that growth. He saw that barbarism and its transformation are individual as well as collective states of consciousness, and that the spoor of that animal man as he moves toward humanity can be traced through language. He found that frenzy and class conflict were more characteristic of heroic culture than reason and light. He discovered, in a word, how different that world was from ours and yet how disturbingly the same. The shock of this difference (and the intervening neglect of Vico) forced Fustel de Coulanges a century later to begin his now classic study *The Ancient City* with thoughts such as these:

> We shall attempt to set in a clear light the radical and essential differences which at all times distinguished these

ancient peoples from modern societies. In our system of education, we live from infancy in the midst of the Greeks and Romans, and become accustomed continually to compare them with ourselves, to judge of their history by our own, and to explain our revolutions by theirs.

He goes on from this to the logical extreme of historicism: to the opinion that, if we study them without thinking of ourselves, "Greece and Rome appear to us in a character absolutely inimitable; nothing in modern times resembles them; nothing in the future can resemble them."[16] Unlike Fustel, however, Vico goes beyond and beneath the changeable intelligence of man, upon which Fustel based his conclusions about classical singularity, to those myth-making powers and psychic states that seem to join in a creative chain the child, the barbarian and the enthusiast as each becomes in turn the adult, the civilized person and the humanist. In comparing rather than contrasting the savage and the epic hero, Vico aligned himself with the missionaries of the Counter-Reformation and the satirists of English and French literature. As Henri Baudet has observed of this contemporary comparison:

Details of the Greeks influenced opinion on the Indian savages; the image of antiquity was coloured by observation of the exotic. Three famous missionaries — Lafitau, Bufier, and Charlevoix — believed that the Homeric Greek lived on in the Indian: lost antiquity in a contemporary setting. The Indian method of bringing up their young was considered to be Spartan, while the Spartan method was found to resemble that of the Severambs. Père Lafitau claimed that a few months sojourn among the Hurons had taught him more about the Trojan War than all the lengthy works of classical scholars combined. Here, too, the historical past gained the upper hand over its mythical counterpart, and the search for a classical Lacedaemon replaced the search for Paradise. Were the autochthonous religions not Homeric in character and older than Moses or

16. Numa Denis Fustel de Coulanges, *The Ancient City*, New York, n.d., pp. 11-12.

the Flood? From then on Lafitau's Indians are clad in tunic or toga. When, presently, the Greek dominates the European scene (cf. Winckelmann), his new status is not solely attributable to a predilection for the classical world. The Romantics cannot forget the highly paradoxical link forged between Greek and savage.[17]

This link binds those two often mistakenly separated eighteenth-century figures, the noble savage and the noble warrior. It was Vico's achievement to suggest that they are alike, not in any deceptive appearance of nobility, but rather in the ignoble realities of savagery.

Vico always emphasizes that mythology is the key to history, and that literature, language and law are the arts and instruments of these new sciences. Early in the *Scienza Nuova* he declares: "It follows that the first science to be learned should be mythology or the interpretation of fables; for, as we shall see, all the histories of the gentiles have their beginnings in fables, which were the first histories of the gentile nations" (para. 51).[18] Notice that Vico distinguishes between providential and gentile (i.e. non-Judaeo-Christian) history. This distinction moves toward a modern conception of history by discarding the figural and hieroglyphic approach to history of the Middle Ages and the Renaissance. It is also a distinction that allows the critical and sceptical attitude toward the past that was common to both the Counter-Reformation and the Enlightenment.

When we follow Vico into his labyrinth of myths and fables this sceptical edge seems to run out everywhere to an ironic or satirical point. Vico on the rapes, incests, perversions and

17. Henri Baudet, *Paradise on Earth: Some Thoughts on European Images of Non-European Man,* tr. Elizabeth Wentholt, New Haven and London, 1965, p. 50. Lafitau's accounts of the Iroquois, published in Paris in 1724, have been acknowledged as a source of Rousseau's noble savage; but the original comparison was with the Homeric Greek.

18. All references are to *The New Science of Giambattista Vico,* rev. tr. of 3rd ed., 1744, ed. and tr. Thomas Goddard Bergin and Max Harold Fisch, Ithaca, N.Y., 1968, p. 33. For the sake of clarity and simplicity, references will be given in the text and keyed to the paragraph numbering of this edition, which is in turn based on the standard edition in *Giambattista Vico Opere,* a cura di Fausto Nicolini, Milan and Naples, 1953.

murders of Olympian mythology suddenly picks out the dark and bizarre shadows that Racine, Dryden, Swift, Fénelon, Fielding and Voltaire discover beneath the fair and poised appearance of Graeco-Roman mythology. To grasp Vico's treatment of the gods is to comprehend suddenly the satirical, historical, and anti-enthusiastic bent of eighteenth-century literature. It is like that shock of discovery felt by the traveller in Athens when he learns that what now seems the bleached purity of Greek sculpture was once tarted up in gaudy colours.

Many of the gods and goddesses in heaven do not contract matrimony at all. One marriage there is, that of Jove and Juno, and it is sterile; and not only sterile but full of atrocious wrangling. Jove indeed fixes in the air his chaste and jealous wife and he himself gives birth to Minerva, who springs from his head. And Saturn, if he begets children, devours them. Such examples, powerful divine examples as they are (though such fables may contain all the recondite wisdom desired by Plato and in our time by Bacon of Verulam in his *Wisdom of the Ancients*), if taken at face value would corrupt the most civilized peoples and would incite them to become as bestial as the very beasts of Orpheus ... (para. 80).

Passages such as this also help to explain why Lucretius, Virgil's great rival and opposite in the classical order of the late seventeenth and eighteenth centuries, then so attracted and disturbed readers he has since lost. Through Lucretius they saw that the creation of nature and culture was sensual, fierce and continuous rather than static, calm and rational.

When Vico turns from the language of the gods and mythology to the language and literature of heroes he outdoes himself in satirical insights worthy of eighteenth-century attacks on the heroic as different as Fénelon's *Les Aventures de Télémaque*, Swift's *Gulliver's Travels*, Fielding's *Jonathan Wild* and Voltaire's *Candide*. Vico noticed that when Achilles rages at Hector in the *Iliad* (XXII, ll. 261 ff.) and boasts "I shall give your body to my hunting dogs to eat," the heroic code has about it something brutal and shocking. And when Vico describes the character of Achilles he shows how easily the knife of satire can slip in between the heroic veneer and its barbarous underwood. In a bluntly colloquial jibe, Vico characterizes Achilles as "a man so arrogant that, as we say nowadays, he will not let a fly pass the end of his nose" — "un uomo orgoglioso, il qual or direbbesi che non si faccia passare la mosca per innanzi alla punta del naso" (para. 667, Nicolini, *Opere*, p. 676). Vico brings his ironic view of the epic spirit even closer to eighteenth-century literature when he compares the battling Greeks and Trojans to "duellists of the returned barbarian times" (para. 667). Vico on the *Iliad* has significantly a great deal in common with the quarrel over Corneille's *Le Cid*, itself an attempt to re-order and re-enact a rambling story concerned with a group of "duellists of the returned barbarian times."

Vico moves finally from the language of heroes to the language of men. As he does so we begin to realize that both his approach and that of eighteenth-century literature tend to integrate poetry and society, myth and history, and the three levels of language. They achieve this integration by making us read every line and every metaphor as a brief fable of the conflicts between levels of verbal usage, class interest, fictional presentation, and historical interpretation.

Let us consider one example that must stand for many. One of the most significant figures (to both his friends and enemies) in eighteenth-century culture was that of the divine-right monarch whose hero's or demi-god's origin was summed up in the emblematic phrase, so deliberately evocative of Christ's heroic role, "descendit de caelis." We come to realize how fully this image results from a myth-making power when we read Vico's account of a parallel myth from Roman history: "For the plebeians in the heroic struggles with the nobles, as ancient Roman history openly tells us, kept saying that the fathers of whom Romulus composed the Senate (and from whom these patricians were descended) *non esse caelo demissos*, 'had not come down from heaven'; that is, that Jove was equal [just] to all. . . . By this reflection the Roman plebeians began to achieve equality with the patricians in civil liberty, until they entirely changed the Roman commonwealth from an aristocratic to a popular form" (para. 415). Any one familiar with works such as Swift's *A Discourse of the Contests and Dissensions between the Nobles and the Commons in Athens and Rome*, Montesquieu's *Les Considérations sur les causes de la grandeur des Romains et de leur décadence* and Gibbon's *Decline and Fall of the Roman Empire* will know, and others can guess from their titles, that conflicting myths corresponded to conflicting social groups, and that the two conflicts merged into the Vichian concept of ancient and modern cyclic patterns, which he called "corsi e ricorsi" in history, poetry, and the human mind itself. And any one familiar with the sacred and blasphemous rhetoric that surrounded the monarch in contemporary England and France will note the social, religious, and poetic implications of the emblem *descendit de caelis* and its obliteration in *non esse caelo demissos*. Especially in an age that opened and closed with acts of regicide, the execution of Charles I in 1649 and of Louis XVI in 1793, and with the revolutionary creation of an English Commonwealth and a French Republic.

The structure of eighteenth-century literature arises from tensions between Vico's language of men and the heaven-sent languages of heroes and gods. These tensions are sometimes resolved comically and satirically. One thinks of the mock-heroic tones of *MacFlecknoe*, the witty zeugmas of *The Rape of the Lock*, the Homeric churchyard burlesque of *Tom Jones*. But they may also remain poised and serious, even tragic. One thinks of Johnson's prose in *Rasselas*, Christopher Smart's *Rejoice in the Lamb*, Bishop Percy's *Reliques of Ancient English Poetry*, Richardson's *Clarissa*, all of which show the revival in the mid- and later eighteenth century of the languages of heroes and gods.

We must in future go beyond formalism in reading individual works and discussing genres in eighteenth-century literature. A work of literature is not only a knowable object. It is also a place where the myth touches us. The formalist approach of the now senile new criticism has always been seriously flawed by its failure to support its interpretations of texts with valid interpretations of literary and cultural history.

Geoffrey Hartman, a critic who has recently gone "beyond formalism" in a book of essays with that title, has also sought to overcome this defect in a spirited article directed "Toward Literary History."[19] Hartman aims at a literary history written from the point of view of the poets, at a point of view that takes into account the poet's nationality and the *rites de passage* he passes through as he creates different kinds of literary works. That approach to literary history seems to me valid for romantic and prophetic poets, for those whose creative impulse drives them toward what Hartman has identified and superbly discussed in his study of Wordsworth, Hopkins, Rilke, and Valéry, *The Unmediated Vision*. But what we find in Racine, Pope, Swift, and Vico is both the literary history and creative achievement of what must be called *the mediated vision*. We have seen that the mediation of language is central to the age's poets. We have seen too that any individual creative use of language is always measured against collective social usage and against the conflicting dialects of gods, heroes, and men. Instead of self-conscious nationality, conscious cultural levels decide the growth of the poet's language and work. The linguist Emile Benveniste has pointed out that the question of level must be answered in any attempt at linguistic or historical analysis,[20] and this is nowhere truer than in interpreting literary styles and works that fuse language and history into poetic vision.

A more valid and fruitful concept of genre may also now be developed. Such a concept should discard the notion of rigid classical models. It should instead adopt the concept of expectations suggested in Chomsky's theory of generative grammar; expectations based upon tensions, clashes, and levels in language that parallel the three levels marked out by Vico. We might go even further in proposing so different a literary history for the eighteenth century. It might be possible to define a literary period as that fusion of history, language, and vision that requires different principles of interpretation from

19. *Daedalus*, spring 1970, pp. 355-383.
20. See his *Problèmes de linguistique générale*, Paris, 1966, p. 119.

those that were valid for what either preceded the growth or followed the decline of that fusion. And eighteenth-century literature, as I have suggested, does require a different literary history from either the Renaissance or the Romantic movement.

But if literary criticism depends upon literary history, both of these activities depend upon cultural history. And the concerns of cultural history, as E. H. Gombrich has recently pointed out, are movements and affinities rather than causes or fantasies based on the Hegelian concept of *Zeitgeist*.[21] We have seen that the literary culture of the eighteenth century was split into two major tendencies, one toward humanism, the other toward enthusiasm. Each tendency or cultural level defined the other, and the conflict between them accounts for the astonishing strength of the age's impulses toward satire and history. When satire and history become one, as in the later poetry of Pope, the concerns of cultural history become the concerns of the mythopoeic imagination. Maynard Mack has shown how this occurs in *The Garden and the City*, and shown too how Pope "managed to fashion from his personal experience and the literary past an enabling myth for himself and his work."[22] The oblique and mediated qualities of eighteenth-century culture are the source of its enabling myths in literature.

Perhaps what finally confronts us is a choice between two different attitudes toward art and life. In thinking about this subject I have repeatedly called to mind two paintings I once saw within minutes of one another at the Prado Gallery in Madrid. The two paintings are by Velazquez and Goya, whose careers mark the two limits of our period. And the styles of the paintings mark the two extremes of vision apparent in eighteenth-century literature. In the first, Velazquez' *Las Meninas*, the light falls on the little Princess Margarita, the painter steps away from his own canvas, courtiers bow and whisper in the background, and the ostensible subjects of the

21. *In Search of Cultural History*, Oxford, 1969, esp. pp. 6-25, 35-45.
22. *The Garden and the City: Retirement and Politics in the Later Poetry of Pope, 1731-1743*, Toronto, 1969, p. vii.

portrait, the King and Queen, are seen only as reflections in a distant mirror. Eveything is framed and reflected. It is all done with mirrors and windows. This is an art dominated by reflection and indirection, both as a quality of light and as a quality of mind. They are the mirrors and the attitudes of the mediated vision.

The second, one of the Black Paintings of Goya, hangs on a lower floor of the Prado in a room that is almost underground; it shows Saturn devouring his son. The old god glares out at us as he numbers the bones and tears the flesh of his son. We see it all, muscle and blood, and we see it plain. Even though the background is dark and the light has no observable source, everything is clear and nothing is explained. This monster and victim have risen out of the sleep of reason. We look straight into the eye of the creative storm, into the gorgon's eye. It is the eye and the attitude of unmediated vision. Its opposite, that of mediated vision, is the sign and glory of eighteenth-century literature. But that civilized vision could not come to exist without a long process in which the savage god learnt human speech and humane reason; just as the cruel Saturn who devoured his son became in a later stage of his myth the civilizer of barbarous tribes, the benevolent creator of a Golden Age.

Peter Hughes

Marivaux
& the Crisis of Literary Forms
in the Early Enlightenment

I

It is difficult to speak of the literary problems of the period 1685-1725 in France without making some reference to the atmosphere of crisis that then was predominant. Twentieth-century criticism of the period has provided us with a vocabulary and an outlook which is at once useful and somewhat misleading. Such terms as "crise," "démembrement," "désagrégation," "décomposition," "dilemme," "problème," etc. have become commonplace thanks to the important studies of Paul Hazard,[1] Raymond Naves,[2] Georges May,[3] and others.[4] These terms are useful in that they attempt to define the temper of a specific, and confusing moment in French history; they are misleading in that they often fail to account for the reverse of the coin, that is, the positive results of the crisis. This latter problem may be rectified most easily by showing the direct relationship between the literary, socio-political and philosophical crises of the early Enlightenment and the attempts of a contemporary writer, in this case Marivaux, to come to grips with them. It is hoped that the result of such an

1. *La Crise de la conscience européenne (1680-1715)*, Paris, Boivin, 1935.
2. *Le Goût de Voltaire*, Paris, Garnier, 1938, especially pp. 7-35.
3. *Le Dilemme du roman au XVIIIe siècle: étude sur les rapports du roman et de la critique, 1715-1761*, New Haven, Yale University Press, 1963.
4. Frédéric Deloffre, "Le Problème de l'illusion romanesque et le renouvellement des techniques narratives de 1700 à 1715," in *La Littérature narrative d'imagination: des genres littéraires aux techniques d'expression.* Colloque de Strasbourg, 23-25 avril 1959, Paris, Presses Universitaires de France, 1961, pp. 115-133.
A. Kibédi Varga, "La désagrégation de l'idéal classique dans le roman français de la première moitié du XVIIIe siècle," *Studies on Voltaire and the Eighteenth Century* 26, 1963, pp. 965-998.

investigation will be to clarify and to particularize the "crisis" itself, as well as to present a fuller and truer portrait of Marivaux, whose versatility and historical importance as a novelist has, until only very recently, been seriously underestimated.

II

The crisis which concerns us was visible on several levels. The political and diplomatic disruptions which helped to create an atmosphere of moral and philosophical uncertainty at the turn of the eighteenth century have been thoroughly examined: the revocation of the Edict of Nantes, in 1685, by Louis XIV, which caused France to be split again over political and religious issues; the advent, in England, of the House of Orange to the throne in 1688, showing the assailability of the "absolute" monarchy, and the inadvisability of religious suppression; the devastating war of the Spanish succession (1700-1714) which caused France to lose its military, diplomatic and mercantile primacy to England, and exposed Louis XIV as an unsuccessful general and a vulnerable king; and, finally, the death in 1715 of Louis himself, who had ruled longer and more forcefully than any other monarch in Europe's history. All of these events showed that the stability which had come to be the hallmark of the great European powers was fast disappearing, and nowhere was this more obvious than in the philosophical and moral speculations of the period. It was an age of criticism, of analysis, of negative attack. As Hazard puts it, "la première tâche était un travail de démolition," and, later, "dans les années finissantes du XVIIe siècle, un nouvel ordre de choses a commencé."[5] Every established tradition and institution came almost simultaneously under attack, and the results were, for a short and crucial period, absolute intellectual chaos.

On the literary level, this crisis, especially in England and France, formalized itself in the Quarrel of the Ancients and the Moderns. Ostensibly, the Quarrel centered on the old argument as to whether Homer and other ancient poets were equal to or better than the poets of the age of Louis XIV. Yet the Quarrel

5. *Op. cit.*, Paris, Gallimard, 1968, 2 vols., I, p. 9; II, p. 303.

was much more complicated than this, for the Ancients and the Moderns were asking some very important questions. They were trying to decide in which direction literature should go and in what ways it had to change in order to be in accord with the new philosophies and the new discoveries which were then being discussed and analyzed all over Europe. The old genres, derived from the canon of ancient literature, and sustained by the dogma of the neo-classical critics, seemed to be losing their vitality. The basic tenets of neo-classicism — perfectability of form, the superiority of reason, the universality of human experience — no longer seemed adequate to the new world view, and at times even seemed contradictory. The Moderns soon found themselves questioning all traditional literary values. At first reacting only negatively to these values, Modern writers soon began to search for new literary forms. Their works during this period carried such titles as *essais, lettres, dialogues, traités, épîtres, entretiens,* etc. as they searched frantically for a new form which could contain their new ideas.

In his excellent study of the esthetics of the early Enlightenment, Raymond Naves has referred to this period of negative criticism and generic chaos as a time of "démembre-ment," as a "crise du Goût classique."[6] At first evident primarily on a purely esthetic level, this dismemberment eventually attained literature and language themselves. The initial battleground was to be that of poetry versus prose. Poetry was seen as a "non-geometric" genre, and as such to be discarded. If kept at all, it should be considered but a game for the intellectually active, for only in prose did truth and reason reside. Ironically, poetry was undergoing the same dilemma that the novel, a little later in the eighteenth century, was to face: "... Si on lui concède le droit de plaire sans instruire, on la réprouve aussitôt pour sa légèrté et son inutilité; si on lui donne la morale pour fondement, on l'expurge de tout ce qui n'est pas proprement utile et on la réduit à la nudité géométrique."[7] The immediate result of this "quarrel within a quarrel" was the weakening of the poetic spirit, and a definite turn in the

6. *Op. cit.,* p. 9.
7. *Ibid.,* p. 28.

direction of prose as the only effective means of literary expression. Hazard has called the Enlightenment "une époque sans poésie."[8] Elaborating on this phenomenon and on the rule of the Moderns who chose prose over Poetry, he continues: "Tous tant qu'ils sont, les Anglais comme les Français, ont donné à la prose une efficacité nouvelle, la chargeant d'idées, la rendant combative et agressive. Ils ont versé dans leurs essais, dans leur lettres, dans leurs dialogues des vivants et des morts, dans leurs voyages imaginaires, toute la morale, toute la religion, toute la philosophie."[9] The unresponsive remains of the once supreme classical aesthetic had left the Moderns no other choice. Prose had become the primary means of literary expression.

The next important question which faced the Modern writers concerned the fictional prose forms available to them, and which ones they would now adopt. During this period, we detect certain attitudinal changes and new technical directions, at times quite subtle, which reflect this concern of the new writers for new forms. Most significant of these new attitudes and directions were the perfection of the *histoire* or *nouvelle* as individual genres,[10] the gradual formulation of a new attitude toward fictional heroes,[11] leading to the eventual separation of the romance and the novel as specific fictional modes,[12] the former not easily adapted to the exigencies of the early Enlightenment's desire for formal and thematic change.

As regards the experimentation with the *nouvelle,* both Deloffre and Godenne show how the formal crisis of this period was fought out within the boundaries of the traditional genre of

8. *Op. cit.*, II, p. 147. For other, fuller analyses of the famous quarrel over poetry, see Margaret Gilman, *The Idea of Poetry in France from Houdar de La Motte to Baudelaire*, Cambridge, Mass., Harvard University Press, 1958, and Raymond Naves' study, already cited above.

9. *Op. cit.*, II, p. 148.

10. Frédéric Deloffre, *La Nouvelle en France à l'âge classique*, Paris, Didier, 1967.

René Godenne, *Histoire de la nouvelle française aux XVIIe et XVIIIe siècles*, Geneva, Droz, 1970.

11. Varga, *op. cit.*

12. For an approach to the comprehension of this problem, see Northrop Frye, *Anatomy of Criticism: Four Essays*, Princeton, Princeton University Press, 1957; reprinted 1966, pp. 303-312.

the short story. A close analysis of these studies and of the works they discuss reveals a mini-crisis which reflects the larger struggle which we have outlined. In an effort to counteract the traditional, romantic and heroic novels still so popular in the late seventeenth century, theoriticians such as Du Plaisir, in his *Sentiments sur les Lettres et sur l'Histoire, avec des scrupules sur le style,* attempt to define a new genre in prose,[13] and the eventual result of these theories will be the novel. The *nouvelle* was an especially fortuitous choice on the part of many prose writers as an experimental ground: short, easily controlled, deprived of most of the formal strictures of classicism, the *nouvelle* provided writers the freedom they needed to discover the novel. Men like Guilleragues, Challes, Marivaux and Prévost would exploit the formal and thematic possibilities of the genre. They saw in the *nouvelle,* and later in the longer prose works of the 1720's and 1730's, an answer to the debilitating themes and techniques of the romantic tradition, exemplified in the novels of d'Urfé, Gomberville, Scudéry and La Calprenède.

In the last decades of the seventeenth and first decades of the eighteenth centuries, it is likewise evident that new attitudes were being formed regarding the qualities and nature of fictional heroes. At first a reaction against the wars of the period, this revaluation of heroism soon attains the very core of fictional expression. The main characters become less universal, less sublime as we move further into the eighteenth century. They also, although at first imperceptibly, move down the social scale. The heroes and heroines are described more concretely: they have dark hair, blue eyes, fair skin; they are tall or short or thin; they are sometimes even of mediocre looks. Obviously, this was an attempt at bringing the reader closer to the fictional character — an important concern of the Moderns who were becoming more and more aware of their public.

The years 1685-1715 were indeed critical. They were years of experimentation and discovery, on every intellectual front. On the literary level, which is our primary concern, old forms

---

13. Deloffre, *La Nouvelle . . . ,* pp. 44-51.
    Arpad Steiner, "A French Poetics of the Novel in 1683," *Romanic Review* 30, 1939, pp. 235-243.

and ideas were being rapidly discarded for new ones. Often the results were not satisfactory, and many less good writers returned to the Classical forms, a practice which perpetuated the tired esthetic of Boileau and Racine until the dawn of Romanticism. Yet there were writers, born and educated in this period, who survived the crisis, and indeed succeeded in their own endeavors because of the lessons it taught them as they searched, in their own turn, to find new ways to express themselves. Among them are such men as Voltaire, Prévost, Montesquieu and Marivaux.

III

Nowhere is this literary dilemma more visible than in the early prose efforts of Pierre Carlet de Marivaux (1688-1763). Marivaux was a member of the Moderns' camp; one of his earliest and most influential protectors was the greatest of all the second generation Moderns, Fontenelle. Yet by the time that Marivaux began writing, the Quarrel was mostly a dead issue, and consequently one of his first published works, *Homère travesti,* a parody of the *Iliad,* was almost totally ignored. Yet Marivaux saw that the Quarrel and its results had brought some fresh air into the stale atmosphere of the decaying neo-classical esthetic, and his first productive years (1712-1719) are defined by a frenetic attempt on his part to find new modes of expression and new subject matter to analyze. Even before the abbé Prévost, the other major French novelist of the first half of the eighteenth century, Marivaux began to clear away some of the accepted dogma surrounding the established literary genres, and his efforts would eventually lead to the primacy of long prose fiction as the dominant form of literary expression in the French Enlightenment.

Marivaux is known to most students of the French eighteenth century as a playwright. Even those most familiar with the literature of the Enlightenment in France know Marivaux only as the author of such fine and subtle plays as *La Surprise de l'amour, La Double inconstance, Le Jeu de l'amour et du hasard, Les Serments indiscrets,* and *Les Fausses confidences.* And in fact Marivaux did write over thirty plays, many of them very successful in the eighteenth century, and many still in the repertories of the Comédie Française and other established French troupes. However, during his early years as a writer Marivaux did not produce many plays, but concentrated rather on prose fiction. In fact, as F. Deloffre has pointed out in his classic study of Marivaux's style,[14] Marivaux seems to have been haunted by the idea of the novel throughout most of his career.

During his first years as a writer, Marivaux wrote, besides the verse parody of the *Iliad* mentioned above, a semi-fictional essay on good company, several short fictional pieces (entitled "Lettres" or "Caractères"), one good play, *La Surprise de l'amour,* and four relatively long pieces of fictional prose, only one of which can be called a novel in the modern sense. The first of these pieces is entitled *Les Effets surprenants de la sympathie, ou les aventures de **** (1712), and was in the tired tradition of the great heroic romances of the sixteenth and seventeenth centuries. It is a piece obviously influenced by Cervantes' last novel, *Los Trabajos de Persiles y Sigismunda*: countless adventures which occur as two young lovers, separated at the beginning of the novel, try to find one another again. The novel is likewise full of interpolated stories (character A meets character B who tells his story about character C who tells his story about D, etc.). Some critics have even seen this work as a parody of the adventure novels themselves, still popular in the early eighteenth century, but there is no internal evidence of this. We do know that Marivaux had probably read and been influenced by many of the great novels that had been written in the Renaissance and the seventeenth century, works such as *Amadis de Gaula, Orlando furioso, Don Quixote* (all most likely in French translation); novels such as Mlle. de Scudéry's *Grand Cyrus* and *La Clélie,* La Calprenède's *Cassandre* and *Pharamond,* Courtilz de Sandras' *Les Mémoires de M. de Bouy,* Fénelon's *Télémaque,* as well as the works of Scarron, Sorel, Lesage and Challes. The influence of these and other works is clearly seen in *Les Effets . . . ,* and such an effort was

14. *Une Préciosité nouvelle: Marivaux et le marivaudage,* 1954, revised edition Paris, Armand Colin, 1967, pp. 72-80.

the logical beginning for an immature and inexperienced artist who wanted to make a name for himself. At the same time, this literary effort most likely had a strong therapeutic effect on its young author. He had worked in an established tradition and had found it unsatisfactory for his purposes. Abandoning the sterile form, Marivaux almost immediately began a parody of it, his major comic novel, entitled *Pharsamon, ou les Nouvelles folies romanesques* (1712; later reprinted as *Le Don Quichotte moderne*). The story is again basically simple: a young French bourgeois who decides he wants to be a knight, and who leaves home in search of his one true love. There is little originality in the story or in the style; what is important to us is the effort by Marivaux to experiment with another traditional form: the romantic parody. Yet he seems still unsatisfied, for such an effort, no matter how successful, did not leave him the freedom that he felt he needed to experiment both formally as well as thematically with prose narrative.

The last two prose works of this extraordinarily productive period were somewhat more original and witnessed a growing sophistication in Marivaux's artistry. *Le Télémaque travesti* (1714) was still in the already well-established tradition of the comic parody. Yet it differs from this tradition, and most noticeably from Marivaux's own *Pharsamon*, in its attempts to treat linguistic and social phenomena in a more *realistic* manner. The hero is a young peasant, who in several ways prefigures Jacob, the hero of Marivaux's *Le Paysan parvenu*. He is honest, of average intelligence, yet inherently comic because of his willingness to point out the obvious discrepancies between appearance and reality. The piece as a whole is a well-controlled parodic effort of Fénelon's very popular romance of the late seventeenth century, *Télémaque*. Marivaux's sophisticated use of dialogue and linguistic distinctions to differentiate between his characters is another of the originalities of the work, and any study of the use of language as a form of characterization must begin with the *Télémaque travesti*. The composition of this novel marks a critical point in Marivaux's career as he makes a decision to remain with prose fiction as a viable literary form, and as he tries to change it into a more serious form, suitable for the themes he wished to analyze.

Almost simultaneously with his composition of *Le Télémaque travesti*, Marivaux was writing another piece which went further than any of his other prose narratives toward breaking with prose tradition. The title of this original work, *La Voiture embourbée* (written c. 1713), reflects the direction in which Marivaux was moving. It is a "realistic" work, relatively short, only fifty-three pages in the original edition, yet its importance in the history of the modern French novel must not be overlooked.[15] Published at the beginning of 1714, it appeared even before the first books of Lesage's *Gil Blas* (1715) which is traditionally considered the first French novel of the eighteenth century. Marivaux's novel is essentially a frame story, centered upon a coach accident: the passengers, after having safely ensconced themselves in a warm inn, decide to make up a "roman impromptu" to while away their time. Of the 50-odd pages of the original edition, twenty deal with the *mise-en-scène*: description of the passengers, of the inn, of the villagers, and of the circumstances surrounding the decision to make up a story. It is in these pages that Marivaux establishes himself as a modern novelist, and shows himself aware of the fictional possibilities of reality. As one critic has said, Marivaux is "le premier romancier français chez qui le monde extérieur est devenu *problématique* pour l'individu." Marivaux's originality lies in "la représentation nouvelle du monde extérieur comme un phénomène humainement significatif."[16] With *La Voiture embourbée*, he has broken away from the traditions of the romance, of the burlesque parody and of the use of "realism" for humorous and picturesque emphasis. There are a few burlesque passages in *La Voiture embourbée* (which occur when some passengers imitate the romantic novels of the past), but, ironically, they serve only as a frame for Marivaux's primary

---

15. One of the best efforts to analyze this early prose effort of Marivaux is an article by Morten Nøjgaard, "Le problème du réalisme dans les romans de Marivaux: Réflexions sur l'introduction de la *Voiture embourbée*," *Revue Romane*, 1, 1967, pp. 71-87.

16. *Ibid.*, pp. 74-75, 76.

interest: the use of prose fiction to analyze contemporary society freely and with a minimum of concern for traditional forms and modes of expression.

Unfortunately, as students of the period know all too well,[17] the road to complete artistic freedom in the domain of the long prose narrative was to be an especially difficult one. Marivaux's experience was no exception. In 1719, because of serious personal financial difficulties, he had no other choice but to become a writer by profession. At this time in France, the only way to make money literarily was through the theater, and it is in this direction that Marivaux turned. Yet, as we have seen, early in his career Marivaux had shown a firm commitment to prose fiction, and, despite his successes as a playwright, he would continue to experiment with the possibilities of prose. He would turn next, not to the novel (he was not to begin his most famous novel, *La Vie de Marianne,* until around 1728), but rather to a much looser form, relatively new and promising, a form that we call the *journal.* In this second major period of his life (1719-1728), it would be through the journal that Marivaux would reveal himself as a superior prose stylist, eager to analyze new ideas in a new prose format.[18]

There is little doubt that Marivaux had been influenced by the satiric tone and unstructured format of both the *Tatler* (1709-1711) and the *Spectator* (1711-1712), the two journalistic works of Joseph Addison and Richard Steele.[19] The journals of Marivaux are entitled *Le Spectateur français* (1721-1724), *L'Indigent philosophe* (1726-1727) and *Le Cabinet du philosophe* (1734).[20] The first and especially the second

17. Georges May, *Dilemme du roman au XVIIIe siècle . . .*

18. One could argue that the *journal* was not all that new, that in fact it was but a modern adaptation of an older, more traditional literary genre, the Menippean satire. This is a valid argument, but does not actually concern us here because Marivaux saw it as a new genre, used it without much attention to any formal criteria, and let it serve primarily as an experimental form as he prepared to write his two major novels.

19. For an analysis of the parallels between Addison and Steele and Marivaux, see the unpublished Ph.D. dissertation of William Wrage, "A Critical Edition of Marivaux's *Spectateur français,*" University of Wisconsin, 1964-65.

20. These works are finally available in a very good edition by Frédéric Deloffre and Michel Gilot, Marivaux, *Journaux et oeuvres diverses,* Paris, Garnier, 1969.

have a superficial narrative structure which keeps the reader's attention as he waits to know and sometimes tries to predict the reactions of the spectator or the philosopher. But these pieces are most interesting and important to our purposes because they show Marivaux still at grips with the basic problems of narrative prose and its potentialities. He used the journalistic format to develop his formal ideas, experimenting with every possible form that prose could take: first- and third-person narration, the epistolary and memoir forms, the short story, the dialogue.[21] The journalistic format continued to fascinate him, even after he had begun his major novels, as is witnessed by the composition and publication of *Le Cabinet du philosophe* in the 1730's.

It is especially interesting to note at this point that the other great novelist of the early Enlightenment in France, the abbé Prévost (who was later to translate Richardson), was going through a similar period of formal experimentation. As early as 1728, Prévost began to think about a journal, in the English "newspaper" tradition, which he even outlines in one of his most famous novels, *Les Mémoires d'un homme de qualité*, t. V. The relative freedom to discuss any and all ideas relevant to contemporary intellectual discourse especially appealed to Prévost. But, at the same time, Prévost saw all the narrative possibilities that such a loose, unstructured form would provide him: "Le dessein de Prévost sera de faire du journal un mode complet d'expression, axé sur la vie contemporaine, accessible à un vaste public. . . . Gagné par ce climat de liberté, par cette forme d'expression réaliste et populaire infiniment souple et mobile, Prévost ira jusqu'à faire de son tome V des *Mémoires et*

---

21. In a number of Prévost's own journalistic venture, *Pour et contre,* Desfontaines gives us a contemporary description of *Le Cabinet du philosophe* which underlines some of the advantages Marivaux saw in this new form: ". . . Il s'agit de la Cassette d'un Philosophe, *Auteur clandestin,* mort il y a quelque tems; & ce sont ses Productions que l'on donne. Elles consistent en morceaux détachez, & en *fragmens de pensées* sur une infinité de sujets, dans *toutes sortes de tournures*: Réflexions gayes, sérieuses, morales, chrétiennes; beaucoup de ces deux derniers: quelquefois des Avantures, des Dialogues, des Lettres, des Mémoires, des Jugemens sur différens Auteurs; & par tout un esprit de Philosophe, dont les réflexions se sentent des différens âges où il a passé. Il écrit ses pensées comme elles se présentent; il ne cherche qu'à les exprimer nettement, sans rien alterer de leur *simplicité brusque & naïve,*" t. II, no. XXX, 1734, p. 340, author's italics.

avantures [*d'un homme de qualité*] une sorte de chronique, une somme de reportages, d'anecdotes, de comptes rendus de spectacles, dans laquelle il nous livre son opinion pour et contre le goût anglais, pour et contre le gouvernement, la religion, les moeurs de l'Angleterre: tout le livre dixième du roman peut passer pour une première ébauche du *Pour et contre.*"[22] No better definition than this could be given for the new novel which would later appear through the efforts of such men as Prévost and Marivaux. The search for formal and thematic realism led them both to the journal, and subsequently to a better idea of what a novel should be. Both *Manon Lescaut* and *La Vie de Marianne* would appear in 1731, after their creators had already outlined (in the case of Prévost) or actually composed (in Marivaux's case) this "loose and baggy monster": the journal.

Not only does Marivaux examine technical possibilities in his journalistic works, but he begins to structure the major theme which will make him one of France's first modern novelists, i.e., the relating of the individual to a specific social context. Prior to his adoption of the journal format, Marivaux had found no form suitable to the new, socially-oriented, Modern, individualistic themes that he had wanted to treat. Prose fiction until that moment had been too romantic, too idealistic to contain these new ideas. The unstructured and unconventional journalistic form afforded him this desired freedom of expression. Lionel Gossman, in an excellent article on Marivaux and the Moderns, has pointed out the originality of this new world view, and how it affected the artistic endeavors of the writers of the early Enlightenment. He explains how "Marivaux's work, like that of all the *Modernes,* is destructive of traditional myths and ideas about literature, about society, about man." Literature was becoming more conscious of its public and of the society in which it existed; it was also "thought of as a means of de-mystification and an exercise in reflection and self-awareness."[23] Marivaux's use of the journal

---

22. Jean Sgard, *Le "Pour et contre" de Prévost,* Paris, Nizet, 1969, pp. 9, 10.
23. "Literature and Society in the Early Enlightenment: The Case of Marivaux," *Modern Language Notes,* 82, 1967, pp. 311, 308.

allowed for this process, giving him also the freedom he desired to develop his new ideas. Yet the formal requirements that he felt he still needed were missing. It was at this juncture, around 1728, that Marivaux turned to the memoir-novel in a final effort to answer the dilemma which had been confronting him for over fifteen years.

It is not my intention to analyze here *La Vie de Marianne* or *Le Paysan parvenu,* but rather to situate them in terms of some of the arguments I have already made. Both of these works are first-person narratives, written in the form of memoirs, a popular novelistic device of the first half of the eighteenth century. They both deal with the problems that two gifted young people face when they try to advance themselves socially. (Marianne is an orphan and Jacob is a peasant.) Both novels are unfinished: the *Paysan parvenu* in fact was written and published between Parts II and III (1734-1735) of *La Vie de Marianne,* which itself was published serially between 1731 and 1741. These few well-known facts bear repeating because they support the premise that Marivaux was in fact developing a new form encompassing new ideas which would become the modern novel of the eighteenth and nineteenth centuries. Some years before Richardson in England,[24] Marivaux had decided to write a story about the problems of social commerce, the difficulties of innocence vis-à-vis the established hypocrisy of social institutions, and the sentimental education of his protagonists as they learn to rely on their wits and their apparent virtue to attain their rightful station in a hostile environment. Through a precise presentation of contemporary society, Marivaux was to formulate one of the basic premises of the modern novel, namely, a moral realism that, when combined with an already established psychological realism, and when sustained by a hesitant picturesque realism (not to be fully developed until much later in the eighteenth century) would provide the verisimilar presentation of reality so ardently

24. This comparison is not made to revive the old, tired argument over the question of influence regarding these two writers. Rather, I want to insist on the fact that almost concurrently, in England as well as in France, efforts were being made by competent artists to develop new forms to express the new world view of the period.

desired by the novelists of the early Enlightenment. These novels, written simultaneously with the abbé Prévost's own efforts in this direction, form a watershed in the invention, if that be the term, and development of the modern novel in France.

That is not to say that Marivaux's novels are without fault. The limitations of the first-person narrative are often telling: for instance, the occasional confusion of the narrator and the subject of the memoirs. Also, the influence of a reactionary criticism on the novel and novelists of the period did not allow for the complete development of the moral and picturesque realism that is but tantalizingly revealed in *La Vie de Marianne* and *Le Paysan parvenu*. Finally, and more particularly for Marivaux, neither of his two great novels are finished, at least from a formal standpoint. Convincing arguments can be made that both works end thematically, that both Marianne and Jacob have reached a certain psychological plateau which reveals the limits and the potential of their actions.[25] But Marivaux did not formally terminate either book. The questions which come to mind at this point are obvious: since neither novel is finished, was Marivaux happy with the new form that he had helped to develop? Or was he a good moralist and social analyst, but not a successful novelist? He left, as far as we know, none of his plays unfinished. Does this mean that he was a better playwright than narrator? The answers to these queries are not nearly so easy as the questions themselves. We are confronted with an artist who was in the process of developing a new form, and yet who, according to our present, post-Jamesian standards, was, in the final analysis, unsuccessful. Marivaux, like many of his contemporaries, was an experimenter. He saw the infinite possibilities that prose narration

25. It will be remembered that each book ends as the major protagonist obtains all the ostensible advantages of a superior social standing: in Marianne's case, acceptance by the aristocracy, a proposal of love from a nobleman, a financially care-free future; in Jacob's story, he has obtained the friendship of the Prime Minister's nephew, wears the clothes and sword of a man of quality, and is invited to sit at the theater with men of noble blood. Yet neither protagonist is satisfied, and both novels end on a note of moral and psychological ambiguity as each character examines the price he has had to pay in order to reach his present social level.

offered to those artists who, like him, were disturbed about the directions that literature was taking in this period of intellectual, moral and philosophical crisis. Convinced of the rightness of their new social and moral principles, these men looked all around them for new ways in which to express themselves, and the one unquestionable result of this period of experimentation was the modern novel. So, to criticize Marivaux for leaving his novels unfinished, for not continuing with his journalistic ventures, for opting finally for the ostensible perfection of the dramatic form is to miss the point. Marivaux introduced and examined possibilities; his failure, if indeed it be that, to follow through completely on these possibilities should be of as little importance to the student of the novel of this period as it most certainly was to those he most palpably influenced, the novelists of the second half of the eighteenth century. Marivaux faced up to the formal and thematic crises of the early Enlightenment, and the result was the birth in France of a new literary form.

Ronald Rosbottom

An 18th-Century View
of Roman Satire

The student of Roman satire who follows his authors as far as the eighteenth century will find himself for the most part on familiar ground, but every now and then he will stumble against an oddity, such as Dennis's *To Matthew Prior, Esq; Upon the Roman Satirists* (1721),[1] that reminds him sharply of the distance he has travelled:

> For is there not Reason to believe that the true *Roman* Satire is of the Comick kind, and was an Imitation of the old *Athenian* Comedys, in which *Lucilius* first signaliz'd himself, and which was afterwards perfected by *Horace*, and that *Juvenal* afterwards started a new Satire which was of the Tragick kind? *Horace*, who wrote as *Lucilius* had done before him, in Imitation of the old Comedy, endeavours to correct the Follies and Errors, and epidemick Vices of his Readers, which is the Business of Comedy. *Juvenal* attacks the pernicious outragious Passions and the abominable monstrous Crimes of several of his Contemporaries, or of those who liv'd in the Age before him, which is the Business of Tragedy, at least of imperfect Tragedy. *Horace* argues, insinuates, engages, rallies, smiles; *Juvenal* exclaims, apostrophizes, exaggerates, lashes, stabbs. There is in *Horace* almost every where an agreeable Mixture of good Sense, and of true Pleasantry, so that he has every where the principal Qualities of an excellent Comick Poet. And there is almost every where in *Juvenal*, Anger, Indignation, Rage, Disdain, and the violent Emotions and vehement Style of Tragedy.[2]

1. *The Critical Works of John Dennis*, ed. E.N. Hooker, Baltimore, 1943, Vol. II, pp. 218-220.
2. Hooker, Vol. II, pp. 218-219.

Dennis's main thesis is unexceptionable: the reader should savour the distinctive qualities of Horace and Juvenal without feeling obliged to champion one against the other. But his categories of comic and tragic satire argue a serious misreading of all three genres. They are an aberration nurtured by intensive controversy and do not deserve to be commended by Mr. Ian Jack as "one of the most intelligent treatments of the main point at issue, that of the style and tone most suitable satire."[3] They read to me like a desperate defence of an untenable antithesis. Horace may have begun as an imitator of Lucilius, but Old Comedy was never a model for his *Sermones* in the sense that Greek lyric was for his *Carmina*. It is true that both Horace and Aristophanes saw themselves as teachers, but teaching was not the primary business of Old Comedy, except in those parts of the *parabasis* where the chorus shattered the dramatic illusion and spoke directly for the poet. Old Comedy is protest, not exhortation; it is a festival, not an arraignment, or even a seminar; its standard finale is a wild, erotic celebration. No one in any century can rise up from seeing or even from reading a play of Aristophanes and proceed at once to the opinion that an agreeable mixture of good sense and true pleasantry are the principal qualities of an excellent comic poet. No comic poet ever won a prize at the Dionysia for mere pleasantry: the mark of the winner was a command of the whole range of humour from the grossly uproarious to the allusively subtle, from the deep comedy of character to the juvenile ebullience of *chaire o Charon, chaire o Charon, chaire o Charon.*[4] And any good sense in Old Comedy outside the *parabasis* had to be mediated through a plot that began in fantasy and went rioting fantastically on for the sheer delight of so doing. There is only one example of fantasy in Horace's *Satires*, 2.5, where the ghost of Tiresias gives Ulysses a lesson in legacy-hunting. It is the least Horatian thing in Horace.

Dennis is roughly right when he says that Horace endea-

---

3. *Augustan Satire*, Oxford, 1952, pp. 102-103. The passage quoted on p. 103 from the *Spectator*, No. 618 shows a deep understanding of Horace and is in a different class altogether.

4. Aristophanes, *Frogs*, l. 184.

vours to correct the follies and errors and epidemic vices of his readers, but quite wrong to apply any such restriction to the invective of Old Comedy, which took all human life for its target, including the pernicious, outrageous passions and the abominable monstrous crimes, to attack which, says Dennis, is the business of tragedy. This last affirmation is so startling that even its author staggers back from it and tries to tone it down by adding "at least of imperfect Tragedy." The attentive reader, who has been following the sharp outlines of the antithesis, suddenly finds himself befogged. He knows that Old Comedy can only mean Aristophanes (the other writers surviving only in fragments), but he cannot pursue the argument any further until he has located at least one imperfect tragedy prior to Juvenal. If he is aware of Dennis's opinion that the only perfect Greek tragedy was Sophocles's *King Oedipus*,[5] he will have plenty of choice, but he must now lose himself in wondering how *King Oedipus* differs from all the rest in terms of Dennis's concept of the business of tragedy. If he knows that *King Oedipus* was not written as an attack on Oedipus, he is equally aware that the *Antigone* was not an attack on Creon. It is quite true that you can find in Greek and Roman tragedy anger, indignation, rage, disdain, violent emotions and vehement style, but none of these is the essence of tragedy. The essence of Attic tragedy was compassion, as Dennis, a good Aristotelian, knew quite well when he was not writing an essay on satire.[6] Now there is not very much compassion in Juvenal. But here and there the harsh and grandiose rhetoric gives way to quiet and even gentle humour, just as in Horace's *Sermones* and *Epistulae* there are depths of seriousness and not a few passages of high poetry.

There are at least three general considerations that should have inhibited Dennis from making his bizarre equations. First,

5. *The Causes of the Decay and Defects of Dramatick Poetry, and of the Degeneracy of the Publick Tast* (1725?), Hooker, Vol. II, p. 287. Cf. *To the Spectator, upon His Paper on the 16th of April* (1711,1712), Hooker, Vol. II, pp. 19-20.

6. *The Usefulness of the Stage* (1697), Part II, Ch. I, Hooker, Vol. II, pp. 150-153, 163-167; *The Advancement and Reformation of Modern Poetry* (1701), Part I, Ch. IX, Hooker, Vol. II, pp. 224-225; *The Impartial Critick* (1693), Dialogue IV, Hooker, Vol. II, pp. 32-33.

Attic tragedy and comedy were highly public forms, and Roman satire a rather private form, of writing. Second, tragedy and comedy were governed by such strict conventions that change came slowly, whereas *Satura*, though a true genre, was so unconfined by rules that it could be swift and sensitive in response to changes both of author and environment. Third, both Horace and Juvenal changed too much in the course of more than twenty-five years of writing to fit easily into so rigid a scheme.

The source of these bizarre equations is, of course, Dryden's *Discourse Concerning the Original and Progress of Satire* (1693),[7] a work which influenced the eighteenth century not only in its preference for Juvenal (". . . the Generality of Readers," says Dennis,[8] "are more delighted with *Juvenal* than they are with *Horace*, because *Dryden* is more delighted with him") but in its whole understanding and appreciation of Roman Satire. If classical students would read it today they would be dazzled by light reflected from facets of Roman satire they had never noticed, they would be stabbed by sharpness of aphorism into asking questions they had never thought of, and they would be assaulted by an almost physical sensation of Roman writers still alive, a solid presence in Augustan England. Best of all, the gusto and body of the writing might shame them out of their own flat, torpid prose. But I should be sorry if Greekless and Latinless students of English were to swallow Dryden whole without ever stopping to beg a spoonful of seasoning from a modern classicist.

"What disreputation is it to *Horace*," asks Dryden,[9] "that *Juvenal* excels in the Tragical Satyre, as *Horace* does in the Comical?" After breathlessly chasing a long, pointed, elaborate, and cumulative contrast,[10] the reader is ready to rest in some

7. *The Poems of John Dryden,* ed. J. Kinsley, Oxford, 1958, Vol. II, pp. 599-670.

8. Hooker, Vol. II, p. 218.

9. *Discourse* 2224-2226.

10. *Discourse* 1741-2224. In 1872-77 he quotes Persius 1.116-117 and says that "by *Vitium,* he means those little Vices, which we call Follies, the defects of Humane Understanding, or at most the Peccadillos of Life, rather than the Tragical Vices, to which Men are hurri'd by their unruly Passions and exorbitant Desires." In 2169 he says of Juvenal, ". . . as his provocations were great, he has reveng'd them Tragically."

such triumphant conclusion, but Dryden has given him no sure grounds: these new-minted categories are a drastic extension of a hint that he picked up from Heinsius (2089-92): "*Heinsius* urges in praise of *Horace*, that according to the Ancient Art and Law of Satire, it shou'd be nearer to Comedy, than to Tragedy; Not declaiming against Vice, but only laughing at it." But, when Horace sat down to write, the art was not all that ancient and the law was not very prescriptive. All Horace had was three preceding satirists, Ennius, Pacuvius and Lucilius, and one older contemporary, Varro: the earliest of them, Ennius, had been born less than two hundred years before. We have nothing of Pacuvius's satires and only fragments of the other three, but quite enough to show both declamation against vice and a rich vein of material that had nothing to do with vice at all. Heinsius knew no more of the matter than we do: his remark is a good example of the renaissance and post-renaissance passion for principles and categories.

But what really knocks the props from under Dryden's antithesis is his explanation of why Horace was not as bloody-minded as Dryden would have liked him to be (1966-71). "After all, *Horace* had the disadvantage of the Times in which he liv'd; they were better for the Man, but worse for the Satirist. 'Tis generally said, that those Enormous Vices, which were practis'd under the Reign of *Domitian*, were unknown in the Time of *Augustus Caesar*. That therefore *Juvenal* had a larger field, than *Horace*." I totter in sheer unbelief and then read bravely on. Three pages later (2082-83) I am poleaxed by the tidings that "*Horace* was a Mild Admonisher, a Court Satirist, fit for the gentle Times of Augustus . . ." Gentle times! A massive proscription, two military dictatorships, and three civil wars. Quite apart from the fact that not even a computer could quantify the comparative wickedness of Horace's and Juvenal's lifetimes, Dryden has his chronology all wrong. Juvenal *lived* under Domitian but he *wrote* under decent emperors, Nerva, Trajan, Hadrian. Horace wrote his first satire soon after the triumviral proscriptions and just before the battle of Philippi.[11] He continued writing satires during the long

11. Horace's poetical whimsy (*Odes* 2.7.9-14) about his own part in the battle

resistance of Sextus Pompeius and the uneasy division of power between Octavian and Antony. He finished them just after Antony's defeat at Actium. But, then, Dryden even thinks that Horace wrote his Odes first and afterwards declined into Satire.[12] He is so captivated by Juvenal's *high* style that he can say (1919-20), plumb in the middle of all manner of splendid observations on Horace, "The low Style of *Horace*, is according to his Subject; that is generally groveling." And who, apart from Casaubon, enabled Dryden to utter such a terrible untruth? Why, Horace himself in his epistle to Augustus, *Epist.* 2.1.250-259. Horace is still at his old game of *recusatio*: "it's not out of preference," he says to Augustus, "that I compose *sermones* that creep along the ground. I'd be delighted to make an epic of your glorious battles, if only I had the talent:

> nec sermones ego mallem
> repentes per humum quam res componere gestas. . ."

This was written between 17 and 13 B.C., that is, about twenty-five years after Horace had first started putting it about that he was not a poet at all, any more than Lucilius had been a poet, but just a simple writer of prose who juggled his words about and made them scan.[13] "Just look at me" he wrote, "no *acer spiritus,* no *uis*; take the metre away and there is nothing left but *sermo merus*,[14] mere talk, the product of a pedestrian Muse."[15] Casaubon, Dryden and Dennis have apparently taken Horace at his word. But contemporary poets were not fooled. Virgil and Varius took him, freedman's son though he was, to meet Maecenas. None of those three would have wasted any

ought not to make us insensitive to what must have been a harrowing experience. Juvenal may have been bullied by Roman soldiers (*Sat.* XVI) but he never had to bear arms against them.

12. *Discourse* 2354-56: "*Holiday* is not afraid to say, that there was never such a fall, as from his Odes to his Satires, and that he, injuriously to himself, untun'd his Harp." Dryden seems to be quoting Holiday with approval, but earlier in the *Discourse* (1036-38) he says, "And *Horace* seems to have purg'd himself from those Splenetick Reflections in those *Odes* and *Epodes*, before he undertook the Noble Work of Satires; which were properly so call'd." The probable publication dates are: Satires I, 35 B.C.; Satires II and *Epodes*, 30 B.C.; Odes I-III, 23 B.C.; Odes IV, 13 B.C.

13. *Sat.* 1.4.6-13, 38-44, 56-62.
14. *Sat.* 1.4.46-48.
15. *Sat.* 2.6.17.

time on a grovelling pedestrian.

Sat. 1.4 is also the *fons et origo* of Dryden's comic and tragic satire. Horace begins it with a reference to the unfettered personal invective of Old Comedy, on which, he says, Lucilius was entirely dependent: all he did was change the metres:

> Eupolis atque Cratinus Aristophanesque poetae,
> atque alii quorum comoedia prisca uirorum est,
> si quis erat dignus describi quod malus ac fur,
> quod moechus foret aut sicarius aut alioqui
> famosus, multa cum libertate notabant.
> hinc omnis pendet Lucilius, hosce secutus
> mutatis tantum pedibus numerisque . . .

When Horace fashioned these lines he would hardly stop and think that ancient, mediaeval, and modern historians of literature would gleefully seize on them as a simple solution to the vexed question of what *satura* was and where it came from.[16] They ought to have paid more attention to context. *Sat.* 1.4[17] was probably Horace's first essay in literary criticism, written in defence of his own early satires, which were quite sharp and personal compared with his later work. So what he noticed in Lucilius, apart from his apparently slapdash style, was the Aristophanic freedom with which he lashed his contemporaries, a freedom that Horace probably began by envying, for it was certainly denied both to him and to every Augustan writer. Hence the carefree exaggeration of *hinc omnis pendet Lucilius. Sat.* 1.10 and 2.1 show how Horace matured to a juster appraisal of his predecessor's many-sided genius.

If "comic satire" can be improperly derived from Horace, *Sat.* 1.4.1-7, an even more specious case can be made out for deriving "tragic satire" from Juvenal 6.634-637:

> fingimus haec altum satura sumente cothurnum

---

16. No sense of historical consistency prevented these same critics, Dryden included (*Discourse* 1101-1226), from falling equally hard for Livy's preposterous theory (7.2) that the tragedy and comedy that Livius Andronicus wrote and directed at Rome in 240 B.C. were the final development of a primitive *satura* domesticated from Etruria.

17. Pope (*Epistle to Dr. Arbuthnot* 283-304) borrows and expands lines 81-85 for a similar defence against similar attacks.

> scilicet, et finem egressi legemque priorum
> grande Sophocleo carmen bacchamur hiatu,
> montibus ignotum Rutulis caeloque Latino?

Dryden does not quote either this[18] or any passage from Juvenal throughout the *Discourse*. But his translation (*The Sixth Satyr* 828-831) is instructive:

> You think this feign'd; the Satyr in a Rage
> Struts in the Buskins, of the Tragick Stage.
> Forgets his Bus'ness is to Laugh and Bite;
> And will, of Deaths, and dire Revenges Write.

His first half-line suggests that he has understood what Juvenal is saying, i.e., "you think that this talk of mothers poisoning their children is pure fiction, the kind you see on the tragic stage. You think that I'm bursting into a Sophoclean lyric, having completely forgotten that Roman satire has always been about real life." The next line and a half will do, though "rage" is not quite right for *bacchamur*. After that Dryden neither translates literally nor interprets the sense, but proceeds to overlay Juvenal's fiction-reality antithesis with an antithesis that is nowhere in the Latin, but which is very much in Dryden's mind, the antithesis between comedy and tragedy. Juvenal goes on (*Sat.* 6.643-646) to draw the conclusion that the tales of the tragedians may now be promoted from fiction to fact. Dryden has already drawn the conclusion that Juvenal is a tragedian *manqué*. But between Juvenal and Sophocles the gulf is as deep and wide as it is between laughing Horace and Old Comedian Aristophanes.[19]

Harold Guite

---

18. C. Witke quotes it without the question-mark in *Latin Satire*, Leiden, 1970, p. 114 in a chapter headed *Juvenal and Saturae Tragicae*.

19. One of the reasons Dryden could not see this is that he was surrounded by clergymen who detected a resemblance between Juvenal and the Prophet Isaiah. In *Discourse* 1660-87 he tells us that the Bishop of Salisbury has recommended ". . . the Tenth Satyr of *Juvenal*, in his Pastoral Letter, to the serious perusal and Practice of the Divines in his Diocese . . ."

Theatrical Satire: A Protest from the Stage Against Poor Taste in Theatrical Entertainment

When we think of the literature of protest we think most naturally of literature which attacks social, political, and economic evils. I have, however, chosen to deal with a little-considered genre which is concerned mainly with satiric attack upon poor taste in its own particular field. For this purpose I shall adopt the term "theatrical satire" to cover all plays which ridicule their own medium, and I am concerned with the reflection of changing tastes in the theatre as they appear in the mirror of this genre between Buckingham's *Rehearsal* and Sheridan's *Critic*.

To begin, and for the purpose of defining the genre, let us look briefly at the question in an historical context. For satire to operate, a writer must share with his audience some common knowledge about the object to be satirized. Thus, while Chaucer could attack, in works like "Sir Thopas," particular fashions in writing, the *terminus a quo* for an attack on theatrical taste in England must, by its very nature, come later. By Shakespeare's time the dramatist could already count on a shared theatrical experience with a settled audience. Thus Shakespeare comments extensively upon the nature of his art, as occurs in the player's scene in Hamlet. Also the plays within plays by amateur theatricals (as in *Midsummer Night's Dream* and *Love's Labour's Lost*) may already augur both the form which many theatrical satires were to take and the satire of either self interest or professional disdain with which some works in the genre were to be concerned.

Insofar as content is the criterion, the first complete play ostensibly fitting the requirements for a theatrical satire is Beaumont's *Knight of the Burning Pestle*. Here the Grocer's taste (and by implication the taste of his class) is undercut with satiric indirection as, seated upon the stage, he makes his highly revealing comments. While the play is in many ways a prototype for the genre, and perfectly capable of successfully holding the stage even in our own times, one ingredient essential for our purposes is lacking. The play failed on its first presentation. F. W. Moorman suggests most plausibly: "perhaps its playful satire may have given offence to the London citizen." However we have no records to help us. Though the play appeared again in 1635 at the Private House in Drury Lane and the court of Queen Henrietta, this would hardly provide a cross cut of the contemporary audience from whose acceptance of the production a change in taste might be deduced.

Mention should also be made of Molière's amusing little piece *L'Impromptu de Versailles* (1663). Molière's play involves the production of a drama in which not only the author himself but also his troupe, including the Béjarts, actually appear on the stage in rehearsal. And while dealing with possible influences for theatrical satire we must not overlook Aristophanes. This writer stands *in loco parentis* to the genre and to him the authors on more than one occasion pay their grateful tributes, though with suitable satiric indirection.

In England, however, the genre clearly starts with Buckingham's *Rehearsal*. Only here do we have a really successful play effectively concerned with protest against the unsatisfactory tastes of another dramatic genre. During the century of theatrical satire with which I am chiefly concerned plays largely or wholly belonging to this genre were written by Buckingham, Duffett, Gay, Carey, Fielding, Foote, Murphy, and Sheridan. I refer for example to Buckingham's *Rehearsal*; Duffett's *Empress of Morocco, Mock Tempest* and *Psyche Debauched*; Gay's *Beggar's Opera*; Carey's *Chrononhotonthologos* and *Dragon of Wantley*; Fielding's *Author's Farce, Tom Thumb, Covent Garden Tragedy, Pasquin* and *Eurydice*; and Sheridan's *Critic*. In addition particular facets of the genre are included in plays like Murphy's *Apprentice*; Foote's *Taste* and *Author*; Jackman's *All the World's a Stage*; Powell's *Private Theatricals*; and the attack on "false sentiment" in the plays of Goldsmith and Sheridan.

Not only was theatrical satire a highly successful genre, but, excepting only the comedy of manners, there are several among these plays which make the best reading today and which of the whole period are most easily staged in our own time. The genre comes to a close with Sheridan's *Critic*. As a result of changing taste during the bourgeois ascendancy, theatrical satire, like other drama of literary substance, was obliged to leave the stage. Thereafter the protest against poor taste in the theatre was confined to such "closet satires" as Hookham Frere's *Rovers*, Tieck's *Gestiefelte Kater*, and Platen's *Verhängnisvolle Gabel*.

Seeking a relationship between the play, the audience, the genre attacked, and the author, I start my study with three hypotheses. These posit that theatrical satire, unlike literary satire, must carry with it the dominant groups in a theatre; that theatrical satire must aggressively attack at least one aspect of the theatre recognizable to the audience of the period; and that theatrical satire has tended to be a tool of conservatives, in the sense that it represented the reaction by an aristocracy of class, of taste, or of special interests.

In general terms, it would appear that all three of these propositions can be justified. Thus the necessity for theatrical satire to carry with it the dominant groups in the audience (be their strength vocal, physical, or social) is demonstrated by the riots of the footmen attending Townley's *High Life Below Stairs* (1759), or the failure of Foote's *Taste* (1752) that attempted a direct attack on the rising bourgeoisie. Moreover, once we are convinced that, in the age of ridicule, theatrical satires will be launched whenever they might be successful, we have acquired a valuable yardstick by which their very absence may be used to measure the strength of public taste. The absence of strong theatrical satire against vulgarity in the Restoration, against opera in the period 1710-1728, or against sentiment right up to the time of *The School for Scandal* will tell us much about the tastes of the times concerned. The absence of satire against Augustan tragedy reflects the expressed ideals of the age. The absence of satire against the comedy of manners, which had instead to be blunted with sentiment, reflects the true tastes of the aristocratic satirists and the call for Aristophanic humour that is found in the theatrical satires right through their century of efflorescence.

In a positive sense, theatrical satire could be relied upon to attack one genre after another, just as soon as the reaction of aristocratic taste might muster enough strength to carry with it the dominant groups in the theatre. Thus, throughout the period, one can trace the reflection of changing tastes in the mirror of theatrical satire. Heroic drama, then Italian opera, pantomimes, pastorals, numerous forms of "spectacle," and finally sentiment itself may be observed as they came within focus of attack. Furthermore, the ridicule of Fielding's *Tom Thumb* against Restoration tragedy is supplementary to Buckingham's attack on the even more baroque heroic drama. Here is reflected a progressive development of taste away from stage histrionics, which was shortly to be further underlined by the exchange of Quinn's style for that of Garrick. Indeed, when Sheridan's turn comes to make the call for Aristophanic humour, he now bewails the very "insipidity" of the stage.

In respect of the need for theatrical satire to have a recognizable object of attack, one can demonstrate that this resulted in the form developing, as a genre, far later than satire in general. Even when censorship problems (to which satire in the theatre is particularly sensitive) had been sufficiently overcome, there still did not appear to be the necessary combination of author, audience, and recognizable dramatic genre that would support a viable satire in the theatre for castigating inferior taste. It was only after the Interregnum that the necessary coincidence of events took place. Thus the killing of the king in 1649 meant that, in the final analysis, the aristocracy would have to fight with satire rather than the sword, and with this England's great age of satire became virtually inevitable. Heroic drama now provided a recognizable genre which was ripe for ridicule, and Buckingham and his associate authors had the requisite skill to launch a full-scale attack in the theatre, with suitable satiric indirection. The fact that Elizabethan domestic drama was not attacked in the Restoration, precisely when this might have been possible, while

Restoration tragedy was attacked in considerable detail as late as Fielding's *Tom Thumb* shows how important it is to theatrical satire that the object of attack shall be recognizable to the audience of the time.

With respect to the question of theatrical satire representing an aristocracy of taste or of special interests, such well known critics as Kernan, Elliott, Worcester, Radin, Rosenheim, Sutherland, and Paulson all support my contention that satirists in general tend to be conservative by nature. It is therefore not surprising that theatrical satirists should have been found by observation to follow this trend. In the class of satires representing an aristocracy of special interest are such works as Duffett's ridicule of the English opera, Murphy's outcry against apprentices who wish to go on the stage, and the satire of Jackman against aristocrats, who having lost their hegemony over the public theatre, were turning toward amateur theatricals. The conflict expressed here is genuine enough, but not one of these works has come down to us with the ring of viable drama.

The great theatrical satires of the century under review — the works of Buckingham, Gay, Carey, Fielding, and Sheridan — are all written by authors in whom an aristocracy of both class associations and taste coincide. Moreover, all carry out an aggressive attack. The extent to which they are progressively obliged to incorporate elements of inferior taste, in order to hold the boards, is a valuable measure of the ground that is being gained by the followers of Queen Ignorance in Fielding's *Pasquin*.

Prologues and epilogues, together with the preludes of author-managers such as Garrick and Colman, are, like the theatrical satires, mines of information regarding the theatre. Yet, only theatrical satire, precisely because it is as aggressive as conditions will allow, provides us with a measure of just how far inferior taste can or cannot be attacked in the theatre at any given moment. Buckingham fights heroic drama with wit alone. However, Gay, in attacking opera, must provide ballads; Fielding and Carey, in fighting the forces of Queen Ignorance, must provide the very entertainment which is represented by her followers; and Sheridan, in ridiculing false sentiment, is obliged to use "true" sentiment as the bench mark of his ideals.

It is important to remember that the aristocratic satirists are highly skilled manipulators of this mode, and that they belong to the greatest age of English and very possibly of world satire. They have adapted their techniques to the theatre in such a way that, if it is at all possible, they will carry the audience with them. First and foremost among these techniques is that of heavily undercutting certain of the characters, and then permitting them to approve of the tastes which are to be ridiculed. It is precisely in this way that satiric indirection is frequently achieved, and that the drama avoids degenerating into mere polemic. The aristocratic satirists, during this period of middle-class ascendancy, no longer make Beaumont's mistake of using such obviously bourgeois protagonists as the London grocer and his wife to be the vehicles for satiric indirection. Most frequently the protagonists are first undercut in a manner which the audience cannot help but approve.

While, in an age of aristocratic cynicism and Restoration gentlemen, Buckingham's Bayes was undercut by falling on his nose and because he wrote for money and grew obsequious before his betters, the later satirists could no longer employ such means. In the eighteenth century we find a variety of methods being used for the undercutting. The Marplays are undercut because they steal plays, Sir Fretful because he plagiarizes them, Chrononhotonthologos because his name is too long, Tom Thumb because his body is too short. Often these characters, who are being prepared as vehicles for praising inferior taste, undercut one another. This is true, for example, of Trapwit and Fustion in *Pasquin,* and of Dangle, Sneer, and Sir Fretful in *The Critic.* The main point is that once the audience has been convinced that anything of which the protagonist approves must, by its very nature, be in poor taste, the battle of the theatrical satirist is half won.

The satirist has other tools with which to fight. His genre is neither the Augustan tragedy nor the Italian opera to which many come merely because this is fashionable. Theatrical satire, if it is to succeed as such, must be both topical and capable of interesting the audience in its own right. Like most good satire it involves itself with layer upon layer of the *lanx satura,* the full dish or hotch-potch. The contents of this *lanx satura* change and in some respects thin out as the period develops. Etherege's Smirk, "my Lady Bigot's chaplain," becomes Goldsmith's Methodist preacher "with a skinful"; patrons turn into objects of satire rather than adulation; and handkerchiefs are eventually as suspect as patriotism. Statesmen, who had been savaged by Gay and Fielding, are merely transformed into painted ancestors in *The School for Scandal.* Priests and citizens' wives, ridiculed heartlessly by the earlier comedy of manners, are but mentioned in passing by Sheridan. Theatrical satire is a veritable gold-mine of changing tastes and conditions in theatre and life. Because this satire is born of conflict, it cuts into the living edge of the audience of its day. Our genre comes far closer to a true representation of the times than any cold repository of historical facts.

As we look back over the century at the three greatest writers of theatrical satire, we find the central focus to have changed in accordance with the perspective of the authors. With Buckingham, writing from the point of view of the amateur critic, it is the author who is undercut, while the management is virtually ignored. Fielding, on the other hand, writes from the perspective of an author, sitting, for the most part, on the outside of the patent theatres. With Sheridan the position is different again, for his is the only viable theatrical satire by an author-manager of the patent houses, and it is now the turn of critic and author to be undercut together.

The very standards that the satirists use — thereby pointing up their satire, in Schillerian terms, as the difference between the ideal and the real — also reflect a change in the nature of the times. Thus Buckingham sets up as his bench mark the aristocratic and epicurean amateur critic, Johnson, whereas Fielding, like Beaumont, uses "The Sermon on the Mount." Sheridan and Goldsmith, in an age where middle-class morality dominates, can only claim true as distinct from false sentiment as their ideal.

In the final analysis, the change in taste and morality during the period with which we are concerned derives very largely from the middle-class ascendancy that came to dominate both literature and life. More than half a decade before the publication of Pope's *Dunciad IV*, Fielding warns us forcefully in *Pasquin* that inferior tastes in the theatre will spread out to become part of the *miaron* (or pollution) of the state. In the modern "era of the common man" he seems to have proved dangerously prophetic. Today, not merely theatrical satire, but also such traditional elements in the *lanx satura* as the ridicule of priests, lawyers, and doctors seem to have been virtually barred from the vehicles for mass media.

Fielding's *Pasquin* describes the fox skulking outside, "while the poor goose in happiness and ease, / Fearless grows fat within its narrow coop, / And thinks the hand that feeds it is his friend." Fearful of the ascendancy of a middle-class morality and taste based almost exclusively on the desire for "progress," Fielding was foreshadowing those dangers that await the man who moves in a centrally heated car from a centrally heated home to a centrally heated office. It is undeniable that such a man enjoys the great material advantages that derive from today's three-cornered arrangements between the entertainment industry, Madison Avenue, and the large corporations. Fielding is suggesting that in the long run it might be better to stay on the outside, lean and cynical like the fox — but how is one to know?

Moreover today, our moral bench marks, like our aesthetic tastes, are closer to those of the goose than those of the fox; at the best they are a combination of both. If we are to understand how this change of taste and morality occurred, we must turn to the literature of the Restoration and the eighteenth century. If we are to hope that one day the alliance between Fielding's Queen Ignorance and commercial entertainment may be weakened, we should take into account the fact that the head which fell in 1649 fell irrevocably. The new aristocracy of taste that will arise, if it arises at all, must be spawned on the campuses of North America, where, like the old aristocracy after the Interregnum, it should seriously consider protesting with ridicule rather than with the sword. We might well be advised to take a new and hard look at the rusty weapons of theatrical satire.

Samuel Macey

An Augustan Monument:
The Opticks of Isaac Newton

Scientific books rarely earn a place in histories of literature. So it is not surprising that few if any accounts of the Augustan Age make even a passing mention of one of the most notable works published in the reigns of Queen Anne and of George I. Yet Isaac Newton's *Opticks*, subtitled "A Treatise of the Reflections, Refractions, Inflexions and Colours of Light," published in 1704, deserves mention, though not a work of imaginative literature, along with Dean Swift's *Gulliver*, the novels of Defoe and the poetry of Alexander Pope. The extraordinary influence Newton's book exerted during the eighteenth century, not only upon science, but upon philosophy, letters and even — as I shall suggest — upon the arts, marks it as an epoch-making Augustan work. Besides the book itself — its composition, publication and subsequent revision in later editions — it is the range and spread of its influence that I propose to discuss.

Chronologically Newton was an Augustan. His apotheosis as a national hero, in the last quarter century of his life, almost exactly coincides with the Augustan Age of English literature. He had left Cambridge in 1696 to assume the post of Warden of the Mint, responsible for the great enterprise of the recoinage. Although for some years he kept his professorship at Cambridge, and his Trinity Fellowship, he resided henceforth in London. Raised to the less exacting and more honorific post of Master of the Mint, a post he held for the rest of his life, he at last severed his connection with his University.[1] The Royal Society of London, whose meetings he had rarely attended up

---

1. The standard biographies are David Brewster, *Memoirs of the Life, Writings, and Discoveries of Sir Isaac Newton*, 2 vols., Edinburgh, 1855, which is still worth consulting, and L.T. More, *Isaac Newton*, New York and London, 1934. Frank Manuel's *Portrait of Isaac Newton*, Cambridge, Mass., 1968, is a psycho-biographical study of Newton's complex and often irritating personality.

to this time became thereafter the center of his life. In 1703, the year after the accession of Queen Anne, he was elected President of the Society, and in April of 1705 he was knighted by the Queen. As President, a post that he held until his death in 1727, he was no mere aging figure-head: he concerned himself actively with the affairs of the Society, taking the lead, for example, in finding a new home for that body. He was, as we have come to recognize, intellectually active in science, and alert to new discoveries, some of which indeed he actively promoted. Most important, perhaps, he brought out new and revised editions of his great classic, the *Mathematical Principles of Natural Philosophy* (1687), and of his *Opticks*. And the changes he introduced into both these works during the last fifteen years of his life show that his philosophy of nature was capable of far from trivial modifications.[2]

Newton's Two Major Books

A comparison between Newton's two great masterpieces is perhaps in order. The *Principia*, more often talked about than read, is a difficult work written, if I may put it this way, in two ancient languages: Latin and geometry. The foundation work in rational mechanics, it is more or less rigorously axiomatic and deductive in form. It treats bodies as if deprived of all qualities or properties except the "primary" ones of extension and mass; abstract theorems about mass points or idealized bodies moving under the influence of "central forces" are applied, in the concluding book of the *Principia* ("The System of the World"), to the real bodies of the solar system.

By contrast, the *Opticks* is written in the language of experiment and was first published in English. To be sure, Newton affects a kind of Euclidean form; beginning with definitions (of "rays of light," "refrangibility," and so on) and with a few axioms (certain basic laws of geometrical optics), the work proceeds as a series of "propositions" and "theorems." But these propositions are not statements of abstract

2. A convenient listing of the editions of these works can be found in George Gray, *Bibliography of the Works of Sir Isaac Newton*, Cambridge, 1907.

mathematical relations; they are assertions of experimental fact, followed by what he calls "proofs by experiment." The axiomatic form is not to be taken seriously; indeed it is systematically followed only in the first of three "books" into which the work is divided. There is little mathematics, and that of the simplest sort. For the most part, the body of the work (exclusive of the famous *Queries* appended to it) consists of a meticulous account of his experiments on light and color. It is no wonder that the book was more widely read, and more accessible to the curious reader, than the formidable *Principia*.

The *Opticks* is in some respects a bibliographical curiosity, and I shall call attention to some of the puzzles it presents to scholars. First of all, contemporaries could have quibbled about the title: the book is not a textbook of optics, but a monograph on color; Newton's purpose is to introduce an exact and quantitative science of color into the ancient and established domain of optics.[3] From his own experiments, and the inferences drawn from them, he explains the colors produced by prisms and droplets of water, the colors of natural bodies, the periodic bands of color ("Newton's rings") observed in thin transparent bodies (bubbles, sheets of mica) and the rainbow.

One puzzle involves the publication date of the *Opticks*. The first edition of 1704 opens with an undated "Advertisement" signed with the initials "I.N." But when, thirteen years later, Newton brought out a second English edition, he added a new preface designated as "Advertisement II"; this too is signed with Newton's initials, and it is dated (July 16, 1717). But the earlier advertisement is reprinted, this time with a date appended. The date — April 1, 1704 — is obviously erroneous, for the evidence is clear that the book had

3. Geometrical optics, spoken of in the seventeenth century as one of the "mixed mathematics," had a long lineage going back through the Middle Ages to such Greek mathematicians as Euclid, Ptolemy and Hero of Alexandria. Despite the well-known preoccupation with the rainbow on the part of medieval scholars, color phenomena long resisted precise mathematical treatment, and remained largely in the domain of crude experiment and speculation. A good introduction to the early history of the subject is Vascho Ronchi, *Storia della Luce*, 2nd ed., Bologna, 1952; tr. into French by Juliette Taton, *Histoire de la lumière*, Paris, 1956. For the rainbow, and early speculations about color, see Carl B. Boyer, *The Rainbow*, New York and London, 1959.

been published more than a month earlier, sometime in February 1704.[4] Newton, as we shall see, was indifferent to such minutiae and rather cavalier in revising his own writings.

To answer such questions as "When was the *Opticks* composed?" or "When did Newton put his manuscript in final form?" is not easy. The work is really a conflate text; it embodies experiments and observations that Newton made at various periods of his life; it seems, indeed, pretty much to recapitulate the sequence of his discoveries. The substance of the "First Book" is an expansion of his classic paper, the letter on his "New Theory about Light and Color," published in the *Philosophical Transactions* of the Royal Society in February, 1672.[5] This famous paper, you will recall, demonstrated by experiments with prisms that white solar light is a "mixture" of rays "differently refrangible" and suggested, although hardly proving, that there is a one-to-one correspondence between the color of the rays and the degree of refrangibility.[6]

Much of the "Second Book" is almost word for word (with some significant emendations) reprinted from a paper sent to the Royal Society in 1675, describing his observations on the ring phenomena, a paper Newton at the time declined to publish.[7]

4. In a memorandum of 1 March 1703/4, David Gregory referred to the *Opticks* as already published. See W.G. Hiscock, ed., *David Gregory, Isaac Newton and their Circle*, Oxford, 1957, p. 15. The Term Catalogues, Arber, III, p. 387, list the book under Hilary Term, 1703/4. Books listed for Hilary Term (January 11-31) were licensed for publication in February. I was led to this bit of information by my colleague, Professor Donald Eddy.

5. Exper. 1 and 2 of the First Book record observations not mentioned in Newton's paper of 1672. Probably the earliest important experiments he made with a prism, they are described in an early notebook (Cambridge University Library, MS. Add. 3975); see A.R. Hall, "Further Optical Experiments of Isaac Newton," *Annals of Science*, 11, 1955, pp. 27-43.

6. In facsimile it may be consulted in I.B. Cohen, ed., *Isaac Newton's Papers & Letters on Natural Philosophy*, Cambridge, Mass., 1958, pp. 47-59; also, as printed "with emendations" based on a transcript by Newton's copyist, in *The Correspondence of Isaac Newton*, ed. H.W. Turnbull, Vol. I, Cambridge, 1959, pp. 92-107; this and subsequent volumes will be cited as *Newton Correspondence*.

7. Called the "Discourse on Observations," it was sent to the Royal Society with a letter dated 7 December 1675. The "Discourse" with few changes makes up Parts I and II and half of Part III of the "Second Book" of the *Opticks*. In its original form it was first printed by Thomas Birch in his *History of the Royal Society of London*, 4 vols., London, 1756-57, III, pp. 272-305; reprinted in facsimile from Birch in *Papers and Letters*, pp. 202-235.

The "Third Book" consists of a short section (about nineteen quarto pages) describing experiments on diffraction, that is: the bending and splitting of light when it passes through narrow apertures, or past the sharp edges of bodies, a phenomenon first described by the Jesuit scientist, Francesco Maria Grimaldi.[8] Newton clearly deemed his own experiments on the subject incomplete or inconclusive, for he wrote: "When I made the foregoing Observations, I designed to repeat most of them with more care and exactness, and to make some new ones. . . . But I was then interrupted, and cannot now think of taking these things into further consideration."[9] Then follow immediately the so-called Queries: shorter or longer suggestions or speculations, framed in the interrogative voice, and proposed, as Newton says, "in order to a further search to be made by others." It cannot be determined with certainty when the diffraction experiments were performed, but evidence points to the years just before 1684-85.[10]

The "Third Book" confronts us with still another puzzle. If we consult the later editions of the *Opticks* (including the modern paperback edition in common use) we find that whereas the First Book is divided into two numbered "Parts," and the Second Book has four, the Third Book is labelled "Part I," but there is no "Part II." This designation of a "Part I" is not to be found in the first edition of 1704; it makes its first appearance in the second English edition of 1717-18, a clue that, as we shall see later on, helps unravel the mystery.

When was the *Opticks* actually put together from its diverse elements? How long before its publication in 1704? We know that Newton had in hand a virtually complete manuscript as

8. In his posthumously-published *Physico-Mathesis de Lumine, Coloribus et Iride*, Bologna, 1665.

9. *Opticks*, 1704, Third Book, p. 132. Unlike the later editions, this quarto first edition has separate pagination for the First Book, pp. 1 - 144, and for the rest of the work: the Second and Third Books and the two Latin mathematical papers appended to the *Opticks*, pp. 1-211. In the Latin *Optice* of 1706, only the mathematical papers have separate pagination.

10. The interruption Newton speaks of was probably occasioned by the writing of the *Principia*, by which time he was familiar with Grimaldi's work, and had himself performed some diffraction experiments. See *Principia*, 1687, p. 231. He probably had not heard of Grimaldi before 1672.

early as 1694, for in that year David Gregory, the Savilian Professor of Astronomy at Oxford, visited Newton in Cambridge and was shown the manuscript of "Three Books of Opticks." This, Gregory noted, would if printed be the equal of the *Principia*.[11] Later the following summer, doubtless at Gregory's instigation, the Fellows of the Royal Society resolved that a letter be written to Newton urging him "to communicate to the Society in order to be published his Treatise of Light and Colours & what other Mathematical or Physical Treatises he has ready by him."[12] There was no response from Cambridge; so the next year John Wallis, the venerable Oxford mathematician, wrote to Newton that he had learned of the completion of "a Treatise about Light, Refraction & Colours; which I should be glad to see abroad." And he went on:

> 'Tis pitty it was not out long since. If it be in English (as I hear it is) let it, however, come out as it is; & let those who desire to read it, learn English.

And Wallis — because of his seniority, eminence and friendship with Newton, he could safely chide that sensitive man — concluded:

> You are not so kind to your Reputation (& that of the Nation) as you might be, when you let things of worth ly by you so long, till others carry away the Reputation that is due to you.[13]

Newton's reply has been lost, but its burden is clear from the exasperated tone of Wallis' next letter:

> I can by no means admit your excuse for not publishing your Treatise of Light & Colours. You say you dare not *yet* publish it. And why *not yet*? Or, if not now, when then? You adde, lest it create you *some trouble*. What trouble *now* more than at another time? Pray consider, how many years this hath lyen upon your hands allready.[14]

11. Memoranda by David Gregory, *Newton Correspondence*, III, p. 336.
12. Journal Book of the Royal Society, 4 July 1694; *Newton Correspondence*, III, p. 340, n. 16.
13. *Newton Correspondence*, IV, p. 100.
14. *Ibid.*, IV, pp. 116-117. Wallis's italics.

Newton's reluctance to publish was, of course, notorious. Only great pressure from the Royal Society, and the direct assistance of Edmond Halley, had brought the *Principia* into being. This reluctance was enhanced by the prolonged controversy — with Robert Hooke and with critics on the Continent — that attended the publication of his first paper of 1672. Not long after, Newton wrote to Henry Oldenburg, the Secretary of the Royal Society:

> I see that I have made my self a slave to Philosophy, but if I get free of Mr. Linus's business I will resolutely bid adew to it eternally, excepting what I do for my privat satisfaction or leave to come after me.[15]

Evidently the composition of the *Opticks* was just such an activity for his "privat satisfaction" and a good part of the work must have been composed after his resolute vow to Henry Oldenburg. Yet, after his move to London, as we saw, Newton remained deaf to the pleas of his friends. Finally a notable delegation paid him a visit. On Sunday, 15 November 1702 (so David Gregory recorded), Newton "promised Mr. Robarts, Mr. Fatio, Capt. Hally [sic] and me to publish his Quadratures, his treatise of Light, and his treatise of the curves of 2^d genre."[16] Newton kept his promise and must have set to work on the final revisions, and dispatched the manuscript to the printer, before the autumn of 1703. In February of 1704 Newton presented a copy of this handsome quarto, its titlepage printed in red and black, to the Royal Society. His name nowhere appears, only his initials appended to the undated "Advertisement" where Newton confessed:

To avoid being engaged in Disputes about these Matters, I

15. Letter of 18 November 1676 in *Newton Correspondence*, II, pp. 182-183. Francis Hall, who called himself Line or Linus, was an elderly professor at the College of Jesuits at Liège, and one of those who attacked the findings of Newton's first paper. Linus died in 1675, but the debate continued with Linus's associate, Anthony Lucas, until Newton brought it to an end in the summer of 1678.

16. Hiscock, *David Gregory*, p. 14. In a later entry, p. 15, Gregory wrote: "Mr. Newton was provoked by Dr. Cheyne's book to publish his Quadratures, and with it, his Light and Colours, etc." George Cheyne, a London physician, published in 1703 his *Fluxionum methodus inversa*, making use of Newton's mathematical discoveries. See Florian Cajori, *History of the Conceptions of Limits and Fluxions in Great Britain*, Chicago and London, 1919, p. 40.

have hitherto delayed the Printing, and should still have delayed it, had not the importunity of Friends prevailed upon me.[17]

Thus appeared one of the most important scientific books ever published in the English language. Its influence can be attributed to the important discoveries it contained, to the clarity and precision of the writing, to the method of scientific inquiry it exemplified and – in the remarkable Queries, as Newton expanded them, and added to them, in later editions – to the bold speculations and suggestions for future investigations which Newton set forth.

Newton and English Style

There was no novelty in publishing a scientific work in English, although Latin was widely favored in the 17th century, especially by physicians who were notably conservative, as the language of scientific communication. Before the middle of the seventeenth century, indeed as early as the late sixteenth, English was employed chiefly in works of a practical nature, such as mathematical works for the surveyor or the navigator, or popular books like John Wilkins' *Discovery of a World in the Moon* (1638). The two earliest classics of English science, William Gilbert's *De magnete* (1600) and William Harvey's epoch-making book on the circulation of the blood, were both written in Latin. But the Royal Society of London, soon after its establishment, profoundly stimulated the use of English, which was the language of its official journal, the *Philosophical Transactions*, and of the majority of the books published under its auspices, for example the *Micrographia* and other writings of Robert Hooke and the *Anatomy of Plants* (1682) of Nehemiah Grew. John Wallis' early mathematical works were published in Latin; but his *Algebra* first appeared in English in 1685 and was only later translated into Latin.[18] This was the common practice

17. *Opticks*, 1704, Advertisement.
18. In the Latin version of his *Algebra*, 1693, Wallis made the first public announcement of Newton's fluxional calculus. He referred to it as "some specimen of what we hope Mr. Newton will himself publish in due time." See *Newton Correspondence*, III, p. 221, n. 1.

of Robert Boyle whose best-known books – his *Spring and Weight of the Air* and his *Skeptical Chemist* – indeed the majority of them, were first composed and published in English but brought out soon after in Latin dress for the benefit of readers on the Continent.[19]

The English style of these early scientific books was often clumsy and cluttered with Anglicized Latin words; none could use them as artfully as Sir Thomas Browne. Boyle is proverbially hard to read; his sentences are long, loose-jointed and rambling. Yet he made a valiant effort to purify his vocabulary from the influence of scientific Latin, and to find, where possible, equivalents in plain English for the technical terms of medicine and chemistry. At all events, he avoids the gibberish of Walter Charleton whose *Physiologia* of 1654 exerted in other respects a profound influence upon his thought. Boyle, to say nothing of Newton, would never have written anything like the following description by Charleton of an experiment with a prism:

> As for the Enodation of the *Later Difficulty*, it is comprehended in the Reasons of the Former. . . . This is easily *Experimented* with a piece of narrow black Ribbon affixt longwise to either side of the Prisme. For, in that case, the light is bipartited into two Borders, or Fringes, the opace part veyled by the Ribbon on each side environed with light, and each border of light environed with two shadows; or, more plainly, between each border of shadows conterminate to each extreme of Light, trajected through the unopacate parts of the Glass: and, therefore, in the commissure of each of the two lights with each of the conterminous shadows, there must be Vermillion to one side, and Caerule on the other.[20]

19. John F. Fulton, *A Bibliography of the Honourable Robert Boyle*, 2nd ed., Oxford, 1961, *passim*.

20. Walter Charleton, *Physiologia Epicuro-Gassendo Charltoniana: or a Fabrick of Science Natural, upon the Hypothesis of Atoms*, London, 1654, pp. 195-196. A facsimile of this work, with an introduction by Robert Kargon, has been published by the Johnson Reprint Corporation in 1966, The Sources of Science, No. 31. For an account of Charleton, London physician and original Fellow of the Royal Society, see Kargon's introduction to the *Physiologia* and his *Atomism in England from Hariot to Newton*, Oxford, 1966, chapter VIII.

Compare this, if you please, with Newton's description of one of his early experiments:

In the Sun's beam which was propagated into the Room through the hole in the Window-shut, at the distance of some Feet from the hole, I held the Prism in such a posture that its Axis might be perpendicular to that beam. Then I looked through the Prism upon the hole, and turning the Prism to and fro about its Axis to make the Image of the Hole ascend and descend, when between its two contrary Motions it seemed stationary, I stopt the Prism that the Refractions of both sides of the refracting angle might be equal to each other . . . In this Situation of the Prism viewing through it the said hole, I observed the length of its refracted image to be many times greater than its breadth, and that the most refracted part thereof appeared violet, the least refracted red, and the middle parts blew green and yellow in order.[21]

There are Anglicized Latin terms, to be sure, but no more than Newton deemed unavoidable. The style is crisp and tight; and here, as throughout his *Opticks*, we find that "close, naked, natural way of Speaking; positive Expressions, clear Senses; a native Easiness" that came to be exacted from the Fellows of the Royal Society.[22]

Newton, of course, could not completely free himself from the academic language of his student days. As we leaf through the *Opticks* we find a number of archaic Latinisms: celerity for speed; conduce for contribute; confine for limit or border; intromit for let in; interjacent for lying between. And here and there we find even stranger words, of the kind that flowed so readily from the pen of Walter Charleton: equipollent, consecution, obliquation.

21. *Opticks*, 1704, First Book, pp. 22-23.
22. Thomas Sprat, *History of the Royal Society*, London, 1667, p. 113. The Royal Society doctrine was only one contribution to simplification of style in the last third of the seventeenth century. The reform in pulpit oratory, distaste for religious "enthusiasm" and the delayed influence of the King James version of the Bible are all factors emphasized by Louis G. Locke, *Tillotson: A Study in seventeenth-century Literature*, Copenhagen, 1954, chap. IV.

Yet there are words first appearing in the *Opticks* that proved of such utility that they were soon domesticated and added to our language, largely through the efforts of Samuel Johnson. Some twenty years ago, Professor W.K. Wimsatt of Yale published a study of Johnson's *Dictionary* and the *Rambler* and the "philosophic words" drawn from the writings of Francis Bacon, Robert Boyle and other worthies, including Isaac Newton, which Dr. Johnson naturalized into the literary language. All the Newtonian words were drawn from the *Opticks*, which Johnson owned and had obviously perused with care. They are words now thoroughly at home in modern prose, at least scientific prose, and which writers have used, and still use, metaphorically: accelerate, assimilate, attraction, luminous, medium, rotation, texture, volatile, and many more.[23]

There is one Newtonian word listed by Johnson that deserves our special attention, for it is a key word in modern physics, commonly used, too, for various metaphorical purposes. This is the word *spectrum* which we usually define as the "band of colors produced by a prism." The O.E.D. cites Newton's classic paper of 1672 as the first appearance of the word in English. But if you look at this early paper, or scan the *Opticks* itself, you find something very peculiar. If, says Newton, you let a beam of light through a hole in a window shutter, and project it upon a screen the "spectrum" will be round and white. If, however, you refract that beam through a prism, and pass the red rays alone through the hole of a second board or screen, projecting it upon the wall, the "spectrum" will be round and red. Newton clearly means by this word any insubstantial, ghostlike optical image.[24] We can see what

23. W.K. Wimsatt, Jr., *Philosophic Words. A Study of Style and Meaning in the Rambler and Dictionary of Samuel Johnson*, New Haven, 1948. For a list of words taken from the *Opticks*, see p. 156.

24. Henry Guerlac, "The Word *Spectrum*: A Lexicographic Note with a Query," *Isis*, 56, 1965, pp. 206-207. Newton, I now think, borrowed an uncommon classical word used once by Cicero in his *Epistulae ad familiares*; Cicero attributes to one Catius, an Epicurean, the use of the word *spectra* for what Democritus and Epicurus called *eidola*. See *Cicero — The Letters to his Friends*, III, Loeb Classical Library, London and New York, 1929, pp. 296-7. In one of his early notebooks Newton referred to the "Phantome" of colors produced by the prism, a fact pointed out to me by Professor Richard Westfall of the University of Indiana. See Hall, "Further Optical Experiments of Newton," *loc. cit.*, p. 28.

transpired to give the word its modern meaning: well into the eighteenth century the band of colors produced by a prism (what Newton himself often called the "coloured spectrum," the "solar spectrum" or the "oblong image") is usually called the *prismatic spectrum.* But when the prismatic spectrum became the chief kind of optical image interesting to physicists, it gradually came to be called *the* spectrum, the adjective being simply dropped.[25]

The Opticks and the Concern with Color

The appeal of Newton's *Opticks* to the nature poets of the English eighteenth century, the best-known literary influence of that book, needs little elaboration from me. Their Newtonian imagery, their preoccupation with color, have been amply described by Marjorie Nicolson in her well-known study, *Newton Demands the Muse.*[26] Miss Nicolson tells us that the keen interest of poets in the *Opticks* began at the time of Newton's death. In the flood of eulogies and elegies published in 1727 and 1728, nearly all the poets mention "Newton's Rainbow" and "Newton's Colours"; yet except for James Thomson's "To the Memory of Newton," and Richard Glover's "Poem on Newton" (from which Miss Nicolson drew the title of her book) she finds these verses crude and undeveloped, "amorphous" is the word she uses. From then on the examples multiply, the quality improves, and poetic allusions to the *Opticks* become more specific, to culminate in Thomson's *Seasons*, Edward Young's *Night Thoughts*, and Mark Akenside's *Pleasures of the Imagination.* To be sure, these poets, while indebted to the *Opticks* for their color language and their prismatic imagery, need not have perused the book itself. They could have read Henry Pemberton's *A View of Sir Isaac Newton's Philosophy* (1728), or a book that dealt chiefly with Newton's discoveries on light and color, Francesco Algarotti's *Il*

25. The abbreviated form already appears in David Hartley's *Observations on Man*, 1749, and in the "Explanation of Technical Terms" in Joseph Priestley's *History and Present State of Discoveries relating to Vision, Light and Colour*, London, 1772.

26. Marjorie Hope Nicolson, *Newton Demands the Muse. Newton's* Opticks *and the Eighteenth Century Poets*, Princeton, 1946.

Newtonianismo per le Dame, brought out in English dress (1739) by Elizabeth Carter.

But whether obtained directly or indirectly, the optical lore of Miss Nicolson's poets was derived from the substance of the first two "books" of the *Opticks*. When Thomson wrote that Newton

> Untwisted all the shining robe of day;
> And, from the whitening undistinguished blaze,
> Collected every ray into his kind,
> To the charmed eye educed the gorgeous train
> Of parent colours.[27]

he was ennobling in verse the prism experiments set forth in the First Book, Part I, of the *Opticks*. And when the poets describe, in embellished Newtonian language, the rainbow, the Iris in a peacock's tail, the permanent colors of natural bodies, it is from Part II of the First Book, and the body of the Second Book that the descriptions are drawn. The Third Book, with its marvellous Queries held its treasures for other and different minds.

Scientists and Painters

If the poets, drawing inspiration from Newton's book, discovered color: color in the natural landscape, color phenomena in the atmosphere, so too did scientists and scientific amateurs. There were efforts to explain in Newtonian terms the colors of the aurora borealis, the blue shadows cast by bodies, and the red color of morning and evening clouds. Others performed experiments on what Buffon called "accidental colors," colors produced by striking the eye, or the vivid after-images seen after strong or prolonged exposure to natural colors, all matters alluded to by Newton.[28]

27. *Ibid.*, p. 12.
28. For Buffon's "Dissertation sur les couleurs accidentelles," see *Histoire et Mémoires de l'Académie des Sciences*, for 1743, Paris, 1746, pp. 147-158. The question of colored shadows and clouds, mentioned by Buffon, is treated by Pierre Bouguer in his posthumous *Traité d'optique sur la gradation de la lumière*, 1760. For the aurora, see Jean-Baptiste Dortous de Mairan, *Traité physique et historique de l'aurore boréale*, 2nd ed., Paris, 1754, Sect. III, Chap. IX, pp. 154-156. Priestley has a general discussion of these problems in his *History of Light and Colour*, pp. 436-449. With due regard for a special point of view, the reader should consult Goethe's

The keen interest in color for its own sake is attested by the ephemeral success of Father Castel's *clavecin oculaire*, or color organ. A severe critic of Newton's celestial mechanics, the Jesuit Louis-Bertrand Castel, for a time accepted, like most Frenchmen of his day, Newton's discoveries concerning color.[29] He drew powerful encouragement from those passages in the *Opticks* where Newton spoke of the prismatic spectrum as exhibiting seven colors, with intervals corresponding to the notes of a musical octave. Color, then, could provide a kind of music; and in the 1750's Father Castel entertained audiences with shifting displays of color, color melodies, played silently on his color harpsichord or with musical accompaniment.

Newton's analogy between sound and color was first fully developed in print in the *Opticks*. Here he tells how he projected the spectrum upon a sheet of white paper and asked a friend, whose color perception was keener than his own, to mark the boundaries of the seven colors by lines drawn across the image. To these intervals he assigned ratios corresponding to the notes of an octave: the tonic, major second, minor third, fourth, fifth, major sixth, seventh and the octave.[30]

Further on, where he reprinted with some changes his early unpublished paper on periodic colored rings, Newton invokes again the musical analogy. He compared the breadths of the rings of different colors to the different thicknesses of the film producing them and found them to be to one another "as the Cube Roots of the Squares of the eight lengths of a Chord,

Materialien zur Geschichte der Farbenlehre, Werke, Hamburg, Band XIV, 1960, pp. 7-269.

29. Father Castel attributed his first ideas to an odd passage in the *Musurgia universalis*, 1650, of Athanasius Kircher, but he refers his reader to the *Opticks* of Newton "pour y voir toutes les couleurs bien diapasonnées avec leurs octaves, quintes, tierces, et septièmes." Later, when he wrote his *Vrai systeme de physique générale de M. Isaac Newton*, 1743, he became convinced that Newton's theory of light and color, like his celestial mechanics, was untenable. See Donald S. Schier, *Louis Bertrand Castel, Anti-Newtonian Scientist*, Cedar Rapids, 1941, espec. pp. 135-138.

30. *Opticks*, 1704, First Book, pp. 91-93. Newton's earliest reference to the analogy of sound and color occurs in his reply to Robert Hooke in 1672, *Newton Correspondence*, I, pp. 174-5. A good discussion of this aspect of Newton's thought is given by Sigalia Dostrovsky in her "Origins of Vibration Theory: The Scientific Revolution and the Nature of Music," unpublished doctoral dissertation, Princeton, 1969.

which sound the Notes in an eighth, *sol, la, fa, sol, la, mi, fa, sol.*"[31]

The ideas of the pioneer psychologist, David Hartley, owe much to the Newtonian passages just quoted, as well as to those in which Newton stated that the periodicity of the rings showed that light rays, for whatever underlying reason, are disposed to display "fits of easy reflexion" alternating with "fits of easy transmission."[32] Hartley's debt to Newton was profound. In his *Observations on Man* (1749) he drew upon the *Opticks* to support his theory of color perception, indeed, as I shall show later on, for his fundamental theory of "vibrations." The sensation of color, Hartley argued, results from vibrations imparted to the retina of the eye. Rays of the seven "primary" colors excite vibrations of different frequencies, and these frequencies are related to each other by the simplest ratios: ratios, he writes that "are also those of the five Tones, and two Semitones, comprehended in the Octave." These ratios are different enough to make at least the five principal colors (red, yellow, green, blue and violet) "appear distinct from each other to the Mind, for the same reasons, whatever they be, as take place in Sounds." Natural bodies reflect all these colors abundantly "and in sufficient Purity for this Purpose," above all the color green, especially what Newton in grading the colors of

31. *Opticks*, 1704, Second Book, pp. 17-18 (Obs. XIV). This musical analogy does not appear in the original, much shorter, version of Obs. XIV in the "Discourse of Observations" of 1675. For Newton's solmization see Christopher Simpson, *Compendium of Practical Musick*, 3rd ed., London 1678, pp. 3-4. Here after describing the old system of Guido d'Arezzo, he writes that four of the old syllables (mi, fa, sol, la) "are necessary assistants to the right Tuning of the Degrees of Sound" but that the other two (ut and re) are superfluous: "We will therefore make use only of Mi, Fa, Sol, La, and apply them to the Seven Letters, which stand for the Degree of Sound." See also John Playford, *An Introduction to the Skill of Musick*, 7th ed., London, 1674, p. 1; Playford remarks that the six syllables were used "for many years past" and in recent times four only are used "being sufficient for expressing the several sounds, and less burdensome for the memory of Practitioners."

32. *Opticks*, 1704, Second Book, Part III, pp. 78-84. Hartley refers especially to Newton's Prop. XVI, *ibid.*, p. 83, where Newton writes that the intervals of the fits of easy reflexion and easy transmission "are either accurately, or very nearly, as the Cube-roots of the Squares of the lengths of a Chord, which sound the notes in an Eight . . . according to the Analogy described in the seventh Experiment of the second Book." See David Hartley, *Observations on Man*, 2 vols., London, 1749, I, Prop. 56, pp. 192-196; I have used the modern facsimile reproduction, with an introduction by Theodore L. Huguelet, Gainesville, Florida, 1966.

successive rings, called the green of the third order, i.e., the color of grass and vegetables.[33]

In a later section Hartley takes up our emotional response to color, a strong source of pleasure in young children, especially when colors are combined together in various ways; yet he doubts that there is anything in the relation of colors to each other which corresponds to consonance and dissonance of sounds. Increasingly, as we grow older, our reaction to "mere colours" becomes "very languid," as compared with our response to more sophisticated and intellectual sources of pleasure; yet the pleasures we receive from colors "remain, in a small Degree, to the last"; moreover the feelings transferred to them by association with other sources of pleasure, Hartley says are "considerable."

> So that our intellectual Pleasures are not only at first generated, but afterwards supported and recruited, in part from the Pleasures affecting the Eye; which holds particularly in respect of the Pleasures afforded by the Beauties of Nature, and by the Imitations of them, which the Arts of Poetry and Painting furnish us with.[34]

And he returns again to the central psychological value of green: the green of Newton's third order:

> It deserves Notice here, that Green, which is the Colour that abounds far more than any other, is the middle one among the primary Colours, and the most universally and permanently agreeable to the Eye of any other.[35]

A generation later the growing interest in color for its own sake is signalized, and was doubtless stimulated, by the publication in 1772 of Joseph Priestley's *History of Vision, Light and Colours*, a work in which discoveries concerning color are carefully recounted, especially from the work of Newton, which he treats at length, until his own time. The book concludes — and not surprisingly when we recall Priestley's debt

---

33. *Observations on Man*, I, p. 194.
34. *Observations on Man*, I, Prop. 60, p. 208.
35. *Ibid.*

to David Hartley — with a summary of Hartley's notions about color and the relation of color vibrations to those of musical tones.[36] Whether artists consulted Priestley's book, I do not know; but it is worth noting that two important figures in the history of aesthetics appear among the subscribers to the *History*: Sir Joshua Reynolds and Edmund Burke, who should be remembered not only as orator and political writer, but as author of the important essay on *The Sublime and the Beautiful* (1757) with its echoes of Hartley and Newton.[37]

In 1780 Priestley moved to Birmingham, where he became an active member of that informal scientific club, the Lunar Society, whose members included Erasmus Darwin, James Watt, Matthew Boulton and Josiah Wedgwood, the potter. Among the varied natural phenomena that occupied these men — and Priestley's book or Priestley himself may have been the stimulus — was color: the "accidental colors" first studied by Buffon, and called by them "ocular spectra"; the color of electrical discharges, of lightning and shooting stars; the phenomenon of colored clouds and other atmospheric color effects.[38]

One interesting series of experiments had its origin in the *Opticks*: experiments with a color wheel or color disc, a device (in its later modifications) variously credited to Thomas Young, Helmholtz or Clerk Maxwell. Yet in its fundamental form it had been suggested by Newton. Divide, Newton wrote, the circumference of a circle into parts "proportional to the seven musical Tones" and paint the pyramidal segments then drawn so that they represent the successive colors, gradations and intensities

---

36. *History of Vision, Light and Colours*, pp. 763-767.

37. Edmund Burke, *A Philosophical Enquiry into the Origin of our Ideas of the Sublime and the Beautiful*, ed. J.T. Boulton, London and New York, 1958, pp. 73, 138 and 159 for Burke's debt to the *Opticks* and to Hartley. The editor of this excellent edition remarks that Burke "clearly owes much" to his study of the *Opticks*; a copy of the 4th English edition, 1730, appeared in the sale of Burke's library.

38. Robert E. Schofield, *The Lunar Society of Birmingham*, Oxford, 1963, pp. 189 and 272-3; Erasmus Darwin, *Botanic Garden*, 4th ed., London, 1799, pp. 262-265. Erasmus Darwin's son, Robert Waring Darwin, published a study of psycho-physiological color effects (Buffon's "accidental colors") in his "New Experiments on the Ocular Spectra of Light and Colours," *Phil. Trans.*, Vol. 76, 1786, pp. 313-348. He cites, among others, Newton, "the celebrated M. de Buffon" and Joseph Priestley. For Erasmus Darwin's possible role in writing this paper, see Schofield, *op. cit.*, pp. 272-273.

of the prismatic spectrum.[39] The colors can be "mixed" when the disc is rapidly whirled. Such color discs, variously painted, were used by a Lunar Society member, Samuel Galton, to demonstrate the primary colors, the production of white and the complementary pairs. Certain of his discoveries, Erasmus Darwin wrote in summarizing Galton's work, "might be of consequence in the art of painting."[40]

If nothing else, these examples attest to the growing interest in color as the eighteenth century drew to a close, a preoccupation that flowered in one of the most famous and controversial books ever written on the subject: Goethe's *Zur Farbenlehre* (1810).[41] Drawn to the problem of color by his interest in painting, and by his sensitivity to the natural landscape, Goethe, like everyone else, inevitably confronted Newton's *Opticks*, but with a difference. Newton, for Goethe, was the antagonist whose experiments he could not, or at least did not, comprehend. Stubbornly rejecting Newton's discoveries, he devoted a long polemical section of his book to refuting them. But Goethe's "science" was idiosyncratic and his errors were legion: he confused, more than he realized, the physical and the psychological aspects of color. Yet in the latter domain he made acute observations and simple experiments that have proved of great interest to modern physiologists and psychologists.

Mention of Goethe brings us to the moment when, as

39. *Opticks*, 1704, The First Book, p. 115 and Fig. 11. Newton does not speak of actually rotating the disc. It may only have been a device to sum up his experiments of mixing prismatic colors.

40. Schofield, *op. cit.*, pp. 270-272 and Darwin, *Botanic Garden*, pp. 258-262. Galton may have been led to these experiments (published long after in the *Monthly Magazine*, Vol. 8, 1799) by reading Priestley's *History*, for Priestley describes Newton's color disc, and reproduces Newton's Fig. 11 in his Fig. 83 of Pl. XII.

41. The *Farbenlehre*, published in two volumes, plus a volume of plates, was the result of Goethe's intensive study of color from about 1790 to 1810. The work is in three parts: the *Didaktischer Teil* (containing Goethe's own observations and theories about color), a *Polemischer Teil*, devoted to attacking Newton, and finally (in the second volume) his long and remarkably detailed *Geschichte der Farbenlehre*, still worth reading. There is a large literature on Goethe as a scientist; the most effective defense is by Rudolf Magnus, *Goethe als Naturforscher*, Leipzig, 1906; Eng. tr. as *Goethe as a Scientist*, by Heinz Norden, New York, 1949. In the same bi-centennial year appeared Sir Charles Sherrington's short but highly critical lecture, *Goethe on Nature & on Science*, Cambridge, 1949.

Professor Gombrich has pointed out, one English painter, John Constable (1776-1837) — who surely had heard more of Newton than of Goethe — dared to brighten his canvasses and introduce, albeit timidly, the color green into his landscapes.[42] Constable, although always the painter, had a curious scientific bent; his early studies of anatomy enthralled him, and he is said to have been fascinated by astronomy. Clouds and cloud-formations obsessed him — their form and their color — and he studied the way in which the ever-changing atmosphere transformed the hues and tones of landscape. In preparation for his Lake District sketches he kept vivid descriptive records of the weather. In a lecture at the Royal Institution in 1836 he remarked, perhaps with his special audience in mind: "Painting is a science, and should be pursued as an inquiry into the laws of nature. Why, then, may not landscape painting be considered a branch of natural philosophy, of which pictures are but the experiments?"[43]

It may be presumptuous, for one not trained in art history, to suggest that at the turn of the nineteenth century — and owing, if only in part, to the varied reverberations of the *Opticks* of Sir Isaac Newton — we can discern the discovery of color, color for its own sake and in the landscape, by the painters. What we might call the Vitruvian aesthetic, a canon derived from classical sculpture and architecture and based on form, mass and proportion, had long held pride of place. Among the Renaissance painters and their followers there were, to be sure, great colorists; but color, when not used (as in Christian subjects) for its emblematic significance, long tended, as Heinrich Wölfflin has put it, to "subserve form." Especially in landscape painting the brighter colors are often wanting: even the landscapes of Claude Lorrain or the Dutch *paysagistes* were rendered — as were Gainsborough's and the scenic backgrounds of his portraits — in muted brownish tones. Constable took the first step in a movement, which has been with us ever since, towards a chromatic aesthetic.

42. E.H. Gombrich, *Art and Illusion*, 2nd ed., New York, 1961, pp. 46-48.
43. Cited by Robert C. Leslie, *Life and Letters of John Constable*, London, 1896, p. 399.

But among the English painters the first true explorer of color was that great artistic revolutionary, J.M.W. Turner. His sketches, his landscapes in water-color and oil – his "pictures of nothing" – were so many excursions into the mysterious world of color: often representations, as Hazlitt put it in a famous essay, "not properly of the objects of nature as of the medium through which they were seen."[44] The chief currents I have been discussing converged upon this extraordinary man: he drew upon, and imitated in his own crude attempts at verse, the color-conscious nature poets: Thomson, Young and especially Akenside.[45] He read and studied Newton's *Opticks*, and he was impressed by the Newtonian analogy between color and sound, although his color organ was his painter's palette. He badgered scientific acquaintances for scientific facts about light and color, and he experimented tirelessly. He studied the effects produced by light filtering through glass balls filled with colored liquids; he observed the way light is reflected from polished metallic spheres; and he explored the problem of color mixing. He clearly grasped the difference between mixing pigments and mixing spectral colors, and he seems to have anticipated Helmholtz, at least to some extent, in distinguishing between "additive" and "subtractive" color mixing. When, later in life, he read and studied Goethe's *Farbenlehre* (in Eastlake's translation of 1840) and annotated his own copy, his admiration was tempered by sharp criticism; he could hardly have gone along with the great poet's misunderstanding of Newton.[46]

The Queries and their Influence

Except for Dr. Johnson and his Newtonian vocabulary,

44. Quoted in Lawrence Gowing, *Turner: Imagination and Reality*, The Museum of Modern Art, New York, 1966, p. 13.

45. Jerrold Ziff, "J.M.W. Turner on Poetry and Painting," *Studies in Romanticism*, III, 1964, pp. 193-215.

46. Eastlake's translation was confined to the "Didactic Part" of the *Farbenlehre*, including Goethe's *Einleitung*, with its several deprecatory references to Newton. For Turner's experiments and his reaction to Goethe see Gowing, *op. cit.*, pp. 21-24. Of considerable importance for Turner's development was his reading of the *Natural System of Color*, written by the entomologist-cum-painter, Moses Harris, published in 1766 and republished in 1811. See for Harris, Gowing, *op. cit.*, p. 23 and Jack Lindsay, *J.M.W. Turner*, London and New York, 1966, p. 208.

most of the influences I have described, whether direct or indirect, derive from the body of Newton's *Opticks*. Let us now turn to the Queries appended to the Third Book; for these Queries mainly influenced the speculations of philosophers and scientists, and came — in a quite different way — to affect such diverse literary figures as Erasmus Darwin and Shelley.

The Queries did not appear all at once; Newton added new ones, and made changes in some of the earlier ones, in the successive editions of the *Opticks*. They have been much discussed and often misunderstood. In particular, they have been used to characterize the entire *Opticks* to which, in fact and in Newton's mind, they form an appendage. Professor I. Bernard Cohen has written: "The *Opticks* differs from the *Principia inter alia*, in that Newton freely indulged in hypotheses and speculations."[47] Except for the Queries, this is a poor description of the *Opticks* which, like the *Principia*, in the body of the text is almost wholly without conjectural matter and speculation.[48] Newton is at pains here, as I believe he was in the earlier *Principia*, to exclude anything he is not convinced he

47. I. Bernard Cohen, *Franklin and Newton*, Philadelphia, 1956, p. 125. Professor Cohen stated this view even more strongly in his preface to the paperback reprint of the fourth edition of the *Opticks*, where he speaks (p. xxvii) of the "progressively conjectural character" of the book and writes that in this work "Newton did not adopt the motto to be found in the *Principia* — Hypotheses non fingo; I frame no hypotheses — but, so to speak, let himself go, allowing his imagination full reign [*sic*], and by far exceeding the bounds of experimental evidence." *Opticks*, Dover Publications, 1952, pp. xxvii and xxiii-xxiv. A similar, but more temperate, view has been put forward by Alexander Koyré; "L'Hypothèse et l'expérience chez Newton," *Bulletin de la Société Française de Philosophie*, 50, 1956, pp. 59-79; reprinted in *Newtonian Studies*, London, 1965, pp. 25-52.

48. The exception occurs at the point where Newton, having described in non-committal fashion "fits of easy reflexion and easy transmission," offers an explanation: "Those that are averse from assenting to any new Discoveries, but such as they can explain by an Hypothesis, may for the present suppose, that ... the Rays of Light, by impinging on any refracting or reflecting Surface excite vibrations in the refracting or reflecting Medium or Substance ... much after the manner that vibrations are propagated in the Air for causing Sound, and move faster than the Rays so as to overtake them." *Opticks*, 1730, p. 280. In his *Newtonian Studies*, p. 50, note 1, Koyré says "it is pretty clear that this medium cannot be anything else" but Newton's hypothetical aether. This is by no means clear: Newton is leaving the question open; the medium might be the aether or the material substance of a refracting body. Newton in one of the early Queries speaks of the rays of light as exciting vibrations in the substance of the retina, which vibrations "being propagated along the solid fibres of the optick Nerves into the Brain, cause the sense of seeing." *Opticks*. 1704, Query 12, p. 135.

can demonstrate mathematically or prove by experiment.

One example should suffice to make my point: throughout the body of the work Newton treats light only as *rays* representable by straight lines. Nowhere does he tell us what the rays physically *are*. Just as nothing in the *Principia* is affected by what we may believe gravitation to be caused by, so in the *Opticks* none of his conclusions, he thought, was in any way dependent upon a theory of the physical nature of light: i.e., whether light is a stream of corpuscles, or a pulse or wave in some ambient medium. In college we were taught that Newton upheld a corpuscular theory of light. But this is simply not the case: Newton makes no such assertions.

Newton had, of course, his private opinions, and the likelihood that light is corpuscular was one of these; but he was largely successful in separating his "scientificall" statements — what he believed he could rigorously prove — from what he deemed possible or even probable. The device he adopted, to separate the two levels or degrees of conviction, was the use of Queries.

The purpose of the Queries of the *Opticks* is clearly set forth in what he says after recounting the experiments on diffraction in Book III and before the first of the Queries:

> When I made the foregoing Observations, I designed to repeat most of them with more care and exactness, and to make some new ones . . . But I was then interrupted, and cannot now think of taking these things into further consideration. And since I have not finished this part of my Design, I shall conclude, with proposing only some Queries, in order to a further search to be made by others.[49]

49. *Opticks*, 1704, Book III, p. 132. My view of the matter is that of Thomas Reid, who wrote in 1785: "Sir Isaac Newton . . . took great care to distinguish his doctrines, which he pretended to prove by just induction, from his conjectures, which were to stand or fall according as future experiments and observations should establish or refute them. His conjectures he has put in the form of queries, that they might not be received as truths, but be inquired into, and determined according to the evidence to be found for or against them. Those who mistake his queries for a part of his doctrine, do him great injustice, and degrade him to the rank of the common herd of philosophers, who have in all ages adulterated philosophy, by

The first edition of the *Opticks* in 1704 has only 16 of these Queries; most of them are quite short, and they set forth notions that occurred to him during the experiments on diffraction. The first, for example, reads: "Do not Bodies act upon Light at a distance, and by their action bend its Rays; and is not this action . . . strongest at the least distance?"[50] From such considerations he was led to questions concerning heat and fire and finally to reveal some of his thoughts about vision. Two years after the publication of the English *Opticks*, Newton brought out the work in a Latin translation, prepared with the help of his disciple, the theologian and philosopher Samuel Clarke. To this Latin *Optice* Newton added seven new Queries, bringing the number up to 23. The first of the new Queries deals with the mysterious phenomenon of double-refraction, as described in Iceland Spar (calcite) by Erasmus Bartholinus and more recently by Christian Huygens. These matters lead Newton to raise objections in Queries 19 and 20 to the theory, favored by Huygens, that light is a pulse or "pression" in the aether. Here, for example, he writes:

Against filling the Heavens with fluid Mediums, a great Objection arises from the regular and very lasting Motions of the Planets and Comets in all manner of Courses through the Heavens.[51]

Such a fluid, he goes on,

can be of no use for explaining the Phaenomena of Nature,

mixing conjecture with truth, and their own fancies with the oracles of Nature." *The Works of Thomas Reid*, ed. Sir William Hamilton, 8th ed., 2 vols., Edinburgh, 1880, I, p. 249. A similar view was earlier expressed by Colin Maclaurin, *An Account of Sir Isaac Newton's Philosophical Discoveries*, 3rd ed., London, 1775, pp. 9-10.

50. Professor Cohen, "Newton's Philosophy of Nature," *Dictionary of the History of Ideas*, article in press, argues that the Queries "are all phrased in the negative and are thus purely rhetorical questions rather than genuine interrogations." I cannot see that this tells us more than that Newton thought the propositions likely (in every case, as Cohen remarks, Newton gives evidence in support of his proposition), yet they are matters he cannot demonstrate, and hopes will be investigated by others.

51. I have used the translation in a later English edition (*Opticks*, 4th ed., 1730, p. 364-5) modifying it only when Newton himself made small but significant changes. The Latin reads: "Praeterea, nulla esse omnino istiusmodi Media fluida, inde colligo, quod Planetae & Cometae regulari adeo & diuturno Motu per spatia caelestia undiq; & quaquaversum & in omnes partes ferantur." *Optice*, 1706, p. 310.

the Motions of the Planets and Comets being better explain'd without it. It serves only to disturb and retard the Motions of those great Bodies.[52]

And a little later he writes:

And for rejecting such a Medium, we have the Authority of those oldest and most celebrated Philosophers of *Greece* and *Phoenicia*, who made a *Vacuum*, and Atoms, and the Gravity of Atoms, the first Principles of their Philosophy; tacitly attributing Gravity to some other Cause than Matter.[53]

In the next Query (Q.21) he asks "Are not the Rays of Light very small Bodies emitted from shining substances?" And he gives reasons for believing that this is the case. In this Query and the one that follows we have the nearest thing to an advocacy of a corpuscular theory of light.[54]

The last Query (Q.23) of the *Optice* is the most famous, the most debated, and the longest. It is, indeed, a small essay on a theory of matter, in which much of the supporting evidence is supplied from Newton's extensive knowledge of chemistry. "Have not," he asks, "the small Particles of Bodies certain Powers, Virtues, or Forces, by which they act at a distance, not only upon the Rays of Light . . . but also upon one another for producing a great Part of the Phaenomena of Nature?" And adducing a large array of fact to show that chemical reactions can be understood as the result of preferential attractions between particles, he concludes: "All these things being consider'd, it seems probable to me, that God in the Beginning form'd Matter in solid, massy, hard, impenetrable, moveable Particles, of such Sizes and Figures, and with such other Properties . . . as most conduced to the End for which he

52. *Opticks*, 1730, p. 368. See *Optice*, 1706, p. 313, where he speaks of "materia illa ficta et commentitia."

53. *Opticks*, 1730, p. 369. The italics are Newton's. His Latin reads: "Istiusmodi autem Medium ut rejiciamus, Auctores nobis sunt antiquissimi illi & celeberrimi Graeciae Phaeniciaeq; Philosophi; qui Principia Philosophiae suae, Spatium inane, Atomos, & Gravitatem Atomorum posuerunt; Tacite attribuentes Vim Gravitatis, alii alicui Causae, a Materia diversae." *Optice*, 1706, p. 314.

54. *Opticks*, 1730, pp. 370-375 and *Optice*, 1706, pp. 315-319.

form'd them." Nature "will be very conformable to her self and very simple, performing all the great Motions of the heavenly Bodies by the Attraction of Gravity . . . and almost all the small ones of their Particles by some other attractive and repelling Powers which intercede [i.e. act between] the Particles."[55]

It is quite evident that Newton's universe, as he conceived it in 1706, is a Lucretian or Epicurean world, in which atoms of matter move in empty space and interact by means of short-range forces of attraction and repulsion. But in the next few years his opinions underwent a profound change.

In 1717 and 1718 Newton brought out a second English edition of the *Opticks*, and to it he added eight new Queries (numbering them 17-24) and moving the Queries of 1706, now revised and translated into English, to the end, and renumbering them, so that the long chemical Query becomes Query 31.

These new Queries set forth a theory quite at variance with Newton's earlier views of 1706.[56] He describes a universe far from empty; on the contrary filled with an aetherial medium "exceedingly more rare and subtile than the Air, and exceedingly more elastick and active." This aether can account for the reflections and refractions of light; by its vibrations it communicates heat to bodies; vision, too, is excited by the vibrations of this medium; and it explains those "fits of easy reflexion and easy transmission," which he had observed in the periodic recurrence of the colored rings.

Newton has returned, with some modifications, to the ideas in a speculative paper which he sent to the Royal Society long before (in 1675) and which he declined to publish.[57] The

---

55. *Opticks*, 1730, pp. 375-6, 400 and 397. *Optice*, 1706, pp. 322, 343, and 340.

56. That major changes occurred in the Queries between the Latin of 1706 and the later English editions was first pointed out by Samuel Horsley when he edited the *Opticks* for his edition of Newton's collected works, *Isaaci Newtoni Opera quae exstant Omnia*, 5 vols., London, 1779-1785. A list of these alterations was given in F. Rosenberger, *Isaac Newton und seine physicalischen Principien*, Braunschweig, 1895. A more detailed analysis is that of Alexandre Koyré, "Les Queries de l'Optique," *Archives Internationales d'Histoire des Science*, 13, 1960, pp. 15-29. This was actually published after April 1961, and I was unaware of it when I wrote my *Newton et Epicure*, Paris, 1963, pp. 27-35, where, independently of Koyré, I called attention to the changes and stressed their significance.

57. "An Hypothesis explaining the Properties of Light," enclosed in the letter of

reasons for this striking reversal of opinion are, I believe, quite evident. Soon after assuming the Presidential chair at the Royal Society he felt the need the reinvigorate the meetings of the Society by appointing a "demonstrator" to perform experiments at the meetings, as Robert Hooke had done in the earlier years. The man chosen was a certain Francis Hauksbee, who carried out this assignment dutifully and brilliantly from 1704 until his death in 1713. The most striking of Hauksbee's experiments — some of them in all likelihood suggested by Newton himself — were electrical demonstrations with a revolving, evacuated globe of glass made to rub against the hand or a piece of cloth. The result was a striking display of electrical discharge under low pressure, the production of a purple electric glow and of remarkable attractive and repulsive effects on nearby light bodies. To Newton, I have argued elsewhere, this demonstrated the existence of a new tenuous kind of matter, "more subtile than the air." He had, in other words, seen the aether, whose existence he had imagined long before, and then rejected.[58] Finally, after Hauksbee's death, the post as the Society's "demonstrator" was taken by Jean Théophile Desaguliers who performed a different sort of experiment, one that Newton suggested and described in one of the new Queries. Desaguliers took two tall cylindrical vessels in which he suspended identical thermometers. One of these vessels was evacuated with the air pump, the other remained full of air. When simultaneously exposed to a source of heat, the experiment, as he reported it in 1717, showed that

the Thermometer *in vacuo* will grow warm as much, and almost as soon as the Thermometer which is not *in vacuo*.

And Newton asked

7 December 1675, and read to the Royal Society at meetings of 9 and 16 December; first published in Birch, *History of the Royal Society*, Vol. III, 1757, pp. 248-260 and 262-269; facsimile reproduction from Birch in *Papers and Letters*, pp. 178-199; reprinted from the copy in the Royal Society Register Book, supplemented and corrected with the original MS, in *Newton Correspondence*, I, pp. 362-386.

58. Henry Guerlac, "Francis Hauksbee: expérimentateur au profit de Newton," *Archives Internationales d'Histoire des Sciences*, 16, 1963, pp. 113-128; also my "Sir Isaac and the Ingenious Mr. Hauksbee" *L'Aventure de la science*, 2 vols., Paris, 1964, I, pp. 228-253.

Is not the Heat of the warm Room convey'd through the *Vacuum* by the Vibrations of a much subtiler Medium than Air, which after the Air was drawn out remained in the *Vacuum*?[59]

You will recall that I mentioned earlier the mysterious indication of a "Part I" of the Third Book of the *Opticks*, but with no subsequent "Part II." A few years ago I turned up in the Cambridge University Library a manuscript draft in Newton's hand of a "Part II." In it are a series of "Observations," among which are references to Hauksbee's experiments and an account of Desaguliers' "two-thermometer experiment." In fact, some of the substance of the so-called aether Queries is given in this draft. It is obvious what happened. Impressed especially by these experiments Newton first believed that he had firm experimental evidence for the existence of a tenuous aether, and proposed to add an account of it to the body of the *Opticks*, as a Part II of Book III in the second English edition. With this in mind, he wrote in pen on the corrected copy of the first edition that he sent to the printer the legend "Part I." But his good sense, or his caution, prevailed; he put the substance of his new ideas in the "aether Queries," but forgot to cancel out the implied promise of a "Part II," where in all subsequent editions it has remained to mystify the reader.[60]

Newton was an indifferent editor. He made a number of rather careless changes in the older Queries to adapt them to his new ideas. Where in 1706 he had argued against filling the Heavens with fluid Mediums, he adds in 1717 the phrase "unless they be exceeding rare." And where he had most strongly advocated the emptiness of space — in referring to the philosophers of Greece and Phoenicia — he now has them attributing "Gravity to some other Cause than *dense* Matter."[61]

It is no wonder that the Queries, in their final form so inherently self-contradictory, have led to quite different interpretations of Newton's theory of matter, both in the eighteenth

59. *Opticks*, 1730, p. 349. The italics are Newton's.
60. Henry Guerlac, "Newton's Optical Aether," *Notes and Records of the Royal Society of London*, 22, 1967, pp. 45-57.
61. *Opticks*, 1730, pp. 364-5 and p. 369. The emphasis is mine.

century and in our day.

By and large the earliest English scientists to be influenced by the *Opticks*, especially by the Queries, ignored Newton's speculations about the aether. This is true of Pemberton and of Desaguliers himself. Nor is the subject of the aether raised in that , great textbook of Newtonian optics, Robert Smith's two-volume *Complete System of Optics* (1728). It is Smith, by the way, who is the real advocate of the corpuscular theory of light, and who devotes his efforts to showing how Newton's theories of attraction and repulsion, the inter-action between light-particles and bodies, can account for all the familiar phenomena of light and color.[62]

The same can be said of the Rev. Stephen Hales who, in his classic book on plant physiology, the *Vegetable Staticks* (1727), quoted from the Queries many times, and spoke of attraction as "that universal principle which is so operative in all the very different works of nature," yet largely ignored the aether.[63]

As for Newton's French disciples — both popularizers and more proficient men of science — they either passed over Newton's aetherial speculations or treated them with disrespect. And so did David Hume. Of all British thinkers none, it can be said, was more influenced by Newton's *Opticks* than Hume. He knew the book thoroughly before he left college; and Newton, the non-speculative Newton, was his inspiration and his model. At the close of his great book, after describing the proper method of scientific inquiry, Newton wrote the lines that may

62. A study of Smith's *System of Optics* was made by Henry Steffens, in "The Development of Newtonian Optics in England, 1738-1831," an unpublished M.A. dissertation, Cornell University, 1965.

63. For Hales's debt to the Queries of the *Opticks* see my "Continental Reputation of Stephen Hales," *Archives Internationales d'Histoire des Sciences*, 15, 1951, pp. 393-404; also Cohen, *Franklin and Newton*, pp. 247, 254-255 and 266-276. Bishop Berkeley in his *Siris*, 1744, that immensely learned but eccentric pamphlet on the virtues of tar-water, several times quoted from the *Opticks* and its Queries. Although he set forth the idea of a universal aether, he identified it with fire or light, conceiving it as a spirit which is neither matter nor mind. In several paragraphs he criticizes Newton's material aether by which "upon later thoughts" Newton explained "all the phenomena and properties of bodies that were before attributed to attraction . . . together with the various attractions themselves." There is no reason "to admit a new medium distinct from light;" to account for the periodic properties of light by vibrations of this medium "seems an uncouth explanation." *The Works of George Berkeley*, V, 1953, pp. 107-109.

well have served as Hume's text:

> And if natural Philosophy in all its Parts, by pursuing this
> Method, shall at length be perfected, the Bounds of Moral
> Philosophy will also be enlarged.[64]

Hume described his first book, his *Treatise on Human Nature*
(1738), as an attempt to introduce the experimental method of
reasoning into "moral subjects." He had no sympathy for the
speculations in the Queries. Newton, he wrote, the "rarest
genius that ever rose for the ornament and instruction of the
species," was particularly to be commended for being always
"cautious in admitting no principles but such as were founded
on experiment."[65] Clearly the Queries should be ignored, with
their conjectures about atoms, interparticulate forces or aetherial mechanisms. And Hume, the rigorous empiricist, tells us
why; in his greatest work, the *Enquiry Concerning the Human
Understanding* (1748), appears this warning:

> It must certainly be allowed, that nature has kept us at
> a great distance from all her secrets, and has afforded us
> only the knowledge of a few superficial qualities of
> objects; while she conceals from us those powers and
> principles on which the influence of those objects entirely
> depends.[66]

Hume is not the first, nor the last, to see Newton as what we
would call a positivist; but he was surely one of the few British
disciples of Newton to do so.[67] If the early admirers had ignored

64. *Opticks*, 1730, p. 405. This passage, I think rightly, has recently been
interpreted in a manner that would not have appealed to Hume: that a "true natural
philosophy must lead to a surer knowledge of God, and thence to a firmly-grounded
moral philosophy." See J.E. McGuire and P.M. Rattansi, "Newton and the 'Pipes of
Pan,'" *Notes and Records of the Royal Society of London*, 21, 1966, pp. 122-123.

65. Cited from Hume's *History of England* by Ernest Campbell Mossner, *The
Life of David Hume*, Austin, Texas, 1954, p. 75.

66. *An Enquiry concerning the Human Understanding*, ed. L.A. Selby-Bigge,
Oxford, 1894, pp. 32-33.

67. Burke should be numbered among them, for he wrote, "When Newton first
discovered the property of attraction, and settled its laws, he found it served very
well to explain several of the most remarkable phaenomena in nature; but yet with
reference to the general system of things, he could consider attraction but an effect,
whose cause at that time he did not attempt to trace. But when he afterwards began
to account for it by a subtle elastic aether, this great man . . . seemed to have quitted
his usual cautious manner of philosophizing . . ." *Sublime and the Beautiful*, ed.
Boulton, p. 129.

the aether Queries, preferring to stress the Newtonian world of particles in empty space, shortly before the middle of the eighteenth century we notice a significant shift of focus. In 1743 the Irish physician, Bryan Robinson (1680-1754), published in Dublin his *Dissertation on the Aether of Sir Isaac Newton.*[68] It opens with a general discussion of this elastic fluid, and treats in succession — with some display of mathematical apparatus — the role of the aether in explaining gravity, elasticity, various phenomena of light and heat, fermentation, and — which was Robinson's chief concern — sensation and muscular motion.

Robinson's source was, of course, the aether Queries of the *Opticks* of 1717-18. But a year after the appearance of his *Dissertation*, there came to light an unknown exposition by Newton of his early aether theory: a letter he had written to Robert Boyle in 1678.[69] Confirmed in his views, Robinson promptly published a compendium entitled *Sir Isaac Newton's Account of the Aether, With Some Additions by Way of Appendix*. In it he reprinted the letter to Boyle, excerpts from the aether Queries, and a further account of his own views on muscular physiology.

Not long after there appeared an even more important convert to the idea of an all-pervading aether. If David Hartley, like Hume, was inspired by the same prognostic passage in the *Opticks* — that the perfection of experimental philosophy can enlarge the bounds of moral philosophy — he took a profoundly different tack. For Hartley, whose vibration theory of color I mentioned earlier, the speculative Queries in the *Opticks* provided him with a physical model, a visualizable mechanism, by which to understand the problems of sensation. He came to his famous principle of the association of ideas from hints he found in the writings of John Locke and the lesser-known John

68. On Robinson, see I. Bernard Cohen, *Franklin and Newton*, pp. 417-419 and Philip C. Ritterbush, *Overtures to Biology*, New Haven and London, 1964, p. 8. I am also indebted to my student, Mr. David Corson, for a careful study of Robinson, as yet unpublished.

69. *The Works of the Honourable Robert Boyle*, 5 vols., London, 1744, I, pp. 70-74. This included Birch's *Life of the Honourable Robert Boyle*, published separately in the same year; here the letter of Newton is given on pp. 234-247.

Gay. But the key passage that led to the vibration theory, and gave it physical meaning, came from Newton's Query 23 — one of the aether Queries of 1717-18 — where Newton wrote

> Is not Vision perform'd chiefly by the Vibrations of this [aetherial] Medium, excited in the bottom of the Eye by the Rays of Light and propagated through the . . . optic Nerves into the place of Sensation?[70]

From this clue Hartley built up his mechanistic psychology in terms of these vibrations: vibrations — as he wrote — excited and propagated by "a very subtle and elastic fluid which Sir Isaac Newton called aether."

It is perhaps significant that this new interest in Newton's aether coincided in time with the discovery of the Leiden jar, the early condenser, and with the dramatic electrical experiments this invention made possible. Newton, we saw, had hinted at the identity of his aether with the mysterious electrical fluid disclosed by Hauksbee's experiments. So it was not long after mid-century that Englishmen, some with impeccable scientific credentials like Benjamin Wilson, F.R.S., and other less qualified persons like Richard Lovett, insisted that the electric matter and the aether were "universally the same thing." Benjamin Martin, a worthy experimenter, held that light, fire, electricity were all different vibratory motions in the aether.[71]

Just as the body of Newton's *Opticks* had inspired the mid-century nature poems studied by Marjorie Nicolson, so the aether Queries left their mark upon such a scientifically curious poet as Erasmus Darwin, and through him upon Shelley in *Prometheus Unbound,* and in the very years when Keats, in *Lamia,* was protesting that Newton had despoiled the rainbow by explaining it. Shelley's notion of a universal fire, of an electrical aether, conceived of as the soul of the world, was not the least of the influences of Newton's remarkable book.[72]

Yet to end on this note would be misleading, for influential

70. *Opticks*, 1730, p. 353.
71. Ritterbush, *op. cit.*, pp. 16-22.
72. Carl Grabo, *A Newton Among Poets*, Chapel Hill, 1930, espec. Chapters III and VIII.

philosophers – like David Hume and the Abbé de Condillac in France – and above all the scientists, found the chief value of Newton's *Opticks* in its exemplification of the only proper method of scientific inquiry. The greatest scientists of the later eighteenth century – men like Lavoisier, Laplace, and the Scots chemists, William Cullen and Joseph Black – were intimately familiar with Newton's discoveries and the compact statement of method with which he ended his last and most famous Query. Rather than repeat, once again, this famous paragraph, I propose to conclude with a more extended statement, a draft of what appeared in Query 31, which has only recently come to light:

As Mathematicians have two Methods of doing things wch they call Composition & Resolution & in all difficulties have recourse to their method of resolution before they compound so in explaining the Phaenomena of nature the like methods are to be used & he that expects success must resolve before he compounds. For the explications of Phaenomena are Problems much harder than those in Mathematicks. The method of Resolution consists in trying experiments & considering all the Phaenomena of nature relating to the subject in hand & drawing conclusions from them & examining the truth of those conclusions by new experiments & drawing new conclusions (if it may be) from those experiments & so proceeding alternately from experiments to conclusions & from conclusions to experiments untill you come to the general properties of things. Then assuming those properties as Principles of Philosophy you may by them explain the causes of such Phaenomena as follow from them: wch is the method of Composition. But if without deriving the properties of things from Phaenomena you feign Hypotheses & think by them to explain all nature you may make a plausible systeme of Philosophy for getting your self a name, but your systeme will be little better than a Romance. To explain all nature is too difficult a task for any one man or even for any one age. Tis much better to do a little with certainty & leave the rest for others that come after you then to explain all things by conjecture without making sure of any thing.[73]

The main thrust of this paragraph, in the familiar but less spontaneous and more condensed form, appeared in all the later editions of the *Opticks*. Clearly, despite the influences I have described — on poets, philosophers and artists — this eloquent draft reminds us that we have been dealing with a work of science; and indeed it was, after all, as a model of scientific investigation, that Sir Isaac Newton's *Opticks* exerted its most profound influence.

Henry Guerlac

73. Cambridge University Library, MS. Add. 3970 (5).

The Pictorial Circuit
& Related Structures
in 18th-Century England

Much has been said of *ut pictura poesis* in the eighteenth century: Rensselaer Lee has shown that painters were taught by the art treatises to paint scenes they read in poems, and Jean Hagstrum has shown that the poets were taught to describe scenes painted by artists.[1] Since the basis of all the arts was thought to be in one way or another the imitation of nature, the results of cross-breeding were often curious, emphasizing differences rather than resemblances. More recently, in his Mellon Lectures, Mario Praz has indicated what seems to me a more fruitful approach to the subject: to seek "sameness of structure in a variety of media," or to make connections not on a mimetic but a formal basis.[2] "Structures" evidently mean to Praz the rococo S curves that appear in garden paths, chair legs, grace notes, and run-on couplets; and in practice he merely produces another Wöllflinian history of styles. It might be more fruitful to use "structure" to mean a significant configuration of elements which serves as a principle of organization in a work of art.

I begin with a garden — the best reflector at this time of what was happening in other visual and verbal forms. The English "poetic" garden in the early eighteenth century was a path through a landscape with benches provided for meditation. The visitor sat on a bench, looked in the direction it was pointed, and saw a carefully-prepared scene, which was a

---

1. Rensselaer W. Lee, "Ut Pictura Poesis: The Humanistic Theory of Painting," *Art Bulletin*, XXII, 1940, pp. 197-269; Jean Hagstrum, *The Sister Arts*, Chicago, 1958.

2. Mario Praz, *Mnemosyne: The Parallel between Literature and the Visual Arts*, Princeton, 1970. The phrase quoted is his title for Chapter 3.

mixture of natural setting and artifacts arranged to look like a painting by Claude and (accompanied by inscriptions) a page from an emblem book. As one followed the path in the direction stipulated, emblem followed emblem in a particular order.

Already in the 1720s, however, Alexander Pope had arranged paths in his Twickenham garden to converge from different directions and terminate on an obelisk to the memory of his mother. An obelisk, urn, or statue could be revealed in different aspects as it was seen down the different garden paths from various directions. By the 1740s pictorial circuits (sometimes called "perimeter belts") had begun to appear in gardens: instead of wandering through the garden, the path made a circuit of it, and the benches revealed a series of perspectives or different points of view on the same scene. There was an embryonic one in Bridgeman's version of Stowe in the 1730s, and then in Wooburn Farm, Stourhead, Hagley, and the Leasowes.[3] In his "Unconnected Thoughts on Gardening," William Shenstone advocated a series of "landskips" one could see from different viewpoints,[4] and the published "Description of the Leasowes" (Shenstone's garden) tells how the seats were placed at intervals from which a cascade or a church steeple could be seen first in one way and then "in a new light." The statue of a piping faun "not only embellishes this scene," we are told, "but is also seen from the court before the house, and from other places." We are referred to a bench that "affords the first, but not most striking, view of the Priory," or one that gives "a nearer view."[5] From different viewpoints the same object might appear under different aesthetic categories: "the grand, the savage, the sprightly, the melancholy, the horrid, or the beautiful"; or "the sublime, the beautiful, and the melan-

---

3. See Derek Clifford, *A History of Garden Design*, New York, 1963, pp. 141-43; Christopher Hussey, *The Picturesque: Studies in a Point of View*, London, 1927, pp. 130-31, and *English Gardens and Landscapes, 1700-1750*, London, 1967, p. 158.

4. "Unconnected Thoughts on Gardening," in *The Works in Verse and Prose of William Shenstone, Esq.*, 2nd ed., 1765, II, p. 116.

5. Robert Dodsley, "Description of the Leasowes," in *Works ... of William Shenstone, Esq.*, II, pp. 291, 296-97, 305. For further on the Leasowes by a contemporary, see Richard Graves' *Columella, or The Distres't Anchoret*, 1779.

choly or pensive."[6]

At Stourhead the Pantheon and the Temple of Flora, seen from the entrance to the garden, were part of a carefully-composed Claude landscape; from the steps of the Temple of Flora, with its emblems of harvest abundance and its inscription from the *Aeneid*, the Pantheon became a symbol of Rome as the New Troy toward which the visitor was progressing — the end of which was the Temple of Apollo, now revealed high on a hill.[7] Thereafter each temple or bridge, each bench, offered a different perspective on one or another of the few basic scenes of the garden.

In a note to his translation of the *Iliad*, Pope drew attention to the literary practice implicit in his variety of alleys converging on a single obelisk. He is speaking of Homer's repetition of similes:

> But may not one say Homer is in this like a skilful Improver, who places a beautiful Statue in a well-disposed Garden so as to answer several Vistas, and by that Artifice one single Figure seems multiply'd into as many Objects as there are Openings whence it may be viewed.[8]

Maynard Mack has noted that this device, offering possibilities for "the disposition of a single figure to answer several points of view," connects with pun and zeugma and is "a species of economy and polysemousness wholly characteristic" of the Augustan mode of poetry.[9] Of course, polysemousness as it appears in pun or zeugma (Queen Anne "does sometimes counsel take — and sometimes tea")[10] was already present in the single closed scene, with its allusions to Claude and to ancient Rome. Pope's converging alleys merely emphasize this new, equally closed view of it, as of the verb "take" when "tea" is

6. Shenstone, "Unconnected Thoughts," *Works*, II, p. 113, 111 n.

7. Kenneth Woodbridge argues (interestingly but not to me convincingly) that a first view of the Pantheon would have included the recognition of both a general and a particular Claude landscape and so an awareness of the *Aeneid* motif. See his "Henry Hoare's Paradise," in *The Art Bulletin*, XLVII, 1965, pp. 83-116.

8. "Essay on Homer's Battles," prefatory to *Iliad* II, 1716.

9. Mack, *The Garden and the City: Retirement and Politics in the later Poetry of Pope, 1731-1743*, Toronto, 1969, p. 28.

10. Pope, *Rape of the Lock*, III, line 8.

added to "counsel." But following the pictorial circuit the viewer passes from one perspective to another, separating the meanings which were simultaneous in Pope's vistas.

While in the 1740s pictorial circuits began to appear in gardens, native English history paintings of the time showed a central figure or action responded to variously in expression and gesture by a number of people. Hogarth's *Pool of Bethesda* and *Paul before Felix* are examples, and as late as the 1760s Wright of Derby's candlelit pictures showed a central object with a circle of observers offering different but equally intense responses. In 1742 Fielding's *Joseph Andrews* employed tableaux in which Joseph or Parson Adams or Fanny is responded to in various ways by different series of people. At the end of the decade Richardson's epistolary novel *Clarissa* was constructed on the principle of an action responded to by the letters of participants, their friends, and mere observers. In the 1760s and 70s — when the pictorial circuit was still the structural unit of many gardens — Smollett's *Humphry Clinker* showed a group of letter-writers moving from place to place along an itinerary describing what they see from their comically divergent points of view. Much the same happens in Sterne's non-epistolary *Tristram Shandy* as one topic after another comes up for discussion by the members of the Shandy household. It is possible over a period of about thirty years to enumerate several avatars of a single structure: one object viewed from multiple perspectives.

A conclusion to draw from these examples is that artists and writers shared with philosophers common assumptions about perception, or a preoccupation with seeing and looking at things, which derived from the current model of the mind vs. reality; and therefore shared some general structures for apprehending reality. Locke's emphasis on experimentation, Addison's on the sight as the most important sense for the "pleasures of the imagination," and the growing assumption that reality was as much in the responding audience as in the work of art were part of the same sweeping change from belief in the primacy of reason to belief in the primacy of experience.

Immediately apparent, however, is a variable in the relative importance attached to object and to viewer. The pictorial circuit set up different and discrete views of an object which was itself various, its different aspects revealed by different contexts. In one sense the circuit is an acknowledgement of nature's variousness, or (to take Pope's sense) of the poet's ability to bring out nature's variousness. But in another it is a paradigm of the eighteenth-century's realization that how something looks, what sort of response it gets, depends on the point of view from which it is seen, and so implicitly by whom it is seen. The same object seen from different angles or distances by the same person is very different from the same object seen by a number of different viewers with different sensibilities. As a radical loosening of the Augustan pun or zeugma takes place, the emphasis shifts from the many-facetedness of the object to the various responses of different observers. One explanation of this shift might be that the world order — the shared myths — having dissolved, or no longer proving viable, polysemous meaning was no longer possible:[11] the viewer could no longer see the object as a whole, and so each brought his own meaning — symbolized by the different viewpoints along the pictorial circuit.

Another explanation may emerge as we relate this change from objectivity to subjectivity to the different media, with their own potentials and traditional structures or topoi, in which the structure of the pictorial circuit was in one way or another reflected. It is in the nature of a garden and the experience it offers that an effect can only be achieved by the arranging of objects and their settings. The viewer himself can be placed at certain distances looking in particular directions, and his responses regulated as skilfully as if by a literary rhetorician like Swift or Pope. But he is not part of the landscape garden: he is a manipulated participant in the total experience of the work, but not an individual responding personally or idiosyncratically, and certainly not several individuals responding in different ways, to a garden. A painting,

---

11. This would be E.R. Wasserman's explanation: *The Subtler Language*, Baltimore, 1959, p. 170.

like an obelisk in a garden, is also itself an object, but being representational it can introduce within itself the viewers as well as the object they are viewing. The two-dimensional nature of the representation, of course, limits the object represented to one facet; and so the other-facetedness of it appears only in the variety of the responses portrayed.

I

In painting one obvious source for the central figure or action responded to variously by a number of people is the category of *l'expression des passions*, the most emphasized doctrine in contemporary art treatises, which Reynolds later summed up, in his seventh Discourse, as "the most essential part of our art"; only the highest art could "aspire to the dignity of expressing the characters and passions of men."[12] Alberti, in his *Della pittura*, had activated the notion by making expression one of the criteria for history painting, the grandest genre a painter could attempt (equated with the epic in poetry). Expression was discussed at great length by Lomazzo, and the French Academy made much of it, conducting regular discussions and classes on the subject. Henri Testelin devoted a third of his *Tables de préceptes* to the passions and Félibien emphasized expression in his introduction to the Academy's *Conférences*. Le Brun spent a whole conference on expression and published a separate illustrated treatise, *Traitée sur les Passions*, which was popular during the eighteenth century among artists, writers, and actors.

What the term came to mean is already implicit in Alberti's assertion that *istoria* should "move the soul of the beholder," and would do so "when each man painted there clearly shows the movement of his own soul." Thus we, the viewers, "weep with the weeping, laugh with the laughing, and grieve with the grieving." This is accomplished through the artist's employment of expression — the movements of the body and of the face, which reveal the "movements of the soul"; and as Alberti's

12. Discourse VII, Sir Joshua Reynolds, *Discourses on Art*, ed. Robert R. Wark, San Marino, 1959, pp. 130-31.

figure suggests, this involves two circles of expression – that of responders within the picture and their reflection in the responders without. Alberti took as his example a Giotto painting of the disciples seeing Christ walking on the water: "Each one expresses with his face and gesture a clear indication of a disturbed soul in such a way that there are different movements and positions in each one."[13] Unfortunately, the example of Christ and the disciples had the effect of dividing the scene into an actor and observers who are not direct participants in the action but surrogates for the viewers of the picture.

The general tendency of art treatises that followed Alberti was toward simplification and rigid formulation along the lines he had laid down. Le Brun pushed expression in the direction of a mere spectrum or catalogue of facial responses. In England the Raphael Cartoons, an ever-present reminder of history painting at its most exemplary, consisted of scenes which could be interpreted as constructed on the principle of response to a central action (Plate 1): each figure responds differently to Paul's action, and the "history" was interpreted as largely the variety of the gestures and facial expressions.[14] A history painter could either expand a central relationship or action to fill his whole canvas, or, if his assumptions remained academic, he could fill out the canvas with figures responding to the central action or relationship, relating only as observer to observed. He could also, of course, emphasize either the

---

13. *Della pittura*, tr. John R. Spencer, New Haven, 1956, pp. 77 (cf. 75), 78.

14. See *The Conference of Monsieur Le Brun . . .*, tr. J. Smith, London, 1701; *A Method to Learn to Design the Passions Proposed in a Conference on their General and Particular Expression*, tr. John Williams, (London, 1734, to which is appended a partial translation of Le Brun's *On Physiognomy*). Le Brun emphasizes facial expression: "the whole man is seen in the head. . . . if man be truly said to be the Epitome of the whole World, the Head may well be said to be the Epitome of the whole Man" (1734 ed., p. 55). For bodily gesture, see Gerard Lairesse, *Groot Schilderboek*, tr. 1738, and in the eighteenth century, Aaron Hill's *Essay on the Art of Acting*, 1746, for adaptations of the art treatises doctrines to the stage. For the stereotypic tendencies of the traditions, see Brewster Rogerson, "The Art of Painting the Passions," *Journal of the History of Ideas*, XIV, 1953, pp. 68-94; and for a general survey of expression as used in painting and on the stage, see Alastair Smart, "Dramatic Gesture and Expression in the Age of Hogarth and Reynolds," *Apollo*, LXXXII, 1965, pp. 90-97.

harmony or the divergence of responses, depending on whether his allegiance lay with classical or baroque schools of painting.

Like other artists of his time, Hogarth was indoctrinated to appreciate the importance of *l'expression des passions*.[15] In his *Paul before Felix* of 1748 he shows the varying responses of Paul's opponent Tertullus, his judge Felix, and Felix's entourage, the scribes, and the Roman soldiers. It is true that Hogarth's characteristic structures, more complex than mere action and response, are studies in choice and responsibility,[16] and the viewer of *Paul before Felix* may wonder whether the picture is about Paul and the range of response to his speech or about Felix the judge who is choosing between Paul and Tertullus (it was painted to hang above the head of the Lord Chancellor in the High Court of Chancery). As if conscious that the conventional structure of expressive response ought to be emphasized in an overt attempt at sublime history (containing echoes of Raphael's *Paul Preaching at Athens* and *Paul and Elymas*), Hogarth added several more responders in the published engraving (Plate 2) than appear in the painting. He also characteristically stepped back and parodied the whole idea of expression in the subscription ticket he issued (Plate 3) in anticipation of the engraving. He shows how Rembrandt might have painted it: Paul's terrifying words elicit a very physical response from Felix, and this in turn is responded to by the people around him.

Naturally, when he attempted the difficult task of raising contemporary genre to the level of history in his "comic history paintings," Hogarth also made response one element of his composition. The *Harlot's Progress* (1732) was ushered into the world with a programmatic subscription ticket in which putti and a faun respond in different ways to a statue of Nature. The first plate, which in fact is about a girl's choice between the passive virtue of the clergyman and the active vice of the procuress and her employer — a kind of Choice of Hercules structure in reverse — was probably regarded by contem-

15. For the influence of these treatises on Hogarth, see my *Hogarth: His Life, Art, and Times*, New Haven, 1971, I, p. 264.
16. This structure is discussed in *ibid.*, I, pp. 272-76.

poraries, also brought up on assumptions about art based on the art treatises and the Raphael Cartoons, as essentially a central action surrounded by vivid responses. The girl is being responded to variously by the parson, procuress, rake, and pimp. Plate 2 shows the responses of a monkey, lover, servant girl, and wealthy keeper to the Harlot's kicking over a tea table; and the final plate (Plate 4), showing the Harlot's coffin surrounded by mourners, is an anatomy of grief — greedy grief, lecherous grief, pretended grief, and unconcern, with perhaps one example of genuine grief. Now the stimulus — the Harlot — has virtually disappeared, and only the responses remain, filling the picture space.

Expression was obviously of great importance to Hogarth, who continually reminded his audience that his faces were expressive without being caricatures, and published more than one print illustrating his own theory of expression. When he turned an engraving over to an assistant, he still, as he publicly noted, engraved the faces himself. His greatest contemporary fame was as a delineator of expression, and this was what Fielding praised in his preface to *Joseph Andrews* when he bestowed on him the title "comic history painter." Whenever a strikingly expressive face was needed, Fielding or another novelist invoked the aid of Hogarth's pen — one more bit of evidence demonstrating the centrality of this aspect of Hogarth's art to his time.

On the other hand, like the painter who wished to raise genre to the level of history, the writer who wished to raise new, uncharted forms of fiction to a respectable eminence and produce a "comic epic in prose," also regarded expression as of the greatest importance. Fielding devoted an essay to the subject, and in *Joseph Andrews* he produced a literary variant of the Harlot's wake when he showed Joseph, robbed and left naked in a ditch, reacted to by a group of gentlefolk who pass by in a coach.[17] "O J-sus," cries a lady, "A naked Man! Dear Coachman, drive on and leave him." "Robbed," cries an old gentleman, "Let us make all the haste imaginable, or we shall be

17. *Joseph Andrews*, ed. M. Battestin, Oxford, 1967, pp. 52-53.

robbed too." A young lawyer responds that "he wished they had past by without taking any Notice: But that now they might be proved to have been *last in his company*; if he should die, they might be called to some account for his Murther. He therefore thought it adviseable to save the poor Creature's Life, for their own sakes, if possible." The coachman objects: "that he could not suffer him to be taken in, unless some body would pay a Shilling for his Carriage the four Miles." And so on: the lady refusing to have a naked man in the coach and the old gentleman "thinking the naked Man would afford him frequent Opportunities of showing his Wit to the Lady." The only sympathy for the poor wretch is shown by the postilion, "(a Lad who hath since been transported for robbing a Hen-roost),"who lends Joseph his greatcoat for covering.[18]

Both Hogarth and Fielding are using expression in a special way, for the spectrum of expression surrounding the Harlot and Joseph is also a satiric exposure of the selfish responses elicited by a foolish or helpless object. The responses, though various, are all bad with one exception – a poor postilion, or an unlucky chambermaid, or a faithful but noseless servant woman. In these vivid scenes a conventional structure of history painting and of satire, an interest in expression and in satiric exposure, coalesce. The satiric structure, however, has the effect of cutting off all of the observers but one from the central object of concern; or put differently, the normative responses are reduced to one.

II

As his burlesque of *Paul before Felix* may have indicated, Hogarth was well aware of the limitations of the categories of expression as promulgated by the art treatises. In *Characters and Caricaturas* (1743), he reacted against the stereotyped expressions of Le Brun's manual by including comic variants

18. I think I am justified in connecting expression as facial and bodily gesture with Fielding's dialogue responses. The important point is the structure and expressive response, not (as Fielding makes clear in his "Essay on the Characters of Men") the details of physiognomy. But Jonathan Richardson, for one, also asks his readers when they look at a history painting to imagine the words spoken, and Aaron Hill's "examples" in his chapters on the passions in *The Art of Acting* are in fact poetic extracts.

that have no place in the austere system that derives from Raphael's idealized faces (shown at the bottom, alongside caricatured faces by Ghezzi and Leonardo); and in the plates of his comic histories he augmented facial and bodily expression with significant objects that reveal aspects of character unobtainable by Le Brun's method.[19]

Fielding's doubts about stereotypic response are also implicit when he describes Tom Jones after his expulsion from Paradise Hall: "He presently fell into the most violent agonies, tearing his hair from his head, and using most other actions which generally accompany fits of madness, rage and despair."[20] Himself something of an antiphysiognomist, Fielding argues in his "Essay on the Characters of Men" that most expressions are difficult to judge; "a formal, stately, austere gravity" tends to make most observers overlook other signs in a person's expression. Though he acknowledges that "the passions of men do commonly imprint sufficient marks on the countenance," he argues that "it is owing chiefly to the want of skill in the observer that physiognomy is of so little use and credit in the world."[21]

His concern with the problematic nature of expression, in both object and observers, leads first to a greater discrepancy between responses — the spectrum of bad responses becomes a mixture of uncomprehending, mistaken ones — and then to the need for another observer, more skilled in physiognomy, who can penetrate behind a face and even words to actions and motives. This, of course, is the Fielding narrator, who shows the reader how to see and judge. Fielding is as interested in the problem of interpreting response as in the exposure of hypocrites and the cruelty under genteel exteriors in a satiric structure.

We must now bring yet another form into consideration, for both Hogarth and Fielding were closely connected with the theater, and actors relied as heavily as painters on the theory of

19. For Hogarth's statements on the problem, see *The Analysis of Beauty*, ed. Joseph Burke, 1955, pp. 136-38, 160-61.
20. *Tom Jones*, Bk. VI, Chap. xii, Modern Library ed., p. 255.
21. Fielding, *Works*, ed. Leslie Stephen, London, 1882, VI, pp. 337, 332.

expression and Le Brun's illustrations of the passions. Though on a stage a series of responses in space could conceivably be presented consecutively in time, in general the theater requires a unified effect which renders action and multiple response temporally synchronous; there is no movement from one point of view to the next, as in the stops of a pictorial circuit, or the responses of people enumerated on a page of *Joseph Andrews*, or even strung across a plate of the *Harlot's Progress*. The exception, significantly, is the rehearsal play, which Fielding made his own: here the scene is discussed and responded to – satirically commented on and interpreted – by an author, a critic, a theater manager, and some actors, who are watching it being performed. In his *Beggar's Opera* paintings of a year or so before Fielding's first rehearsal play, Hogarth achieved a related effect by showing people looking at a play being performed, with quite different responses and degrees of involvement; the inscription "Velute in speculum" above his stage made the implicit connection with the topos of life as a stage. He repeated the effect in portrait groups like *A Scene from 'The Indian Emperor,'* but also in the interplay of action and observation in his comic histories, which are in a sense about play-acting, and about the actress or actor (who is always assuming some inappropriate role) surrounded by multiple spectators to the performance.

When Fielding turned to prose fiction, he kept the context of the "life is a stage" topos, constructing his novels on circles of response. Beginning with Joseph himself responding to Lady Booby, he worked his way out to the fools and knaves who respond to Joseph as he makes his way back to Booby Hall, and to the author and readers who (as patently part of the fictive structure as in the rehearsal plays) respond to them. In *Tom Jones* (1748/9) the action is dominated by the theatrical metaphor and structured on the assumption that an actor – Tom himself – playing a role (sometimes congenial, sometimes not) is variously applauded and damned by an audience of different characters within the novel as well as by the audience of readers – of the pit, boxes, and galleries – without. The Hogarthian work that sums up this aspect of *Tom Jones* is *The*

Laughing Audience (Plate 5), which omits the performance altogether and shows only the pleased responses of the pit, the disinterested ones of the box, and the businesslike ones of the orchestra. As Partridge shows when, at a performance of *Hamlet*, he cannot distinguish the ghost until he sees Hamlet-Garrick's response to it, the response may define the object. Tom's actions finally exist largely in terms of the responses of the grave, sneering, prudent, virtuous, or critical auditors (or, as the metaphor shifts to that of a courtroom, to the judge and jurors), and Hogarth's etching is prophetic of the direction writers would take toward elimination of the performance altogether.

A variety of expressions responding to a central situation is also one explanation for Richardson's epistolary structure in *Clarissa* (1747). His friend Aaron Hill's drama treatises would have made him familiar with the relevance of expression to acting,[22] but he was also interested in expression in a broader sense. He began his literary career by writing typical epistolary responses to the usual situations, and from these letters of gratitude or bereavement he moved into responses to unusual situations, and ultimately conceived the letters of Pamela (1740).[23] For Richardson, who interposes no commentator or series of commentators as does Fielding, the primary aim is less understanding than the excitement of expressive response – its psychology and variety, expressed in "writing to the moment." Much more than Fielding, he was concerned with the visual possibilities of writing; not only are the letters visual units, rendered more expressive by exclamations, dashes, and breaks, but Pamela conveys what she sees through the description of expressions and gestures, heightened by her emotion of the moment, and often with visual prototypes (in some cases from Hogarth's prints).[24]

22. See Hill's *Prompter*, 1734-36, and *Art of Acting*, 1746.
23. See Robert Adams Day, *Told in Letters: Epistolary Fiction before Richardson*, Ann Arbor, 1966, for an account of one source of Richardson's epistolary form in the passionate speech derived from Ovid's *Heroides* and its many imitators including *The Letters of a Portuguese Nun*.
24. There are two kinds of response in *Pamela*: those of the characters to Pamela herself, which often sounds like Joseph and the coachload of people; and

In *Clarissa* Richardson abandoned the letter-journal of *Pamela* for the group of letters from different writers portraying responses to actions from their individual points of view. The letters reveal different aspects of a complex situation: how Clarissa's departure from the garden looked to her, how it looked to Lovelace, how his elaborate machinations affected the results, how Anna Howe responds from a distance, how the Harlowes respond, and how the "editor" responds (emphasizing Lovelace's control over events) in the notes — all fragmented, separated in time, and equally passionate and prejudiced. But we never see the scene itself, as we do the obelisk in a garden, or the Harlot or Joseph Andrews surrounded by exploiters. The scene in the garden is only conveyed by reflections. Clarissa's rape —the crux of the novel — is conveyed to us only by Lovelace's terse response ("The affair is over. Clarissa lives.") and then by Clarissa's own feverish, incoherent jottings, with lines running at random angles across the page; only much later by her attempt to recall for Anna what actually happened. The complexity of the situation is revealed indirectly, but that of the responding mechanisms directly, vividly, and visually.

As Clarissa writes at one point to Anna: "I fancy, my dear, . . . that there would hardly be a guilty person in the world, were each *suspected* or *accused* person to tell his or her own story, and be allowed any degree of credit."[25] The reader begins to recognize the problematic nature of the actions, as he does in *Tom Jones*, by trying to determine the problematic extent of truth in Clarissa's or Anna's or Lovelace's response. The criterion of expression, if not of truth, is distance from the object — the degree of empathy or selfishness (or subjectivity) in the responder.

Here acuity of perception and subjectivity come together. At the same time that Fielding was trying to educate his reader to the most sophisticated sort of understanding by enumerating the possible responses to one action, Hogarth was arguing in his

those of the characters to Pamela's journal when it is circulated. The former is plainly the situation of a group of people (mostly wicked or selfish) reacting to Pamela's vulnerable chastity.

25. *Clarissa*, London, 1905, I, p. 263.

Analysis of Beauty (1753) that the individual should put aside all that he has read in treatises on art, and see with his own eyes and judge for himself. Richardson's practice was not very different: the tragedy of Lovelace is that he responds always within the stereotype of himself as machinating rake, and even Clarissa often seems blinkered by her own view of herself as daughter, rake-saver, or spiritual paragon.

In retrospect, all of the encounters we have explored have served to explode some stereotype, whether that of the simple "idea" of an object or the stereotype of response itself. Inappropriate roles assumed, words that confuse or conceal, and inaccurately appraised "character," have been fragmented to expose their real complexity or reduced to their relative unimportance vis à vis the complexity of human experience.

Related also is an alteration of conventional narrative method which allows the writer to move beyond the hampering linear structures he inherited from his medium. In the same way, a garden of perspectives tends to reduce the fixed quality of the view necessary for "reading" the moral exemplum, turning the two-dimensional into the undeniably three-dimensional; it opens up the setting, making the garden less a series of set pieces than a fluid experience of nature for the viewer. Richardson's use of epistolary form and the landscape gardener's of perspectives loosen the linear structure embodied in a garden as on a printed page in a beginning, middle, and end. Rational narrative control — whether of an omniscient author or of a memoirist who can tell the story in a traditional, more or less chronological sequence — gives way to a series of responses or insights that tend to circle around an object rather than advance in a straight line. Even a protagonist is slightly subordinated when she is only one of a number of letter-writers, who perceive her and the events.

In Smollett's *Humphry Clinker* (1771), the complex discrimination among the epistolary points of view in *Clarissa* has been expanded into comic incongruity. Here a group of grotesquely diverse travellers visit a series of places (Bristol, Bath, London, York) and write letters on each spot that register their different responses. Lydia Melford sees everything through

a romantic haze; Jery Melford through the eyes of a sophisticated Oxford graduate; and Matthew Bramble through the
eyes of a sick, crotchety old man. Tabitha Bramble sees no Bath
or London at all but only her house in Wales and a projected
husband, and Winifred Jenkins' servant's-eye view reveals sex
and scatology in whatever it touches. There are similarly
opinionated observers within the letters (Lismahago, Mickle-
whimmen, Humphry Clinker himself, and even S------t), who also
fall somewhere along a spectrum of acceptance and rejection of
what is seen. None of these views is valid in itself but a special
circumstance of illness, callow youth, or young love, and must
be sublimated, dehumored, or in some way corrected – as many
are by the end of the novel.

By implication there is a *real* Bath these views distort; or
rather a Bath the reader reconstructs out of the sharp though
partial view of Bramble, the less true one of Lydia, and so on.
However, in Sterne's *Tristram Shandy* (1759-67), the object
itself has virtually disappeared. Here too the members of a
family respond discordantly to situation after situation – the
more emphatically because they seldom venture out of the
family parlor or each other's company. An object or even a
word – the death of brother Bobby, "curtins and horn works,"
a nose, a bridge, sash weights – is responded to and misunderstood in as many different ways as there are people trying to
understand it. But Bobby himself never appears, and his death
remains only a series of completely subjective responses; even
the hat Trim drops is not a hat to Trim or to his audience but
"the sentiment of mortality." Unlike Clarissa's rape or the city
of Bath, "nose" is never more than a word, distinct from the
nose on Tristram's face, and exists quite literally only in the
minds of the various people who talk about it.

If Smollett exploits the comic possibilities in *Clarissa*'s
epistolary structure, Sterne carries the doubts about the relationship of observer and object in *Tom Jones* to their logical end.
The satiric structure too remains, the paradigm being in this
case a scene like the one in which Bridget Allworthy, Deborah
Wilkins, and Squire Allworthy respond to the discovery of the
foundling Tom. The two rational but discordant and utterly

selfish responses of the women (equally hobbyhorsical but with opposite ends) are followed by Allworthy's feeling the "gentle pressure" of Tom's little hand, which seemed "to implore his assistance, [and] certainly outpleaded the eloquence of Mrs. Deborah." The one good response becomes in *Tristram Shandy* the occasional intuitive understanding that leaps the barrier of conventional words and actions to unite Toby and Walter Shandy — as when Toby, his system having been verbally castigated by Walter, puffs vigorously on his pipe, causing Walter to choke on the fumes, which makes Toby leap to his assistance regardless of the pain in his groin; and for a moment the two brothers are one. Though it never brings the object under observation any closer, this moment reveals that the real relationship is between subjects, not between a subject and some imaginary or misconceived, perhaps non-existent object.

III

At this point we must put our structure alongside an equally radical structure projected by the philosophy of Hume: "Beauty is no quality in things themselves: It exists merely in the mind which contemplates them; and each mind perceives a different beauty." To which he adds: "One person may even perceive deformity, where another is sensible of beauty; . . . To see the real beauty, or real deformity, is as fruitless an enquiry, as to pretend to ascertain the real sweet or real bitter."[26] Behind Hume is the skeptical idealism of Berkeley,[27] and behind both (in this particular respect) the old relativist topos, "Man is the measure of all things," which Cicero glossed in his *Academia* as: "One view of the criterion [of reality] is that of Protagoras, who holds that what seems to each person is true for each person." Or as Socrates glossed it, in words echoed by Hume and Berkeley, "The same wind is blowing, and yet one of us may be

---

26. "Of the Standard of Taste," originally in *Four Dissertations*, 1757, no. xxii in *Essays, Moral, Political, and Literary*, ed. T.H. Grose, London, 1882, II, pp. 268-69. See also, *An Enquiry concerning the Principles of Morals*, ed. L.A. Selby-Bigge, Oxford, 1894, Appendix I.

27. Berkeley, *Principles of Human Knowledge*, 1710, ed. A.C. Fraser, Oxford, 1901, I.14.

cold and the other not, or one may be slightly and the other very cold," and so "the wind is cold to him who is cold, and not to him who is not."[28]

Hume offered two solutions that may apply in the cases of Smollett and Sterne. The first was simply that different evaluations and estimates of a situation may be equally valid; "they do not contradict one another; they supplement each other."[29] Either skepticism or a kind of happy comic acceptance may be the result of the spectrum of discrepant perspectives. The second solution to the problem of relativist misunderstanding (and of all misunderstanding through structures of reason and the understanding) is feeling, which we have seen Sterne apply to interpersonal relationships rather than to the clarification of the meaning of an object.

Hume's is a view that is better suited to prose or poetry than to the visual arts: the writer need never show the object at all. If the painter represents the subject, he must also represent the object; otherwise he will have only a gallery of portraits.[30] The tour de force of Hogarth's *Laughing Audience* (or a century later Daumier's pictures of responding audiences) is as far as an artist can go in the direction of representing subjectivity. The tendency toward multiple perspectives appears in painting, as in the garden, not as an expression of subjectivity but as a way of eliciting a variety of responses from a viewer. From the 1750s onward rooms in houses, people posing for their portraits, and experience in general was portrayed through no uniform style but rather through a whole spectrum of them. As studies of the period show that try to designate it neoclassical or romantic or whatnot, no one style dominates in the way the rococo and the

28. Protagoras' aphorism appears in Diogenes Laertius, *Lives of the Eminent Philosophers*, 9.51. See Cicero, *Academia*, 2.142, and Plato, *Theaetetus*, 152a, tr. Jowett, II, p. 153. See also, Aristotle, *Metaphysics*, 3.5; Berkeley, *Siris*, pp. 270, 274, 290; Bernard Mandeville, *Fable of the Bees*, ed. F.B. Kaye, Oxford, 1924, I, pp. 325-26; David Hartley, *An Enquiry into the Origin of Human Appetites and Affections*, 1747, p. 117; *Observations on Man*, 1801, p. 442.

29. Ralph Cohen, "David Hume's Experimental Method and the Theory of Taste," *ELH*, XXV, 1958, p. 283. See "Of the Standard of Taste," p. 281.

30. Edmund Burke wrote of poetry (vs. painting) that its business is "to display rather the effect of things on the mind of the speaker, or of others, than to present a clear idea of the things themselves," *Philosophical Enquiry into our Ideas of the Sublime and Beautiful*, 1757, ed., J.T. Boulton, London, 1958, p. 172.

baroque dominated earlier periods or the *oeuvre* of earlier artists. A landscape painter moved easily from the forms and conventions of Claude to those of Salvator Rosa or of Ruisdael or Rembrandt. Reynolds might paint one sitter in the style of Rembrandt, another in the grand style of Titian or Rubens, as he painted Garrick's Tragic Muse in the Bolognese style and his Comic in the style of Correggio. An architect might decorate a set of rooms in a country house so that a Greek-style room opened into a Chinese and that into a Gothic, each eliciting a different but conditioned response from the visitor. The basis of this phenomenon probably lies in the principle of decorum — proper style, proper subject matter; but now the tendency was to let the style, or a variety of styles, shape the subject, whether a portrait, a landscape, a garden, or a suite of identical rooms. Some of the best poetry of the time too, extending as far as forgery, was written in Scottish, Gothic, Classical, Biblical, or Ossianic styles. On the one hand there was the acceptance of several different formal vocabularies as legitimate, as extending the expressive possibilities of an art. On the other there was the feeling that the multiplicity of points of view — as the procedure might come to be regarded — represented only a widening gap between the individual and the real world.

Subjectivity could appear in painting in another, more concrete way by putting in question the status of the represented object of response without actually omitting it. In the late 1760s Joseph Wright of Derby (who, incidentally, painted illustrations to Sterne) began to produce his candlelit pictures in which a central object — a scientific mechanism or an art object — is responded to and meditated upon by a group of people of various ages and temperaments, and their expressions intensified by the candlelight.[31] More than any other pictures we have considered, Wright's dissociate the object from the many-faceted responses of its viewers. Though Sterne seems sometimes close behind him, he is best understood as continuing the tradition of expression of the passions, which from the start cut off its central action from the spectrum of

31. I have dealt with Wright in detail elsewhere: "Zoffany and Wright of Derby," *Eighteenth-Century Studies*, III, 1969, pp. 278-95.

responses. He is another artist like Hogarth who is trying to find ways to maintain the criterion of expression and produce a history painting for his time, and his solution (consonant with that of the novelists) is to turn expression into perception, and emphasize the dissociation of subject from object.[32]

Wright, however, also draws on the old tradition of meditation in which the source of light was originally a divine or miraculous object or a candle lighting it and the meditators' faces. Or, if the object was not divine, it was a memento mori — a skull lit by a candle, or the candle itself used as an emblem of self-consuming time. Wright keeps the candle and the intense light, but now it is only a candle, and the object is a man-made imitation of a miracle.

In *A Philosopher giving a Lecture on the Orrery* (Plate 6), it is an imitation solar system, the candle simulating the sun. The group around it may be portraits, but the presence of a young lady and children serves to set off the contraption and the philosopher's books with a contrary indication of life as it is lived. To the children the Orrery is merely a plaything, and the young lady is thinking of something else. The roughly emblematic arrangement of the divergent responses in the *Orrery* is made schematically clear in *An Experiment on a Bird in the Air Pump* (Plate 7). At the center is a bell jar, being drained of air, with a living — or dying — bird in it, to illustrate the principle of the vacuum. The candle that illumines it is now contrasted with a natural source of light, the moon, seen through the window. Behind the air pump, demonstrating it, is a disheveled-looking scientist. An interested student and an awestruck boy look at

32. Wright's generation arrived at an intensification of expression through Burke's *Philosophical Enquiry into . . . the Sublime*, which places the efficient cause of beauty and sublimity in the observer — in "certain affections of the mind, that cause certain changes in the body." When he takes the examples of pain, fear, terror, or love, his descriptions of the physiognomic responses involved come straight out of Le Brun's manual (ed. Boulton, pp. 130, 133). Burke's theory, however, presupposes one stimulus-one response. Although in his second edition (1759) he did begin with a Hume-like discussion of the multiplicity of points of view that prevents a universal taste, and admitted, after his account of the physiological response to "such objects as elicit love," that "These appearances are always proportioned to the degree of beauty in the object, and of the sensibility of the observer," he ended by presupposing certain physiological responses elicited by the same objects in all people (p. 149).

the experiment. One little girl looks up at the fluttering bird with sympathetic eyes, and another covers her eyes, as a fatherly-looking man tries to explain its meaning to her. The rest are cut off completely. A pair of lovers turn their eyes away from the experiment to each other. An old man, his eyes turned inward, is submerged in his own thoughts. And a boy near the window looks straight at the final viewer, ourselves.

Wright uses responses that are as subjective as Sterne's or Smollett's, and he starts with the same cross-section of ages and sexes, arranging them in a formal order according to the Ages of Man: children, lovers, a parent, and an old man. Against the wild-eyed, wild-haired scientist, and his man-made mechanism, their responses constitute something of a comment. Like the philosopher in the *Orrery* with his candle a substitute sun, the scientist here embodies the topos of star knowledge vs. knowledge of man. The observers show the unbridgeable distance between the two.

In Wright's *Academy by Lamplight* (Plate 8) the central object is the statue of a girl. One student has put down his drawing and is merely gazing with rapt attention into her eyes, forgetting the distinction between flesh and stone. Another has finished his drawing and is turning away. Others are still making their copies. One little boy at the right looks straight ahead, uninterested in such things, catching the eye of the viewer. Our first response as viewers may be: is she a model or a statue? is she looking at the boy or he at her? We are reminded that Wright's photographic technique is also part of the effect. In this picture even the statue is part of a circle of response, which includes everything except the one missing element: the real girl called to mind by the statue.[33]

33. It is useful to remember, especially in the light of Wright's groups, that the dominant form in which English painting expressed itself during almost the whole of the period we have been discussing was, of course, the portrait or the portrait group. (Hogarth's comic histories of the 1730s too had been closely connected with the conversation pictures — small portrait groups — he painted between 1728 and 30.) Portraiture, in short, was at least by the time of Wright all mixed up with the problem of expression, and one finds many portraits of two or more gentlemen or ladies looking at some object, usually aesthetic. Ultimately there is Zoffany's *Tribuna* of the 1770s, in which little circles of connoisseurs, artists, and hangers-on examining works of art are scattered about the canvas. Zoffany reverses the ratio of object to

Contemporary with Wright's pictures were history paintings that depicted observers responding to a death. As with Wright's candlelit meditations, there is a long tradition of death-and-response in art, secular and religious: the former recommencing in the 1750s with Gavin Hamilton's deaths of Hector and Patroclus (derived from Poussin's *Death of Germanicus*) and the latter beginning again in the 1770s with West's modern-dress *Death of General Wolfe* (with its conscious echoes of a Pietà). I only wish to notice that the picture of a dead or dying person surrounded by mourners (which was also popular in France from the 1750s onward)[34] begins to flourish again at a time when writers and artists are portraying responses around an empty or ambiguous center.

The difference from the structure we have been following is obvious. There is no question in *The Death of General Wolfe* (Plate 9) about the unity of responses and, in a sense, of subject and object. Burke's *Philosophical Enquiry into the . . . Sublime and Beautiful* (1757) may be reflected with its emphasis on certain physiological responses being elicited by the same object in all people. But West is also part of the tradition of multiple styles we referred to earlier, in which Reynolds and others harmoniously joined contemporary Englishmen to the forms of heroic history painting or Greek antiquity. Wolfe is seen by West as a Christ in a Pietà, with no sense of discrepancy, and with all the responders united in their grief. This is very different from the other tradition, beginning in England with Hogarth's comic histories, which showed how inappropriate history painting was to contemporary life. A glance back at the harlot's wake, with its shattering echo of *The Last Supper*, its twelve mourners plus the son sitting in the center, emphasizes the discrepancy and the unrelatedness of the responses from the

observer, and we almost lose the observers among the paintings and sculpture. His picture is about art and artists and connoisseurs, only one aspect of which is the way they look at sacred pictures or profane, classical or moden, Venuses or Madonnas; more importantly, it is about how they appear alongisde them.

34. Not long before West began these pictures, Diderot was remarking admiringly on the varying nuances of grief on each face in Greuze's *Death of the Paralytic* (Salon, 1763), each showing a different response and relationship to the dying man. (See Michael Levey, *From Rococo to Revolution*, London, 1966, pp. 150-51.)

object, and of response from response; as too in Wright's forge paintings where the blacksmith's forge replaces the Nativity scene, its glowing ingot the Christ Child, and the spectators respond with the same variety of expressions shown in the *Air Pump*.

The interesting fact, however, is that a dead figure becomes the center of the circle of response in history paintings celebrating the rise of the British Empire.[35] In some sense death is parallel to the object in *Tristram Shandy* that has no independent existence of its own, or the artifact, patently false, at the center of Wright's candelit pictures. West's mourners are all in harmony with each other, sharing a common grief, and West is doing something quite different from either Sterne or Wright; and yet the mourners' very grief now expresses their alienation from the object. Being cut off is part of the experience of these pictures — if not by death or disaster, then by an ontological barrier. In all of them the object is of an ambiguous status; whether it is absent, non-existent, a fabrication, or dead, the emphasis is on the responses of the periphery, which has lost touch with its center.[36]

Ronald Paulson

35. In Copley's *Death of Chatham*, at the end of the decade, the sense of discrepancy is even clearer than in West. Copley moves away from the static West composition toward a more baroque and flowing one with a larger perspective. From the right, where Chatham lies, a series of shock waves emanate as from a pebble dropped in the water. Chatham's death is reflected intensely in the immediate circle of grieved heads and becomes less and less apparent until Lord Mansfield is found still sitting, unaffected. In *The Death of Major Pierson* of 1782 the emotion is so intense at the center that one mourner does take action, breaking the barrier between subject and object, by avenging his leader; but the agitation gradually subsides as it reaches the edges of the canvas. An intense activity round the center — which is death — dissipates until at the periphery there is no expression at all.

36. If we recall that *Tristram Shandy* is a work of the late 1750s and that these paintings of epistemological alienation date from the 1760s and 70s, we might hazard a speculation that from Sterne onward they reflect a public or social as well as a personal sense of dissolution of the external world, which can be documented in many tracts and pamphlets of the Seven Years' War period, and in the 1760s was felt by members of both parties, for the empire and against it, and became real in the 1770s with the decline of the empire and in 1780 with the Gordon Riots, which materialized the Wilkes and Liberty that may have been implicit in *Tristram Shandy* once and for all in bloodshed.

The Dawn of British
Romantic Painting, 1760-1780

As resistant as Romanticism may be to tidy definitions in any of the arts, there is no doubt that any number of new subjects, forms, and emotions which well up in the late eighteenth and early nineteenth centuries produce today a unanimous response that is articulated by the word "Romantic." Problems of semantics and categories aside, it would seem that in the history of art, as in the history of literature, music, and philosophy, the first rumblings of these changes are heard in the second half of the eighteenth century. The task at hand is not so much to re-define these changes in the hopes of arriving at yet a new interpretation of Romanticism, but simply to examine, somewhat less ambitiously, a particular time and a particular place in the hopes of discerning how, rather than why, these changes were wrought. The place is Britain and the time is the twenty-year period, 1760 to 1780, during which, to judge from the pictorial evidence, almost every innovation later to be associated with full-blown Romantic art occurred.

In looking for symptoms of change, one might well begin with the most direct vehicle of psychological expression, the portrait, and in particular, with the portraiture of the most officially prominent painter of the period, Sir Joshua Reynolds (1732-92), the first president of the Royal Academy, newly founded in 1768.[1] The official academic image and the public psychological facade of Reynolds' portraiture are familiar enough, especially in the many allegorical portraits he executed of aristocratic women who wished to be personified, as if at an erudite masquerade, in the guise of such classical deities as *Juno Receiving the Cestus from Venus* (Lady Anabelle Blake, R.A. 1769) or *Three Graces Adorning a Term of Hymen* (The

1. For the most recent study of these events, see Sidney C. Hutchison, *The History of the Royal Academy, 1768-1968*, London, 1968.

Misses Montgomery, R.A. 1774).[2] Yet now and again, Reynolds would abandon this gallery of learned charades (analogous to the modish neo-Greek ladies of Reynolds' French contemporary, Joseph-Marie Vien) in order to paint a portrait of surprising directness and emotional intensity, even within the restrained decorum expected of aristocratic portraiture. Such is the case in a portrait of c. 1775 of Lady Charlotte Spencer (Plate 10) where, most surprisingly, the sitter is represented with an immediacy of feeling that undermines the well-mannered proprieties of the usual "grand style" portrait. Her hair tousled by the wind, her gaze stormy and directed outward to some unseen point beyond the picture's confines, Lady Spencer stands in strange emotional proximity to her horse, whose huge head demands, especially in its large, wet, and staring eye, a startling degree of empathy for a dumb animal.

Such emotional chinks in the psychological armor of Georgian portraiture were, in fact, to be felt in many portraits of the 1760's and 1770's, but nowhere more conspicuously than in the work of that cantankerous and ambitious Irish painter, James Barry (1741-1809), a friend and disciple of Edmund Burke, whose *Philosophical Enquiry into the Origin of our Ideas of the Sublime and the Beautiful* (1756) was to inflame the imagination of so many young artists who began their careers in the 1760's.[3] As early as 1767, in a self-portrait executed at the beginning of his Roman sojourn (1767-71), Barry locates himself in a strange, imaginative world that confounds his empirical self with profile portraits of two artist friends (Paine and Lefevre) and a glimpse of the Belvedere Torso, all painted on the murky canvas behind.[4] By the next

---

2. These two portraits (R.A. 1769, no. 90; R.A. 1774, no. 216) are most conveniently illustrated in the standard modern monograph on the master: E. K. Waterhouse, *Reynolds*, London, 1941, Pls. 126, 152. For important insights into Reynolds' allegorical portraiture, see also Edgar Wind, "Borrowed Attitudes in Hogarth and Reynolds," *Journal of the Warburg Institute*, II, 1938-39, pp. 182-185.

3. The fundamental study of the "Sublime" as an aesthetic category is Samuel H. Monk, *The Sublime; a Study of Critical Theories in XVIII-Century England* (new ed.), Ann Arbor, Mich., 1960. For a more specific study of the relation of Burke and Barry, see Robert Wark, "A Note on James Barry and Edmund Burke," *Journal of the Warburg and Courtauld Institutes*, XVII, 1954, pp. 382-384.

4. On this portrait, see also the exhibition catalogue, *British Self Portraits, c. 1580-c 1860*, Arts Council, 1962, no. 42.

decade, this will to transform a portrait situation into a dreamlike adventure was fully realized in an extraordinary allegorical portrait of the artist himself and his friend Burke, exhibited at the Royal Academy in 1776 (Plate 11).[5] Here Barry has terrorized, so to speak, the classical allegorical disguises of Reynolds' sitters by imagining Burke and himself in the role of Ulysses and his companions escaping from the cave of Polyphemus. This weird setting, with its irrational confusions of scale and its fantastic *dramatis personae*, was to provide, as in some Homeric version of a Gothic novel, a wildly imaginative environment into which the sitters and the spectators could expand their own sensations of dread and adventure. It was a path that Barry, in the greater loneliness of his later life, was to explore to an extreme degree of hallucinatory portraiture.[6]

Just as the long tradition of British portraiture began to disclose, between 1760 and 1780, new dimensions of subjectivity, so too did another venerable tradition in British art, landscape painting, begin to investigate at exactly the same time what might be called the objective correlative of these states of feeling. In the most famous mid-eighteenth-century master of landscape, Richard Wilson (1714-82), one can already observe how the search for more rugged, erratic facts in nature tended to strain the more harmonious landscape formulae he inherited from the seventeenth-century tradition of Claude Lorrain. At times, these traditions could easily be adapted to accommodate such of his native Welsh facts as a view of the River Dee,[7] lucidly organized by a large foreground tree that frames a quiet vista of receding planes; but elsewhere, wilder topography, like the dramatic Welsh site, Cader Idris, tended to unbalance this serene natural order. Thus, in Wilson's painting of a view of the lake Llyn-y-Cau at Cader Idris of c. 1774 (Plate 12),[8] the ragged

5. R.A., no. 18. For further bibliography, see the exhibition catalogue, *Irish Portraits, 1660-1860*, Dublin, National Gallery of Ireland, 1969, no. 64.

6. Most specifically, in the haunting *Self Portrait* of c. 1803, on which see *ibid.*, no. 68; and the fuller discussion by Robert Wark, "The Iconography and Date of Barry's Self-Portrait in Dublin," *Burlington Magazine* XCVI, May 1954, pp. 153-154.

7. On Wilson's several versions of this native scene, transcribed into Claude-like vistas, see W. G. Constable, *Richard Wilson*, London, 1953, pp. 173-175.

8. For a detailed discussion of this painting, see *ibid.*, pp. 171-172.

contours of the crater, moving ever higher toward the picture's edge, and the startlingly Lilliputian scale of the human spectators at the crater's rim introduce untamable natural data that threaten earlier landscape conventions in terms of both formal and emotional structure. And in the works of other, younger landscape painters active between 1760 and 1780 these threats are even greater. A particularly telling case in point is the work of an Irish painter, George Barret (1732?-84), who like Barry was a disciple of Burke.[9] Already in the 1760's, he sought out the stronger stuff of wild landscape, such as could be found in the British Isles, and attempted to convey, for example, the overpowering spectacle of the Powerscourt Waterfall in Ireland. In one version of this Sublime subject (Plate 13), possibly that exhibited at the Society of Artists in 1764,[10] Barret locates a group of tiny figures at the foot of these torrential falls, whose height and power are in part screened by the dark, irregular shapes of enormous trees in the foreground. Such overwhelming natural phenomena (of a kind that produced, according to Burke's aesthetic, the experience of the "Sublime") continued to capture Barret's imagination on his travels throughout the British Isles in search of awesome scenery. Thus, in 1777, he painted a stormy vista of Llanberis Lake in North Wales, where a group of spectators and horses (painted by Sawrey Gilpin) are strongly silhouetted against an awesome view of a hazy, remote mountain range that is made still more craggy by the picturesque ruin of Dolbardarn Castle at the right (Plate 14).[11] With its sense of vast distance, obscuring mist, and dizzy altitudes, such a landscape pushes to

9. Barret is important and needs study. For some preliminary comments, see Thomas Bodkin, *Four Irish Landscape Painters*, Dublin, 1920. A longer encyclopaedic account may be found in Colonel Maurice Harold Grant, *A Chronological History of the Old English Landscape Painters (in oil)* ... (new ed.), III, Leigh-on-Sea, 1958, pp. 193-198. For a recent effort to locate him within the context of Romanticism, see James White, "Irish Romantic Painting," *Apollo* LXXXIV, October 1966, pp. 268-275.

10. No. 3. Another version of the painting is in the National Gallery of Ireland.

11. It was exhibited at the R.A. in 1777, no. 16, under the title, *A Storm; the scene, Llanberies Pool, in the Mountains of Wales*. The site was popular with painters and was later illustrated by Loutherbourg (R.A. 1787, no. 94; Nottingham, Castle Museum and Art Gallery). For further comments on Barret's painting see the exhibition catalogue, *The Romantic Movement*, Arts Council of Great Britain, 1959, no. 12.

an extreme the fantastic potential of native British scenery.

Artists of Barreṭ's generation, however, often traveled to the Continent, in search not only of wider artistic experience and of wealthy patrons enjoying the Grand Tour, but also of the picturesque and sublime sites of European landscape. For example, Joseph Wright of Derby (1734-97), during his Italian sojourn of 1773-75, paid considerably more attention to the wonders of volcanoes and caverns than to the ideal beauties of antique and Renaissance art. Thus, with the eye of both a scrupulous observer of natural fact and a sensate tourist seeking out experiences of the strange and the marvelous, he could record among other natural spectacles the eruptions of Mount Vesuvius (Plate 15)[11a] — which, obligingly for the origins of the Romantic Movement, was particularly active in the 1770's — or the strange rock formations of stalactitic grottoes on the coast near Naples.[12] Later, back in England, this raw material of observed natural fact was to be aggrandized to yet more spectacular views that could combine Vesuvius' sulfurous eruptions with the no less eerie light of a full moon glistening behind passing clouds.[13] Wright's response to the wonders of Continental scenery was shared, in the 1760's and 1770's, by many lesser British masters of whom William Marlow (1740-1813) may serve as a typical example.[14] During his own Continental tour of 1765-68, Marlow recorded, among such other sights as Vesuvius itself,[15] the mirror-like stillness of Lake Geneva (Plate 16), whose awesome dimensions, crowned by distant snowcapped mountains, are emphasized by the speck of a sailboat in the foreground.

The search for ever more strange, marvelous, and terrifying

11a.   On Wright's many views of Vesuvius, see Benedict Nicolson, *Joseph Wright of Derby, Painter of Light*, I, London, 1968, pp. 254 f. and Appendix B, pp. 279 ff.

12.   On these grotto paintings, see *ibid.*, pp. 255-259.

13.   As in, for example, such later versions of Vesuvius' eruptions illustrated *ibid.*, II, Pls. 170, 214, 291.

14.   For others, see such a work as Loutherbourg's *Falls of the Rhine at Schaffhausen* of c. 1775, illustrated and discussed in Frederick Cummings and Allen Staley, *Romantic Art in Britain; Paintings and Drawings, 1760-1860*, Philadelphia Museum of Art, 1968, no. 59; or the many studies of the Alps made by John Cozens on his trip to Italy with Richard Payne Knight in 1776-77.

15.   Marlow exhibited two views of Vesuvius at the Society of Artists: 1768, no. 95; 1768 (Special), no. 67.

facts of landscape was enormously stimulated by the voyages of
Captain Cook in the 1770's; for he took with him, during his
second expedition of 1772-75, a skilled landscape painter,
William Hodges (1744-97),[16] who recorded many of the
wonders of the South Seas for subsequent exhibition in
London. Indeed, his topographical and anthropological
repertory introduced all kinds of themes into Western art that
would have enormous issue in the nineteenth and twentieth
centuries.[17] On the one hand, he could literally expand the
awesome dimensions of his teacher Richard Wilson's *Llyn-y-
Cau: Cader Idris* in his view of a much larger crater in the South
Pacific that pushes the rectilinear confines of the canvas almost
to the breaking point and that dwarfs even more vertiginously
the scale of man against the scale of nature (Plate 17);[18] on the
other, he could record a view of Tahiti,[19] whose seductive
foliage, gentle breezes, and nude bathers conjure up an exotic
Garden of Eden that would continue to exert its lure in the
Tahitian landscapes of a more famous Western artist in the
South Seas, Paul Gauguin. And elsewhere, he could present, as a
cultural and visual curiousity, the strange totems of Easter
Island (Plate 18),[20] artifacts whose remoteness and crude power
must have planted, in late eighteenth-century imaginations, the
seeds of that fascination with primitive art which maintained its
inspirational source in modern art from Gauguin's own totemic
sculptures to Brancusi's more abstract idols.

The magic of exotic landscape, so enriched by Cook's
explorations, had its human counterpart in the growing variety
of races represented in British portraits of the 1770's. From the
South Pacific itself came such portraits as that of the Princess

16. Hodges is now the subject of a doctoral thesis being completed by Mrs.
Isabel Stuebe of the Institute of Fine Arts, New York University.

17. For a study of the broad ramifications of these new geographical and
cultural contacts, see the basic study by Bernard Smith, *European Vision and the
South Pacific, 1768-1850; A Study in the History of Art and Ideas*, Oxford, 1960.

18. For more on this painting, see Cummings and Staley, *op. cit.*, no. 74.

19. The painting is probably to be identified with R.A. 1776, no. 134, *A View
Taken in the Bay of Otaheite, Peha*, of which another version is now in the collection
of Mr. and Mrs. Paul Mellon. The Arcadian implications of this Tahitian landscape are
discussed in Smith, *op. cit.*, pp. 46-47.

20. For more on this painting, see *ibid.*, pp. 51-52.

Poedooa, recorded by another artist, John Webber (1752-93), who had joined Cook on his third expedition. The Polynesian princess had in fact been taken as a hostage on the S. S. Resolution for five days in November 1777,[21] but she is recorded in her native tropical setting, a newly-discovered Eve or Venus, nude to the waist with flowers adorning her hair and a frond-fan in her hand (Plate 19). This ancestor of Gauguin's Tahitian models had her male complement in the famous Omai, a young Polynesian who was brought back from Huahine to England on the S. S. Adventure in 1774 and who charmed the British aristocracy during his year-long sojourn.[22] As represented by Reynolds in a majestic, full-length portrait exhibited at the Royal Academy in 1776,[23] Omai appears to be a Polynesian reincarnation of that antique marble most venerated by the late eighteenth century, the Apollo Belvedere (Plate 20).[24] Reynolds has, of course, been certain to include the exotic paraphernalia that gave Omai his luster — the turban, the native robes, the tattoo marks and pointed fingernails — and he has located him in a setting of tropical palms, but the image also strikes one as that of a noble human being, both graceful and heroic. The association the late eighteenth century could make between a "Noble Savage" and the ideal beauties exemplified by antique statuary had already been borne out amusingly by the legend of Benjamin West (1738-1820) and his first encounter in Rome, in the early 1760's, with the Apollo Belvedere. To an audience of cognoscenti who must have been curious about the response of an American colonial artist who had come from a land of redskins to so sublimely beautiful a work of antiquity, West remarked, "My God, how like it is to a

21. She was the daughter of Oree, Chief of Ulietea in the Society Islands, and was taken with her brother and brother-in-law on board the S. S. Resolution in November 1777 until a seaman and midshipman were returned to the ship. See *The Voyages of Captain Cook*, III, London, 1846, pp. 205 ff.

22. For the story of Omai's visit, see Thomas Blake Clark, *Omai, First Polynesian Ambassador to England*, San Francisco, 1941.

23. No. 230, under the title *Omiah*.

24. Reynolds had already used this antique model as a support for grand-style portraiture in *Commodore Keppel* of 1753 (National Maritime Museum, Greenwich), as already pointed out in Smith, *op. cit.*, p. 59.

young Mohawk warrior."[25] Indeed, in West's own work of the 1770's, American Indians appear like Noble Savages, whether viewed in Poussinesque contemplation as in the *Death of Wolfe* of 1770 or in stoical stillness and majesty as in the figure of the Indian, Joseph Brant, the companion of Colonel Guy Johnson, Secretary of Indian affairs, in a portrait of c. 1775.[26] To the growing anthropological variety of Polynesian and Indian sitters in the 1770's (not to mention the Negro so prominent in Copley's *Watson and the Shark* of 1778) could also be added the Chinese, most conspicuously in Reynolds' portrait of the young Wang-y-Tong, painted c. 1776 (Plate 21). The Chinese youth was, in fact, somewhat occidentalized, having been brought up with a good classical education by the Duchess of Dorset at Sevenoaks;[27] but in Reynolds' portrait his exotic aspects are underlined, not only by the cross-legged posture, but by the fan he holds and the bamboo settee upon which he is seated. Such portraits of exotic peoples seemed to provide the human counterpart to the equally exotic garden pavilions — Chinese, Moorish, Hindu — that began to spice such landscape vistas of the 1760's as Kew Gardens. Indeed, beginning in the late 1770's, even ideas for Tahitian garden follies and North American reed huts were introduced.[28]

The zoological parallel to this growing curiosity about other races, other cultures, other landscapes, other architecture was the increasing variety of then unfamiliar animals that began to be recorded in the 1760's and 1770's, above all by the great British animal painter, George Stubbs (1724-1806). For one, he exhibited at the Society of Artists in 1763[29] a painting of a female zebra which, together with a male, was sent up from the

25. West had then gone on to explain, with the help of his translator, Mr. Robinson, that he had often seen Indians in that attitude. The story is told in John Galt, *The Life and Studies of Benjamin West*, I, London, 1816, pp. 105 f.

26. For more comments on this painting, see Grose Evans, *Benjamin West and the Taste of His Times*, Carbondale, Ill., 1959, p. 46.

27. On Wang-y-Tong, see Hugh Honour, *Chinoiserie; the Vision of Cathay*, London, 1961, p. 185.

28. On these, see Robert Rosenblum, *Transformations in Late Eighteenth Century Art*, Princeton, 1967, p. 143, n. 140, fig. 166.

29. No. 121. The painting is discussed in *Painting in England, 1700-1850; Collection of Mr. and Mrs. Paul Mellon*, Virginia Museum of Fine Arts, Richmond, 1963, no. 315.

Cape of Good Hope as a gift to George III; for another, he painted in the 1760's a cheetah, again a gift to the King, this time from the Governor of Madras;[30] and surely most strange, he painted c. 1771-72 the very first kangaroo in Western art (a creature brought back to the West from Captain Cook's first voyage around the world) and exhibited this pictorial record of a bizarre new animal at the Society of Artists in 1773 (Plate 22).[31]

Such odd animals are painted by Stubbs with the scrupulous objectivity of a zoologist studying natural facts; indeed, the paintings might almost substitute for illustrations in an eighteenth-century treatise on natural history. Yet often, especially in dealing with animals that are both less exceptional and more closely related to man on the evolutionary ladder, Stubbs begins to reveal an intense empathy into the life and mysterious emotions of such dumb creatures. James Barry's comment on one of Stubbs's paintings of a tiger of the 1760's (Plate 23)[32] is telling, for he described it as "a tyger lying in his den large as life, appearing as it were disturbed and listening."[33] The possibility of emotional projection into the feelings of subhuman beings — what Ruskin was later to call the "pathetic fallacy" — was made even greater in Stubbs' many variations on the theme of a white Arab stallion attacked by a lion, a motif that, beginning in the 1760's, he treated often as a terrifying narrative sequence in which we first watch the lion stalking the horse, then confronting it suddenly, and finally leaping upon its back and clawing its flesh (Plate 24).[34] At times, even the landscape reverberates with the terror emanating

30. On this painting, see George Clutton, "The Cheetah and the Stag," *Burlington Magazine* CXII, August 1970, pp. 536-539.

31. No. 318. It was there titled *A Portrait of the Kongouru from New Holland, 1770.* For further comments on the painting, see the exhibition catalogue, *George Stubbs,* London, Whitechapel Gallery, 1957, no. 52. A pencil drawing of a kangaroo (now in the British Museum) was made on the voyage by Sydney Parkinson.

32. There are, in fact, many variants of Stubbs' paintings of tigers that need disentangling. This one may be that exhibited at the Society of Artists, 1769, no. 175.

33. *The Works of James Barry*, I, London, 1809, p. 23.

34. The fullest effort to clarify the origins of this motif in Stubbs' art and to compile his many variations upon it is Basil Taylor, "George Stubbs: 'The Lion and Horse' Theme," *Burlington Magazine* CVII, February 1965, pp. 81-86.

from this brutal drama.

Such an awakening of sympathy with the suffering and passions of animals — so characteristic a symptom of the new (Romantic) sensibility — could be exemplified at the same time in Joseph Wright of Derby's famous *Experiment on a Bird in an Airpump*, exhibited at the Society of Artists in 1768 (Plate 7).[35] Especially by comparison with a contemporary French version of the same scientific experiment, that by Charles-Amédée-Philippe Van Loo (1719-95), exhibited at the Salon of 1771 (Plate 25),[36] Wright's interpretation reveals a wholly new sympathy with the plight of this victim to science. In the French Rococo painting, none of the aristocratic spectators seems to care about the bird in the glass bell, who must gradually suffocate in order to demonstrate that the oxygen being pumped from its vitreous prison is necessary to sustain life; whereas in Wright's record of the same experiment, in which so many animals suffered cruel deaths in the late seventeenth and early eighteenth century, we are acutely aware of the two young girls' responses to the fluttering of the expiring bird. The younger child looks up innocently, naive and confused; but the elder one cannot bear the spectacle and must shield her eyes. Such new sensibilities toward other than human feelings are the pictorial manifestations of the new anti-Cartesian attitudes toward animals in the mid-eighteenth century, exemplified not only in the poems of Richard Jago and William Shenstone, but in such a humanitarian treatise as that of 1776 by the Reverend Humphrey Primatt, *A Dissertation on the Duty of Mercy and the Sin of Cruelty to Brute Animals*.[37] And it might be added that the consequences of this new

35. No. 193. For more on this painting, see Nicolson, *op. cit.*, I, cat. no. 192. For some remarks on the scientific history of the experiment, see Ruthven Todd, *Tracks in the Snow*, London, 1946, pp. 10 ff.

36. No. 25. *L'Expérience Physique d'un Oiseau privé d'air, sous le récipient de l'ancienne Machine Pneumatique.* For some contemporary critical comments on this painting, complaining of the indifference of the spectators present at the experiment, see Jean Seznec, ed., *Diderot Salons*, IV, Oxford, 1967, p. 132. I am indebted to Mr. Peter Walch for providing me with a photograph of this painting.

37. My information about these early Romantic attitudes toward animals stems mainly from Dix Harwood, *Love for Animals and How it Developed in Great Britain*, New York, 1928.

empathy toward animals, expressed with fresh poignancy in the period 1760-80, were enormous, not only in pictorial art but in cultural manifestations ranging from the establishment of Humane Societies to the popular mythologies of Walt Disney.

Just as it explored with new sensibility unfamiliar landscapes, peoples, and animals, British painting began to reveal, in the same decades, a rapidly growing empathy with a wide variety of historical times and places, which were pictorially reconstructed with the increasing accuracy characteristic of the later eighteenth-century penchant for accumulating precise encyclopaedic data. The work of Benjamin West provides an especially telling example of this new mobility of historical fact and feeling; for at the Royal Academy Exhibition of 1773, he followed his earlier, innovative *Death of General Wolfe* (Plate 9) — a scene from contemporary history that represented, in the guise of a traditional Pietà group, the martyrdom of the 32-year-old British general, dead for his country on September 13, 1759 on the Plains of Abraham outside Quebec[38] — with two other paintings that represented the deaths of great historical military heroes. One was that of Epaminondas, the Theban general who died fighting the Spartans at Mantinea in 362 B.C., (Plate 26); the other was that of the Chevalier Bayard, the noble French warrior, "sans peur et sans reproche," who died in A.D. 1524, fighting the Italians at the Battle of the Sesia (Plate 27).[39] The trio of paintings therefore took the same mournful motif — the tragic expiration of a great national hero in battle — and simply transposed it, as it were, from one historical milieu to another, providing in each case an effort to reconstitute the historical truth about costumes, decor, *et al.*[40]

38. Exhibited R.A. 1771, no. 210. For an excellent discussion of the *Death of Wolfe*, including a comparison with Van Dyck's *Pietà*, see Charles Mitchell, "Benjamin West's 'Death of General Wolfe' and the Popular History Piece," *Journal of the Warburg and Courtauld Institutes*, VII, 1944, pp. 20-34.

39. R.A. 1773, nos. 304, 305. For further details on the *Epaminondas* and *Bayard*, see the catalogue entries in Oliver Millar, *The Later Georgian Pictures in the Collection of Her Majesty the Queen*, London, 1969, nos. 1156, 1157. For comments on the importance of Bayard for late eighteenth-century painting, see also Rosenblum, *Transformations* . . . , p. 34, n. 107.

40. The classic treatment of these changes is that of Edgar Wind, "The Revolution of History Painting," *Journal of the Warburg Institute*, II, 1938-39, pp. 116-127. For an amplification of some of these ideas see Rosenblum, *op. cit.*, pp. 34 ff.

Such themes from Greco-Roman history were to be sure familiar enough in the Western tradition of painting, though resurrected with new enthusiasm by West and other British artists in the 1760's; but the paralleling of such themes in terms of contemporary history and medieval history[41] inaugurated the new historical mobility of the later eighteenth century, which was to leave so thorough a mark on all later attitudes toward the recording of historical events, past or present.

Moreover, the same kind of mobility extended to more imaginative literary or mythological themes. Thus, the same motif − a tragic death in some remote setting − could be found in the 1770's in the context of a Greek mythological theme, as in James Barry's *Death of Adonis*, a brooding lamentation in a bleak and agitated landscape, exhibited at the Royal Academy in 1775 (Plate 28);[42] or in the context of an Ossianic legend, as in the *Death of Oscar* by Alexander Runciman (1736-85), a drawing of 1772 that reflects the artist's painted decorations, now destroyed, at Penicuik House in Scotland, where the first important illustrations to James Macpherson's collection of poetic forgeries, *The Works of Ossian* (1765), were to be found, long before this archaizing fantasy swept the imaginations of so many Continental artists.[43]

In the 1760's and 1770's, British artists began to explore with new zeal, curiosity, and passion an ever-growing repertory of literary sources that, more and more often, were chosen to provide dramatic themes which demanded of artist and specta-tor an intense involvement with emotions of pity and terror. Strong feelings like these were, of course, hardly new to Western art, but they were virtually new to British and even

41. The turn to medieval history in British painting of the 1760's and 1770's is a phenomenon traditionally associated with early Romanticism in a kind of false opposition (i.e. Romantic versus Neoclassic) to the revival of Greco-Roman history at exactly the same time. However, these historical period pieces, whether classical or medieval, are two sides of the same coin. For a useful list of the growing number of medieval subjects in British painting, beginning in 1769, see Anthony Blunt, *The Art of William Blake*, New York, 1959, p. 7, n. 16.

42. No. 20. Horace Walpole commented that it was "very strange and glaring."

43. The basic study of Ossianic illustrations is that by Henry Okun, "Ossian in Painting," *Journal of the Warburg and Courtauld Institutes*, III, 1967, pp. 327-356. The Penicuik House decorations are discussed *ibid.*, pp. 331-334.

Continental art of the eighteenth century, whose first six decades only rarely produced paintings that investigated fully the potentials of human suffering, violence, horror, and helplessness. For one, the theme of a human being exposed to malevolent nature suddenly appears in multiple literary guises. Already in the 1760's, Richard Wilson illustrated legends of heavenly destruction, as couched, for example, in his several versions of the tragic myth of the deaths of the children of Niobe, pitted on earth against the airborne fury of Apollo and Diana in stormy landscape of blasted trees;[44] or in the modern literary stimulus of James Thomson's *Seasons* (1726-30), where in the section, *Summer* (vv. 1191-1214), the pathos-ridden story of the lovers Celadon and Amelia is told (Plate 29).[45] Like a modern daughter of Niobe, Amelia was struck dead by lightning in a summer storm in the very arms of her lover Celadon, a theme of tragic destiny and evil nature that had great issue in later Romantic painting. Indeed, another version of the subject by William Williams (active 1763-94),[46] probably exhibited at the Royal Academy of 1778 (Plate 30),[47] may suggest not only the continuing popularity of the theme, but the way in which the dramatic apparatus of wild nature and extravagant passions tends to be inflated as one traces a Romantic motif from its origins in the 1760's into later eighteenth- and nineteenth-century decades.

Comparable in its stirring drama of furious nature and human suffering is the newly popular theme of King Lear in the Storm, a Shakespearean subject already essayed by several artists in the 1760's. A precocious version of c. 1762 by George Romney (1734-1802) is remarkably clumsy, almost the work of a primitive painter, but the very fact of its existence attests to

44. This version is probably that exhibited at the Society of Artists, 1760, no. 72. For comments on Wilson's other variants of this theme, see W. G. Constable, *op. cit.*, pp. 160-163.

45. This version is probably that exhibited at the Society of Artists, 1765, no. 157: *A Summer Storm with the Story of the Two Lovers from Thompson* [sic] *(Celadon and Amelia)*. See *ibid.*, p. 165.

46. On this little-known artist, see the basic biography in Colonel Grant, *op. cit.*, III, p. 227.

47. No. 346. A later version, signed and dated 1784, is in the Tate Gallery, London, and is still more extravagant in its landscape.

the strong new emotions sought out by artists in this innovative decade (Plate 31).[48] Far more convincing is the small, but torrential interpretation of the theme by John Runciman (1744-68), executed in Rome in 1767 (Plate 32). Here, the literal details of the text are drastically altered — Shakespeare's scene, after all, should take place on a heath, not by a stormy sea that washes up drowned bodies — in order to convey not a literal record of a staged production but rather the artist's totally imaginative and passionate response to the plight of Shakespeare's King.[49]

Other literary sources produced similar dramatic collisions of man against an overpowering nature. Once more, Macpherson's Ossianic poems could provide such a subject in the episode of Fingal Engaging the Spirit of Loda, a moment of legendary battle between a human hero and a tempestuous, godlike spirit who lives in clouds. It was a scene again included in Alexander Runciman's decorations at Penicuik House, now known only through a drawing of 1772 (Plate 33),[50] but one whose cataclysmic waves and idealized archaic warrior established an aura of elemental heroism and primitive nature that was to reverberate in such later, Continental illustrations to Ossian as those by the German-Danish master, Asmus Jakob Carstens.[51]

Even more heroic in its legendary grandeur was James Barry's interpretation, also of the 1770's, of the almost unbearable suffering of the hero of Sophocles' tragedy, *Philoctetes,* who was abandoned on the Island of Lemnos to the brutality of nature. A classical Robinson Crusoe, Philoctetes is seen in savage isolation, his long hair and beard windswept against a stormy sky and blasted tree, his left foot bandaged after

48. On this painting see the exhibition catalogue, *George Romney, Paintings and Drawings,* Kenwood, Iveagh Bequest, 1961, no. 5.

49. The basic study of this painting is that by W. M. Merchant, "John Runciman's 'King Lear in the Storm'," *Journal of the Warburg and Courtauld Institutes,* XVII, 1954, pp. 385-387. The most conspicuous later interpretation of this subject is that by Benjamin West of 1789 for the Boydell Shakespeare Gallery, discussed in Cummings and Staley, *op. cit.,* no. 51.

50. See Okun, *ibid.*

51. For Carstens' illustration to this scene, a painting of 1797, see Alfred Kamphausen, *Asmus Jakob Carstens,* Neumünster in Holstein, 1941, p. 214, Pl. 26.

the bite of the snake, his only means of survival (a bird shot down with an arrow) lying beneath his ragged draperies. Characteristically, Barry's engraving of 1777 (Plate 34) is even more dramatic than his first painted version of the theme of 1770.[52] If anything, nature has become yet more savage and Philoctetes' expression still more agonized and heroic.

Indeed, the 1770's seemed to establish a rivalry among artists for subjects of uncommon anguish and horror. In their search for literary stimuli of unfamiliar grisliness, British artists freshly examined, for one, Spenser's *Faerie Queene*, which, for Benjamin West, yielded not only such an agreeable allegorical theme as Una's mastery of a lion,[53] but more to the horrific point, the blood-curdling description of the Cave of Despair (I, ix, 28 ff.). Probably following the macabre visual clues first offered by the Swiss-born Henry Fuseli (1741-1825), who, at the very end of his first London sojourn (1763-69), illustrated both this[54] and another fantastic theme from Spenser (the vision of the Faerie Queene to the sleeping Prince Arthur), West introduced to the Royal Academy in 1773,[55] a full-scale painted illustration, reeking with Gothic horror, of the passage in question (Plate 35). His work shows Una preventing the Red Cross Knight from taking his own life with a dagger, confronted as he is by the melancholic spectacle of Despair, a medieval Philoctetes who sits like a benumbed madman beside a grim array of suicidal instruments: fire, rope, poison. A new victim of suicide ("a drearie corse ... all wallowed in his own yet luke-warme blood") is seen in the righthand corner, while

52. This earlier painted version of 1770 (Bologna, Accademia di San Lucca) is illustrated and discussed in David Irwin, *English Neoclassical Art*, London, 1966, pp. 39-40, Pl. 18. For further comments on the theme of Philoctetes in Romantic art, see Rosenblum, *Transformations* ... , p. 13, n. 35.

53. West's *Una and the Lion* was exhibited at the R.A., 1772, no. 74. It is now in the Wadsworth Atheneum, Hartford.

54. The subject of Fuseli's weird drawing was first recognized in Helmut von Erffa, "An Unidentified Subject by Fuseli Identified," *Burlington Magazine*, LXXXIX, August 1947, pp. 106-107. Further information about this work, in particular, and Fuseli, in general, will be available shortly in the large monograph and catalogue scheduled for publication in 1971 and kindly made available to me in proof stage by its author: Gert Schiff, *Oeuvre-Katalog, Johann Heinrich Füssli, 1741-1825*, cat. no. 338.

55. No. 309. Horace Walpole called it "outré."

above, a hideous armored skeleton is crowned by "a ghastly owle."

At the same Royal Academy exhibition, that of 1773,[56] these medieval horrors were duplicated by Reynolds himself, in his illustration to that most harrowing passage from Dante's *Inferno* which describes the Count Ugolino's incarceration with his children in the Tower of Famine (XXXIII, vv. 37 ff.) (Plate 36). Although Reynolds' subject paintings of the early 1770's generally conformed to the more Rococo taste suggested by such a title of his as *Venus Chiding Cupid for Learning to Cast Accompts*, a painting exhibited two years earlier at the Royal Academy,[57] here he turned to a completely contrary mode that not only rejected the usual eroticism of his subject paintings but even their Greco-Roman sources. In 1719 Jonathan Richardson had in fact already spoken of the possibility of this horrific passage in Dante as a subject for a painter, as it once had been for a Renaissance sculptor,[58] but it was not until 1773, upon the first wave of Romantic awakening, that any eighteenth-century artist, British or Continental, essayed this theme. Reynolds shows us the awful moment that followed the closing of the prison door behind the Count and his children, a moment at which the youngest son Anselmo asks, with poignantly childish innocence, what has happened. The despair of the elder children at the right and the glazed, nearly mad stare of Ugolino himself prepare the spectator for the even greater horrors of starvation and possibly even cannibalism that followed in Dante's text. How precocious Reynolds was in illustrating this theme, so popular in later Romantic art through Rodin, is suggested by the fact that the first painting of this subject in

56. No. 243, entitled *Count Hugolino* [sic] *and his children in the dungeon* (with the relevant passage from Dante quoted in the catalogue). The original painting is at Knole, but in such poor condition that much of it is illegible.

57. R.A. 1771, no. 156. The painting is in the Iveagh Bequest, Kenwood.

58. In his *Discourse on the Science of a Connoisseur*, pp. 25 ff. The sculpture he had in mind is a relief now attributed to Pierino da Vinci, but considered in the eighteenth century to be by Michelangelo. For a discussion of Richardson, Reynolds, and other Ugolinesque matters, see the basic article by Frances A. Yates, "Transformations of Dante's Ugolino," *Journal of the Warburg and Courtauld Institutes*, XIV, January-June 1951, pp. 92-117. For further references to Dante illustrations see Rosenblum, *Transformations* . . . , p. 169, n. 76.

France did not appear until the Salon of 1800.[59]

Modern literature as well could provide the dreadful motif of a particularly brutal imprisonment, a subject that was sure to elicit the spectator's most heartfelt empathy. Thus, a passage from Sterne's immensely popular *Sentimental Journey* of 1768 stimulated the imagination of at least two British artists of these early Romantic decades, John Hamilton Mortimer (1740-79) and Wright of Derby. In 1774, the former artist exhibited a drawing at the Society of Artists (now lost, but preserved in an etching of 1781) that illustrated the scene of "The Captive," i.e., Yorick's imaginary projection of himself as a prisoner, deprived of liberty and left to languish in a dungeon.[60] In the same year, Wright, then in Italy, made the first of his several painted versions of the theme, one of which was finally exhibited at the Royal Academy in 1778.[61] Both artists included some of the literal details in Sterne's description of prison horrors, whether the "little straw," which served alternately as the captive's chair and bed, the "little calendar of small sticks," or the "rusty nail" with which he etched "another day of misery to add to the heap." Again, such British innovations of the 1770's, in which the spectator was suddenly to imagine himself immersed in the full horrors of incarceration, prophesied the prison and madhouse milieus that were to become so ubiquitous a setting for later Romantic art, opera, and literature.

The emotional and thematic range of these new horror paintings of the 1760's and 1770's was the same as that of the new Gothic novel, and like that literary genre, included the spine-chilling apparatus of the supernatural. Thus, themes of sorcery and hallucination begin to rear their fantastic heads at exactly this time; and again, the iconographic sources are far-reaching. From Spenser, Fuseli could seize, in a drawing of

---

59. This painting, by Fortuné Dufau, is discussed in R. Rosenblum, "Who Painted David's 'Ugolino'?" *Burlington Magazine*, CX, November 1968, pp. 621-626.
60. Mortimer's version is discussed by Benedict Nicolson in his exhibition catalogue, *John Hamilton Mortimer, A.R.A., 1740-1779*, Towner Art Gallery, Eastbourne and Iveagh Bequest, Kenwood, 1968, no. 82.
61. No. 360. On Wright's versions of this subject, see Nicolson, *Joseph Wright of Derby* . . . , pp. 60-61, 150-151, and cat. nos. 216-217.

c. 1769, the visionary appearance of the Faerie Queen to the sleeping Prince Arthur (I, ix, 13)[62] in a composition dependent upon that famed seventeenth-century Italian master of the horrific, Salvator Rosa (Plate 37);[63] and the Old Testament itself could provide a passage of eerie necromancy in the theme of Saul and the Witch of Endor, who conjures up the ghost of Samuel (First Book of Samuel, XXVIII, 1-14), a passage illustrated by Benjamin West in a painting of 1777[64] that again depends closely upon Rosa's prototype for its repertory of ragged silhouettes and terrified reflexes (Plate 38).[65]

Other scenes of necromancy, classical or medieval, may be exemplified in such works as Mortimer's *Sextus the Son of Pompey Applying to Erictho to Know the Fate of the Battle of Pharsalia*, a painting exhibited at the Society of Artists in 1771 (Plate 39)[66] which, combining zeal for both classical tradition and Romantic horror, selects a particularly ghastly passage from Lucan's *Pharsalia* that described the witch Erictho resurrecting a mangled corpse by lashing it with snakes; or in Wright of Derby's *Alchemist* (also exhibited in 1771 at the Society of Artists[67]), a scene of medieval magic that locates us in a spooky Gothic interior which, with its dark vaults and eerie illumination by phosphorus, candlelight, and full moon, provided

62. On this drawing, see Schiff, *op. cit.*, cat. no. 337.

63. Fuseli's drawing borrows from Rosa's *Dream of Aeneas* (now in the Metropolitan Museum of Art, New York). It is illustrated, together with a related drawing and print, in Luigi Salerno, *Salvator Rosa*, Milan, 1963, figs. 67a, b, c. Rosa's importance for the development of British Romantic horror painting is enormous, as it is for the development of the wilder aspects of Romantic landscape painting. For a discussion of Rosa's impact on a particular Romantic artist, see John Sunderland, "John Hamilton Mortimer and Salvator Rosa," *Burlington Magazine*, CXII, August 1970, pp. 520-531.

64. For further data on West's painting, see the exhibition catalogue, *The World of Benjamin West*, Allentown Art Museum, Allentown, Pa., 1962, p. 11.

65. Rosa's painting of this subject, a popular one in Romantic art, is in the Louvre (illustrated in Salerno, *op. cit.*, Pl. XXIV).

66. No. 84. For further comments on this painting, see Rosenblum, *Transformations . . .*, pp. 11-12. In the preceding year, 1770, Mortimer exhibited at the Society of Artists another scene of sorcery (no. 88, *An Incantation*). A mezzotint after this painting, now destroyed, is illustrated in the catalogue, *John Hamilton Mortimer . . .*, no. 100.

67. No. 207. For a detailed discussion of Wright's painting, which was reworked by the artist in 1795, see the interpretation by Frederick Cummings, "Folly and Immutability in Two Romantic Paintings: *The Alchemist* and *Democritus* by Joseph Wright," *Art Quarterly*, XXXIII, Autumn 1970, pp. 247-275.

exactly the kind of ambiance that would have thrilled visitors to Walpole's new Gothic folly, Strawberry Hill, or readers of his Gothic novel, *The Castle of Otranto* (1764) (Plate 40).

Within this new pictorial ambiance of shuddering and terror, Death itself often appeared in many new guises. In Reynolds' own work, usually rational and witty, one finds an unexpected intrusion of the macabre as early as 1768-69 in a mysterious allegorical painting (Plate 41).[68] Here, a sick child, held by a mother who resembles a secularized Titian Madonna, has been saved by an angel from the assault of Death in the form of a shadowy skeleton, scythe in hand, who stalks off defeated. A similar deathly apparition is found in Wright of Derby's illustration to Aesop's fable of *The Old Man and Death*, a painting exhibited at the Society of Artists in 1774,[69] in which a weary woodchopper idly asks that death relieve him of his burden, which request is instantly granted in the form of a skeleton bearing the arrow of death (Plate 42).

The thematic similarities of Wright's and Reynolds' works may also help to emphasize the growing stylistic polarity that emerged in British art of these two crucial decades, i.e., on the one hand, a highly abstract mode of vision that created an unreal ambiance for scenes of imaginary grandeur, terror, fantasy, and allegory (a current pursued by Barry, Mortimer, Fuseli, and Blake, among others[70]); on the other, an intensely empirical mode of vision that created a growingly factual ambiance of sharply focused, literal detail which, in the case of such an apparitional scene as Wright's, almost produces a proto-Surrealist effect. The contrast between these two divergent pictorial modes can again be seen in two other works of the 1770's that deal with the horrific theme of death's sudden appearance. *Watson and the Shark* (Plate 43), the famous painting by John Singleton Copley (1738-1815) first exhibited

---

68. This strange work, listed in Waterhouse's catalogue (*Reynolds* . . . , p. 60), needs study.

69. No. 321. For the most recent consideration of this often-discussed painting, see Nicolson, *Joseph Wright of Derby* . . . , pp. 55-56 and cat. nos. 220-222.

70. This horrific, abstract trend in British painting of the late eighteenth century was first defined in Geoffrey Grigson, "Painters of the Abyss," *Architectural Review*, CVIII, October 1950, pp. 215-220.

at the Royal Academy in 1778,[71] offers, as it were, the documentary, journalistic counterpart to such scenes of apocalyptic horror as Mortimer's *Death on a Pale Horse* (Plate 44), a drawing first exhibited in 1775 at the Society of Artists[72] and then circulated, after the artist's death, in an etching of 1784. Copley chills the spectator's spine by illustrating, as the Royal Academy catalogue defined it, "a fact which happened," i.e., the hairbreadth escape of Sir Brook Watson, later to be Lord Mayor of London, who, in 1759, as a fourteen-year old boy, was attacked by a shark while swimming in the harbor of Havana. In two assaults the beast bit off Watson's lower right leg, but was then, like Reynolds' menacing death, diverted. Mortimer's sudden vision of thundering death is another matter, culled as it is, not from journalistic truth, but from the Book of Revelations (VI, 8). Visionary rather than empirical, it plunges us into a domain of imaginary horror that, indeed, was to set afire the imagination of many Romantic artists and even poets to come, from Benjamin West himself, who, beginning in the 1780's, made many versions of the theme, including one that crossed the Channel for the Paris Salon of 1802,[73] to Turner, in his spectral fantasy of c. 1830,[74] to Baudelaire, who, in *Les Fleurs du Mal*, included a poem inspired by Mortimer's engraving.[75]

Such an evolutionary pattern – in which a Romantic seed first planted in the 1760's and 1770's continues to bear fruit into the nineteenth century – is, indeed, as typical in the history of art as in the history of literature. Again, in a British

71. No. 65. For a full discussion of the painting and its variant versions, see Jules David Prown, *John Singleton Copley (in England, 1774-1815)*, II, Cambridge, Mass., 1966, pp. 267 ff. and 459-460.

72. No. 183. For the fullest discussion of this visionary drawing and print, its sources and consequences, see Norman D. Ziff, "Mortimer's 'Death on a Pale Horse'," *Burlington Magazine*, CXII, August 1970, pp. 531-535.

73. This version is amply discussed in Fiske Kimball, "Benjamin West au Salon de 1802, *La mort sur le cheval pâle*," *Gazette des Beaux-Arts*, VII, June 1932, pp. 403-410.

74. For a brief discussion of Turner's painting, see *The Romantic Movement*, Arts Council of Great Britain, 1959, no. 358. The painting, generally called *A Skeleton Falling off a Horse in Mid-Air* (Tate Gallery, no. 5504), appears to be an imaginative variation on the more literal earlier illustrations of *Death on a Pale Horse*.

75. See Ziff, *op. cit.*, pp. 532 f.

context, one may consider a precocious painting by the Welsh artist, Thomas Jones (1742-1803), an illustration to Thomas Gray's *The Bard* exhibited at the Society of Artists in 1774 (Plate 45).[76] Following closely the literal detail of Gray's Pindaric ode of 1757, a work that tells of the vengeance of the one Welsh bard who survived the slaughter inflicted upon his brethren by the conqueror Edward I, Jones evokes the sublime mood of a desolate, primitive landscape (complete with Stonehenge-like menhirs and dolmens); of a breathtaking precipice that looks down "O'er old Conway's foaming flood"; of "affrighted ravens" and a "famished eagle"; and of the legendary bard himself, with his "beard and hoary hair / Streamed like a meteor, to the troubled air." The pictorial translation of these early Romantic poetic tremors was only the beginning of a long series of British artists' painted and drawn illustrations to Gray's windswept, melancholy theme, which ranged from works by Fuseli and Blake to Corbauld and John Martin.[77]

In fact, such later Romantic deductions were drawn from almost every Romantic premise of the period, 1760-80, discussed in these pages. For example, the sudden emergence of sublime landscape in this period in the works of Wilson, Barret, Hodges would be aggrandized even further in such High Romantic gargantuanism as James Ward's immense painting of the Yorkshire wonder, *Gordale Scar* of 1811-15 (Plate 46),[78] a sublime site already admired, "not without shuddering," by Thomas Gray in 1769;[79] and the blinding whirlpools of malevolent nature, found as early as John Runciman's *King*

76. No. 123. For further references to this painting, see the exhibition catalogue, *Thomas Jones (1742-1803)*, Marble Hill House, Twickenham and National Museum of Wales, Cardiff, 1970, no. 8; as well as the *Annual Report, National Museum of Wales*, LVIII (1964-65), Cardiff, 1965, p. 31.

77. For some considerations of British Romantic artists' illustrations to Gray, see Arthur Marks, "The Source of John Martin's 'The Bard'," *Apollo*, LXXXIV, August 1966, suppl., pp. 1-2; and Irene Tayler, *Blake's Illustrations to the Poems of Gray*, Princeton, 1971.

78. On Ward's gigantic painting (R.A. 1815, no. 255), see also *The Romantic Movement*, Arts Council of Great Britain, 1959, no. 369.

79. For Gray's famous description, see the journal entry of 13 October 1769 in *Correspondance of Thomas Gray* (eds. P. Toynbee and L. Whibley), III, Oxford, 1935, pp. 1106-1107.

Lear in the Storm of 1767 (Plate 32), would reach their climax some seventy years later in the engulfing vortices of Turner's storms. Nor should the later reverberations of these first stirrings of British Romantic art be restricted to Britain herself; for again and again, an international history of Romanticism tends to disclose that the innovations in British art of the 1760's and 1770's preceded, often by decades, the Continental absorption of these new forms, new subjects, and new emotions.[80] One need only remember, in this light, that Stubbs' visions of savage animals as metaphors of strange, subhuman passions were not to have full-scale issue in France until the work of Géricault and Delacroix some fifty years later; or that those literary heroes of international Romanticism — Ossian, Dante, Shakespeare — were first illustrated in Britain; or that the pioneers of the new late eighteenth-century wave of history painting, whether Greco-Roman, medieval, or contemporary were active in a predominantly British milieu. But such questions of the international priority of these innovations for the later development of Romantic art on the Continent are complex and can only be evoked, rather than explored, in this paper's narrower restriction to one country and two pivotal decades.

Robert Rosenblum

---

80. For some preliminary thoughts on the relation of British Romantic art to the Continent, see R. Rosenblum, "British Art and the Continent, 1760-1860," in Cummings and Staley, *op. cit.*, pp. 11-16.

Chin Nung & the
18th-Century Eccentric View

It is common enough in studying a painter that the bare facts of his life do not tell us much about his work. This, one finds, is particularly trying with regard to a Chinese painter. The Chinese biographies are especially frustrating in this respect for, as one goes through almost all of them, one ends with a few meagre facts which in the long run reveal little about what actually made him the man he was. With a Western artist we often have many important clues as to why a man acted in a certain way and how his life affected his work — as it so often did; a love affair, a trip to Rome or to the South Seas, illness, aberration, social reaction, and so on. Just to think of the wealth of material we have on the lives of the artists of the second half of the nineteenth century makes one yearn for similar material with respect to Chinese artists, for without any doubt they also were subject to social and personal influences just as strong as their counterparts in the West. Scholars of Chinese painting have barely scratched the surface of the Chinese artists' backgrounds.

The period in which the Eccentrics lived, China of the seventeenth and eighteenth centuries, in certain respects re-sembled Europe in the nineteenth century. The artistic, like the intellectual scene, was then far more complicated than in the earlier periods. In the earlier periods indeed opinions and styles changed, but far more slowly, as a great wide river shifts its banks while its main course remains comparatively stable. With the seventeenth and eighteenth centuries Chinese painting seems to have come to an area of rapids, the great river splitting up into a number of streams going like quicksilver in all directions. Traditions made sacred by repetition were being broken, rules were thrown overboard or at least questioned by a number of artists — the most noted, of course, being men like the famous Hsü Wei (1521-1593), Pa-ta-shan-jen (ca. 1625-1700) and Tao Chi (ca. 1630-1714). These men were no longer satisfied with formulae worked to death during the Ming Dynasty — the traditional *wên-jên* attitudes, those amateur scholar-official modes which in their time had added a great deal to the long achievements of Chinese painting but which now seemed lifeless. They had, in fact, reached the end of one line and started along others.

The aspirations which characterised the group of Individualists who inherited their revolutionary ideas were formulated at the beginning of the eighteenth century in a number of centres, the most important being the southern city of Yang-Chou. They considered this exciting cosmopolitan city their spiritual home and they found there during these decades the culture, the wealth and the stimulating and sympathetic atmosphere in which, within certain limits, they could work independently of economic want and intellectual restriction. The most famous group of the eighteenth-century Individualists, "The so-called Eight Eccentrics of Yang-Chou," all had their own very marked and different styles, and in speaking mainly of Chin Nung, who lived from 1687-1764, I would like to try to describe a little the atmosphere in which they lived, the social pressures on them, and how they thought. As well as saying something of their work, we should look at a few of the cultural and economic influences acting on them, to gain a deeper picture of the society in which they lived, a lively, fascinating world which is little known to the West. When I first started studying this group of painters over twenty years ago, it was necessary to persuade an audience that Chinese painting in the eighteenth century was anything but dead, or at best very sick. Fortunately this is no longer necessary. A number of outstanding scholars have recognised their efforts. James Cahill, who worked in the Freer and is now Professor at Berkeley, has taken a special interest in them, and the exhibition which he recently put on for Asia House, New York, was an eye-opener to many in the West. Even before this, Yen Shih helped Mr. W. Finlayson put an equally striking collection together in Toronto.

It is important to appreciate that Chin Nung, like so many before him, was essentially a poet as well as a calligrapher and painter. He was, in his time, a typical intellectual product of Chinese traditional education – a man of many parts and versed in many arts. During the first fifty years of his life he gained fame as a calligrapher and poet before taking up the art of painting. In fact he only started to paint when he was about sixty. It is from his poetry and from the inscriptions on his painting, these often recorded in poetic form, that we gain the most valuable insights into his life and thought. It is difficult to study the one without the other. These painters on the whole tended not to write treatises on painting or aesthetics – one must look for the clues to his social and intellectual world among what sometimes appear almost chance remarks – and believe me, as anyone who has delved into this subject well knows, this is not always an easy matter.

Chin Nung (Plate 47) was born in Hang-chou in 1687. He took his first pen name Tung-hsin or "Cold Heart," a name by which he is generally known throughout the East, in 1716, after a night of sickness. During the night of suffering he recalled a line by the T'ang poet Ts'ui Kuo-fu: "Afflicted, I nurse my Cold Heart."

During his long life of seventy-seven years he took many other fancy names, and in translating them, however inadequately such names translate, we gain some insight into his wayward personality – "The Man Detained in the Forests," "The Unofficial Historian of the Winding River," "The Old Man whose Heart is Converted to Becoming a Monk with a Begging Bowl," "The Old Man Rich in a Hundred Ink Stones," "The Fisher Master of Chin Chiang," and sometimes just simply "The Old Man."

He was fortunate to live in a wealthy, stimulating period of Chinese history. The K'ang-hsi emperor (1662-1722) was well established on the throne and peace reigned. With this peace came a prosperity which China had not known for a hundred years. The memory of the native Chinese Ming Dynasty which collapsed in 1644 had, to a certain degree, faded. There were of course loyalists and memories of loyalists who refused to be subjected to the yoke of the Manchu barbarians from the North – and, at times of strain, the Ming served as a nostalgic rallying point. Everybody revered these loyalists as models of probity but I suspect that few took them very seriously – somewhat in the way those in England regard Stuart royalists. The protests against the Manchus, which at times would be troublesome, were more often secret than overt. In the overall political scene they were relatively insignificant. Nobody could deny that China was prosperous under these barbarians who in time-honoured ways were rapidly becoming more Chinese than the Chinese. Compared with many Europeans of former dynasties, certainly many of the late Ming, the K'ang-hsi Emperor ruled with firmness but with justice. He supported traditional Chinese culture more, for instance, than the Mongols of the Yüan Dynasty. And after all, the Civil Service remained the principle means of earning a living for the educated man and it usually happened that those who *could* get in *did* get in. The overt protest was small and, in a typically Chinese way, it expressed itself in unusual and subtle ways to which I shall refer later.

It is easy to over-simplify a background as unfamiliar as that of eighteenth-century China. I must digress a little here and describe one important aspect of Chinese life at this time, which is the great Chinese Civil Service system. Each area of China was allowed to produce its quota of officials – that is to say recruiting was on a territorial rather than on a population basis. An area with a sparse population appointed as many officials as a densely populated area. Arizona say would produce as many as New York. Alaska as California. Thus in areas like the South, where our painters came from, with its great wealth and thriving culture, the scholars faced terrific competition. It is quite understandable that the Manchus arranged it thus – for the South was the last area to submit to their rule and they always regarded it with suspicion as a centre of sedition. But the system created a problem which the Manchus were never able to solve – that of the unemployed scholar; and, as we have seen even recently, unemployed scholars who feel that they are being deprived of their rights to civil service employment are always dangerous. Even employed scholars can be dangerous, but unemployed ones are pretty lethal.

This concerns us here because it exerted an influence on the concept of the scholar-official painter. Hitherto the ideal scholar-painter had been considered as an official who painted purely as an amateur and for his own pleasure. Painting, like calligraphy and poetry, was regarded as the expression of his loftiest, other worldly spirit. Thousands before, safe in administrative jobs large and small, had held to this hallowed tradition but from this time onwards many of the scholars were condemned to be much less favoured, less pampered creatures. They were often scholars without jobs who painted and practised calligraphy for a living and they found that this, as in the West, was often an extremely precarious way of keeping body and soul together, unless fame came early — as, I may say, it seldom did. They did, in fact, become professionals, which was against all the rules of propriety. I have dwelt a little on this important point because we must appreciate that it introduced into Chinese painting in these centuries a new element — the need of a painter to find or even create a clientele which appreciated his style. This in its turn made it difficult for an artist to remain outside the society to which he looked for support and heedless of its demands. He could no longer work in an ivory tower as had so many scholar-painters before him. We see these forces sharply reflected in the thoughts of these men. One feels the spectre of hunger in Chin Nung's lines such as:

> I love bamboo no less than I love beautiful women. Recently I again brandished and swept (i.e. 'painted') — often painting (or being forced to paint) for my own amusement. Occasionally I formed a plan for bartering my paintings for rice, but there have never been any successful men sending me rice in strings of boats.

— and one is touched by the number of times the mention of food comes into his comments, recurring as often as for example thoughts of sleeplessness come into the works of Shakespeare.

Chin Nung's life falls into three periods. The first ended

when he was about thirty and he spent this in his home and birthplace town of Hang-chou and devoted himself to study. The second was one of seemingly ceaseless travel during which, as many a painter before him, he saw much of China. It ended when he was sixty and was devoted mainly to poetry and calligraphy but included some painting. The third and closing period of his life, what one can call "the Yang-chou period" lasted till his death at the age of seventy-seven. During this period he led a quiet life earning a living by painting and calligraphy.

The first period was passed in a semi-rural existence. He does not mention his means of support as do many others who gained fame in this period. He does not seem to have been forced to work for a living. He speaks of a studio in a little plot of land and says he never lacked the necessities of life. His studio faced the river as he sat by its banks feasting his eyes. Later in life when things seemed far less comfortable he often referred to this idyllic time of his youth.

"South of Nan-shan," he says "in our Hang-chou the woodcutters' roads and paths along the mountain torrents all have beauty spots with bamboo thickets. Men walk beneath them and the greenness of the bamboo soaks into their garments. Now, far away, staying as a guest in Yang-chou, every time I think of them I paint their appearance and compose short poems," and he goes on to add the kind of poem which these memories inspire:

After the rain the tall bamboos are unusually green,
The cold wind whistles through them as I pass the pavilion
  by the ferry,
Everything in the world is apathetic,
There are only the autumn sounds I most love to hear.

We do not hear any of the fanciful stories of Chin Nung being an infant prodigy — as we do about so many other Chinese painters. He seems to have been a delicate child. He started his study of poetry when he was seventeen with a local teacher of no great distinction. But when he was twenty-one he was received as a student in the home of a famous scholar best known as Ho I-mên. Ho I-mên was a very talented man, distinguished principally in the field of essay writing, but also a calligrapher and a painter. This brilliant but traditional-style writer significantly enough for the life of Chin Nung also failed to get into the Civil Service. He spent most of his life as a teacher — the principle source of support for the failed civil servant. One of this man's main contributions to scholarship was in the field of *textual criticism* of which he was one of the foremost early practitioners. This subject, remote as it may seem from our interest, requires a short digression because it had a profound effect on Chinese intellectual life in the first period of the Manchu dynasty.

When the Manchus conquered China they adopted the Chinese administrative system and supported the concept of the Confucian state. They were almost inevitably forced to support the most traditional and conservative aspect of Chinese intellectual life. There then emerged from the welter of Chinese scholasticism the famous scholar Ku Yen-wu and his followers, who attributed the fall of the Ming to the empty philosophising of the Sung school of Confucianism founded by the almost canonised Chu Hsi and the Ch'en Brothers. Ku Yen-wu and his many disciples, whose names I will spare you, took their interpretations of the sacred Confucian texts from the Han dynasty nearly two thousand years before and a thousand years before the Sung dynasty of Chu Hsi. They supported their proposed rectifications of these texts with scientific and philological studies and textual criticism in the European fifteenth-century spirit. This, of course, is putting the whole important movement in a few brief words but parallel with this interest in the oldest writings, and of particular interest to us, went another movement which concentrated on the search for and study of old inscriptions on stone and metal which could support the textual criticism. The movement had influence on the Eccentric painters, who sought in these old inscriptions the justification for their own rather extraordinary calligraphy styles.

More widely speaking, the effect of the whole movement was to split the ranks of the scholars into two — the supporters of the old and of the new. It created an iconoclastic atmosphere which provided fertile fields for new ideas – especially new ideas which, and this is most vital to the understanding of these Eccentrics, could claim an antiquity of seemingly impeccable ancestry. Most of the employed scholars, the civil servants who had passed their examination to the Service on the *old* syllabus of Confucian tradition, had a vested interest in supporting the old ideas and the Sung School of commentary which the Manchus supported. Among the partisans of the new school one found most of the unemployed and original thinkers of the time. Chin Nung and his contemporaries were the immediate inheritors of the new thought founded by men like Ku Yen-wu who tried to inject new life into Chinese thought. These men introduced him to the fascinating study of old inscriptions. Two characteristic styles of Chin Nung's calligraphy which brought him fame are shown in Plates 48 and 49. One hardly needs the discipline of years of Chinese scholarship to look at them simply as works of the brush and appreciate their distinctive vitality and personality. Plate 48, in *Li Shu* style is the style by which he is best known and it springs directly from the characters cut into stone in some of the early stone inscriptions – seeming to reject the finesse and elegance of the traditional brushstrokes which fade into delicate lines and sweep in mellifluous curves. Instead of dancing over the paper this seems to sit strong and square, almost defiant.

An intimate friend of Chin Nung's early years named Li E in his book of collected poetry mentions "Chin Nung showed me a book of rubbings of inscriptions on bells of the Chin-ling period" (A.D. 707-710). The notes to the poem show it was written in 1714 when Chin Nung was twenty-seven. Now this Li E was one of the most eminent poets of his time and noted for his originality and his independence of the models formed by the two most eminent poets of this time, Wang Shih-chen and Chu Ts'un. Li E gained fame much earlier than Chin Nung and it was he who was able to introduce Chin Nung into the full intellectual life of the time at its most active. And we must assume that it was this *entrée* which enabled our painter to earn his living by teaching and enjoying the hospitality of the rich and enthusiastic patrons of the arts who were so vital to the life of the period – for we must remember that poor Chin Nung never did succeed in the examinations. He was in fact a typical *manqué* personality of a type with which we are very familiar.

These patrons played a very vital role indeed and one must mention in particular the Ma brothers of Yang-chou. These two men had amassed a large fortune from the salt trade and they spent a considerable part of it in gathering together a huge library which they installed in their garden. They lavished hospitality on their friends – on literary men and artists of all kinds, and in particular on the many poor scholars who were attracted by their open-handed hospitality and by the facilities for work and study that they provided. A history of their house, "The Little Lattice-work Pavilion in the Hills," would form a fascinating chapter for a book on patronage in Chinese art which still awaits an author.

In 1718 he began the second period of his life – his travels throughout the length and breadth of China. In 1750 he wrote a preface to his collection of inscriptions on his paintings in which he records "It is now forty years since I began my travels. I am now old and tired [he was sixty-three] and he goes on to recount all the places he had visited by land and water "sometimes travelling by chair and sometimes by boat. There were times when I sat quietly in one house without worldly desires, sometimes I had three or four students, sometimes six or seven." What a charming picture this makes of a relatively carefree life, ministered to and supported by a few pupils, generally with enough to keep body and soul together, wandering over the vast, amazing Chinese country with its endless variety, selling his work to connoisseurs and sometimes instructing pupils in it. Known as a man of genius with whom one could entrust one's children, he seems to have succeeded in supporting himself from private resources, by teaching and by selling his calligraphy which had by now become famous.

In 1735 he lived for a while in the house of a governor of a district in Chekiang who recommended him for the examination of Scholars of Wide Learning to be held in Peking in 1736. Despite the suspicion with which the ruling house regarded many of the unemployed scholars, the Manchus made a token

effort in 1736 to appease them and to bring some of the more
eminent into public life, men who, for some reason or other,
had not passed the customary exams. Many attended the
examination at Peking — most of them failed and among them
poor Chin Nung, but he records the fine time he had in the
capital that year visiting friends and seeing collections of
paintings which were later to inspire his own work. It is
interesting that the most trenchant dislikers of the regime
refused, on some excuse or other, to attend the examination
and indeed there was no shame in having failed. One suspects
that there may even have been a certain distinction attached to
having failed — anyway there was a definite cachet attached to
having been invited at all.

At this time Chin Nung started his collection of ink-stones.
He later explained his pen name "Old Man Rich in a Hundred
Ink-Stones" as "a flattering term for a vulgar peasant — I have
used my inheritance of a single ink-stone to pass my life
ploughing with the brush and weeding with the ink. What is
more I wandered everywhere and fed myself and my yearly
income is not meagre."

But like so many independent artists throughout the world,
we find on the one hand pride in independence but on the other
regrets for seeming failure. "Here I am," he says "an old man
with white hair, not having succeeded in life — I grow old and
ugly without having been married" (and by this I must hasten
to add that he is not thinking about the pleasures of conjugal
bliss but the absence of a job). But there must have been many
consolations — travels with great men and fellow artists like the
lovable painter of bamboos, Chêng Hsieh whom I shall mention
again later.

He must have been nearly sixty when he settled down in
Yang-chou for the last long period of his life — though he had
often visited the city. Jüan Yüan in his book of biographies of
Chekiang poets says, "He enjoyed hospitality for twenty years
and his writings brought in a thousand pieces of silver which he
spent as it pleased him." But according to the artist himself
things were not so easy: "I am now in Yang-chou where I have
watched the moon wax and wane five times. There is a good

handful of dust on my robe. Everyday I paint bamboos in the hope of selling them but I cannot avoid the danger of eating only three times in nine days." Even his love life seems to have been a failure, for his wife, tired by his desertion of her while he travelled around, left him and returned to her family. When she died he took a concubine but later he confesses, "Since my former wife died I have lived alone, chaste of body. Formerly I had a dumb concubine but now I have sent even *her* away" — and often he experiences the loneliness of the creative artist, as a poem of self-pity written in 1751 shows:

> As a guest my body turns a thousand times,
> Thinking of home, my heart revolves,
> In a Yang-chou kitchen with wine,
> How pitiful is this lonely cup.

or in a sad little poem on a bamboo thicket:

> One group has grown into a thicket on this bitter bamboo
>   islet,
> Branches and leaves in the cold autumn
> Acquire an air as if they were smiling gently
> They smile at me — a homeless old man with white hair.

But on the other side many monks and wealthy men helped him and he could not have been an easy guest for he went to stay with his sister for a while but couldn't stand it. Nor I suspect could she, so he turned more and more to Buddhism and lived with the monks — though I suspect that the more profound aspects of the faith meant very little to him. "I live and eat with the monks. . . . I am a decrepit old man of seventy who does not seek either prosperity or happiness. My only wishes are to enjoy the following — a deep peace and to gaze my fill on the colours of the river in front of the monasteries on the Southern bank." In fact he seems to have become so much of a recluse and a pretty testy recluse at that, that many of his friends thought he was dead — friends like Chêng Hsieh and Ting Ching, the seal carver, when they heard that he was still alive wrote to congratulate him that he had not, as they put it, "responded to the disastrous constellation." As far as we know he died a peaceful death in a Buddhist hut in Yang-chou during the autumn of 1764, and his remains were taken for burial in the family vault at Hang-chou.

Now, what I have said of Chin Nung here is the merest vignette of his interesting and long life. However, we know so little of a Chinese painter's thought and actions that, by providing some background to this extremely human character, we may appreciate his work a little more.

He did not start to paint until the last thirty or thirty-five years of his long life, towards the end of a critical period in Chinese painting. The traditional styles, the kind of elegant accomplished workmanship that we associate with the Four Wangs were the accepted form just as much as any academy styles anywhere in the world, and they received the approbation of the same kind of people we see nodding over their port and cigars at any academy dinner. To understand the new boys one has to put oneself into the kind of context that prevailed in late nineteenth-century France and twentieth-century England. We have now fully accepted or are afraid to reject what was considered revolutionary a few years ago, and the way-out, the op, the pop and what-have-you we accept today with a smile rather than a foam at the mouth — and in case we may be tempted to feel superior or complacent about this, we must remember that it has taken us nearly a century to do so.

In China, the movement away from the conventional, the kind of work which ended in the famous manuals of painting which purported to instruct anybody who could read and write in the mysteries of painting, began in serious in the sixteenth century. There were what the Chinese call I-p'in and we translate as "Untrammeled Painters" way back in the history of the art. These were the men the Chinese could not fit into any of their favourite categories. Shimada wrote about them, and Cahill translated his most interesting articles in the periodical *Oriental Art*. The Chinese never quite accepted them, and since they could not ignore them, they got the special category "untrammeled." The famous Tung Ch'i-ch'ang (1555-1636) had experimented with forms, but intellectually rather than emotionally as did the Eccentrics. As Levenson has pointed out, the Ming dynasty raised high the Confucian literati and they cherished an ideal of social stability. As a corollary, in matters of taste generally they deprecated the idea of change and the quest for originality. They were in fact classicists. Ming culture was, as Levenson indicates, the apotheosis of the amateur — and it is by no means surprising that many of the early Ch'ing artists were professionals in one way or another — though, I am sure, they would have fought to the death anybody who accused them of so being. Sometimes I think that our terms "amateur" and "professional" have little validity in this context.

And it is equally certain that the work of the Eccentrics offended their more academically-minded contemporaries. Wang Shih-min for instance, who produced landscapes, writes censoriously, "Then there came men with superficial spirits who knew nothing of the ancient traditions and who wished simply to put their own ideas into practice. They have spread false customs which have been adopted by their contemporaries and these have caused the complete abandon of the rules and traditions of preceeding generations — a tendency which has become more and more widespread." This is the kind of pontification with which many a generation has tried to stem the rising tide of the next. I do not think that Chin Nung would have accepted such a criticism for he says: "I take the brush and I paint with all seriousness. And what is more I do not violate the rules transmitted by the ancient masters." We shall try later to see what he meant by the ancient masters.

One of the main problems facing the historians at the time was, of course, the bewildering number of schools springing up — and the more "individualism" became the touchstone, the more this was bound to happen, as indeed we see about us now in the West. Wang Shih-min on this very point complains: "The students of painting these days are as numerous as the trees in the forest, and everyone of them boasts of being a great master — and nevertheless the majority do nothing more than follow the fashion of the day, there are few who know how to profit from the study of the ancient"; and Wang Hui, another of the favoured group, added: "The decline is due to the numerous schools which have abandoned the traditions during the last periods." Wang Yuan-ch'i, yet another of this group, adds his complaint that some painters were daring, as he puts it, "to question the significance of these things and they have returned towards the past, thereby becoming heterodox." The past to which he refers is, I suspect, not the hallowed past carefully traced through the traditional schools but the far-distant past to which the Individualists appealed.

I must confess that it comes as quite a shock to hear a traditional painter complaining about other painters returning to the past. These barbs were no doubt aimed at painters like Hsu Wei of the late Ming, Kung Hsien and Tao Chi, the individualist master of the seventeenth century, late-Ming-early Ch'ing. It is interesting to note here in passing that Chin Nung's friend Chêng Hsieh greatly admired Tao Chi but Chin Nung himself never mentions his work, though he certainly knew of him and felt the same way — as, for instance, he says, "My painting follows no master." We find on a bamboo painting a more explicit confession of faith: "Men of former times said that to equal the talent of others was not as valuable as having been the first to do something," or again "To follow everybody in criticising something is not as worthy as being the only one to appreciate it. I too, when I paint a bamboo, I do not follow a fashion nor do I seek a reputation for myself." He is delighted when two of his painter friends, Wang Shih-shên and Kao Hsien, praised one of his prunus paintings because, as they said, "He had the ancients before his eyes, because he did not try to obtain a realistic representation and because he was not restrained by any bonds."

We can now see a little more clearly what he was aiming at — a complete break with the past as envisaged by his contemporaries. What he calls his "strange taste" and "eccentric imagination" can be summarised by one of his maxims "The essence lies in the first impression one receives from an object beyond its external appearance."

I mentioned earlier the iconoclastic atmosphere in scholarship at this time created by the discovery of old inscriptions and texts. This gave Chin Nung what he considered a purer source for his work than that which had inspired others working around him. One piece of calligraphy done about 1736 resembles the stone carving which he studied, and is quite unlike the well-defined elegance of the model scripts. Later work, also in *Li Shu* style, is even more personalized and powerful, and we know that he used a worn out brush for this type of calligraphy which has traces of the graduated lines familiar from traditional writing.

It is important to understand this calligraphy style for it established him as a revolutionary, and when he was to turn to painting his public expected something which, in modern jargon, we would call "way out." But this is as difficult if not more difficult in painting than it is in calligraphy. The bonds of the past are never stronger than in the purely representational. Thus, in the first painting we have by him we see something which foreshadows his independence but is not overwhelmingly original (Plate 50). It is a portrait of a "Bodhidharma Crossing the River on a Branch." The date is difficult to decipher but it is probably 1744 when he was fifty-seven or fifty-eight years old — and we are told that he started to paint when he was about sixty. He says that "on the second day of the first month he washed his hands respectfully and painted it." The lines are traditional but the emphasis is placed firmly on the piercing expression, a fairly new departure but one which looks back to the untrammeled painters of the T'ang dynasty like Kuan Hsiu.

Three years later he did another painting of a monk (Plate 51) with an inscription not found in his collected works, which reads:

Very quiet and still are the empty mountains
Sufficient in themselves to cut off mundane thoughts.
How much more so are the minds of the mountain people
Transcendent and crystal clear!
Standing in solitude he forgets morning and meal-time
Nothing forced about his trance.

and he goes on to say:

Alas the people of this world
Bustling and worrying, heading towards the net of dust
I ask you — but you are silent — not a single word
How can I fathom your depth and breadth?

Here the lines are stronger and more what one would expect of his worn out brush.

Thirteen years later he did another Bodhidharma in 1758 on which he writes:

In the eighth month of the Autumn of the year *wu-yu*, I was staying in the southern part of the city. While resting from my work of painting the Buddha, I fell into a deep sleep during which I had a dream. In the dream I saw the Master Ta Mo coming across the river on a reed. He had a noble and inspiring countenance which caused my scalp to prickle. I thought I would paint a scroll of him and present it to some eminent temple where it could be worshipped forever. That dawn I arose, incensed myself, bathed and fasted. I reverently drew a portrait of the master just as I had seen him in my dream. I shall take it to the Shao-lin Monastery on Mount Kao and compare it with the true image of Master Ta-mo on the face of the rock there and see whether or not it agrees with it in every feature. If it does agree then men will not be able to say that what I have done is merely the wild dream of a foolish old man.

I must confess to my regret that I have not been able to make that same pilgrimage myself to check on Chin Nung, and there is no record of whether in fact he did so, but the power of the face is undeniable and quite unusual for Chinese painting.

Finally in this series there is a Buddhist monk painted one year later in 1759 (Plate 52) which is one of the boldest and most striking of all his works, and one which I found many years ago on a postcard in the Library of Congress. This one is as powerful as a blow in the face, its outline done with three brush strokes full of ink and a penetrating face to match. What more can one ask of an eccentric as applied to portraiture?

While on this subject I must add that the whole group were interested in portraiture and the odder the subject, the better. One of the men who played a large part in his life was a certain Ting Ching whom I mentioned briefly before. He was, according to those who wrote about him, a man of compelling personality, forthright, outspoken and not afraid of giving offence, quick of temper, especially when things did not please him. Hang Shih-chun, his son-in-law, wrote that Chin Nung used to visit him and that they studied old inscriptions together. He records, "They lived close together and at their frequent meetings Chin Nung surpassed Ting Ching in fine words and elegance, but Ting Ching excelled in logic and reasoning" and that when he let himself go he could not be restrained even by Chin Nung. He was most famous as a carver of seals and many of the group of Eccentrics came to him for seals and for frank comments on their work — discussing them in the humble hut in which he lived outside the city wall of Yang-chou. Their pleasures, we learn, were reading poetry aloud to each other and enjoying the beauties of the countryside around them.

A portrait of the famous Eccentric Seal Carver Ting Ching (Plate 53) was done by Chin Nung's most faithful pupil, Lo P'ing, one might almost say his disciple, and a man who, as Chin Nung says, "with poems for presents came to my door" at about the age of twenty-five or twenty-six and stayed with him most of his life, acting later as literary executor. He learned poetry, calligraphy and painting from the old master. The portrait of Ting Ching by Lo P'ing is human and affectionate and far removed from the stiff artificiality of traditional portraiture. It carries the idea of the Eccentrics one step further and epitomizes their interest in personality, the accent on the man as he was, an unwillingness to conceal anything behind an empty idealisation. And we see here too a typical unconventional man of the group — staff to hand to help him through the countryside, ready to stay and quote poetry or discuss painting and, one likes to think, many other things besides. In fact the atmosphere must have been much like it is in any turbulent artistic circle — hard living, hard drinking, artistically daring, non-conforming. The picture is a pretty familiar one which, transferred a few thousand miles and a century, becomes the familiar vie-de-Bohème of Paris in the nineteenth century, or anywhere.

To turn for a moment to another favourite subject of Chin Nung — that of bamboo. We know that our painter was an intimate friend of and loved that delightful reprobate, the all too human Chêng Hsieh, brilliant poet, painter, resigned Civil Servant, wine bibber, womaniser. The story is told of how he used to drink too much in "The Land of the Flowers," as they called the houses of pleasure, and when he was drunk the girls used to take rolls of paper from their sleeves and press him to paint — girlish entreaties which in his happy state he found it difficult to resist. He was expelled from the Civil Service after some floods when, seeing the misery of the peasants, he wanted to cancel all debts. This was sedition indeed — an unsanctioned New Deal if ever there was one. After that, with a few friends he travelled about the country in peasant dress, on drinking tours as they called them, sometimes painting orchids, rocks, bamboos on the verandahs where they drank or poems on temple walls. He had a modest scale of charges ranging from five cash for a fan to six taels for a large scroll — and the records leave it in no doubt that he was extremely popular. As I mentioned earlier, he admired Chu Ta and Tao Chi and he was a great friend of Li Shan, another of the eight Eccentrics. Orchids and bamboo were his constant subjects. Chin Nung thought his work "scattered" and said that he carried incoherence to the extreme without ever losing refinement. Thus Chin Nung's early bamboos are somewhat in the Chêng Hsieh style, but this kind of refined elegance was not in the Chin Nung vein and he abandoned it. An album leaf of 1755 is very Chêng Hsieh but has an amusing inscription in poetry:

> During the night the spring thunder beats out its first sounds,
> The full mountain of new bamboo shoots are like facets of jade,
> I bought them and stewed them together with the meat of a piebald pig,
> I did not ask my kitchen maid to cook them for me but asked the Old Monk.[1]

In 1760, four years before his death, he did a bold bamboo (Plate 54) in which he claims that he emulated the spirit of the T'ang dynasty painter Wang Shih-ch'eng as far as he knew what

1. A sly reference to a friend more gourmet than himself.

this meant, and he says he used the red ink of the Sung dynasty Su Tung-p'o, who did a famous red bamboo, in order, as he says, to cause those who see them to admire "this gentleman [the usual synonym for bamboo] with his empty heart, lofty character and face as if touched with rouge." He was now seventy-four.

Another popular subject was, of course, prunus and most painters tried their hand at this. Here too he started in a fairly traditional course enjoying the purity and the subtle skill of Yüan dynasty painters like the famous Wang Mien. "To paint plum trees" he says "one must paint their approaching coldness in the evening, in such a way that the trees will have no ugliness in their appearance and their fragrance will saturate the sleeves." "They must be like herons standing in a frozen shallow." "Sparse and graceful" he said they must be, and on another inscription he says, delightfully I think,

The sparrows are twittering, suddenly a fragrance is blown into my house. A single blossom catches the eye. Is it snow? Is it a plum blossom?

He admires the purity of the cold fragrance of a masterpiece. I quote almost at random from the inscriptions on his plum blossom:

The shadows of the slanting plum blossoms are on the West side of the wall,
Eight or nine out of ten of the flowers are already open,
By perverse chance the East wind is full of frolics,
It blows them in confusion, in confusion drops them and in confusion contaminates them with the wet earth.

With the passing of time, again we see the vigour of his brush and mind strengthening what had always been such a delicate subject. With the comparison of an old gnarled trunk with a few flowers on a young branch, (Plate 55) he intensifies the emotion, dramatises the theme, breaks down the barriers of gentility which had always surrounded this subject.

It is not possible here to cover all the facets of Chin Nung's production and before considering the landscapes I would like to draw attention to one example from his group of horse paintings (Plate 56). Throughout the paintings on horses he frequently mentions his admiration for the horse paintings of the Sui and T'ang dynasties, but in this particular painting I suspect he is pulling the legs of his stuffy contemporaries more than just a little. The inscription reads "To sweep a galloping horse with a worn brush" — that is the superb quality of the horse paintings done by Wei Hou Yen (a T'ang dynasty painter from whose hand, we must add, nothing has survived). "In the first year of Ch'ien-lung [1736] I saw a scroll by him of a horse covered with a red saddle blanket in the house of the Vice-Minister Wang in the capital[2] and I wrote a poem on the left of it. After the death of the Vice-Minister this painting was stolen by a lowly servant and came into the possession of a gruel shop in the Inner City. Now, snatching up my brush and recalling its idea of what is called 'with one dot for the head and one sweep for the tail' I have reproduced it on this plain silk. Whenever I come to the festival of the third day of the third month, the occasion of washing one's cloth, I cannot help cherishing the idea that in the slanting sun and fragrant grasses, the scented wheels of some beauty are retreating farther and farther into the distance." The painting is dated 1760 and is in the famous Abe Collection in Osaka.

I have not been able to determine what he means by "the scented wheels of some beauty retreating into the distance," but to understand this old nag one must have read an earlier inscription on a horse painting where he makes a joke at what he calls the two "firsts" in his family. Two of his ancestors came out top in the examinations and, as was the custom, were led round the capital on a fine steed, bedecked with almond blossoms, the admiration of the world, their future guaranteed and a minister's daughter to wed. But then he asks "Why is so much importance attached to a 'first'-class honours. In three years time anyway there will be another one. Scholars, anybody and everybody can do it. What is really unusual lies in the achievement of a man's life not decaying after him." And here, instead of painting a handsome horse, he does an old broken

---

2. I imagine this was when he was in Peking for the Scholars of Wide Learning Examination which he failed.

down nag, a comment on himself perhaps, broken down at the age of seventy-four and a little cynical of success.

Finally in this almost random survey of his work we must consider a few landscapes. The earliest I have dates from 1750 when he was sixty-six and shows an immortal seated on a rock:

The wind in the wood blows unceasingly
The autumn shade fades as the evening approaches.

It is a nostalgic sketch of no great pretensions but presaging the intimacy and affection which give his work so much appeal — at least to me.

About four years later, if my dating is correct, in about 1754 we find in an album a scene which is perhaps only part landscape but which, in an unpretentious way is quite unlike other Chinese painting (Plate 57): the sleepy buffalo herdsman, back to us, dozing away in the heat of the sun, and the heavy beast, shown in unusual foreshortening, tied up and resentful — a quick sketch which catches the atmosphere of noon as surely in a Chinese way as do the Impressionists in some of their paintings of French landscape.

He could do larger landscapes, as we see in Plate 58 from the collection of Wango Wang in New York. The inscription says:

The lotus flowers have opened
On the silver bank it is still — the new coldness came early,
How plentiful the jade-winged dragonflies.
Six by six the water windows open, a faint breeze stirs
    beneath her fan,
I remembered that lady with whom I sat, her delicate
    hands peeling the seed cases of the lotus.

This is a typical scholar-painting of a type which he could do but rarely did. Plate 59 is autobiographical in that it shows him at the age of seventy-five enjoying his leisure by the river he loved. The touch is that of an old man — the synthesis of a leisurely solitary life devoted to calligraphy and painting — a boat boldly placed across a river in a most original way. The key to an understanding of it lies in the little white duck which swims unconcernedly in front of the boat and the old man who pensively looks at it. And what does he say here?

I wonder if people know that I am the Fishmaster,
In the springtime boat, the white duck leads me on.

And I have often wondered what these seemingly simple lines really mean.

To end I have chosen a plaintive little scene which is somehow the very essence of Autumn (Plate 60). A man, himself no doubt, stands alone in an open thatched hut braving the first chill wind, the branches above his head bending as if they did not wish to let their last leaves escape them. A few swirl about the figure whose calm contrasts with the tension of the branches. "In the empty pavilion" he says, "I stand for a long time not without thoughts." The six leaves form the link to the various elements, the calligraphy seems to share the angular stubbornness of the tree, the hut and the figure which oppose the forces of approaching Winter, a Winter which triumphs over him as well as the countryside.

Peter Swann

Dr. Mandeville: "A Thinking Man"

"Religion is one Thing, and Trade is another."

It was Thomas Hobbes who dictated the terms and topics of philosophical debate in eighteenth century Britain. No metaphysician nor theologian, no moralist nor political writer could afford to ignore his opinions, and few could tolerate them. Hobbes was a materialist, and a pretty crude one. Since he did not aspire to the honour of martyrdom, he denied being an atheist. It is clear, nonetheless, that in his mechanical cosmos providence has been replaced by the laws of motion. He took the low view of man, a revealing perspective even if a narrow one. He sized men up as egoistic creatures moved by vanity and restrained by fear. He thought of them as discrete centres of power, each one struggling alone against the counter force of competitors toward material prosperity and social prestige. He was an ethical relativist who derived his rather unedifying moral code "from the single dictate of reason advising us to look to the preservation and safeguard of ourselves."[1] Virtue is prudence, and its aim, which he detaches from any extra-terrestial concern, is "peaceable, sociable, and comfortable living."[2] Hobbes conceived of society as an artificial arrangement for reducing the hazards of human association which is inherently competitive, mistrustful and hostile. "All society therefore," he writes, "is either for gain, or for glory; that is, not so much for love of our fellows, as for love of ourselves."[3] It is not benevolence which inhibits man's lust for power, but fear of retaliation.

According to Hobbes's anthropology, human reason

1. *Philosophical Rudiments*, Vol. II, p. 44 of *The English Works of Thomas Hobbes*, ed. Sir William Molesworth, II vols., John Bonn; Longmans Green, London, 1839-45.
2. *Leviathan, English Works*, Vol. III, pp. 146-147.
3. *Philosophical Rudiments, English Works*, Vol. II, p. 5.

emerged from the primitive depths of violent instincts as the agent of racial survival. It prescribes the laws of the secure society wherein alone each man can realize his over-riding interest in his own preservation. Since Hobbes did not exaggerate the strength of most men's reason, he delegated its repressive function to the sovereign. The citizen, who has exchanged freedom of action and conscience for the government's protection, has only one duty, and that is to obey the law. In Leviathan, moral responsibility for all other decisions is reserved for the sovereign alone.

Hobbes's ideas were generally considered detestable — wicked, blasphemous and dangerous falsehoods. Mandeville, who had been reading Hobbes during his student days at Leyden, was exceptional in responding favourably. In his own time he was regarded as a pot-house Hobbes, and it is not uncommon now for scholars to speak of the Hobbes-Mandeville view of human nature. To call Mandeville a disciple of Hobbes would be, perhaps, to exaggerate the influence of the older man. There were many other literary influences working on Mandeville, for he read widely, especially, as his faithful editor, F.B. Kaye, has shown, in French scepticism, in Bayle, La Rochefoucauld, Esprit, Montaigne, Nicole, Abbadie, Saint-Evremond. Unlike Hobbes, Mandeville was not an original thinker, but he was an original writer. He assimilated congenial ideas in bulk, readily and completely, and after retempering they appeared in his tough, racy prose with the glitter of novelty. Neither was Mandeville a systematic thinker, nor a metaphysician, whereas Hobbes was both. It is upon comparing their views of human nature, their perceptions of the volatile psychological basis of human community, that one feels Mandeville's affinity for Hobbes. Mandeville sometimes differs from Hobbes in what he says about these things, but he does not disagree with him. It is a matter of his inventing a new fable or allegory to convey an essentially Hobbesian truth about the corruption lurking at the heart of civilization.

Mandeville said that he wrote for the reader's diversion, and I conjecture that he was always glad to hear that those who were not amused were annoyed, very annoyed. The injured tone in which he complains of his book being presented by the Grand Jury of Middlesex and of being abused in journals and sermons strikes me as affected. I think that outrage was precisely the effect which he intended, a sign that his barbs had found their mark and were deeply imbedded under his victim's skin. Hobbes, who had lived through the violent times that went before Mandeville's tranquil era, had not written to divert his reader, but to teach him how society had been brought, and must be kept, under rational control. I do not think that Hobbes ever wrote expressly to shock or to scandalize. He impresses me as having that lovable ingenuousness and candour often found in exceptionally gifted thinkers. I imagine him being dismayed by the uproar provoked by his anxious reasoning about the human predicament. He only wanted to help. Mandeville's was a different case. He had somewhere lost his innocence before he began to write. He saw in Hobbes a fit accomplice in his plot to harass polite readers whose sentiments about human kind were refined and edifying but delusory.

In his native Holland Bernard de Mandeville studied philosophy and medicine. After immigrating to England he continued to practise both disciplines and in both he was a specialist. As a physician he specialized, like his father, in nerve and stomach complaints, as a philosopher in human motives and social mores. In 1711 he published *A Treatise of the Hypochondriak and Hysterick Passions*, a learned dialogue between a physician (himself, called Philopirio) and two patients, and nineteen years later a revised and expanded version, *A Treatise of the Hypochondriak and Hysterick Diseases*. This work has all the intimate charm to be expected of a four hundred page transcript of consultations between a family doctor and an ailing couple whose teen-age daughter exhibits the most unpleasant symptoms of gastric disorder. His philosophical career was inaugurated almost surreptitiously with the publication in 1705 of twenty-four pages of doggerel, *The Grumbling Hive: or, Knaves turn'd Honest*. The verse depicts the decline and fall of a once thriving bee hive after the vices that had fired industry were quenched. Before ill-considered prayers for virtue on a national scale were answered

Luxury
Employ'd a Million of the Poor,
And odious Pride a Million more:
Envy itself and Vanity,
Were Ministers of Industry;
Thus every Part was full of Vice,
Yet the whole Mass a Paradise . . .

Economic ruin follows in the wake of moral reform:

As Pride and Luxury decrease,
So by degrees they leave the Seas.
Not merchants now, but Companies
Remove whole Manufactories.
All Arts and Crafts neglected lie;
Content, the Bane of Industry,
Makes 'em admire their homely store,
And neither seek nor covet more.

Enter mass unemployment, a decimated population, an en-feebled army. The hive is overrun; the virtuous survivors fly off to a hollow tree. Mandeville draws the moral:

Then leave Complaints: Fools only strive
To make a Great an honest Hive
T'enjoy the World's Conveniencies,
Be fam'd in War, yet live in Ease,
Without great Vices, is a vain
Eutopia seated in the brain.

Nine years later, 1714, Mandeville reprinted the poem and set about explaining it through an essay, *An Enquiry into the Origin of Moral Virtue*, and twenty Remarks on various lines, although, so far as I know, no one in the meantime had asked for clarification. After another nine quiet years Mandeville brought out a new edition with further Remarks and two more essays, *A Search into the Nature of Society*, and the one which provoked the fight he had been looking for, *An Essay on Charity and Charity-Schools*. In 1728 these explanations were in turn explained by his spokesman, Cleomenes, in the six long dialogues which compose Part II of the *Fable*. Abuse of the book in the press and pulpit naturally stimulated interest, and the numerous editions and translations into French and German—are evidence of Mandeville's popularity in the eighteenth century.

Mandeville's urge to elucidate his poem by prose commentary seems to have been frustrated at the very start by a failure of communication on the title page:

The

Fable

of the

Bees:

or,

Private Vices, Publick Benefits[4]

Seventeen years later, on the last pages he ever wrote, he was still trying to straighten out the meaning of that verbless formula: "Private Vices, Public Benefits." What he meant, as he had tried to explain in 1723, by quoting the last line of the *Fable* in "A vindication of the Book," was "that Private Vices, by the dexterous Management of a skilful Politician, might be turn'd into Publick Benefits" (*Dion,*[5] 36; cf. *Fable* I, 369, 411-412). He gives as a plausible illustration a law enacted in Britain which enabled the pardoning and rewarding of an arrested felon who would impeach two or more of his accomplices or other malefactors on a capital offense. "There is no Doubt but that this is a good and wise Law" (*Dion,* 43), he says, for it reduces the criminal population. The viciousness of the defector's treachery is undeniable, but the effectiveness of the expedient has been proven:

> This shows the Usefulness of such a Law, and at the same Time the Wisdom of the Politician, by whose skilful Management the Private Vices of the Worst of Men are made to turn to a Publick Benefit (*Dion,* 45).

Mandeville agreed that another construction could be put upon his words to yield the more general and difficult thesis

4. Ed. F.B. Kaye, Oxford, Clarendon Press, 1924, 2 vols. All references to *The Fable of the Bees* are to this edition and follow quotations in parentheses.

5. *A Letter to Dion,* ed. Bonamy Dobrée, University Press of Liverpool, 1954, here called *Dion.*

that "the Vices of Man . . . are . . . inseparable from the Earthly Felicity of the Civil Society" (*Dion*, 37). Although Mandeville here calls this "the worst Construction," it is actually the one which he had acknowledged in his Preface to the *Fable*:

> For the main Design of the Fable, (as it is briefly explain'd in the Moral) is to shew the Impossibility of enjoying all the most elegant Comforts of Life that are to be met with in an industrious, wealthy and powerful Nation, and at the same time be bless'd with all the Virtue and Innocence that can be wish'd for in a Golden Age; from thence to expose the Unreasonableness and Folly of those that desirous of being an opulent and flourishing People, and wonderfully greedy after all the Benefits they can receive as such, are yet always murmuring at and exclaiming against those Vices and Inconveniences, that from the Beginning of the World to this present Day, have been inseparable from all Kingdoms and States that ever were fam'd for Strength, Riches, and Politeness, at the same time (6-7).

On the last page of the *Fable* Mandeville rephrases his proposition that depravity is a necessary condition of the great society, and adds "I flatter my self to have demonstrated" it (I, 369). "Demonstration," in the logical sense, is too strong a word to be claimed by a writer who avoids abstract, formal argument. Mandeville relies for persuasion upon a massive array of observations reported in graphic style. He is the counterpart in prose of the clever photographer whose candid camera reveals the meaning and truth of characters, acts and events. Or, to revert to his own comparison, he is the skilful anatomist who makes a deft incision in smooth white skin to display the less alluring organs beneath. In this sense, a laboratory sense, he demonstrates — he shows the concealed aim, the disguised intent, the crooked wish which underlie well rationalized, respectable behaviour. But the deeds of men are ambiguous signs of their motives, and social goals are controversial. If Mandeville is to convince his reader, he must first reach an agreement with him upon the definition of vice and upon a conception of the public good.

His first move is a master-stroke from which opponents do not quickly recover. He endorses the ascetic morality extolled by Christians, paying sly tribute to the values of self-denial and renunciation. He writes in the *Origin of Honour* "That no Practice, no Action or good Quality, how useful or beneficial soever they may be in themselves, can ever deserve the Name of Virtue, strictly speaking, where there is not a palpable Self-denial to be seen"[6] and in the same book, still in the spirit of the *Fable*, that "There is no Virtue that has a Name, but it curbs, regulates, or subdues some Passion that is peculiar to Human Nature."[7] These are plain statements of the premises declared or implied by Christian moralists who taught that the conquest of passion by reason is the essence of moral virtue. Even Hobbes, whose life-work was given over to displacing theology by psychology as the theoretical basis of ethics, had not broken this particular strand in the tradition. Hobbes always viewed the passions darkly as forces of barbarism, blind and violent and disruptive. He saw civilization resting first and finally upon the inhibitions imposed by reason. He professed not to judge the unrestrained hedonism of men ruled by instinct, mood and inclination within a state of nature. Their egocentric behaviour, however threatening and self-defeating, was perfectly natural, and no more to be condemned than are the elliptical orbits in which the planets move. Such tolerance did not suit Mandeville's strategy. He moves to a loftier plane where he will meet his adversaries, amongst them members of the Intellectual School, whose leader, Samuel Clarke, had denounced

> . . . all rational Creatures, whose Wills are not constantly and regularly determined, and their Actions governed, by right Reason . . . , according to the eternal and invariable Rules of Justice, Equity, Goodness and Truth, but suffer themselves to be swayed by unaccountable arbitrary Humours, and rash Passions, by Lusts, Vanity and Pride, by private Interest, or present sensual Pleasures.[8]

6. *An Enquiry into the Origin of Honour and the Usefulness of Christianity in War*, John Brotherton, London, 1732, p. vi.

7. *Ibid.*, p. ix.

8. *A Discourse of Natural Religion*, 1706, *British Moralists*, ed., L.A. Selby-Bigge, Bobbs-Merrill, Indianapolis, 1964, Vol. 2, pp. 14-15.

Mandeville does not contest this sternly rationalistic conception of morality; rather he disarms his opponents by adopting it. As he says of the *Fable* in his *Vindication*, "It is a Book of severe and exalted Morality, that contains a strict Test of Virtue, an infallible Touchstone to distinguish the real from the counterfeited . . ." (I, 405). "Exalted," to be sure; so exalted that no one is likely to pass the test, least of all a productive member of the great society. For in order to qualify as virtuous by this high-flying standard, a man must inhibit all behaviour to which his desires or sense of self-interest incline him and act from a purely rational determination to promote the welfare of society.

So much for motives. But acts have consequences also, and moral philosophers have felt compelled to take account of them. The real possibility of dissonance in moral value between motives and consequences has caused them considerable trouble. The worthiest, most altruistic motive — to promote international peace, say — may impoverish a society profiting from the sale of arms. The basest, most selfish motive — to line one's pocket — may benefit a society in need of clever, ambitious industrialists. The Benthamite resolution is to disqualify motives altogether, for they are unfathomable, and to evaluate observable, social effects. The Kantian solution is to discount consequences, which need not accord with the agent's intention, and to admit only motives as morally relevant. Francis Hutcheson, a younger contemporary of Mandeville, tried to handle both factors by issuing a moral sense theory of motives by which to judge agents and a utilitarian theory of consequences by which to evaluate acts. The difficulty with this double standard is that it allows the possibility of a commendable society made up of moral degenerates or of an iniquitous society composed of virtuous men. Adherents to the tradition of natural law were not perplexed by such logical possibilities. They believed in a pre-established harmony between moral motives and social effects. If citizens acted out of respect for the moral law, society benefited; if they did not, it suffered. The "Law of Nature," Berkeley said in his discourse on *Passive Obedience*, "is a system of such rules or precepts as that, if they be all of them, at all times, in all places, and by all men observed, they will necessarily promote the well-being of mankind, so far as it is attainable by human actions."[9] These philosophers, Cumberland, Cudworth, Locke, Clarke, Wollaston, and countless others often spoke along with Berkeley of the common, general or public good, but so abstractly that it would be hard to say, on the basis of their writing, what counted for them as a Public Benefit. Mandeville decides for them, after observing what they really pursue, enjoy, and pray for:

> . . . the National Happiness which the Generality wish and pray for, is Wealth and Power, Glory and Worldly Greatness; to live in Ease, in Affluence and Splendour at Home, and to be fear'd, courted and esteem'd Abroad . . . (*Fable* II, 106).

It would be very hard to adjust an ascetic concept of personal virtue to a utilitarian standard of social value. But philosophers have cheerfully undertaken even more hopeless tasks quite often, and if Mandeville had been a truly earnest reasoner, he could have come up with some reconciling project, some panoramic scheme in which the great society was shown to be the natural result of collective integrity. If he had failed, he could then either have relaxed the severity of his test of personal merit as being unsuited to human frailty, or he could have renounced materialistic social values as unworthy of human dignity. He does none of these things, of course, for he has no incentive to resolve a resounding discord which yields the richly satiric themes of human duplicity and self-deception. Comic writers, who are nourished by absurdity, are always grateful for displays of inconsistency, of actual practice contradicting professed principle. To have uncovered hypocrisy operating on a national scale was an auspicious find, and Mandeville therefore takes the last remaining option of accrediting an ascetic morality of motive and a utilitarian ethic of social consequence while insisting upon their incompatibility.

9. *The Works of George Berkeley*, ed. A.C. Fraser, Oxford, Clarendon Press, 1901, Vol. Iv, p. iii.

He can now proceed to show how the social benefits men acquire in practise result from the private vices which they renounce in theory.

It is not only the peripheral amenities which Mandeville traces to their vile source in passion, the luxuries in which men indulge themselves to gratify vanity, the status tokens which flatter pride. Society itself, as such, the whole elaborate scheme of custom and convention, sanction and taboo, reward and penalty is an artificial arrangement for accommodating vice. What passes in the world for a moral order is a system of pressures which conditions people to repress and sublimate socially disruptive passions and cultivates those through which men can be domesticated. Preeminent amongst the socially manageable passions are pride and shame, as was recognized by the first politicians who (in their own interests, of course) first undertook to tame this "extraordinary selfish and headstrong, as well as cunning Animal" (Fable I, 41-42).

> They thoroughly examin'd all the Strength and Frailties of our Nature, and observing that none were either so savage as not to be charm'd with Praise, or so despicable as patiently to bear Contempt, justly concluded, that Flattery must be the most powerful Argument that could be used to Human Creatures (Fable I, 42-43).

Thus "the Moral Virtues are the Political Offspring with Flattery begot upon Pride" (Fable I, 51).

To confirm society's debt to the evils of human nature, Mandeville conducts a series of psychological analyses of socially acceptable and beneficial behaviour to uncover its selfish motives; and thus, by the ascetic standard adopted, he reduces conventional morality to vice. These investigations serve also to show how society capitalizes on those vicious qualities of human nature which it officially condemns. A typical specimen of reductive analysis is found in Remark C, where Mandeville traces honour to its affective basis in self-love.

His aim there is to show that honour and dishonour are social concepts whose content or meaning is dictated by considerations of social convenience. The sense of honour, a complex of habits and attitudes induced by custom and education, is culturally conditioned. What is innately there to be conditioned are pride and shame, two aspects of self-love which are responsive to the opinions of others, in other words susceptible to flattery and contempt. Mandeville recognizes only purely conventional, artificial criteria of honour, by which term, he says "we mean nothing else but the good Opinion of others, which is counted more or less Substantial, the more or less Noise or Bustle there is made about the demonstration of it" (*Fable* I, 63-64). Morally, the value of honour so defined is "imaginary." Its efficacy as an instrument of social control, however, presupposes passions which are real. From the side of those who are in a position to confer or withhold honour, human vanity supplies ready-made a means of manipulation, and the politician's exploitation of this weakness is perfectly justifiable from a utilitarian standpoint. The pursuit of honour is motivated by pride, a passion gratified by having one's vanity rubbed and therefore of no moral worth.

Mandeville goes on to talk about the social utility of shame. This passion is a "Frailty in our Nature," but it is in the interest of society to cultivate it. Since passions cannot be totally repressed (and some are essential to racial survival), they must be tamed, diverted, sublimated, trained in ways conducive to public order. Social relations are controlled by conventions which regulate the gratification of passion. No real self-denial or renunciation is demanded but only a certain amount of restraint. The inhibitions engendered by education and social sanctions are of no moral value for they depend upon one passion, shame, for example, overcoming some other, sexual desire, let us say. But virtue is recognized in the ascetic view only when passion is actually subdued by reason:

> The Multitude will hardly believe the excessive Force of Education, and in the difference of Modesty between Men and Women ascribe that to Nature, which is altogether owing to early Instruction: *Miss* is scarce three Years old, but she is spoke to every Day to hide her Leg, and rebuk'd in good Earnest if she shews it; while *Little Master* at the same Age is bid to take up his Coats, and piss like a Man. It is Shame and Education that contains the

Seeds of all Politeness, and he that has neither, and offers to speak the Truth of his Heart, and what he feels within, is the most contemptible Creature upon Earth, tho' he committed no other Fault. If a Man should tell a Woman, that he could like no body so well to propagate his Species upon, as her self, and that he found a violent Desire that Moment to go about it, and accordingly offer'd to lay hold of her for that purpose; the Consequence would be, that he would be call'd a Brute, the Woman would run away, and himself never be admitted in any civil Company. There is no body that has any Sense of Shame, but would conquer the strongest Passion rather than be so serv'd. But a Man need not conquer his Passions, it is sufficient that he conceals them. Virtue bids us subdue, but good Breeding only requires we should hide our Appetites. A fashionable Gentleman may have as violent an Inclination to a Woman as the brutish Fellow; but then he behaves himself quite otherwise; he first addresses the Lady's Father, and demonstrates his Ability splendidly to maintain his Daughter; upon this he is admitted into her Company, where, by Flattery, Submission, Presents, and Assiduity, he endeavours to procure her Liking to his Person, which if he can compass, the Lady in a little while resigns her self to him before Witnesses in a most solemn manner; at Night they go to Bed together, where the most reserv'd Virgin very tamely suffers him to do what he pleases, and the upshot is, that he obtains what he wanted without having ever ask'd for it (*Fable* I, 71-73).

The point of this cynical squib is underscored a bit later:

Because Impudence is a Vice, it does not follow that Modesty is a Virtue; it is built upon Shame, a Passion in our Nature, and may be either Good or Bad according to the Actions perform'd from that Motive. Shame may hinder a Prostitute from Yielding to a Man before Company, and the same Shame may cause a bashful good-natur'd Creature, that has been overcome by Frailty, to make away with her Infant. Passions may do Good by chance, but there can be no Merit but in the Conquest of them (*Fable* I, 74).

Perhaps after two and a half centuries Mandeville is beginning to sound a bit old-fashioned. Only recently the straight-forward approach of "the brutish Fellow" has come to seem no more unnatural than the dalliance of the "fashionable Gentleman." To see whether or not comparable changes in the outlook upon war also tend to antiquate Mandeville's sociology, let us consider Remark R. Here he displays a fair sample of the derivation of public benefits from private vices by analysing honour, as that concept would be understood in a military academy.

Evidently courage is the chief distinguishing quality of whoever would pass as a man of honour in an officers' club. Mandeville wants to show that military valour is not animal courage, but an artificial social virtue synthesized out of waste materials by "Moralists and Politicians" in the interests of national security. Mandeville was a pioneer in the now fashionable science of ethology, and this comparative study of animal and human aggression is a remarkable anticipation of recent work by Konrad Lorenz. He begins with a Hobbesian statement of the Law of Self-Preservation:

> There is nothing so universally sincere upon Earth, as the Love which all Creatures, that are capable of any, bear to themselves; and as there is no Love but what implies a Care to preserve the thing beloved, so there is nothing more sincere in any Creature than his Will, Wishes, and Endeavours to preserve himself. This is the Law of Nature, by which no Creature is endued with any Appetite or Passion but what either directly or indirectly tends to the Preservation either of himself or his Species (*Fable* I, 200).

Like Hobbes, who made "appetite and aversion" (approach and withdrawal) the fundamental concepts of his theory of motivation, Mandeville immediately infers a pleasure principle upon which to construct his model of human nature:

> The Means by which Nature obliges every Creature continually to stir in this Business of Self-Preservation, are

grafted in him, and (in Man) call'd Desires, which either compel him to crave what he thinks will sustain or please him, or command him to avoid what he imagines might displease, hurt or destroy him (*Fable* I, 200).

Animal behaviour is mainly a matter of responding to the stimulation of hunger and lust. Responses are controlled by two passions, fear and anger. Predators would be inhibited in their pursuit of edible and sexual objects by fear of competitors if they were not also roused by anger by the prospect of having their desires frustrated. When the odds are not overwhelmingly against an animal, his fear will be subdued by anger and he will fight for gratification. "From whence it must follow," says Mandeville, "that what we call Prowess or natural Courage in Creatures, is nothing but the Effect of Anger, and that all fierce Animals must be either very Ravenous or very Lustful, if not both" (*Fable* I, 205).

Viewed as a physical specimen, no man, undressed, would impress an impartial observer as a particularly formidable beast of prey. Nor would his sexual performance, except perhaps in his own imagination, compare favourably with that of a Bantam rooster or a Black Angus bull. His thin, vulnerable skin, lack of fangs or horns or hoof, his small brittle nails, poor balance, unremarkable speed and unimpressive musculature all suggest that if left naked in the woods, he would have been, as Mandeville says, "a timorous creature." But civilization offers him almost limitless opportunities for novel self-indulgence. "Hence it must follow," as Mandeville points out, "that he will often be cross'd in the Pursuit of them, and meet with abundance more disappointment to stir up his Anger in this than his former Condition, and Man would in a little time become the most hurtful and noxious Creature in the World, if let alone, whenever he could over-power his Adversary, if he had no Mischief to fear but from the Person that anger'd him" (*Fable* I, 206). It is therefore the chief responsibility of every government to instil fear of the consequences of uninhibited behaviour provoked by anger. The balance of fear and anger instinctively maintained in a state of nature is thus reinstated in society by punishing violence.

In solving one problem the "Moralists and Politicians" have created another. By the arts of moral persuasion, religious indoctrination and judicial control they have reduced antagonism to a tolerable level. Having multiplied men's desires and then, by threats of punishment, suppressed their anger at being often thwarted, the rulers have eliminated the animal courage which would disturb the internal peace of society. But every great society needs vast numbers of men who can overcome both their fear of death and their inhibition against killing members of their own species. The management of this residual problem is a tribute to the dexterity of politicians. The people are first made to clearly understand the distinction between the horrible crime of murder and the patriotic act of killing strangers in the defense of their country's interests.[10] Animal courage can no longer be relied upon; even if it had not been eradicated, depending as it did upon the fleeting passion of anger, it would have been too unstable to sustain a soldier through a long, hazardous campaign. The politician who has his country's interest at heart must therefore find some other trait of human nature to manipulate, as Mandeville explains:

> Whoever would civilize Men, and establish them into a Body Politick, must be thoroughly acquainted with all the Passions and Appetites, Strength and Weaknesses of their Frame, and understand how to turn their greatest Frailties to the Advantage of the Publick. In the Enquiry into the Origin of Moral Virtue, I have shewn how easily Men were induc'd to believe any thing that is said in their Praise. If

---

10. Cf. Berkeley, *Passive Obedience*, S. 32: "If it be said that some negative precepts, e.g. 'Thou shalt not kill,' do admit of limitation, since otherwise it were unlawful for the magistrate, for a soldier in a battle, or for a man in his own defence, to kill another; I answer, when a duty is expressed in too general terms, as in this instance, in order to a distinct declaration of it, either those terms may be changed for others of a more limited sense, as *kill* for *murder*; or else, from the general proposition remaining in its full latitude, exceptions may be made of those precise cases which, not agreeing with the notion of murder, are not prohibited by the law of nature. In the former case there is a limitation; but it is only of the signification of a single term, too general and improper, by substituting another, more proper and particular, in its place. In the latter case there are exceptions; but then they are not from the law of nature, but from a more general proposition, which, besides that law, includes somewhat more, which must be taken away in order to leave the law by itself clear and determinate." (*Works*, ed. Fraser, Vol. IV, pp. 121-122.)

therefore a Law-giver or Politician, whom they have a great Veneration for, should tell them, that the generality of Men had within them a Principle of Valour distinct from Anger, or any other Passion, that made them to despise Danger and face Death it self with Intrepidity, and that they who had the most of it were the most valuable of their kind, it is very likely, considering what has been said, that most of them, tho' they felt nothing of this Principle, would swallow it for Truth, and that the proudest feeling themselves mov'd at this piece of Flattery, and not well vers'd in distinguishing the Passions, might imagine that they felt it heaving in their Breasts, by mistaking Pride for Courage. If but one in Ten can be persuaded openly to declare, that he is possess'd of this Principle, and maintain it against all Gainsayers, there will soon be half a dozen that shall assert the same. Whoever has once own'd it is engaged, the Politician has nothing to do but to take all imaginable Care to flatter the Pride of those that brag of, and are willing to stand by it, a thousand different ways: The same Pride that drew him in first will ever after oblige him to defend the Assertion, till at last the fear of discovering the reality of his Heart, comes to be so great that it out-does the fear of Death it self. Do but increase Man's Pride, and his fear of Shame will ever be proportion'd to it; for the greater Value a Man sets upon himself, the more Pains he'll take and the greater Hardships he'll undergo to avoid Shame.

The great Art then to make Man Courageous, is first to make him own this Principle of Valour within, and afterwards to inspire him with as much Horror against Shame, as Nature has given him against Death . . . (*Fable* I, 208-209).

As soon as the Notions of Honour and Shame are received among a Society, it is not difficult to make Men fight. First, take care they are persuaded of the Justice of their Cause; for no Man fights heartily that thinks himself in the wrong; then shew them that their Altars, their Possessions, Wives, Children, and every thing that is near and dear to them, is concerned in the present Quarrel, or at least may be influenced by it hereafter; then put Feathers in their Caps, and distinguish them from others, talk of Publick-Spiritedness, the Love of their Country, facing an Enemy with Intrepidity, despising Death, the Bed of Honour, and such like high-sounding Words, and every Proud Man will take up Arms and fight himself to Death before he'll turn Tail, if it be by Daylight. One Man in an Army is a check upon another, and a hundred of them that single and without witness would be all Cowards, are for fear of incurring one another's Contempt made Valiant by being together. To continue and heighten this artificial Courage, all that run away ought to be punish'd with Ignominy; those that fought well, whether they did beat or were beaten, must be flatter'd and solemnly commended; those that lost their Limbs rewarded, and those that were kill'd ought, above all, to be taken notice of, artfully lamented, and to have extraordinary Encomiums bestowed upon them; for to pay Honours to the Dead, will ever by a sure Method to make Bubbles of the Living (*Fable* I, 210-211).

The signs are clear in the great societies of our generation that the old techniques of manipulation are no longer as effective as once they were. More and more of the aggressive violence that should be reserved for export is being consumed locally. National strength depends upon finding new incentives for being docile at home and bloody abroad.

The time has come to move toward a conclusion. A question about Mandeville's own moral commitment remains alongside another about how he intended these sociological studies to be taken. By way of answering, the following alternatives are proposed:

1. Mandeville was perfectly sincere in his professed asceticism and really believed that true virtue can be realized by subduing selfish passions through a rational decision to promote the welfare of others. Credited with this conviction, his writing

may be understood as a satirical critique of prevailing social values through which corrupt men of power exploit human weakness.

2. Mandeville was a convinced utilitarian who heartily approved of the material benefits that can be realized only in a rich industrial society. On this view, his work can be understood as a *reductio ad absurdum* of ascetic morality, which over-rules motives that are both natural and indispensible for commercial and military success.

3. As a student of moral philosophy and religious ethics and a disinterested observer of the mores of his society, Mandeville was struck by the discrepancy between the approved ideal of mankind as rational beings selflessly seeking virtue and the spectacle of their passionate striving for self-gratification. So taken, his work should be read as an indictment and a plea: an indictment of the hypocrisy of preaching self-denial while practising self-indulgence, and a plea for self-awareness and honest speaking about human nature.

It is easy to quote Mandeville in support of each of these interpretations, and equally easy to find each contradicted somewhere in his writings. Like all great satirists, Mandeville is wilfully ambiguous and therefore elusive. In the end, the commentator must make a decision about how to read him, and forego the comfort of having conclusive textual evidence for his interpretation.

The first, ascetic, interpretation is favoured by the unflattering colours by which Mandeville's depictions of society highlight the frivolous vanity of the wealthy, the boorish stupidity of the poor, and the cynicism of the rulers. There is, in addition, his explicit avowal that "If I have shewn the way to worldly Greatness, I have always without Hesitation preferr'd the Road that leads to Virtue" (*Fable* I, 231, 407). However, when F.B. Kaye, whose understanding of Mandeville commands the highest respect, quotes this remark, he comments shortly that "he is simply not to be believed" (*Fable* I, lv). Why not? Presumably because a writer does not spend twenty-seven years showing people how to proceed in one direction when he prefers them to take an opposite course.

It requires no great straining at the text to extract evidence for Mandeville's being a utilitarian who denounces asceticism as unrealistic and impractical. The collapse of the Grumbling Hive through the insidious spread of virtue is presented as a disaster, and the Moral exhorts us not to renounce "the World's Conveniencies" but to stop complaining about the associated immorality. Furthermore, the main effect of his stressing irrational forces in psychology is to discredit optimism about man's moral perfectibility through reason. On the other hand, a note of contempt is insinuated into Mandeville's comments upon the great society. Very often he appears to disassociate himself from the materialistic values which he attributes to his generation. In fact he says, "I would prefer a small peaceable Society, in which Men, neither envy'd nor esteem'd by Neighbours, should be contented to live upon the Natural Product of the Spot they inhabit, to a vast Multitude abounding in Wealth and Power, that should always be conquering others by their Arms Abroad, and debauching themselves by Foreign Luxury at Home" (*Fable* I, 13).

The third position suggested for Mandeville is also exposed to uncertainty by his conflicting statements. It is true that Mandeville says of Cleomenes, and therefore of himself, that "He took uncommon Pains to search into human Nature, and left no Stone unturn'd, to detect the Pride and Hypocrisy of it" (*Fable* II, 18). And later, through his spokesman, Cleomenes, he explains himself as "only pointing at or labouring, to detect the Inconsistency of others with the Principles they pretend to" (*Fable* II, 102). It might be expected, however, that his reforming zeal would be defused by his belief that dissimulation is a congenital defect amongst civilized men. "For," he says, "we are ever pushing our Reason which way soever we feel Passion to draw it, and Self-love pleads to all human Creatures for their different Views, still furnishing every individual with Arguments to justify their Inclinations" (*Fable* I, 333). And he also says flatly that "it is impossible we could be sociable Creatures without Hypocrisy. . . ." "In all Civil Societies," he continues, "Men are taught insensibly to be Hypocrites from their Cradle, no body dares to own that he gets by Publick Calamities, or even by the loss of Private Persons. The Sexton would be stoned should he wish openly for the Death of the Parishioners, tho' every body knew that he had nothing else to live upon" (*Fable* I, 349).

Despite this difficulty, I think that the third proposal comes closer to fixing Mandeville's position and stating his intention than the other two. I do not think that he was preaching asceticism, because he thought the practice of it impossible; and I do not think that he was teaching utilitarianism, because he considered such lessons unnecessary. Except for a few aberrant specimens, human beings are disqualified by their instinctual and emotional endowment from the ascetic life. And they need no encouragement to pursue the useful and enjoyable things to which they are already compulsively attracted. I do think that Mandeville regarded hypocrisy, in the specific form that involves self-deception, dispensable, and that throughout all his work he is arguing for clear-headed honesty about one's own motives. I have not forgotten his opening statement of intention and expectation in the Preface to the *Fable*, where he declares that he is writing simply for the reader's diversion. He professes there not to expect that his work will bring about a reduction in the level of hypocrisy or any increase in self-knowledge, for mankind is incorrigible. But perhaps this conventional cynicism expresses Mandeville's first word rather than his last. After all, he is forever claiming to have undeceived himself, and self-analysis did not hinder him from enjoying a useful, sociable life.

Although self-knowledge is rare, it is attainable, for no constitutional infirmity stands in its way. Hypocrisy, which is unknown in the animal world, is a social disease spread through education. The prognosis is not hopeless if the patient will undergo a strict course of self-examination such as Cleomenes prescribes for his friend Horatio, and such, I think, as Dr. Mandeville prescribes for us.

James Noxon

The Theory of Conspicuous Consumption in the 18th Century

The theory of conspicuous consumption was first given that name by Thorstein Veblen in 1899, but the idea behind the theory is as old as human nature. No less a figure than Shakespeare has King Lear provide us with one of the most eloquent defences of conspicuous consumption:

> O reason not the need! Our basest beggars
> Are in the poorest things superfluous.
> Allow not nature more than nature needs,
> Man's life is cheap as beast's. Thou art a lady;
> If only to go warm were gorgeous,
> Why, nature needs not what thou gorgeous wear'st,
> Which scarcely keeps thee warm.

When it came time to elevate Shakespeare's insight to the level of an economic theory, Veblen reached for the same images to illustrate his notion that consumption occurs for motives very different from those of everyday utility. Conspicuous consumption, as he defines it, means consumption as visible evidence of wealth, or of the master's superiority over his servant. As he says, "The basis on which good repute in any highly organised industrial community ultimately rests is pecuniary strength; and the means of showing pecuniary strength, and so of gaining or retaining a good name, are leisure and a conspicuous consumption of goods."[1] Veblen devotes a whole chapter of *The Theory of the Leisure Class* to clothes, which, as Shakespeare noticed, provide the chief distinction between the king and the beggar:

> The pleasing effect of neat and spotless garments is chiefly,
> if not altogether, due to their carrying the suggestion of
> leisure — exemption from personal contact with industrial

1. Thorstein Veblen, *The Theory of the Leisure Class*, New York, 1926, p. 84.

processes of any kind. Much of the charm that invests the patent-leather shoe, the stainless linen, the lustrous cylindrical hat, and the walking-stick, which so greatly enhance the native dignity of a gentleman, comes of their pointedly suggesting that the wearer cannot when so attired bear a hand in any employment that is directly and immediately of any human use. Elegant dress serves its purpose of elegance not only in that it is expensive, but also because it is the insignia of leisure. It not only shows that the wearer is able to consume a relatively large value, but it argues at the same time that he consumes without producing.[2]

We have heard from the nineteenth and the seventeenth centuries; it is time now to hear from the eighteenth. One thinks of the clothing metaphor which dominates *A Tale of a Tub*, and of the glittering artifice of Belinda's dress in *The Rape of the Lock*. But the true echo of Veblen is to be found in Bernard Mandeville's *The Fable of the Bees*, where, in Remark "M," Mandeville says:

> But whatever Reflexions may be made on this head, the World has long since decided the Matter; handsome Apparel is a main Point, fine Feathers make fine Birds, and People, where they are not known, are generally honour'd according to their Clothes and other Accoutrements they have about them; from the richness of them we judge of their Wealth, and by their ordering of them we guess at their Understanding. It is this which encourages every Body, who is conscious of his little Merit, if he is any ways able, to wear Clothes above his Rank, especially in large and populous Cities, where obscure Men may hourly meet with fifty Strangers to one Acquaintance, and consequently have the Pleasure of being esteem'd by a vast Majority, not as what they are, but what they appear to be: which is greater Temptation than most People want to be vain.[3]

2. Veblen, p. 171.
3. Bernard Mandeville, *The Fable of the Bees: or, Private Vices, Publick Benefits*, ed. F. B. Kaye, Oxford, 1924, I, p. 127.

I begin with Veblen and Mandeville because they so clearly demonstrate the way in which the theory of conspicuous consumption has been discussed. Both men are moralists and satirists, however vehemently they may deny the roles. The very definition of conspicuous consumption implies a value judgment and a consideration of motives. It is no accident that clothing, that favorite metaphor of the satirist, should be a recurring image for both Veblen and Mandeville. The men are linked in another way as well, coming as they do at the beginning and end of the great period of liberal, laissez-faire, non-judgmental economics. Mandeville used conspicuous consumption to show the irrelevance of traditional ethics to the economic realities of the new money-dominated society of Augustan England; Veblen set about to reintroduce ethical and aesthetic considerations into economic discussion, at a time when the failures of liberal economics, of the self-regulating mechanism, were becoming everywhere obvious.

To enter into the economic and ethical controversies of the end of the nineteenth century is beyond the scope of this paper, and beyond my capabilities, so for the time being we should abandon Veblen and look more closely at the milieu which produced the peculiar satirical mixture contained in *The Fable of the Bees*, and in particular its defence of conspicuous consumption.

The conventional literary attitude of the eighteenth century maintained an ascetic primitivism which made conspicuous consumption, or "luxury," its favorite target. Goldsmith's famous lines in "The Deserted Village" sum up the century's usual ethic:

> O luxury! Thou curst by Heaven's decree,
> How ill exchanged are things like these for thee!
> How do thy potions with insidious joy,
> Diffuse their pleasures only to destroy!
> Kingdoms by thee, to sickly greatness grown,
> Boast of a florid vigour not their own.
> At every draught more large and large they grow,
> A bloated mass of rank unwieldy woe;
> Till sapped their strength, and every part unsound,

> Down, down they sink, and spread a ruin round.

This was the commonest ethical attitude of the century, but there were dissenters, one of the most famous being Dr. Johnson, of whom Boswell once said, "He as usual defended luxury; 'You cannot spend money in luxury without doing good to the poor. Nay, you do more good to them by spending it in luxury, than by giving it: for by spending it in luxury, you make them exert industry, whereas by giving it, you keep them idle.' "[4] In the statements of these two close friends, Goldsmith and Johnson, we have the great dilemma of the eighteenth century neatly expressed, a dilemma which demands at the same time an increase in frugality and an increase in trade. Frugality meant not using the luxurious products of foreign nations; a frugal nation, therefore, would be a nation which could depend on its own resources and get by without trade. By the same token, a nation anxious to expand its trade should expand the desires of its citizens by encouraging conspicuous consumption.

In general the most fervent ascetics were the Tory landowners, the enemies of trade and the merchant class. In the early years of the eighteenth century there was even a demand for sumptuary laws. John Dennis complained in 1711 that ". . . neither the Clergy, nor the Lay-Societies for the *Reformation of Manners*, can employ the effectual Method . . . for the immediate Suppression of bare-fac'd Luxury, the spreading Contagion of which is the greatest Corrupter of the Publick Manners, and the greatest Extinguisher of *Publick Spirit*."[5] Jonathan Swift, too, describing "The true way of multiplying Mankind to publick Advantage in such a Country as *England*," argued that it would be necessary "To enact and enforce Sumptuary Laws against Luxury, and all Excesses in Cloathing, Furniture, and the Like."[6] This is part, of course, of a general

4. James Boswell, *Life of Johnson*, ed. George Birkbeck Hill, revised and enlarged by L. F. Powell, Oxford, 1934, III, p. 291.
5. John Dennis, *An Essay upon Publick Spirit: being a Satyr in Prose upon the Manners and Luxury of the Times, The Chief Sources of our present Parties and Divisions*, London, 1711, p. v.
6. Jonathan Swift, *The History of the Four Last Years of the Queen*, in *The Prose Works*, ed. Herbert Davis, Vol. VII, Oxford, 1951, p. 95.

Tory fear of trade and the moneyed class. Swift mourned that "that *Power*, which, according to the old Maxim, was used to follow *Land*, is now gone over to *Money*,"[7] and an often-quoted tract, *Britannia Languens*, reminded its readers that it must "be of dangerous Consequences if the Trade of a Nation run into over-much *Shop-keeping*."[8] It is worth quoting at length from John Dennis, as he describes his forefathers and in the process gives us a glimpse of a Tory Arcadia:

> As they were sincere in their Religion, they were sound in their Morals: The Men were at once both just, and generous, sincere, faithful, laborious; the Women modest, obedient, chast, and diligent: Both Men and Women frugal, liberal, temperate, hospitable. Their Conversation and their Diet were like their Manners simple; their Conversation without Fraud, and their Diet without Artifice. Both their Meat and their Drink, for the most part, were of the native Growth of their Country, and the costly Juice of the Grape was us'd oftner for Physick, than it was for Pleasure.... They were the Tutelary Gods of the Poor, who in Sickness had Physick from them, and in Health their Food, and in both their Habitations. Their way of Living in the Country, their Diet, their Air, their Oeconomy, and their rural Diversions and Exercises confirm'd their Healths, and improv'd their Estates, and supply'd them both with Strength of Body, and with Vigor of Mind. So that their Minds were serene, or their Passions moderate; their Distempers neither frequent nor violent, and their Children healthful, lively, robust, and nervous.[9]

We have here an ideal society, ideal because trade is unnecessary and no money changes hands. It is a description which is no less beautiful because it also happens to be Tory propaganda.

On the other side of the argument the mercantilist trading classes were just as busy wrapping the cloak of morality around

---

7. *The Examiner*, No. 13, Nov. 2, 1710.

8. *Britannia Languens, or A Discourse of Trade*, London, 1680, in J. R. McCulloch, ed., *Early English Tracts on Commerce*, London, 1856, p. 302.

9. Dennis, *Essay upon Publick Spirit*, p. 8.

their own money-making. In the seventeenth century John Evelyn had provided a marvelously baroque defence of trade, implying that trade must be God's will because the earth had so obviously been designed for commerce:

> The earth, and every prospect of her superficies, presents us with a thousand objects of utility and delight, in which consists the perfection of all sublunary things: And, though through her rugged and dissever'd parts, rocks, seas, and remoter islands, she seem at first, to check our addresses; yet, when we ag'en behold in what ample baies, creeks, trending-shores, inviting harbours and stations, she appears spreading her arms upon the bordures of the ocean; whiles the rivers, who repay their tributes to it, glide not in direct, and praecipitate courses from their conceil'd, and distant heads, but in various flexures and meanders (as well to temper the rapidity of their streams, as to water and refresh the fruitful plains) methinks she seems, from the very beginning, to have been dispos'd for trafick and commerce, and even courts us to visit her most solitary recesses.[10]

If the earth is designed for trade, then surely the most exalted profession must be that of merchant. Whig propaganda was not long in making this very claim, perhaps most eloquently through Richard Steele:

> ... there is no man whom I so highly honour as the Merchant. This is he who turns all the Disadvantage of our Situation into our Profit and Honour. His Care and Industry ties his Country to the Continent, and the whole Globe pays his Nation a voluntary Tribute due to her from his Merit. His Handwriting has the Weight of Coin, and his good Character is Riches to the rest of his Countrymen. All other Subjects of our Island, from the highest to the lowest, are as much below the Merchant in political Merit,

---

10. John Evelyn, *Navigation and Commerce, their Original and Progress*, London, 1674, in J. R. McCulloch, ed., *A Select Collection of Scarce and Valuable Tracts on Commerce*, London, 1859, p. 33.

as that ravenous Worm in the Entrails of the State the Stock-Jobber.[11]

One of the reasons, therefore, for the recurrence of luxury as a theme in Augustan literature was that it was a fundamental issue in the political controversies of the time. Most Englishmen, however, were probably neither convinced Whigs nor convinced Tories. They retained a distrust of luxury, but enjoyed the benefits of trade. And it was precisely on this personal level that the ethical dilemma was most acute. If it is moral for the state to amass wealth, is it also moral for the individual to consume conspicuously? Conversely, if individuals are to rely solely on the land, should the state survive by taxation alone? The conflict between private morality and public advantage was one of the most vexing ethical problems of the time. Charles Davenant reflects sadly on the ethical compromises he and others were forced to make:

> Trade, without doubt, is in its nature a pernicious thing; it brings in that Wealth which introduces Luxury; it gives a rise to Fraud and Avarice, and extinguishes Virtue and Simplicity of Manners; it depraves a People, and makes way for the Corruption which never fails to end in Slavery, Foreign or Domestick ... But, the Posture and Condition of other Countries consider'd, 'tis become with us a necessary Evil.[12]

Defoe is much happier with the new wealth:

> The same trade that keeps our people at home, is the cause of the well living of the people here; for as frugality is not the national virtue of *England*, so the people that get much, spend much; and as they work hard, so they live well, eat and drink well, cloath warm, and lodge soft! in a word, the working manufacturing people of *England* eat the fat, drink the sweet, live better, and fare better, than

11. Richard Steele, *The Englishman*, ed. Rae Blanchard, Oxford, Clarendon Press, 1955, p. 20 (from No. 4, October 13, 1713).

12. [Charles Davenant], *An Essay upon the Probable Methods of making a People Gainers in the Ballance of Trade*, second edition, London, 1700, p. 102.

the working poor of any other nation in *Europe*.[13]

Defoe rejoices in worldly comfort, while Davenant regards it as corrupting. Behind this conflict lies the transition from the medieval God-centred universe to the modern secular state, and, in economics, the transition from a feudal to a mercantilist and ultimately to a liberal laissez-faire economy. The shift embodied by mercantilist thinking is well described by Eli Heckscher:

> Mercantilism rejected in principle any ethical attitude towards luxury. The only consideration that carried weight was how far a particular measure furthered or obstructed economic life in the direction which mercantilism tried to lead it. Thus, finally, in strictest contrast to the medieval standpoint, there arose a conscious and frankly admitted tendency to justify luxury, indeed to stimulate it, quite irrespective of the status of the purchaser, in all cases in which it guaranteed a market for the country's products and 'put money into circulation.'[14]

To justify luxury meant, of course, to justify conspicuous consumption in the face of all the moral appeals to ascetiscism and moderation with which the century was filled. As Alexander Pope said,

> What Nature wants (a phrase I much distrust)
> Extends to Luxury, extends to Lust:
> And if we count among the Needs of life
> Another's Toil, why not another's Wife?[15]

Pope serves nicely to reintroduce us to Mandeville, who in addition to defending luxury provided a defence of lust in his *A Modest Defence of Publick Stews*. Mandeville defines luxury as everything "that is not immediately necessary to make Man subsist as he is a living Creature."[16] While admitting that this is a rigorous definition, he says ". . . if we are to abate one inch of

13. [Daniel Defoe], *The Complete English Tradesman*, 3rd edition, London, 1732, I, p. 318.

14. Eli F. Heckscher, *Mercantilism*, trans. Mendel Shapiro, London, 1955, II, p. 290.

15. "Epistle to Bathurst," ll. 25-8.

16. *Fable of the Bees*, I, p. 107.

this Severity, I am afraid we shan't know where to stop." His definition is broad, but from the economic point of view his intentions are clear enough. In any case, his definition is not so very different from Pope's. By luxury he means conspicuous consumption as opposed to saving; a large part of the *Fable of the Bees* is devoted to the praise of spending and the denunciation of frugality, which he says is "like Honesty, a mean starving Virtue, that is only fit for small Societies of good peaceable Men."[17] The ironic implication is that in a society which does not consist of "good, peaceable Men," prodigality is an absolute necessity. Like Veblen, he is more concerned to describe human nature than to promulgate economic doctrine.

Mandeville's primary interest is in separating ethical from practical considerations, in differentiating between virtue and the inevitable consequences of fallible human nature. To accomplish this separation he first dismisses the fears of luxury's enervating effect:

> As long as Men have the same Appetites, the same Vices will remain. In all large Societies, some will love Whoring and others Drinking. The lustful that can get no handsome clean Women, will content themselves with dirty Drabs; and those that cannot purchase true *Hermitage* or *Pontack*, will be glad of more ordinary *French* Claret.[18]

In other words, the conspicuous expenditure of money on one's vices does not make them any worse; if anything, the vices of the poor are more degrading and enervating than those of the rich. The direction of Mandeville's irony is obvious. Wherever ethical standards have traditionally been applied to economics, he is careful to show their irrelevance.

He goes farther, however, to argue that a prosperous state depends on the exploitation of human passions and vices by "wary Politicians." He reminds us that man in the ideal Arcadia of "a fertile soil and a happy climate, a mild government, and more Land than People" will be "easy, loving, honest and sincere," but also "poor, ignorant, and almost wholly destitute

17. *Ibid.*, I, p. 104.
18. *Ibid.*, I, p. 118.

of what we call the Comforts of Life," since "all the Cardinal Virtues together won't so much as procure a tolerable Coat or a Porridge-Pot among them." He sums up his argument as follows:

> Would you render a Society of Men strong and powerful, you must touch their Passions. Divide the Land, tho' there be never so much to spare, and their Possessions will make them Covetous: Rouse them, tho' but in Jest, from their Idleness with Praises, and Pride will set them to work in earnest: Teach them Trades and Handicrafts, and you'll bring Envy and Emulation among them: To increase their Numbers, set up a Variety of Manufactures, and leave no Ground uncultivated . . . would you moreover render them an opulent, knowing and polite Nation, teach 'em Commerce with Foreign Countries, and if possible get into the Sea, which to compass spare no Labour nor Industry . . . Then promote Navigation, cherish the Merchant, and encourage Trade . . . This will bring Riches, and where they are, Arts and Sciences will soon follow, and by the Help of what I have named and good Management, it is that Politicians can make a People potent, renown'd and flourishing.[19]

In such passages as this Mandeville sounds very much like a precursor of laissez-faire economic liberalism, but his emphasis on the controlling power of "Politicians" reminds us that he has not totally abandoned the mercantilist view of the all-powerful state. Mandeville is a mercantilist in his acceptance of the role of the state, but the mercantilists were never quite prepared to say that a wealthy state should contain wealthy people. On this issue Mandeville is closer to laissez-faire economists, who saw the state as a collection of individuals, whose private prosperity caused the prosperity of the state. The advocates of laissez-faire saw a positive virtue in conspicuous consumption and rapid spending, and argued that economic power would automatically come to that state which left its citizens freest to fulfill their desires. Any economic imbalance which might result would be

19. *Ibid.*, I, p. 184.

overcome by the workings of natural law. It is on this point of individual freedom, as well, that Mandeville differs from the economic liberals. Human passions, he argues, can only be harmonious after the civilizing process has taken place, and this process, far from depending on natural law, requires the disguising of nature by means of the laborious propaganda of skilful politicians. This is an idea subtler than the mercantilists' taxes and regulations, but not nearly so flattering to human nature as laissez-faire trust in natural law. Thus we find Mandeville maintaining a view of human nature close to that of Swift and Pope and the propagandists against luxury, while accepting the prevailing Whig economics of the time, the economics of mercantilism gradually yielding to laissez-faire liberalism, and in particular of conspicuous consumption as an essential part of the economic process.

Conspicuous consumption as defined by Veblen, however, implies more than simple luxury. It is also an important means of class distinction, which provides a way of differentiating worker and man of leisure, master and servant, and even man and woman. Each class has its own standard of consumption, or what Veblen calls "pecuniary decency," which differentiates it from other classes. Sometimes this standard of consumption creates anomalies, as in the life of the scholar:

> In any modern community where there is no priestly monopoly of these occupations, the people of scholarly pursuits are unavoidably thrown into contact with classes that are pecuniarily their superiors. The high standard of pecuniary decency in force among these superior classes is transfused among the scholarly classes with but little mitigation of its rigour; and as a consequence there is no class of the community that spends a larger proportion of its substance in conspicuous waste than these.[20]

This matter of consumption as a distinguisher of class, and indeed the whole question of class distinction, is generally either taken for granted or ignored in the eighteenth century. As Harold Laski once said,

20. Veblen, p. 113.

What, indeed, is singular in the English political thought of this period is the absence of any sense, at least in a notable expression, of what the social problem implied. A barely noticed pamphlet of William Ogilvie, some scattered reflections of Dr. Wallace, the satirical comments of Mandeville in his *Essay on Charity Schools,* these are the main comments of the age upon the problem.[21]

Ogilvie's pamphlet was published in 1781 and Dr. Wallace's reflections in 1761, so that Mandeville's *Essay,* published in 1723, is by far the earliest statement of what Laski calls "the social problem," the problem of class distinction defined in part by consumption. In the *Essay on Charity and Charity-Schools* Mandeville attacks one of the most sacred of Augustan cows, the schools set up to teach the children of the poor the basic skills of reading and writing and arithmetic, so that they would make better servants. The Bishop of London, preaching one of the annual charity-school sermons in 1714, reminded his listeners that "It is doubtless your Intention, that these Objects of your Charity be so educated, as that they may hereafter become useful in inferior Stations."[22] In most of what was written and spoken about the charity schools, this purpose was taken for granted. Mandeville almost alone saw that the schools could only create unfulfillable expectations, that a society which insisted on maintaining a wealthy class with a high level of pecuniary decency had to keep the poor both ignorant and abject. "Abundance of hard and dirty Labour is to be done," he tells us, "and coarse Living is to be complied with: Where shall we find a better Nursery for these Necessities than the Children of the Poor? none certainly are nearer to it or fitter for it."[23] This sounds brutal and unfeeling, but it is brutal only in the same way that *A Modest Proposal* is brutal. The true Mandevillean sentiment emerges when he says,

---

21. Harold J. Laski, *The Rise of European Liberalism*, London, 1936, p. 206.

22. John Robinson, *The Benefits and Duty of the Members of Christ's Kingdom. A Sermon Preach'd ... May 20, MDCCXIV,* in *Twenty Five Sermons Preached at the Anniversary Meetings of the Children Educated in the Charity-Schools in and about the Cities of London and Westminster,* London, 1729, p. 248.

23. *Fable of the Bees,* I, p. 311.

I know it will be ever urged against me, that it is Barbarous the Children of the Poor should have no Opportunity of exerting themselves, as long as God has not debarr'd them from Natural Parts and Genius more than the Rich. But I cannot think this is harder, than it is that they should not have Money as long as they have the same Inclinations to spend as others.[24]

Mandeville will not allow the wealthy to salve their consciences by promoting a little free education for the poor. He sees clearly enough that genuine betterment can come to the poor only with increased powers of consumption, whereas the charity schools operate only to encourage servitude and class distinction. The necessity of a docile and orderly servant class was assumed in most of the arguments for the schools.

The charity schools were a form of consumption by the poor on behalf of the rich, or of what Veblen calls "vicarious consumption." In showing how this works, we can return to the clothing imagery of the beginning of the paper. Veblen tells us that,

Where leisure and consumption is performed vicariously by henchmen and retainers, imputation of the resulting repute to the patron is effected by their residing near his person so that it may be plain to all men from what source they draw. As the group whose good esteem is to be secured in this way grows larger, more patent means are required to indicate the imputation of merit for the leisure performed, and to this end uniforms, badges, and liveries come into vogue. The wearing of uniforms or liveries implies a considerable degree of dependence, and may even be said to be a mark of servitude, real or ostensible.[25]

From Veblen's point of view, the defenders of the charity schools were full of unconscious ironies. Take Samuel Chandler, for example, preaching in January, 1728:

The very garments that in some schools are given them to

24. *Ibid.*, I, p. 310.
25. Veblen, p. 78.

wear, and their maintenance in all of them by charity, are the constant badges and proofs of their dependence and poverty; and should therefore teach *them* humility, and *their parents* thankfulness; the frequent contributions made for their support, shews them their obligations to their benefactors and friends, and naturally leads them to gratitude and submission; and must, if any thing, inspire them with a desire to please, by their faithfulness, diligence, and industry, that they may not forfeit the protection and assistance they need in any future station of life.[26]

Mandeville's essay is full of ironic comments on the smug hypocrisy of the wealthy as they admire their charity to the children of the poor:

It is diverting to the Eye to see Children well match'd, either Boys or Girls, march two and two in good order; and to have them all whole and tight in the same Clothes and Trimming must add to the comeliness of the sight; and what makes it still more generally entertaining is the imaginary share which even Servants and the meanest in the Parish have in it, to whom it costs nothing; Our Parish Church, Our Charity Children.[27]

There is no more savage comment on this particular manifestation of vicarious consumption until we come to William Blake at the end of the century, who gives us his two images of the charity children in the *Songs of Innocence* and the *Songs of Experience*. On the one hand, in the *Songs of Innocence,* we have the orderly spectacle, with the ominous beadles in the background:

'Twas on a Holy Thursday, their innocent faces clean,
The children walking two and two, in red and blue and green,
Grey-headed beadles walked before, with wands as white as snow,
Till into the high dome of Paul's they like Thames' waters flow.

26. Samuel Chandler, *Doing Good recommended from the Example of Christ. A Sermon Preach'd for the Benefit of the Charity-School in Gravel-Lane, Southwark, Jan. 1727/8*, London, 1728, p. 20 (misnumbered 28).

27. *Fable of the Bees*, I, p. 282.

Then, in the *Songs of Experience*, Blake gives us the truth behind the orderly procession:

> Is this a holy thing to see
> In a rich and fruitful land,
> Babes reduced to misery,
> Fed with cold and usurous hand?

If we demand the right for some classes to consume conspicuously, Mandeville tells us, we must recognise that this right can be bought only by forcing other classes into subservience. Like Veblen, he makes no overt moral judgment, but again like Veblen, he leaves no doubt about the satirical thrust of his comments on human nature and society:

> It is impossible that a Society can long subsist, and suffer many of its Members to live in Idleness, and enjoy all the Ease and Pleasure they can invent, without having at the same time great Multitudes of People that to make good this Defect will condescend to be quite the reverse, and by use and patience inure their Bodies to work for others and themselves besides.[28]

The theory of conspicuous consumption, then, is not only an economic theory but a satirical device. Its two chief advocates, Mandeville and Veblen, use it primarily to perform the ancient satirical task of stripping away illusions, of revealing the hypocrisy of society. In the process they make some profound comments on human nature and on the nature of the social system, comments all the more impressive because of the lightness of touch with which they are presented. The offhand manner of both men is the mark of the true satirist, as when Mandeville says, in words which must conclude this paper, "The *Fable of the Bees* was designed for the Entertainment of People of Knowledge and Education, when they have an idle Hour which they know not how to spend better."[29]

Gordon Vichert

28. *Ibid.*, I, p. 286.
29. *Ibid.*, I, p. 404.

Adam Smith's Approach to Economic Development

We are concerned in this essay with Adam Smith's attitude towards economic development, defined in terms of rising *per capita* income. The first issue to be examined is the "desirability" of development bearing in mind the approaches taken both in the *Theory of Moral Sentiments* and the *Wealth of Nations*. In the second and third sections we consider the role envisaged by Smith for government in the developmental process including, particularly, the financing of education. We turn to alternative policy objectives to development in the fourth section with special reference to national defence.

The Desirability of Economic Development

The *Theory of Moral Sentiments* (1759) contains a formal downplaying of economic development, for any surplus income (over some undefined "minimum") is said to be meaningless to the recipient. Thus the ambitious poor man may exhaust himself in acquiring wealth only to discover that "wealth and greatness are mere trinkets of frivolous utility, no more adapted for procuring ease of body or tranquility of mind, than the tweezer-cases of the lover of toys."[1] The inability of high command over goods and services to provide genuine happiness is only recognized when it is too late:

> Power and riches appear then to be, what they are, enormous and operose machines contrived to produce a few trifling conveniencies to the body, consisting of springs the most nice and delicate, which must be kept in order with the most anxious attention, and which, in spite of all our care, are ready every moment to burst into pieces, and

1. *The Theory of Moral Sentiments* (1759), New York, 1966, p. 261.

to crush in their ruins their unfortunate possessor.[2]

The real costs of acquiring higher income in terms of mental and physical effort thus far exceed the real benefits which are derived therefrom. But mankind tends to be misled, runs the argument, by the apparent "fitness" of commodities and services to generate wellbeing: "If we consider the real satisfaction which all these things are capable of affording, by itself and separated from the beauty of that arrangement which is fitted to promote it, it will always appear in the highest degree contemptible and trifling."[3]

Yet the error of judgment, Smith continues, has the fortunate effect of stimulating economic activity: "it is well that nature imposes upon us in this manner. It is this deception which rouses and keeps in continual motion the industry of mankind." What requires notice is the precise nature of the advantages of growth which here evidently relates to *aggregative* rather than average income; for the emphasis is placed upon the large population which can be maintained by a large national product: "The earth, by these labours of mankind, has been obliged to redouble her natural fertility, and to maintain a greater multitude of inhabitants."[4] Since it is presumed that total "happiness" increases along with the increase in total population — at "subsistence" — the expansion of the total national product is a desirable objective.

The argument is intimately bound up with the view that the distribution of income, apparently severely unequal, is in actuality more-or-less egalitarian. For the wealthy landlord can consume scarcely more than the "meanest peasant" and accordingly distributes the means of subsistence to his servants and others who are "employed in the economy of greatness; all of whom thus derive from his luxury and caprice that share of the necessaries of life which they would in vain have expected from his humanity or his justice." In consequence, "the produce of the soil maintains at all times nearly that number of

2. *Ibid.*, p. 262.
3. *Ibid.*, p. 263.
4. *Ibid.*, p. 264.

inhabitants which it is capable of maintaining."[5]

In addition, as already pointed out, the poor are in any event at least as well equipped psychologically as the rich to attain genuine happiness. It is indeed in this context that the celebrated term "invisible hand" appears long before its use in the *Wealth of Nations*:

> [The rich] are led by an invisible hand to make nearly the same distribution of the necessaries of life which would have been made had the earth been divided into equal proportions among all its inhabitants; and thus, without intending it, without knowing it, advance the interest of the society, *and afford means to the multiplication of the species*. When providence divided the earth among a few lordly masters, it neither forgot nor abandoned those who seemed to have been left out in the partition. These last, too, enjoy their share of all that it produces. In what constitutes the real happiness of human life, they are in no respect inferior to those who would seem so much above them. In ease of body and peace of mind, all the different ranks of life are nearly upon a level, and the beggar, who suns himself by the side of the highway, possesses that security which kings are fighting for.[6]

It is sometimes suggested that Smith's concern in the *Wealth of Nations* was with the "economic man" devised as a construct of the mind or an abstraction which removes part of his psychological make-up and retains only the economic

---

5. *Loc. cit.* Economically Smith's error lies in failing to recognize that the landlord is enjoying *his* income and the servants their incomes.

Cf. *loc. cit.* a further uncomplimentary reference to the rich: "The rich only select from the heap what is more precious and agreeable. They consume little more than the poor; and in spite of their natural selfishness and rapacity, though they mean only their own conveniency, though the sole end which they propose from the labours of all the thousands whom they employ be the gratification of their own vain and insatiable desires, they divide with the poor the produce of all their improvements."

de Mirabeau in the *Tableau Economique avec ses explications* (1760; tr. 1766) expressed a similar optimism, based on much the same grounds, regarding the inequality of income. Cf. E. Cannan, *A Review of Economic Theory*, ed. 2, London, 1964, p. 294.

6. *Theory of Moral Sentiments*, pp. 264-5. My emphasis.

motive.[7] This interpretation may seem unlikely in light of the trivial nature accorded to the economic end in the *Theory of Moral Sentiments*.[8] An alternative view, which in this regard is less troublesome, is that Smith was concerned in the *Wealth of Nations* with the "entire man" but in the "anonymous" market place where there is little scope for the various social sentiments.[9] Whether or not this latter interpretation better reflects Smith's intentions, we must take into account the fact that even in the earlier work he did *not* recommend an abysmally low standard of living for the poor. Smith's apparently complacent attitude towards the poor was qualified.

We derive support for this view in part from criticism in the *Theory of Moral Sentiments* of Mandeville according to whom, Smith contended, "everything . . . is luxury which exceeds what is absolutely necessary for the support of human nature, so that there is vice even in the use of a clean shirt, or of a convenient habitation."[10] Moreover, the legitimate object of government, we are also told, is or should be, "to promote the happiness of those who live under them" and to assure that the people "are better lodged, that they are better clothed, that they are better fed." Smith accordingly approved of subsidies and the like granted to the linen and woollen manufactures, and of the "patriot," that is the individual who exerts himself in the public interest, for example by the repair of high-roads.[11] It would, accordingly, be justified to regard Smith's position in the *Theory of Moral Sentiments* as one in support of economic

7.   Cf. H. T. Buckle, *History of Civilization in England*, II, New York, 1885, pp. 351 f.

8.   Yet it should also be borne in mind that in the *Wealth of Nations* Smith's conception of economic self-interest refers not merely to the accumulation of wealth strictly defined but every motive to action, including a desire for leisure, for honour and so forth, except those designed to promote the well-being of others. Cf. Jacob Viner, "Adam Smith and Laissez Faire," in J.M. Clark *et al.*, *Adam Smith 1776-1926*, Chicago, 1928, pp. 132-3; and Glenn R. Morrow, *Ethical and Economic Theories of Adam Smith*, (1923), New York, 1969, pp. 75-6.

9.   Viner, "On the Intellectual History of Laissez Faire," *Journal of Law and Economics* III, October, 1960, p. 60; Morrow, "Adam Smith: Moralist and Philosopher, in J.M. Clark, *et. al.*, *Adam Smith 1776-1926, op. cit.*, p. 167; and Morrow, *The Ethical and Economic Theories of Adam Smith, op. cit.*, pp. 7-9.

10.   *Theory of Moral Sentiments*, pp. 456-7.

11.   *Ibid.*, pp. 265-7.

development as a prerequisite for an increased population at a "reasonable" level of subsistence, and as a denigration of any surplus income over this (undefined) minimum. Insofar as attention is paid to the material requirements of the poor Smith diverges from mercantilist doctrine.[12]

We must also allow for a change in emphasis in Smith's attitude towards economic development in the *Wealth of Nations*. In the first place, of course, the opening paragraphs of the work place the emphasis squarely upon average annual income: "According, therefore, as this produce, or what is purchased with it, bears a greater or smaller proportion to the number of those who are to consume it, the nation will be better or worse supplied with all the necessaries and conveniencies for which it has occasion."[13] Equally important, the index was not intended to serve as a mere statistical fiction; capital accumulation was desirable at least in part because it raised the living standards specifically of the *labouring* class. It is true that in consequence, population was expected to respond and — in the absence of further increase in the demand for labour — wages per head to decline; yet the initial upward pressure on wages of itself was regarded as desirable:

> The liberal reward of labour, therefore, as it is the effect of increasing wealth, so it is the cause of increasing population. To complain of it, is to lament over the

12. Cf. a similar conclusion by Lord Robbins that Smith's argument according to which the distribution of happiness is less unequal than the distribution of wealth need not conflict with the view that *ceteris paribus* the beggar would benefit from an increase of real income. *The Theory of Economic Development in the History of Economic Thought*, London, 1968, p. 164. The admission by Smith of the necessity for minimum living standards, even in the earlier work, is discussed at some length by James Bonar, *Philosophy and Political Economy*, ed. 3, 1922, London, 1967, pp. 170 f. (Similar views are attributed to Francis Hutcheson and David Hume, *ibid.*, p. 113.)

A.L. Macfie, "The Invisible Hand in the 'Theory of Moral Sentiments,'" *The Individual in Society: Papers on Adam Smith*, London, 1967, p. 107, emphasizes that "the optimistic theism" of the *Theory of Moral Sentiments* conflicts with Smith's grasp in the same work of the "seamier side of human nature and life." Thus "the suffering and injustices that are never reconciled or recompensed here on earth are a constant theme in the *Moral Sentiments*, though Smith's common sense does lead him to recognize that a considerable amount of justice and due reward is achieved." (See also *ibid.*, p. 117.)

13. *Wealth of Nations*, Modern Library ed., New York, 1937, p. lvii (referred to hereafter as *WN*).

necessary effect and cause of the greatest public prosperity.

It deserves to be remarked, perhaps, that it is in the progressive state, while the society is advancing to the further acquisition, rather than when it has acquired its full complement of riches, that the condition of the labouring poor, of the great body of the people, seems to be the happiest and the most comfortable. It is hard in the stationary, and miserable in the declining state. (81)

The advantages of rising average wages are even more graphically expressed in Smith's laudatory comments upon the observed contemporary upward trend:

Is this improvement in the circumstances of the lower ranks of the people to be regarded as an advantage or as an inconveniency to the society? The answer seems at first sight abundantly plain. Servants, labourers and workmen of different kinds, make up the far greater part of every great political society. But what improves the circumstances of the greater part can never be regarded as an inconveniency to the whole. No society can surely be flourishing and happy, of which the far greater part of the members are poor and miserable. It is but equity, besides, that they who feed, cloath and lodge the whole body of the people, should have such a share of the produce of their own labour as to be themselves tolerably well fed, cloathed and lodged. (78-9)

In this regard it will be recalled that seventeenth- and eighteenth-century writers frequently emphasized the national importance of a *large* population at low living standards; despite a concern with pauperism it was assumed typically that the population was too small for the territory.[14] In the *Wealth of Nations*, by contrast, the emphasis is upon the desirability of circumstances generating a *growing* population: "The most

14. This is especially true after the mid-seventeenth century. Cf. D.C. Coleman, "Labour in the English Economy of the Seventeenth Century," *Economic History Review*, VIII, 1956, reprinted in E.M. Carus-Wilson, ed., *Essays in Economic History*, II, London, 1962, p. 305.

decisive mark of prosperity is *the increase* of the number of its inhabitants."[15] Thus, while China is described "as one of the richest, that is, the most fertile, best cultivated, most industrious, and *most populous* countries in the world" living conditions are said to be frightful,[16] providing an illustration of the proposition that it is *not* "in the richest countries, but in the most thriving, or in those which are growing rich the fastest, that the wages of labour are highest."[17]

Moreover, although there is no suggestion that private property should in any way be seriously interfered with, Smith did not hesitate to approve of some induced alteration in the pattern of income distribution in favour of labour. We may refer to two instances. In the first place, he recognized approvingly the element of progression inherent in the taxation of house-rents (insofar as the proportion of the budget of the rich devoted to housing exceeded that of the poor): "A Tax upon house-rents, therefore, would in general fall heaviest upon the rich; and in this sort of inequality there would not, perhaps, be any thing very unreasonable. It is not very unreasonable that the rich should contribute to the public expence, not only in proportion to their revenue, but something more than in proportion."[18] Secondly, Smith recommended higher tolls on the luxury carriages of the rich than upon freight whereby "the indolence and vanity of the rich is made to contribute in a very easy manner to the relief of the poor, by rendering cheaper the transportation of heavy goods to all the different parts of the country."[19]

We also recall numerous statements to the effect that landed proprietors as well as capitalists "love to reap where they have not sown"; that in old-established and slowly expanding or stagnant countries "rent and profit eat up wages, and the two superior orders of people oppress the inferior one"; and

15. Cf. *WN.*, p. 70; my emphasis. This view was adopted too by Malthus: "there is not a truer criterion of the happiness and innocence of a people than the rapidity of their increase," *Population: The First Essay*, (1798), Michigan, 1959, ch. vi, p. 38.
16. *WN.*, pp. 71-2. My emphasis.
17. *WN.*, p. 69.
18. *WN.*, p. 794.
19. *WN.*, p. 683.

particularly that social inequality gives masters the advantage in bargaining in conditions of economic stagnation. There is no complacency or "optimism" in these remarks and there can be little doubt that economic development was considered to be a desirable objective as the means of raising the living standards of labour.

Finally, we should note, in the present context, Smith's insistence that in contemporary circumstances rising wages would stimulate workers to greater effort, in contrast to current mercantilist notions which implied a backward-bending labour supply function:

> The liberal reward of labour, as it encourages the propagation, so it increases the industry of the common people.... Some workmen, indeed, when they can earn in four days what will maintain them through the week, will be idle the other three. This, however, is by no means the case with the greater part. Workmen, on the contrary, when they are liberally paid by the piece, are very apt to over-work themselves, and to ruin their health and constitution in a few years.[20] (81-2)

We do not, however, intend to suggest that there are no references to the advantages of a large population in the *Wealth of Nations*. The division of labour is related — although infrequently — to population size: "What takes place among the labourers in a particular workhouse, takes place, for the same reason, among those of a great society. The greater their

20. This may be compared with the position of Arthur Young (*Farmer's Tour Through the East of England* (1771), IV, p. 361): "Every one but an idiot knows that the lower classes must be kept poor or they will never be industrious"; and with Smith himself, as recorded in student notes of his lectures (1763) (*Lectures on Police, Justice, Revenue and Arms*, ed. E. Cannan, New York, 1964, p. 257), who had emphasized the primitive nature of working-class aspirations and the effect thereof upon effort: "We find that in the commercial parts of England, the tradesmen are for the most part in this despicable condition; their work through half the week is sufficient to maintain them, and through want of education, they have no amusement for the other, but riot and debauchery." It must be noted, however, that ultimately the low behavioural standards are ascribed by Smith to a *lack of education*.

Smith's altered position in the *Wealth of Nations* is similar to that adopted by the French school of Physiocrats.

number, the more they naturally divide themselves into different classes and subdivisions of employment."[21] But in light of Smith's expressed concern with the serious distributional implications of a "populous" and "stationary" economy, it is unlikely that great weight could have been placed upon the productivity advantages as such forthcoming therein. It should be emphasized however, that in a *growing* economy the efficiency advantages might be increasingly assured while at the same time high average wages are maintained.

We note further that the celebrated maxim relating the division of labour to "the extent of the market" may indeed imply the desirability of a large population.[22] But the preceeding observation again applies; it is expansion rather than the dimensions of the economy that assures against a depression of *per capita* wages. It may be added that although a growing population might indeed generate an extension of the market it is not clear to what degree Smith explained contemporary extensions in these terms, and to what degree he ascribed them to rising average incomes since both forces were in fact recognized.[23]

21. *WN.*, p. 86.

22. *WN.*, p. 17 f. Although brief reference is made to population size as a determinant of the market, almost the entire discussion concerns the significance of satisfactory transportation facilities.

We note, however, elsewhere an emphasis upon the magnitude of the domestic *urban* population as a particularly significant determinant of the market for *agricultural* products. This issue is raised in the context of a criticism of constraints imposed upon industry and trade in the supposed interest of agriculture: "Whatever, besides, tends to diminish in any country the number of artificers and manufacturers, tends to diminish the home market, the most important of all markets for the rude produce of the soil, and thereby still further to discourage agriculture." (*WN*, p. 650). Similarly, "the greater the number and revenue of the inhabitants of the town, the more extensive is the market which it affords to those of the country." (*WN.*, p. 356).

23. A reference to expanding markets in North America in consequence of rapid population expansion casts some light on the issue (*WN.*, p. 202): "as its advances in agriculture, industry, and population, are much more rapid than those of the most thriving countries in Europe, its demand must increase much more rapidly." The fact is, however, as Smith never tired of emphasizing, that average incomes were rising also with particular rapidity in the colonies.

The account of land-utilization patterns in developing countries also depends upon the increasing demands for various commodities — hitherto free goods — generated by growing population and rising *per capita* income. (*WN.*, p. 235.)

Compare conflicting positions on this matter adopted by Adolph Lowe, "The Classical Theory of Economic Growth," *Social Research*, XXI, 1954, pp. 136-7; and

Our discussion thus far suggests that Smith regarded as desirable the expansion of national income as a means of assuring adequately high *per capita* wages and at the same time of permitting and stimulating the *growth* of population. The emphasis is upon the advantages of change in, rather than the absolute dimension of, national income. At this point we wish, however, to draw attention to a sense in which the magnitude of the capitalist sector as such — and accordingly growth in the aggregative sense — had in Smith's view certain desirable consequences. These relate to various personal characteristics typical of the capitalist sector. Thus "whenever commerce is introduced into any country probity and punctuality always accompany it," in consequence not of "national character" but of "self-interest, that general principle which regulates the actions of every man, and which leads men to act in a certain manner from views of advantage."[24] Similarly, Smith ascribed greater "security" to the capitalist sector: "Nothing tends so much to corrupt mankind as dependency, while independency still increases the honesty of the people."[25] But even in this case the ultimate cause of the differential behaviour pattern relates to the higher *per capita* earnings in the capitalist sector compared with those "paid out of revenue": "The establishment of commerce and manufactures, which brings about this independency is the best police for preventing crimes. The common people have better wages in this way than in any other, and in consequence of this the general probity of manners takes place through the whole country."[26]

It is revealing, in the present context, to examine Smith's recognition of an element of "surplus" available for taxation even in wage income. The imposition of excise taxes upon the "luxury" goods consumed by labourers (such as tobacco, tea,

J.J. Spengler, "Adam Smith's Theory of Economic Growth — Part II," *Southern Economic Journal,* XXVI, July 1951, pp. 7-8.

24. *Lectures, op. cit.,* p. 252.

25. *Ibid.,* p. 155. Cf. *Wealth of Nations,* p. 319. In these terms Smith explained the lower capital-crime rate of Glasgow compared with Edinburgh.

26. *Lectures,* pp. 155-6. The poverty of those dependent upon the spending of revenue by the wealthy is similarly emphasized in the *Wealth of Nations, loc. cit.*; thus in the various court towns of the Continent "the inferior ranks of people . . . are in general idle, dissolute, and poor."

sugar, and beer) will have no effect, it is said, upon the rate of population growth. This proposition is applied only to the "sober and industrious poor" who, it should be carefully noted, "principally supply the demand for useful labour" in contrast to the "dissolute and disorderly." Evidently, the entire population mechanism was defined specifically in the productive (or capitalist) sector. Moreover, in this sector high *per capita* wages were envisaged as generating population growth to the extent only that expenditures were devoted to the consumption of "necessaries" towards which indeed the "sober and industrious" might be attracted by raising the relative price of "luxury" goods. The argument thus defines certain fundamental demographic implications of the differential behaviour pattern of productive as distinct from unproductive labour and suggests a further reason for Smith's approval of an expansion of the productive sector:

> The high price of such commodities does not necessarily diminish the ability of the inferior ranks of people to bring up families. Upon the sober and industrious poor, taxes upon such commodities act as sumptuary laws, and dispose them either to moderate, or to refrain altogether from the use of superfluities which they can no longer easily afford. Their ability to bring up families, in consequence of this forced frugality, instead of being diminished, is frequently, perhaps, increased by the tax. It is the sober and industrious poor who generally bring up the most numerous families, and who principally supply the demand for useful labour. All the poor indeed are not sober and industrious, and the dissolute and disorderly might continue to indulge themselves in the use of such commodities after this rise of price in the same manner as before; without regarding the distress which this indulgence might bring upon their families. Such disorderly persons, however, seldom rear up numerous families; their children generally perishing from neglect, mismanagement, and the scantiness or unwholesomeness of their food. If by the strength of their constitution they survive the hardships to which the bad conduct of their parents exposes them; yet the example of that bad conduct commonly corrupts their

morals; so that, instead of being useful to society by their industry, they become public nuisances by their vices and disorders. Though the advanced price of the luxuries of the poor, therefore, might increase somewhat the distress of such disorderly families, and thereby diminish somewhat their ability to bring up children; it would not probably diminish much the useful population of the country. (823-4)[27]

We conclude that Smith's concern was with rising *per capita* income partly for its own sake and above all to assure adequate average wages, and partly as a means of encouraging population expansion and consequently the extension of the productive or capitalist sector. Expansion of the productive sector, in turn, was recommended in part because of the productivity advantages of large scale, and in part because of the desirable social and personal characteristics engendered therein. The two-fold objective imposed mutual restrictions. On the one hand, the nature of the real income increase which was considered to be desirable was constrained, for the extensive enjoyment of high average income in certain "luxury" forms would fail to stimulate population growth. On the other hand, mere magnitude of dimension in terms of capital, population, aggregate output — as distinct from the expansion thereof — did not guarantee high *per capita* incomes for labour despite high productivity.[28]

It is true that Smith in the *Wealth of Nations* reverts upon

27. The precise classification of "luxuries" as distinct from "necessaries" certainly dilutes somewhat the mercantilist flavour of parts of the passage:

"By necessaries I understand, not only the commodities which are indispensably necessary for the support of life, but whatever the custom of the country renders it indecent for creditable people, even of the lowest order, to be without.... All other things I call luxuries; without meaning by this appelation, to throw the smallest degree of reproach upon the temperate use of them. Beer and ale, for example, in Great Britain, and wine, even in the wine countries, I call luxuries. A man of any rank may, without any reproach, abstain totally from tasting such liquors. Nature does not render them necessary for the support of life; and custom nowhere renders it indecent to live without them." (*WN.*, pp. 821-2).

Cf. Smith's criticism of Mandeville referred to earlier.

28. Our analysis conflicts with a recently expressed view of Smith's position according to which the concern was with aggregate — as distinct from *per capita* wealth — mainly because of the *large* population which might be maintained thereby. See Jacob Viner, "Adam Smith," *International Encyclopedia of the Social Sciences*, vol. 14, 1968, p. 325.

occasion to a denigration of material well being reminiscent of the *Theory of Moral Sentiments*. We call attention to his discussion of the institutions required to curb "cowardice" and to develop "martial" attitudes among the masses. "Happiness and misery," runs the contention, "which reside altogether in the mind, must necessarily depend more upon the healthful or unhealthful, the mutilated or entire state of the mind, than upon that of the body."[29] Similarly, in a discussion of the desirability of complete freedom of trade in corn — with particular reference to exportation — Smith conceded in an extraordinary comment that some degree of control might be necessary to satisfy an unjustified concern of the public with its material welfare: "The people feel themselves so much interested in what relates either to their subsistence in this life, or to their happiness in a life to come, that government must yield to their prejudices, and in order to preserve the public tranquillity, establish that system which they approve of."[30]

29. *WN.*, p. 739.
We may also refer to Smith's enthusiastic endorsement of the division of labour — despite severe inequality of income — on the grounds that the workman "even of the lowest and poorest order, if he is frugal and industrious, may enjoy a greater share of the necessaries and conveniencies of life than is possible for any savage to acquire," (*WN.*, p. lviii) or that the peasant lives better than an African king (*WN.*, p. 12). There are even stronger statements to the same effect in the "Early Draft of the *Wealth of Nations*" (c. 1763) in W.R. Scott, *Adam Smith as Student and Professor*, Glasgow, 1937, pp. 325-7. For example: "If we consider, I say, all those different conveniences and luxuries with which he [the labourer] is accommodated and consider what a variety of labour is employed about each of them, we shall be sensible that without the assistance and cooperation of many thousands, the very meanest person in civilized society could not be provided for, *even in what we very falsely imagine*, the easy and simple manner in which he is commonly accommodated." (*ibid.*, p. 325; my emphasis).
It is perhaps of relevance that Smith himself was "most Spartan in his mode of life," (cf. W.R. Scott, *op. cit.*, p. 325 n.), and much admired certain of the institutions and practises of ancient Greece and Rome (*Wealth of Nations*, p. 738 f.) as did David Hume (cf. "Of Commerce," *Political Discourses* (1752) in E. Rotwein, ed., *David Hume: Writings on Economics*, London, 1955, p. 7 f.).
30. *WN.*, p. 507. (But he insisted that the price above which restrictions on corn exports are imposed should be at a very high level.) Smith's comments were motivated by a bill of 1773 which retained the substance of earlier legislation on grain exports. In a later edition, probably the second (1778), Smith added (*ibid.*, p. 510): "So far, therefore, this law seems to be inferior to the ancient system. With all its imperfections, however, we may perhaps say of it what was said of the laws of Solon, that, though not the best in itself, it is the best which the interests, prejudices, and temper of the times would admit of. It may perhaps in due time prepare the way for a better." This addition is sometimes attributed to the influence of Edmund

These comments are apparently in conflict with the general course of the argument in the *Wealth of Nations*. For, as we have seen, Smith applauded the contemporary upward trend in *per capita* wages and deplored the pitiable living standards of labour in those contemporary societies which, while possessing great populations, were stagnant. But we may to some degree overcome the disaccord if we once again ascribe to Smith disapproval of *excessively* high average incomes on "moral" grounds, and because of certain social disadvantages such as the weakening of the nation's "martial" spirit and, we might add, possibly because of the implied failure of the population mechanism. To take this view of Smith's position, however, suggests that the *desiderata* of policy cannot be defined unambiguously but depend upon the particular circumstances which happen to rule. It also follows that the difference between Smith's two major works with regard to the desirability of economic development (in terms of rising average income) is one of degree rather than of kind, for the former after all justified a *"comfortable"* standard of subsistence for labour. But the difference is nonetheless sufficient to permit a particular concern with the absolute magnitude of wealth and population in the earlier work only.

Government Intervention in Economic Development

Throughout the *Wealth of Nations* Smith makes use of a presumptive case in favour of laissez-faire based upon the "natural right" of individuals not to be interfered with. (Amongst numerous applications, this principle is strikingly utilized in the condemnation of the Settlement Acts – as a "violation of natural liberty and justice" – and of interference with colonial enterprise, and in defence of the regulation of paper money as the exception which proves the rule.[31]) Whether

Burke, who was critical of Smith's professional argument for free commerce, referring to various frictions of interest. (Cf. Viner, *Guide to John Rae's Life of Adam Smith*, New York, 1965, p. 23 f.) But in light of Smith's concession noted in our text, which appeared in the first edition of 1776, and of other concessions to retaliatory measures, mentioned below, there seems little reason to believe that any significant change in attitude on his part occurred.

31. *WN.*, p. 308: "Such regulations may, no doubt, be considered as in some

an extensive program of government intervention *in the interest of economic development* would have to be rejected on the grounds that it conflicted with the principle of natural liberty is a question which Smith rarely raised formally, although the general tenor of his work would suggest a rejection of far-reaching control. It is true that a passage in the *Theory of Moral Sentiments*,[32] already referred to, implies that the government itself represents an arm of the natural order: "The perfection of police, the extension of trade and manufactures, are noble and magnificent objects. The contemplation of them pleases us, and we are interested in whatever can tend to advance them. They make part of the great system of government, and the wheels of the political machine seem to move with more harmony and ease by means of them." Yet despite this view of the role of government Smith subsequently formulated his celebrated assault upon the "man of system" implying severe disapproval of excessive intervention: "The man of system . . . is apt to be very wise in his own conceit; and is often so enamoured with the supposed beauty of his own ideal plan of government, that he cannot suffer the smallest deviation from any part of it . . ; in the great chess-board of human society, every single piece has a principle of motion of its own, altogether different from that which the legislature might choose to impress upon it."[33]

Further evidence may be drawn from Smith's treatment of the corn trade, already referred to, which established the general rule that completely free trade in corn was in principle desirable to assure that "the scarcity of any one country" may be "relieved by the plenty of some other," and, it will be noted, *to assure the farmer his natural right not to be interfered with*: "To hinder, besides, the farmer from sending his goods at all

respect a violation of natural liberty. But those exertions of the natural liberty of a few individuals, which might endanger the security of the whole society, are, and ought to be, restrained by the laws of all governments."

32. *Op. cit.*, p. 265.

33. *Ibid.*, pp. 342-3. Cf. *Wealth of Nations, op. cit.*, p. 423: "The statesman, who should attempt to direct private people in what manner they ought to employ their capitals, would not only load himself with a most unnecessary attention, but assume an authority which could safely be trusted, not only to no single person, but to no council or senate whatever, and which would nowhere be so dangerous as in the hands of a man who had folly and presumption enough to fancy himself fit to exercise it."

times to the best market, is evidently to sacrifice the ordinary laws of justice to an idea of public utility, to a sort of reasons of state."[34]

Yet intervention in the interest of expansion was not rejected out of hand.[35] It is well known that Smith recommended the maintenance of the current maximum rate of interest imposed by the usury laws to prevent "prodigals and projectors" from cornering the supply of loans: "Sober people, who will give for the use of money no more than a part of what they are likely to make by the use of it, would not venture into the competition. A great part of the capital of the country would thus be kept out of the hands which were most likely to make a profitable and advantageous use of it, and thrown into those which were most likely to waste and destroy it."[36] Furthermore, as a means of encouraging agricultural investment and experimentation, Smith recommended tax abatements for those landlords who cultivated part of their own land: "It is of importance that the landlord should be encouraged to cultivate a part of his own land. His capital is generally greater than that of the tenant, and with less skill he can frequently raise a greater produce. The landlord can afford to try experiments, and is generally disposed to do so."[37] Thirdly, we note that Smith approved of British colonial practise which had restrained the engrossing of uncultivated land by obliging proprietors to improve and cultivate a certain proportion of their property within a limited time.[38] And as a further instance we recall that Smith suggested the use of excise taxes to alter the pattern of

34. WN., pp. 506-7.

35. Even in the case relating to free corn exportation, he conceded that if some countries imposed constraints, others — particularly small states rather than England or France — may legitimately find it prudent to follow suit and limit exportation to assure adequate supplies for the domestic market; and he accepted some slight control in the interest of public order as we have seen.

36. WN., pp. 339-40. Whether Smith ultimately accepted the force of Bentham's criticism of his case for a legal maximum, as is sometimes suggested, is an open question. Cf. Viner, Guide to John Rae's Life of Adam Smith, op. cit., pp. 18-19.

37. WN., p. 784. Conversely, the landlord who charged a fine for the renewal of the lease should be penalised because he "takes from the tenant so great a part of his capital, and thereby diminishes so much his ability to cultivate the land." (WN., p. 783.)

38. WN., p. 539.

working-class consumption as a device to assure population expansion.

These instances of legitimate intervention, it will be noted, are largely directed at the encouragement of *investment* at the expense of luxury outlays, speculative ventures and the like. This accords with Smith's disapproval of excessive consumption expressed even in the case of labour and *a fortiori* – in light of his consistent assaults – in that of the upper classes.[39] But they should not be exaggerated as evidence of support for an extensive governmental programme.[40] Moreover, what requires particular emphasis is Smith's overwhelming rejection of policies designed to stimulate more rapid expansion by altering the allocation of a given capital stock as distinct from intervention concerned with the stimulus of net capital accumulation. It is precisely the attempt to demonstrate on analytical grounds that such forms of intervention can only slacken the rate of growth which represents his fundamental challenge to mercantilist thinking.[41]

---

39. It is true that Smith contrasted "parsimony" with "prodigality" which refers to consumption actually encroaching upon capital (*WN.*, p. 322), but the contrast seems to be merely a formal one for he appears to disapprove of excessive consumption as such as, for example, in the dictum (*WN.*, p. 489) – in a section added to the third edition of 1784 – that "in public, as well as in private expences, great wealth may, perhaps, frequently be admitted as an apology for great folly."

See too Smith's view that excessively high profits are likely to have a *negative* effect upon savings (*WN.*, p. 578): "The high rate of profits seems everywhere to destroy that parsimony which in other circumstances is natural to the character of the merchant. When profits are high, that sober virtue seems to be superfluous, and expensive luxury to suit better the affluence of his situation."

40. In fact Smith summarized his position regarding policies suitable for agriculture by calling for complete freedom of enterprise (*WN.*, p. 785): "The principal attention of the sovereign ought to be to encourage, by every means in his power, the attention both of the landlord and of the farmer; by allowing both to pursue their own interest in their own way, and according to their own judgement; by giving to both the most perfect security that they shall enjoy the full recompence of their own industry; and by procuring to both the most extensive market for every part of their produce, in consequence of establishing the easiest and safest communications both by land and water, through every part of his own dominions, as well as the most unbounded freedom of exportation to the dominions of all other princes."

41. See a forthcoming paper by the present writer, "Some Implications of Adam Smith's Analysis of Investment Priorities," *History of Political Economy*, III, 2, Fall 1971

Vocational Training[42]

Smith recognized institutional impediments to the process by which wages in different occupations were kept in line, particularly contemporary apprenticeship and corporation laws. But apart from these artificial constraints he was confident that the market process could be relied upon to generate appropriate supplies of skilled labour. We may illustrate the extent to which he tended to play down the restraints imposed on mobility by the difficulty of acquiring the necessary skills. For example, in a discussion of the consequences of abolishing trade barriers, Smith denied that long-term unemployment would result on the grounds that workers may easily transfer from one trade to another: "Though a great number of people should, by thus restoring the freedom of trade, be thrown all at once out of their ordinary employment and common method of subsistence, it would by no means follow that they would thereby be deprived either of employment or subsistence.... To the greater part of manufactures ... there are other collateral manufactures of so similar a nature, that a worker can easily transfer his industry from one of them to another."[43] It was in fact precisely upon these grounds that Smith condemned contemporary practises relating to apprenticeship: "Long apprenticeships are altogether unnecessary. The arts, which are much superior to common trades, such as those of making clocks and watches, contain no such mystery as to require a long course of instruction ... How to apply the instruments and how to construct the machines, cannot well require more than the lessons of a few weeks, perhaps those of a few days might be sufficient. In the common mechanical trades, those of a few days might certainly be sufficient."[44]

In fact, according to Smith the degree of skill required in

42. This section is drawn from my article entitled "The Role of the State in Vocational Training: The Classical Economists' View," *Southern Economic Journal*, XXXIV, April 1968, pp. 513-525.

43. *WN.*, pp. 436-7. Cf. pp. 134-5.

44. *WN.*, p. 123. This may have been an error of judgment. It was partly because the Carron ironworks could not supply the skilled artisans whose help was essential that Watt's experiments on the steam engine could not be easily completed. See T.S. Ashton, *The Industrial Revolution, 1760-1830*, London, 1966, p. 68.

manufacturing was less than that in agriculture where the system of apprenticeship was not applied:

> The policy of Europe considers the labour of all mechanics, artificers, and manufacturers, as skilled labour; and that of all country labourers as common labour. It seems to suppose that of the former to be of a more nice and delicate nature than that of the latter. It is so perhaps in some cases; but in the greater part it is quite otherwise. . . . (101)

> There is scarce any common mechanic trade . . . of which all the operations may not be as completely and distinctly explained in a pamphlet of a very few pages. . . . Not only the art of the farmer, the general direction of the operations of husbandry, but many inferior branches of country labour, require much more skill and experience than the greater part of mechanic trades. The man who works upon brass and iron, works with instruments and upon materials of which the temper is always the same, or very nearly the same. (126-7)

Smith recognized *geographical* immobility apparently unrelated to the laws of the land. In commenting on an observed permanent difference between real wages paid to town and to country labourers he remarked: "After all that has been said of the levity and inconstancy of human nature, it appears evidently from experience that a man is of all sorts of luggage the most difficult to be transported."[45] In his highly optimistic treatment of *occupational* mobility Smith apparently believed that this observation was irrelevant.[46] The equalization process whereby money-wage differentials compensate for subjective evaluations of work and other non-monetary characteristics attached to each occupation requires of course the assumption of "mobility," or rather *enough* mobility to meet the conditions of net equalization without creating chaos. Some degree of inertia and of attachment to locality relating to the risk and

45. *WN.*, p. 75.
46. This problem is mentioned by Francis A. Walker, *The Wages Question*, New York, 1875, p. 193.

cost of moving must exist. Yet Smith's references to geograph-ical immobility imply a degree of inertia in *excess* of this required amount.[47]

Although Smith emphasized the ease with which skills may be acquired by the working class he was, at the same time, acutely aware of the fact that workers could not afford a costly education: "the common people . . . have little time to spare for education. Their parents can scarce afford to maintain them even in infancy. As soon as they are able to work, they must apply to some trade by which they can earn their subsistence."[48] Smith did not evidently fear that the exclusion of workers from occupations requiring a heavy preliminary "investment" in education in any way prevented the process of net equalization of returns. He apparently presumed that a sufficient number of relatively wealthy individuals were available to assure that, in the long run, excessive returns in such occupations would be eliminated.[49]

The classical economists, in general, based a case for government intervention in education on the grounds of a divergence between social and private returns. So far as *vocational* training is concerned, however, Smith considered that private and social returns coincide so that the market can be relied upon to generate adequate investment. Consider for example Smith's references to an earlier discussion by David

47. Insofar as Smith was writing a "tract for the times" his position may be understood as calling for the removal of the *grossest* institutional impediments to mobility first. Remaining obstacles would be of relatively smaller significance and could be dealt with afterwards.

48. *WN.,* p. 737.

49. The Smithian analysis was severely criticized by J.S. Mill. Although Smith had recognized that monetary returns in any occupation must in equilibrium suffice to indemnify education costs, he had failed to consider the possibility that returns might persist which exceed the amount required, apart from instances of excessive returns due to institutional constraints upon entry into skilled trades. In fact, Mill argued, both *financial and social obstacles* prevented the attainment of skills by sufficiently large numbers to assure the eradication of monopoly returns in skilled trades even in the absence of institutional constraints. In the *Wealth of Nations* the analysis of the wage structure referred essentially to the earnings of the "working class"; professional men were a non-competing group. The recognition by Mill that *within* the working class there were non-competing groups was the essence of the change. Cf. *Collected Works of John Stuart Mill*, vol. II, *Principles of Political Economy*, Toronto, 1965, pp. 386-7.

Hume to this effect:

'Most of the arts and professions in a state,' says by
far the most illustrious philosopher and historian of the
present age, 'are of such a nature, that while they promote
the interests of the society, they are also useful and
agreeable to some individuals; and in that case, the
constant rule of the magistrate, except, perhaps, on the
first introduction of any art, is, to leave the profession to
itself, and trust its encouragement to the individuals who
reap the benefit of it. The artizans, finding their profits to
rise by the favour of their customers, increase, as much as
possible, their skill and industry; and as matters are not
disturbed by any injudicious tampering, the commodity is
always sure to be at all times, nearly proportional to the
demand.' (742)[50]

A clearer statement to the effect that normally social and
private returns may be presumed to coincide cannot be
imagined. Yet the allowance that government aid might be
called for "on the first introduction of any art" should be noted
carefully for it is possible that Hume and Smith would have
adopted a different attitude in an economy undergoing rapid
changes in products and processes.

Some reference may be made at this juncture to Smith's
recommendation that a modernized curriculum was desirable
for working-class children. Elementary education should be
extended to "geometry and mechanics": "If in those little
schools . . . they were instructed in the elementary parts of
geometry and mechanics, the literary education of this rank of
people would perhaps be as complete as it can be. There is
scarce a common trade which does not afford some opportunities of applying to it the principles of geometry and
mechanics, and which would not therefore gradually exercise
and improve the common people in those principles, the
necessary introduction to the most sublime as well as the most

50. The reference is to the *Discourses on the First Decade of Titus Livius*, Book
III, ch. i.

useful sciences."[51] To some extent it may appear that vocational training is implied in the above recommendation and indeed that Smith was implicitly recognizing the impediments to mobility created by limited educational opportunities. Although on balance it would appear that the emphasis is upon elementary education rather than on the training of specific skills, it is nonetheless significant that a relatively ambitious program was recommended in order to raise the productivity of the working force; moreover, attention was paid in arguing the case for more or less public aid to elementary schooling not only to beneficial "social" effects of a general kind resulting from literacy, but also to specifically economic advantages. In fact, to the extent that many workers were initially receiving no education, or very little education, or education of very low quality, the introduction of adequate elementary training would tend to increase mobility. Indeed, starting from an illiterate base it is difficult to distinguish elementary from vocational training since, frequently, the former is a necessary prerequisite of the latter.

The economic advantages are implied in the elementary-school curriculum recommended by Adam Smith which included, as we have just seen, "the principles of geometry and mechanics . . . the necessary introduction to the most sublime as well as the most useful sciences." It is also the case that amongst the stultifying effects of specialization — which could be countered by education — Smith included the danger that the industrial worker would find it ultimately impossible to operate "in any other employment than that to which he has been bred."[52] We conclude that Smith's optimism regarding the high degree of mobility — upon which was based his confidence in the operation of the free market in the provision of skills — was contingent upon a necessary minimum degree of elementary training, towards which government was advised to contribute.

51. *WN.*, pp. 737-8. The government would establish parish schools. But the teacher would be paid only in part from public funds. Fees would be charged to assure against the "deriliction of his duty."

52. *WN.*, p. 735.

Alternative Policy Objectives

A few words are in order regarding alternative and possibly conflicting goals of policy to that of development. Smith recognized the legitimacy of certain instances of governmental interference designed to encourage particular industries, on grounds of "defence." Thus the Navigation Acts, introduced in the interests of British shipping — by imposing restrictions on the use of foreign shipping in the British import and coastal trades, and in the colonial trade — although quite illegitimate from the point of view of growth were justified: "The act of navigation is not favourable to foreign commerce, or to the growth of that opulence which can arise from it. . . . As defence, however, is of much more importance than opulence, the act of navigation is, perhaps, the wisest of all the commercial regulations of England."[53] A similar justification (albeit somewhat half-hearted) is given for the granting of subsidies to particular defence industries: "if any particular manufacture was necessary, indeed, for the defence of the society, it might not always be prudent to depend upon our neighbours for the supply; and if such manufactures could not otherwise be supported at home, it might not be unreasonable that all the other branches of industry should be taxed in order to support it. The bounties upon the exportation of British-made sail-cloth, and British-made gun-powder, may, perhaps, both be vindicated upon this principle."[54]

Whether these concessions should be emphasized is, however, another matter. In defining the nature and scope of the investigation undertaken in the *Wealth of Nations* Smith, after all, wrote that "the riches, and so far as power depends upon riches, the power of every country, must always be in

---

53. *WN.*, p. 431. The emphasis here is upon the economic disadvantage to foreign traders of arriving in British ports without cargo, which causes a reduction in the number of foreign sellers and correspondingly of foreign buyers with the consequence that we "are thus likely not only to buy foreign goods dearer, but to sell our own cheaper, than if there was a more perfect freedom of trade."

54. *WN.*, pp. 488-9. This precise formulation appeared in the third edition of 1784. In the first two editions the bounty upon the importation of American "naval stores" was similarly justified. (Cf. Cannan, *op. cit.*, p. 485 n.)

proportion to the value of its annual produce."[55] It was Smith's objective in this context to show that, at least as a first approximation, the two ends are not in conflict, so that governments concerned with national power do not generally need to interfere with the allocation of capital. For the foundation of national power lay in the taxation capacity of the state which was defined in terms of the rental, profit and wage income in excess of subsistence and which, it was envisaged, would be maximized in a competitive economy in the absence of intervention.[56] Moreover, Smith in fact recommended that Britain relinquish her monopoly in the colony trade, one of the key features of the Navigation Acts, on the grounds that it "depresses the industry of all other countries, but chiefly that of the colonies, without in the least increasing, but on the contrary diminishing, that of the country in whose favour it is established."[57] Indeed he recommended the abandonment of the American colonies entirely if they could not be justified on *economic* grounds:

> The rulers of Great Britain have, for more than a century past, amused the people with the imagination that they possessed a great empire on the west side of the Atlantic. This empire, however, has hitherto existed in imagination only. It has hitherto been, not an empire, but the project of an empire; not a gold mine, but the project of a gold mine; a project which has cost, which continues to cost, and which, if pursued in the same way as it has been hitherto, is likely to cost, immense expence, without being

55. *WN.,* p. 352. Cf. *WN.,* p. 397. "Political economy, considered as a branch of the science of a statesman or legislator ... proposes to enrich both the people and the sovereign." A similar position was adopted by David Hume, "Of Commerce," *op. cit.,* p. 5: "The greatness of a state, and the happiness of its subjects, how independent soever they may be supposed in some respects, are commonly allowed to be inseparable with regard to commerce; and as private men receive greater security, in the possession of their trade and riches, from the power of the public, so the public becomes powerful in proportion to the opulence and extensive commerce of private men."

56. More specifically we read: "In modern war the great expence of fire-arms gives an evident advantage to the nation which can best afford that expence; and consequently, to an opulent and civilized, over a poor and barbarous nation." *WN.,* p. 669.

57. *WN.,* p. 577.

likely to bring any profit; for the effects of the monopoly of the colony trade ... are, to the great body of the people, mere loss instead of profit.... If the project cannot be completed, it ought to be given up. If any of the provinces of the British empire cannot be made to contribute towards the support of the whole empire, it is surely time that Great Britain should free herself from the expence of defending these provinces in time of war, and of supporting any part of their civil or military establishments in time of peace, and endeavour to accommodate her future views and designs to the real mediocrity of her circumstances. (899-900)

We may discern on Smith's part the objective of goading the government to reform, in order to justify the retention of the colonies. But the emphasis upon the economic criterion is clear. It is, therefore, likely that Smith's approval of the Navigation Acts was severely limited (perhaps to those sections only relating to the British import and coastal trades). And we deduce that the formally straightforward dictum "defence is much more important than opulence" was after all maintained subject to a degree of "cost control."[58]

It is of relevance for any evaluation of Smith's attitude towards goals of policy to recall his concern with the potentially dehumanizing effects upon the labourer of one of the key requisites for growth, namely specialization. Yet what must be emphasized in this regard is the recommendation that governments should subsidize education as a countervailing measure: "His dexterity at his own particular trade seems ... to be acquired at the expense of his intellectual, social, and martial virtues. But in every improved and civilized society this is the

---

58. However, some commentators have discerned a greater element of "dualism" (that is inconsistency) in Smith insofar as he condemned mercantilist protection while maintaining an "equivocating" interest in defence and power. Cf. Charles Wilson, "'Mercantilism': Some Vicissitudes of an Idea," *Economic History Review*, X, 1957, pp. 182-3.

Although the charge of serious "dualism" is in our view exaggerated, we can find no justification for the view expressed by E. Heckscher that power for Smith "was only a means to the end" of opulence (*Mercantilism*, II, ed. 2, London, 1955, p. 17).

state into which the labouring poor, that is, the great body of the people, must necessarily fall, unless government takes some pains to prevent it."[59] There is no suggestion that economic growth should be slackened on these grounds. (At the same time — if our earlier interpretation reflects accurately Smith's intentions — any permanent increase in average income beyond some ill-defined minimum level in fact met with disapproval on moral and social grounds. It may only be surmized that under certain conditions Smith might have recommended an alternative approach.)

There are other costs of economic development implied in the *Wealth of Nations* as far as the growth of towns is a concomitant phenomenon. For the town labourer is said to be in danger of losing the support and control exerted by his neighbours, typical in the small village, and consequently might "abandon himself to every sort of low profligacy and vice."[60] Smith accordingly lauded the small religious sects which tended, in his evaluation, to provide the labourer with the necessary social contacts. And the state might contribute by the encouragement of "public diversions."[61] Once again, there are solutions to the negative aspects of growth.

Summary and Conclusion

Our discussion of economic development in the *Wealth of*

---

59. *WN.*, p. 735. Indeed Smith insists that even if the state did not benefit from the education of the poor in matters of defence, there would still be an obligation to assure that the poor "should not go altogether uninstructed." (*WN.*, p. 740.) In fact the argument has implications for the matter of income inequality. For it is specifically the poor who are the victims of the various disadvantages of specialization.

Cf. *Lectures, op. cit.*, p. 255. In his discussion of the "inconveniencies arising from a commercial spirit," Smith refers not merely to the effects of specialization but to the neglect of the education of the young who enter the work force at a very early age. Here too, education is recommended for its beneficial social effects.

60. *WN.*, p. 747.

Malthus was to make a related though not identical observation: "The unwholesomeness of towns, to which some persons are necessarily drawn from the nature of their trades, must be considered as a species of misery. . . ." (*Population: The First Essay, op. cit.*, p. 38.)

61. *WN.*, p. 748. Smith was careful to insist that this "encouragement" should merely take the form of "allowing perfect liberty to all those who for their own interest would attempt, without scandal or indecency, to amuse and divert the people." Yet even this position conflicts with typical mercantilist doctrine.

Nations reveals the significance to Smith of various extra-economic objectives. While in contemporary circumstances, rising average income was desired particularly as a means of assuring labour an "adequate" standard of living, Smith at the same time disapproved on "moral" and "social" grounds of excessively high consumption, and clearly found undesirable a constant population in the face of significant capital accumulation and a rapidly rising demand for labour. On the other hand, we have noted that the optimism of *The Theory of Moral Sentiments* which served as rationale for the desirability of a large population in that work is severely qualified in the *Wealth of Nations*. Our conclusion, therefore, is that a *large* population was not in itself regarded as a particularly desirable objective. On the contrary, the unfavourable income distribution, from the point of view of labour characteristic of stagnant economies, however large, is much emphasized despite the potential for productivity increase deriving from scale. Scale economies might, however, be obtained in an *expanding* economy while at the same time wages per head are maintained at a satisfactory level.

A central feature of Smith's writings upon the issue of development is the relative weight attached to possibly conflicting goals. Indeed he formally insisted that the fundamental concern of policy should be with national power recognizing a potential conflict in certain cases with development. His preoccupation with the "martial" spirit of the masses — threatened to some degree both by excessively high consumption itself and by specialization, a fundamental prerequisite of growth — his support for a standing army, his allowance of a case for intervention in favour of British shipping and various other industries, all illustrate the dictum that "defence is much more important than opulence." But the interpretive problem is less serious than it may appear. In the first place, we have noted Smith's presumption that as a rule the objective of defence would best be served by those same processes of the freely-operating market which generate a maximum net revenue product from the community's resources; intervention in favour of particular industries was recommended in very few cases.

What, however, requires emphasis above all is the fact that where a conflict between the objectives of "defence" and "opulence" is recognized, the foregone opportunities (that is the alternative costs) in following the former objective are made quite explicit. It will finally be recalled that certain of the social disadvantages inherent in the developmental process might be overcome by various forms of government intervention particularly in the elementary education of the poor, also required to assure the necessary minimum knowledge essential for the operation of the free market in the provision of vocational skills.

Samuel Hollander

The Via Media
in an Age of Revolution:
Anglicanism in the 18th Century

When the question is asked, what happened to Anglicanism in the hundred years between the British "Glorious Revolution" of 1688 and the beginning of the French Revolution in 1789, a period punctuated by the American Revolution in the 1770's, I suppose the obvious answer is that, like the Abbé Siéyès, it survived. That this is not so frivolous an answer as it may at first seem, I will presently try to show; it is even more to the point in the Abbé's original French — "J'ai vécu"; "I went on living." Surviving some of its later historians, however, has proved a harder task.

The history of religion in the eighteenth century generally — not merely in England — has received scandalous treatment at the hands of the historians of that century, and I do not think that we can feel much confidence that we possess any sound general knowledge of the history of the century's life and culture until some of the neglect and distortion has been repaired. To document this charge is all too easy. As a more or less random example, there is the recently published very large and sumptuous volume edited by the late Alfred Cobban, one of the most deservedly distinguished names among historians of the time, entitled simply *The Eighteenth Century* — though with the somewhat ominous subtitle, "Europe in the Age of Enlightenment."[1] It contains ten chapters, by other eminent historians, on various aspects of life in the century — government, science and technology, agriculture and industry, exploration, the arts, and so on. Does it contain a chapter on religion? Those who have had some experience with works bearing the

1. London, Thames and Hudson, 1969.

word "Enlightenment" in their titles will smile at the naiveté of
the question. Even a search through the very detailed index for
an entry for "religion" reveals none. There *is* one for "religious
conflicts," listing references to a total of five pages. One of
these passages (in the chapter entitled "Reform and Revolution") contains what may be said to be the only formal
treatment of the religious history of the century in the book –
captions to a series of illustrations, of which the following is a
fair selection: "Religious hatred still contributed to unrest in
almost every country of Europe. The Church . . . was inevitably
interlocked with the State . . . . Minorities suffered in both
Catholic and Protestant centres. . . . Anti-catholic bigotry in
England – the Gordon Riots of 1780. . . . 'Enthusiasm,' derided
by the Enlightenment, was the life-blood of the dissenting
Churches which sprang up in most Protestant countries as a
reaction against the apathy and complacency of the establishment. . . . The Jews in the West were still open to unfair
discrimination" (pp. 322-23).

There is some truth in all this, of course. To be sure, the
dissenting churches did not spring up in Protestant countries as
a reaction against the apathy and complacency of the establishment, as a glance at the history of Presbyterianism and
Congregationalism and the Baptists will show, nor was "enthusiasm" – a belief in the extraordinary inspiration of individuals
by the Holy Spirit – their life-blood, or even accepted by them,
or by John Wesley as far as that goes. But I suppose one must
not expect too much erudition on such points from students of
"the Enlightenment," the very definitely anti-clerical movement
on the Continent of which men like Voltaire, Diderot, and
D'Alembert are the key figures. No one will deny that this
movement was one of the highest importance in the intellectual
history of the century. But to continue to insist, as the title of
this volume seems to, that "the Enlightenment" *is* the eighteenth century is absurd. It is now even a little old-fashioned:
the veteran historian of ideas, George Boas, in a rather curious
"agonizing reappraisal" entitled "In Search of the Age of
Reason" – Boas is now not even sure that there ever was one –
recently conceded,

However one defines the Age of Reason, however revolutionary and anti-authoritarian one estimates its spirit to have been, it should be noted that neither the Roman Catholic nor the Anglican nor the Lutheran communions ceased their ministrations in 1750. Moreover, in England, men like Burke and Johnson and Goldsmith, as much earlier Pope and Addison, continued to believe in the religion and philosophy of their forefathers.[2]

We may readily agree, at the same time reserving our judgment of Boas's implied assumption that the essence of Roman Catholicism and Anglicanism and Lutheranism is authoritarianism and counter-revolution. Are the teachings of the Gospel which it is, in theory at least, the function of these bodies to propagate, in fact authoritarian and counter-revolutionary?

The history of Roman Catholicism and Lutheranism in the eighteenth century will have to be left to others to trace: our present concern is with Anglicanism. Returning to the index of the Cobban volume, we find no entry for the Church of England; we do find, under "Anglicanism" three references to separate pages of the work, which however turn out to contain only the barest incidental mention. No student trying to form a picture of what life in that century was like would ever guess, from reading the book, that perhaps ninety per cent of the population of England were connected with the established church (and most of the rest were Christians of other denominations, Roman Catholics or nonconformists), that most of them were baptized, married, and buried by it, that most of them learned its Catechism, and attended its services at least once a week most of their lives — and, as a result, had the language of its magnificent Prayer Book almost by heart; that the unit of local civil administration was the parish, so that even the weekday life of the average citizen was therefore closely linked to the church; that his life, civil as well as spiritual, was punctuated by its great festivals of Christmas and Easter and the lesser ones of Whitsunday and Trinity Sunday and Michaelmas;

2. In Earl R. Wasserman, ed., *Aspects of the Eighteenth Century*, Baltimore, Johns Hopkins University Press, 1965, p. 18.

that the government of the country on the larger scale was likewise closely linked to it — the sovereign was solemnly crowned in Westminster Abbey in an ancient religious ceremony, periods of public thanksgiving or mourning were signalized by services in St. Paul's Cathedral and other churches, Parliament at stated times attended its church of St. Margaret's, Westminster, as a body, the hierarchy of the church were selected and appointed by the Government. It was a great age of preaching; the sermons of men like South and Tillotson, Clarke and Butler and Secker had a large sale — not to mention the thousands who were attracted to the open-air preaching of Wesley and Whitefield. It was a great age — very probably the greatest — of hymn writing, the age of Watts and Doddridge and Ken, of Charles Wesley and John Byrom and Cowper and John Newton: the best known and best loved hymns of English-speaking Protestantism come from the eighteenth century. It was an equally great age of church architecture, that of Wren and his gifted successors, men like Gibbs and Hawksmoor and Archer; Gibb's novel design of St. Martin's-in-the-Fields set the pattern for the hundreds of white, steepled village churches of New England and elsewhere in North America; even Westminster Abbey as we know it today is a product of the eighteenth century, since its tall western towers were erected by pupils of Wren. It was a notable age of church music, headed by the magnificent achievement of Purcell and Handel, and with such lesser but highly competent practitioners as Boyce, Greene, Croft, Blow, and Samuel Wesley.

The vast majority of important English writers, thinkers, and artists of the century were sincere, professing, often devout Christians. To Boas's "short list" of Burke, Johnson, Goldsmith, Pope, and Addison, could be added dozens more — Dryden, Bunyan, Defoe, Steele, Richardson, Fielding, Sterne, Smart, Cowper, above all the towering figure of the Very Reverend Jonathan Swift, Doctor of Sacred Theology, one of the two deans of the Anglican church who are among the great names of literature and, in my opinion, no less authentic a Christian than his fellow dean, John Donne. The two greatest scientists of the age, Newton and Boyle, were devout Anglicans; so were two of the three greatest philosophers, Locke and Bishop Berkeley. The list of avowed enemies of orthodox Christianity among the literary figures of the time is a very small one: one thinks only of Hume and Gibbon among writers of the first rank, though there was a handful of other smaller ones who evince some skepticism but keep quieter about it — Prior, Gray, Horace Walpole. A few of the Christian writers I have mentioned, like Pope and the later Dryden, were Roman Catholics, and a few, like Bunyan and Defoe, were Protestant nonconformists. Of these, Dryden and Defoe, to be sure, engaged from time to time in controversy with their Anglican colleagues over matters of church government and the civil rights of dissenters; but on the great central matters of Christian doctrine, their differences were small. Bunyan was a man of little formal education and the humblest social position, a member of an obscure Baptist sect who was jailed by the authorities for unlicensed preaching — not a man, one would think, who would much appeal to the Anglican "establishment." Yet it is interesting to note the attitude toward him of the two great "High Church" writers of the eighteenth century. Swift, in his "Letter to a Young Gentleman Lately Entered into Holy Orders," giving his protégé good advice about composing sermons, counsels him to avoid imitating learned philosophical treatises, and remarks "I have been better entertained and more informed by a chapter in the Pilgrim's Progress than by a long discourse upon the Will and the Intellect, and simple or complex Ideas."[3] And there is the charming story of Johnson's taking Bishop Percy's little daughter on his knee, and asking her whether she had read *Pilgrim's Progress*. When she replied that she had not, " 'No?' said the Doctor. 'Then I would not give one farthing for you'; and he set her down and took no further notice of her."[4]

I have tried to sketch, in the brief time available, the outline of what seems to me a *prima facie* case for affirming that the Christian religion in its Anglican form is to be taken seriously as a highly important force in the social and intellectual history of

3. Swift, *Prose Works*, ed. Herbert Davis, Oxford, Blackwell, 1948, IX, p. 77.
4. Boswell, *Life of Johnson*, ed. G.B. Hill and L.F. Powell, Oxford, Clarendon, 1934-50, II, p. 238, n. 5.

England in the eighteenth century — quite as important a force as in other centuries, certainly as in the nineteenth and twentieth. That case now has to be defended against the innumerable attacks that have been made on it, attacks found in the great majority of the standard social and literary histories of the century. The origin of this hostile attitude is obscure, and one can only speculate about it, though the question is important enough to warrant a full scale investigation. One possible theory stems from the fact that the later eighteenth and early nineteenth centuries in England saw a number of vigorous reform movements in religion — the Methodist and Evangelical movements, later the Oxford Movement. Any church here on earth, being a collection of sinful human beings, is of course always in need of reform — is *semper reformanda,* always falls short of its heavenly ideal, is always rightly subject to denunciation by reformers. The denunciations of the early nineteenth century reformers took place at a time when the eighteenth century, because of the "generation gap," was in general bad odor anyway, and they were eagerly seized on by writers of popular histories and textbooks for the vastly expanded reading public and the host of new schools and colleges founded in the mid-nineteenth century. Having found their way into such textbooks, these clichés get passed on from one textbook writer to the next without any real investigation into their soundness, and attain a prescriptive right to existence. The eighteenth century, too, was a great age of the comic, and the inevitable discrepancy between the moral ideal the clergyman is supposed to embody and the fallibility of its human representatives makes fine material for the literary satirist like Swift and Fielding or the satiric draughtsman like Hogarth and Rowlandson. Yet Swift and Fielding considered themselves, with justice, loyal and sincere Anglicans; and it might well be argued that their assiduous pillorying of "dull divines" — Swift's phrase — in an attempt to improve the standards of intelligence and sincerity among the clergy of their church is a sign of health and liveliness in that church; that it is a church in which no such self-criticism takes place that is in a state of dangerous decadence.

At any rate, there has been no lack of modern historians to repeat the old charges. J. H. Plumb's little handbook in the Pelican series, *England in the Eighteenth Century* (1950), much used in schools and colleges for "background" of the century, will do as well as any:

> There is a worldliness, almost a venality, about eighteenth-century prelates which no amount of apologetics can conceal. The clerical duties of visitation, ordination, and confirmation were done only as political duties allowed.... The greatest danger to the Church lay not only in its refusal to reform but in its attitude to life. The way to success was in discretion and man-pleasing and the worldly virtues became heavenly ones. . . . Evil and guilt, sin and redemption — the whole personal drama and appeal of religion — was forgotten or rationalized away and the eupeptic optimism of politicians pervaded the teaching of the Church (pp. 43-44).

Plumb, to be sure, is in general no admirer of Christianity — and this is true of a number of popular and influential writers who have had much to do with fixing the picture of the eighteenth century that exists in the minds of modern readers, Sir Leslie Stephen, that militant agnostic, for one, Sir Walter Raleigh for another. But even those who profess a Christian outlook have at least equally harsh things to say. Hoxie Neale Fairchild, who in the introduction to his *Religious Trends in English Poetry*,[5] proclaims himself an Anglo-Catholic, begins by quoting Boling-broke — no great authority on the subject, one would think —

> 'There is no profusion of the ethereal spirit among us.' . . . Few students of the age of Queen Anne would dispute the accuracy of that statement. Religion — especially religion of that emotional and imaginative sort which inspires poetic expression — was at low tide. Large numbers of intelligent and cultivated men were at best indifferent, at worst hostile, to faith in the supernatural (I, 3).

5. New York, Columbia University Press, 1939-69, 6 vols.

The next chronological period in his work, that from 1720-1740, fares no better:

> The period included some able prose writings in defense of Christianity against deism, but it is generally admitted that at this time the emotional and imaginative aspects of Christianity receded to a lower level than at any other period in English history (I, 265).

Professor G. R. Cragg, of Andover Theological Seminary, often regarded as the foremost specialist today in the ecclesiastical history of the eighteenth century, is quite as severe:

> This kind of involvement with society encouraged worldliness. Perhaps the most savage indictment of the eighteenth-century Church is Hogarth's damning portrait of Bishop Hoadly. 'The lust of the flesh, the lust of the eyes, and the pride of life' have seldom been depicted with such merciless candor.[6]

One member of the conference at which this was delivered was moved to protest, in defence of poor Hoadly, that the traits that displeased Professor Cragg in Hogarth's portrait might have been the product of his notorious ill health.

How does one go about answering all this, which is only a small sampling of the invective that has been heaped on the head of eighteenth-century Anglicanism for the last century or more? One might begin by objecting that these charges are all very vague and general, and ought to be supported by more specific evidence than appears here. The facial lineaments of an individual in a Hogarth portrait are a shaky structure from which to launch an attack on "the eighteenth-century Church," or even on the individual himself. The saintliness of the late Pope John XXIII might have been hard to deduce from the photographs of his obese body and fat, jolly, relaxed face — formed rather along the same lines as Hoadly's, indeed. Is it really true that, in a church which continued to use the Book of Common Prayer in its services throughout the century, evil and

---

6. James L. Clifford, *Man Versus Society in Eighteenth-Century Britain*, Cambridge, Cambridge University Press, 1968, p. 59.

guilt, sin and redemption were forgotten and its parishioners were taught to please men rather than God? To rebut the charge of worldliness, one would have to ask how worldliness is to be defined. A bishop, after all, is appointed to administer the affairs of a diocese, and there is no guarantee that if, through his "unworldliness," he maladministers it, the spiritual welfare of his flock will be advanced. And, of course, one must inquire whether the comparative aspects of the investigation have been fully considered. It can readily be granted that the church in the eighteenth century, as in others, was very far from perfect. But were its bishops really more worldly and politically and materially minded than, say, King James I's, or the long succession of medieval episcopal lords chancellor and lords treasurer, culminating in Wolsey, or — to take a later instance, if a fictional one — Bishop Proudie of Barchester? Was there really more emphasis on "man-pleasing" and the "worldly virtues" of discretion and outward decency and conformity with values in society in the average eighteenth-century parish than in, say, the glimpses of medieval ecclesiastical life that we get in Chaucer's *Canterbury Tales* and Langland's *Piers Plowman,* or in the average prosperous, middle-class suburban American parish today?

The answers to these questions were in fact given before any of the critiques I have quoted were written, in the superb scholarship of the Very Reverend Norman Sykes, late Dean of Winchester — Hoadly's old diocese, incidentally — and before that Dixie Professor of Ecclesiastical History at Cambridge University. In his Birkbeck Lectures, printed as *Church and State in England in the Eighteenth Century,*[7] and in his fine biographies of Archbishop Wake and Bishop Gibson and other writings, he carefully collects the concrete evidence — dates and durations of episcopal visitations, dates of confirmation tours and numbers of confirmations, divisions in the House of Lords — which establishes the falsity of such charges as Plumb's (and Plumb's book appeared sixteen years later than Sykes' *Church and State!*). There is time to quote only a few of Sykes'

7. Cambridge, Cambridge University Press, 1934; rep. Hamden, Conn., Archon Books, 1962.

conclusions, whose sobriety of tone is refreshing after the hectic extravagance of the critics:

> Granting the occurrence of a few scandals, such as the elevation of Hoadly [and, I may interject, there is much more to be said for Hoadly than Professor Cragg admits], and the presence of sundry episcopal mediocrities (from which few ages are even predominantly free), it would not appear that a general charge against the kings or their ministers of trafficking in spiritual dignities for unworthy ends can be sustained.

> . . . The particular misfortune of the eighteenth-century episcopate indeed has lain in the public and ubiquitous parading of the names of Hoadly and Watson and the representation of their careers as normal and characteristic of the bench. It may be contended with justice that such a judgment is unfair; and that it would be as equitable to asperse the Caroline episcopate by the unworthy examples of Barlow, Smith, Crewe, and Beaw, as to pillory that of the succeeding epoch by the constant mention of these two bishops. Even numerically they did not constitute a majority of the bench, and their negligence was not copied by the generality of their brethren.

> . . . A century which embraced amongst the English episcopate alone such names as Tillotson, Burnet, Hough, Tenison, Nicholson, Wake, Potter, Gibson, White Kennett, Tanner, Benson, Secker, Herring, Butler, Pearce, Hume, Warburton, Hurd, Porteus, and Hallifax, together with the avowed high churchmen Sharp, Dawes, Atterbury, Sherlock, and Horsley, may not be accounted deficient either in learning or piety. Against a bench adorned by such talents it would seem eccentric indeed to frame an indictment of infidelity and secularity.

> . . . It is singular . . . that few historians of the nineteenth century in praising the high standard of episcopal duty set by Bishop Samuel Wilberforce of Oxford and Winchester offer the obvious comparison with Gilbert Burnet of Sarum during the reigns of William III and Anne. Yet that

indefatigable pastor anticipated in his own person and diocese most of the reforms of Wilberforce more than a full century later, in regard to confirmation tours, regular and frequent preaching in the parish churches, the solemn observance of ordination embertides, the personal examination of candidates and the emphasis upon the pastoral office, and even the attempted establishment of a theological college. . . (pp. 411-413).

So much — perhaps it is safe to say — for the charges against the eighteenth-century episcopate. The more generalized charges against the whole "attitude to life" of the church — pastors and flock together — as materialistic, worldly, lacking in spirituality, lacking, indeed, in religion itself in the true sense of the word, since they are harder to pin down, are harder to refute. No doubt it is possible to define religion in as many ways as it is possible to define poetry, and Fairchild seems to equate it, or at least associate it very closely, with romantic poetry — "religion of that emotional and imaginative sort which inspires poetic expression." Samuel Johnson, who doubted that religious experience was suitable material for poetry, would have disagreed; so would T. S. Eliot, though for somewhat different reasons; so, I imagine, would most good modern theologians. It is, indeed, somewhat shocking to suggest that there is a hierarchy of different "sorts" of Christian religion, and that the sort which would make a Shelley (if he were a Christian) burst into song is somehow superior to that achievable by a humble, illiterate, and unpoetic carpenter or fisherman. Curiously, Bishop Stephen Neill, whose treatment of Anglicanism in his book with that title in the Pelican series is usually so admirable, seems to take a similar position. He describes "the general eighteenth-century attitude towards poetry" as

What is there that can better be expressed in poetry than in prose? Inevitably the honest eighteenth-century attitude was "Nothing." . . . Poetry can have only an ornamental value in rendering agreeable that which can in reality be better expressed in other forms. The true understanding of poetry is that it is the vehicle for the expression of those immensities of the human spirit for which symbolic and evocative language alone is appropriate. True religion is far more akin to those immensities than to the neat Palladian architecture and the formal gardens in which eighteenth-century man delighted.[8]

But of course he is as wrong about the eighteenth-century attitude toward poetry as he is about its delight in formal gardens. How hard the old myth about the "age of prose and reason" dies! If the good bishop were informed that, far from delighting in formal gardens, eighteenth-century Englishmen contemned them, and that it was the "neo-classicist" writers Pope and Addison who led the attack on them and the movement toward the "natural" garden, would he concede that there was a chance that they might be capable of "true religion"?

Two pieces of writing in particular have, I think, been responsible for keeping us from seeing, what strikes me more and more forcibly the more carefully I study the documents of the time, both literary and theological, that there is no essential difference between the orthodox Anglicanism of the eighteenth century and that of the preceding century, the seventeenth, the century of Donne and Herbert and Andrewes, or that of the sixteenth, the century of Latimer and Hooker and Spenser — or, for that matter, of the following century, the century of Coleridge and Wordsworth. Why should there have been? Again we have a strong *prima facie* case, which the onus is on the dissentients to overturn. There were no proclaimed changes in doctrine: the same Prayer Book — at least with only minor changes — was used every Sunday, the same Catechism was taught, the same Creeds were repeated, the same Thirty-Nine Articles were subscribed. There was, to be sure, toward the end of the century, a movement, never powerful and in the end unsuccessful, to abolish subscription to them, but this, I think, was part of the movement of religious toleration which

8. *Anglicanism*, Harmondsworth and Baltimore, Penguin Books, 1960, rev. ed., p. 183.

culminated in the repeal of the Test Act in 1828, rather than evidence of a desire for change in Anglican doctrine.

Nevertheless, the continuing prestige of Leslie Stephen's *English Thought in the Eighteenth Century*[9] has tended to perpetuate the belief that virtually every literate, or, at most, intelligent, person in eighteenth-century England was a deist, or at least heterodox in some way or other. The title of the book is, of course, a flagrant misnomer. Its first, and better, half is an excellent history of English deism; its second half is rather a mish-mash of matters that interested Stephen — utilitarianism, economics, a good deal of general literary criticism. Orthodox Anglicanism, which Stephen had formally repudiated as a young man, interests him hardly at all, and the representatives of it whom he picks out for some extended treatment, Hoadly, Warburton, and Paley, are not very attractive ones. Butler, who is much more attractive, is there as part of the treatment of deism. One finishes the book with the impression that Anglicanism was a minor phenomenon of the century, a relic of bygone times, rather like Roman paganism just before Constantine's proclamation, held by a few not very bright fuddy-duddies, and soon to be swept away by the tide of newer thought. But of course this is just not so, as anyone knows who reads widely and unselectively in the literature of the century — not merely in the major literary figures, from Defoe and Richardson up to Cowper and Jane Austen (and, for that matter, Wordsworth), but in the general writings of any decade of it, the histories, the treatises, the steady flow of sermons, and, best of all for getting an authentic picture of the time, the newspaper and magazines. It was the deists who were a small band of unpopular eccentrics, and their writings received very short shrift at the hands of the not-very-silent majority of orthodox.

The other work which has caused trouble is an article by the late Ronald Crane, for whom I have the deepest admiration as one of the acutest students of the eighteenth century that the twentieth century has produced, a critic seldom taken in by

9. New York, Harcourt, Brace, and World, 1962. First ed., 1876.

myths and clichés about the period. Nevertheless, his article, "Suggestions Toward a Genealogy of the 'Man of Feeling,'" published as long ago as 1934,[10] has always disturbed me. It has had a tremendous influence on later literary studies of the century, especially studies in Swift and Fielding, in which it is often cited as though it were unshakable gospel about the religious history of the century. It should some day be subjected to a thoroughgoing analysis, for which there is not time here; in particular, the dozens of eighteenth-century sermons that it so impressively cites in its footnotes should be unearthed and carefully read to determine whether the context justifies the use that Crane makes of the quotations and paraphrases of passages from them to support his thesis. That thesis, briefly, is that "the earliest impulse which led to the popular triumph of 'sentimentalism' toward 1750" is to be found in "the combined influence of numerous Anglican divines of the Latitudinarian tradition who from the Restoration onward into the eighteenth century had preached . . . essentially the same ethics of benevolence, 'good nature,' and 'tender sentimental feeling' as was expressed in the passages from Fordyce and his anonymous contemporary quoted at the beginning of this paper." These passages — one from David Fordyce, professor of moral philosophy at Aberdeen, and a layman, the other an anonymous contribution to a periodical bearing the curious title of *Man: a Paper for Ennobling the Species* — appeared in the 1750's and hymn the joys of sympathizing with others.

There are a number of points to be made about this. First, it is odd of Crane to say that this is "not a philosophy which the eighteenth century could have derived full fledged from ancient or Renaissance tradition. It was something new in the world — a doctrine . . . which a hundred years before 1750 would have been frowned upon, had it ever been presented to them, by representatives of every school of ethical or religious thought." It may not have been presented to them by classical or

10. Rep. in his *The Idea of the Humanities*, Chicago, University of Chicago Press, 1967, I, pp. 188-213.

Renaissance tradition, but it certainly had been presented to them in the New Testament — in the Sermon on the Mount, in the parable of the Good Samaritan, in the "great commandment," "thou shalt love thy neighbor as thyself." Thus it is understandable that Crane should have had no trouble finding expressions of it in sermons from 1650 onward; and one imagines that if he had searched with equal care, he could have found expressions of it in sermons and devotional works long before 1650 — in, let us say, works by and about St. Francis of Assisi.

There are differences, however, between the recommendations of benevolence by Fordyce and his contemporary, and the exhortations to charity (*caritas*) by the clergymen Crane cites. One is Fordyce's statement that one of the rewards of benevolence is a "self-approving joy." I do not think that this motive to altruism — which is also found in Shaftesbury — is one that the Christian preachers offer. They remembered too vividly the parable of the self-approving Pharisee. One thinks of that sturdy Anglican Samuel Johnson's scathing comment on the Shaftesburian philosopher in Chapter 22 of *Rasselas,* who, after haranguing his students about the desirability of living "according to nature, in obedience to that universal and unalterable law with which every heart is originally impressed," then "looked round him with a placid air, and enjoyed the consciousness of his own beneficence."

Another, and basic, difference, of course, is that Fordyce and the contributor to *Man* clearly believe that human nature is, or can be, intrinsically good, without assistance from outside itself — that, as the periodical's subtitle suggests, the "species" can "ennoble" itself. That is to say, they reject the Augustinian doctrine of original sin, as stated in Article IX of the Anglican church, and adopt its converse, the heresy of Pelagianism. Many scholars have readily followed Crane in attributing such Pelagianism or near-Pelagianism to the Anglican divines of the late seventeenth and early eighteenth century whom he mentions, and indeed to the clergy of the time generally. I suggest, however, that a careful reading even of Crane's carefully selected quotation from them reveals no serious evidence to support such a charge, and that the orthodox Anglican attitude throughout the century, as earlier in Donne and Herbert, remains that which is summed up in two lines of a modern Christian poet, W. H. Auden, "You shall love your crooked neighbor/ With your crooked heart."[11] The moment you alter it to "You shall love your crooked neighbor with your intrinsically pretty admirable and meritorious heart," you are in a different and highly dangerous world, as not only every Anglican clergyman, but every intelligent Anglican layman of the century brought up on the Book of Common Prayer, was well aware. From a rejection of Article IX follows a rejection of Articles XI to XIV, which state the doctrine of justification by faith alone and deny the doctrine of justification by works. Though, as in general Protestantism, Anglicanism affirms that "good works, which are the fruits of faith, follow after justification," it insists that "works done before the grace of Christ and the inspiration of his Spirit" — works like the Pharisee's fasting and tithing, motivated by need for self-congratulation, self-approval — "are not pleasant to God ∴ .. but they have the nature of sin." Again, I submit that nothing that Crane cites from the orthodox Anglican clergy of the time furnishes evidence that any such rejection by them took place.[12]

As a result of these misapprehensions, Crane further confused the already confused question of what is meant by the term "latitudinarianism" by ascribing to it doctrinal divergences from orthodoxy which in fact never took place. Contrary to what probably the majority of modern eighteenth-century English literary scholars think, the term has no doctrinal significance. What it does signify is the desire of many Anglicans of this period — very often bishops and archbishops — to

11. "As I Walked Out One Evening," in *Collected Poems*, New York, Random House, 1945, p. 198.

12. Crane quotes (p. 192) Joseph Glanvill on the Latitudinarians' emphasis on "doing the works of real Righteousness towards God, and our Neighbour," and uses this as evidence that they were "hostile ... to the Puritan dogma of justification solely by faith in the imputed righteousness of Christ, with its corollary of the worthlessness of 'our *Good Works* and Christian Vertues.'" The dogma (which is equally an Anglican dogma) carries no such corollary, nor is Glanvill's position in any way inconsistent with Articles XI to XIV, which few, if any, literary students writing on such matters seem to have studied or absorbed.

broaden the terms on which adherence to the Church of England was possible, so that it could again "comprehend" the many Protestants, differing little if at all in essential doctrine, who had been forced out of it by the restrictive legislation of 1662. But their efforts to effect this, led by Archbishop Tillotson in the 1690's, met determined resistance from High Church exclusivism, and were defeated.

Latitudinarianism in this sense continues to be treated hostilely by modern historians. In this they are blindly following the men of the Oxford Movement, over a century ago, without considering that the attitude seems somewhat inappropriate today, when one realizes that the modern synonym for "comprehension" is "ecumenism." That attitude is amusingly illustrated by Norman Sykes, who quotes[13] the annotations of an early nineteenth-century editor, S. H. Cassan, on an autobiographical fragment by a latitudinarian bishop of the 1680's and 1690's, Kidder of Bath and Wells. Kidder had "charitable sentiments towards presbyterians," Sykes reports; but "Before all his references to the presbyterian ordinations of that [the Commonwealth] period, his editor was careful to prefex the epithet 'Mock' to 'ordinations,' and, lest the meaning of this rebuke should be lost upon the reader, to append the observation that 'to call by the venerable name of "Orders" the self-appointed office of a presbyterian teacher, is an unaccountable misnomer, and I cannot but wonder how Kidder could have let the word drop from his pen.'" When Kidder speaks of "dissenters," Cassan thinks he should have called them "schismatics, whereby their sin would be intimated." When Kidder finds some of his parishioners unwilling to receive the Communion kneeling, he consults his bishop and receives his approval for administering it to them nevertheless. Cassan denounces such scandalous laxity: "Bishop Henchman should have been brought before the Convocation for such uncanonical advice." And so on. What we think of latitudinarianism will depend on whether we side with Kidder or his editor in such differences of opinion. If we side with Cassan, we may well go

13. Sykes, *op. cit.*, pp. 4-5.

on accusing the latitudinarians, as modern histories still do, of laxity, indifference, negligence, sloth, failure to give evidence of genuinely devout Christian conviction. On the other hand, if we believe the charity (*caritas, agape*) recommended in I Corinthians 13 and the love of one's neighbor inculcated by Matthew 22 to be the essential touchstone of true Christianity, we might just possibly decide that Bishop Kidder was a better Christian than his critic.

Alexander Pope, that jaundiced critic of the degeneracy of England (as he saw it) under Walpole, composed a complexly ironic epigram "On the Large Sums of Money Given in Charity in the Severe Winter of 1740-41":

> 'Yes, 'tis the time,' I cried, 'impose the chain,
>   Destin'd and due to wretches self-enslaved';
> But when I saw such charity remain,
>   I half could wish this people should be saved.
>
> Faith lost, and Hope, our Charity begins;
>   And 'tis a wise design in pitying Heav'n,
> If this can cover multitude of sins,
>   To take the *only* way to be forgiv'n.[14]

If one attempted to isolate the characteristic teaching of the Anglicanism of the eighteenth century, I think it would be charity − not in the narrow sense of giving alms, though its record there is a fine one, but in the wider one of the *agape* of Matthew 22 and I Corinthians 13. Here the key dates of the period would be, not those of political revolutions, but those of the passing of the Toleration Act of 1689 and the Catholic Relief Act of 1829 − this in spite of such unpleasant incidents as the Gordon Riots of 1780 and the passing of the Occasional Conformity and Schism Acts of 1711 and 1714. But the latter remained a dead letter and were repealed in 1718, and the Gordon Riots lasted only a week − not to be compared with the deadly violence of the religious dissension of the sixteenth and seventeenth centuries; not even to be compared with the

14. *Poems*, Twickenham ed., 1954, VI, p. 389.

violence which has vexed, say, Ireland, in the twentieth. Also included in such a consideration would have to be the great missionary movements, marked by the founding of the Society for Promoting Christian Knowledge in 1699, the Society for the Propagation of the Gospel in Foreign Parts in 1701, and the Church Missionary Society in 1799; the ecumenical efforts of Bishop Compton and Archbishop Wake to establish liaison between the English Church and Swiss Protestants, French Huguenots and Gallicans, German Lutherans and Reformed; the inception of the great movements that were to lead, early in the next century, to the abolition of Negro slavery, the mitigation of the criminal law, and the regulation of child labor. The last trial for witchcraft in England took place in 1712 (the accused was acquitted). Advances of this kind are often said by historians to be manifestations of the growing spirit of rationalism, and no doubt this is true. But how does one distinguish, in such cases, between what is "rational," and the teaching of the Gospel about charity and doing to others what one would want done to oneself? Are they not one and the same?

As a student of the literature of the century, what interests me most in this matter is the way in which (it seems to me) the biblical teachings regarding one's inner motivation in one's behavior toward one's neighbor and to society in general are reflected in the great imaginative writing of the century. Lionel Trilling said of the modern novel — "the most effective agent of the moral imagination in our time" — that "Its greatness and its practical usefulness [lie] in its unremitting work of involving the reader himself in the moral life, inviting him to put his own motives under examination, suggesting that reality is not as his conventional education has led him to see it."[15] It is perhaps no coincidence that the modern novel had its origin in eighteenth-century England, among men (and women) accustomed every Sunday to hearing such exhortations as "If we say that we have no sin, we deceive ourselves, and the truth is not in us," and "Enter not into judgment with thy servant, O Lord; for in thy

15. In his *The Liberal Imagination*, New York, Anchor Books, 1953, p. 215.

sight shall no man living be justified," and confessing "We have erred and strayed from thy ways like lost sheep; we have followed too much the devices and desires of our own hearts. . . . We have left undone those things which we ought to have done, and we have done those things which we ought not to have done, and there is no health in us; But thou, O Lord, have mercy upon us, miserable offenders." One thinks of Richardson's minute probings of the innermost thoughts and feelings of Clarissa and Lovelace; of Fielding's acute exposés of the innumerable ways in which pride, lack of charity, and self-deception manifest themselves; of the great self-revelation scenes in Jane Austen's novels, the moments of *anagnorisis,* the turning-points in their action — for instance, in *Pride and Prejudice,* a title which few readers take seriously enough:

> How despicably have I acted. . . . I, who have prided myself on my discernment! . . . who have often disdained the generous candour of my sister, and gratified my vanity, in useless or blameable distrust.—How humiliating is this discovery! —Yet, how just a humiliation! Had I been in love, I could not have been more wretchedly blind. But vanity, not love, has been my folly. . . . I have courted prepossession and ignorance, and driven reason away. . . . Till this moment I never knew myself.[16]

Fully to expound this theme, that of the Christian ethic as manifested in eighteenth-century English literature would take much longer than we have time for here. A discussion of it in any one of Johnson or Cowper or Christopher Smart or Sterne, to mention a few, would alone require a substantial paper, even a book. I cannot conclude, however, without calling brief attention to one very important writer, who I think has been much misinterpreted and still baffles many modern readers, partly at least because they have been misled by the mistaken teachings of intellectual historians about the nature of Anglican doctrine in the eighteenth century. This is Jonathan Swift, Dean

---

16. Chapter 36. Other similar passages are coveniently collected in C.S. Lewis, "A Note on Jane Austen," in his *Selected Literary Essays*, Cambridge, Cambridge University Press, 1969, pp. 175-76.

of St. Patrick's. We are not without critics and historians — A. L. Rowse, for instance — who still follow the old Victorian line of hinting that he was not a Christian at all. But I should like very briefly to call attention to four pieces of writing by him, and leave them for you to ponder. First, in spite of the innumerable books and articles presenting infinitely subtle interpretations of that undoubtedly complex work *A Tale of a Tub,* is not the key passage in it, a passage by no means difficult to comprehend, the one in Section VI, where Martin and Jack, having broken away from Peter's tyranny, begin to remove the illicit embroidery from their coats. "Ah, good brother Martin," cries Jack,

'do as I do, for the love of God; strip, tear, pull, rent, flay off all, that we may appear as unlike the rogue Peter as it is possible.' ... But Martin ... begged his brother, of all love, not to damage his coat by any means; for he never would get such another: desired him to consider that it was not their business to form their actions by any reflection upon Peter's, but by observing the rules pre-scribed in their father's will. That he should remember Peter was still their brother, whatever faults or injuries he had committed; and therefore they should by all means avoid such a thought as that of taking measures for good and evil from no other rule than of opposition to him.

Second, is not the key passage in the fourth book of *Gulliver's Travels,* which scholars puzzle and dispute over even more than the *Tale,* the quiet scene in Gulliver's little garden at Redriff, five years after the traumatic experience of his expulsion from Houyhnhnmland as a Yahoo, where, as Swift puts it in the last chapter heading, "The author ... proposeth his manner of living for the future"? This consists of three things,

to apply those excellent lessons of virtue which I learned among the Houyhnhnms, to instruct the yahoos of my own family as far as I shall find them docible animals, to behold my figure often in a glass, and thus if possible habituate myself in time to tolerate the sight of a human creature.

Is not this the perennial program of the Christian ethic: to attempt to practice the highest lessons of virtue — the imitation of Christ — knowing that we, as sinful human beings, can never attain that perfection; to try to teach others around us to do the same; frequently to examine our own imperfections — to remind ourselves that ever since the Fall we have been Yahoos — and thus to mortify our pride? "If we say that we have no sin, we deceive ourselves, and the truth is not in us," as Swift, an ordained Anglican clergyman, would have repeated to himself daily out of his Prayer Book.

The other two works are verse, one very short, but quite hair-raising, "The Day of Judgment." It was, understandably, not published until long after Swift's death. You may remember it: the day arrives, the last trumpet sounds, the living and dead gather before Jove's throne for judgment. Jove addresses them:

> Offending race of human kind,
> By nature, reason, learning, blind;
> You who through frailty stepped aside,
> And you who never fell — *through pride.*

The parable of the Pharisee is neatly summed up in this last line.

> You who in different sects have shammed

(other, apparently equally authoritative readings from the early versions, are "You whom the different sects have shammed," and "You whom the different churches shammed")

> And come to see each other damn'd.
> (So some folks told you, but they knew
> No more of Jove's designs than you.)

Jove, in fact, has a surprise for them.

> The world's mad business now is o'er,
> And I resent these pranks no more.
> I to such blockheads set my wit?
> I damn such fools? — Go, go, you're bit.[17]

Never has the kind of "religion" which consists of sectarian partisanship been more effectively satirized, except, possibly in

17. *Poems*, ed. Harold Williams, 1958, pp. 578-79.

the discussion in *Gulliver's Travels* of the controversy between Big-Endianism and Little-Endianism, in which, so far, eleven thousand people have been killed.

Finally, I would like to call attention to a much better known poem, the "Verses on the Death of Doctor Swift."[18] It has often been analyzed and discussed, but I wonder whether the main point in it has been fully appreciated. This is the opening discussion of La Rochefoucauld's maxim, "In the adversity of our best friends, we find something that doth not displease us." Swift's versification of this is brilliant —

> We all behold with envious eyes,
> Our *equal* raised above our size;
> Who would not at a crowded show
> Stand high himself, keep others low?

One recalls the opening of *A Tale of a Tub*, where the hack instructs us, "Whoever hath an ambition to be heard in a crowd, must press, and squeeze, and thrust, and climb with indefatigable pains, till he has exalted himself to a certain degree of altitude above them."

> To all my foes, dear fortune, send
> Thy gifts, but never to my friend:
> I tamely can endure the first,
> But this with envy makes me burst.

When his friends hear that Swift's health is precarious and that he may not last till spring, they

> hug themselves, and reason thus,
> 'It is not yet so bad with us.'

All this has, of course, been called "cynical," and it is well known that the standard label to be affixed to Rochefoucauld is "cynic." Yet when one stops to think about it, it is the most orthodox analysis of the deadly sin of envy, one of the offspring of the original sin of pride, of our built-in craving for oneupmanship, which makes complete love between human beings impossible. I have sometimes thought that Swift was one

18. *Poems*, ed. Harold Williams, 1958, pp. 553-72.

of the few who would be able fully to understand that parable of Jesus which is most difficult for the modern reader to accept, the parable of the laborers in the vineyard.[19] You will recall how it goes: the owner of the vineyard, at harvest time, goes out in the morning and engages a number of workmen for the day, at an agreed-on wage. At noon, seeing that the work will not be finished, he engages more — at the same wage. An hour before sunset, he engages still another group — also at the same wage. The work is finished; the laborers come for payment; they all receive the same sum, whether they have worked the whole day, half the day, or a single hour. Needless to say, there is bitter discontent and complaint. The owner says to the complainers, "Friend, I do thee no wrong: didst not thou agree with me for a penny?" But one suspects that few of us would immediately grasp the point, but would go away with a gnawing grievance fed by our egotism.

To conclude, and to oversimplify, one could almost say that the essentials of the ethic taught by orthodox eighteenth-century Anglicanism, by its imaginative writers as well as its divines, are contained in this handful of passages from Swift. Could one go further and assert that the answer, or at least one answer, to the often-debated question "Why did England, at the end of the eighteenth and beginning of the nineteenth centuries, not undergo such revolutionary violence as afflicted so many other European countries?" is that, through this teaching, something at least of those essentials penetrated into the minds and emotions of a substantial number of those who were exposed to it? There is no possible way of proving anything of the kind, but at least it is a hypothesis that may be worth pondering.

Donald Greene

19. St. Matthew, xx: 1-16.

Religion & Society
in America's Revolutionary Era:
Some Preliminary Reflections

The revolutionary era from 1776 to 1815 was of crucial importance not only for the general political development of British North America, but for the history of religion and the adjustment of the relations between religion and society. It was indeed "the hinge upon which the history of Christianity in America really turns."[1] In the United States and, to a lesser degree in the continuing British colonies, these years encompassed the growth of traditions and understandings that would help to shape the character and the role of religion in America throughout the nineteenth century. The magnitude of the contrast between the state of religion in the 1770's and in the post-Napoleonic period will illustrate this statement. Some comments on the changes that had occurred should indicate their significance.

When the Revolution began, the outward religious condition of the colonies could have been summed up under four headings: orthodoxy, establishment, indifference, and limited diversity. Despite the winds of the Enlightenment and the first Great Awakening, Calvinism and Roman Catholicism were still the most powerful theological currents in America; the latter being confined almost exclusively to the new province of Quebec. Throughout the colonies the concept and the reality of establishment, though severely strained in practice, were still officially accepted and enforced; in Quebec the state intended to establish the Church of England, a design which was already being frustrated by Royal connivance in the maintenance of the privileged position of the Catholic Church.[2] Apart from Quebec,

1. S.E. Mead, *The Lively Experiment*, New York, 1963, p. 52.
2. H. Neatby, *Quebec: The Revolutionary Age, 1760-1791*, Toronto, 1966, pp. 107-124.

however, the proportion of church members may have been as low as five per cent, mute testimony to the frustration, hostility, and dissatisfaction of the majority with respect to the traditional churches.[3] Nonetheless, these forces had not yet been effectively harnessed by new religious organizations: in the thirteen colonies and Nova Scotia, Anglicanism, Congregationalism, and Presbyterianism were dominant; the Methodists and Baptists were still relatively insignificant groups.

By 1815, the position of religion in the United States and British North America had been dramatically transformed. The former was now officially committed to the separation of church and state, and in the individual states the bare remnants of establishment persisted.[4] In the Maritime Provinces and Upper Canada, the aspirations of Inglis and Strachan were evidently becoming forlorn hopes.[5] The debris of the establishments reflected the downfall of the Congregational and Anglican churches, and the emergence on the tide of the second great awakening of the Presbyterians, Baptists, and Methodists as the most important Protestant denominations in both old and new states and provinces.[6] Evangelical Protestantism was well on the way to becoming the new orthodoxy, and the proportion of its adherents in the total population was steadily rising. In the United States, the churches had severed their transatlantic ties and had turned resolutely inward towards the vista of an expanding nation.[7] Those in the British North American colonies, in contrast, were still dependent on their

3. F.H. Littell, *From State Church to Pluralism*, New York, 1962, p. 32.
4. Article VI and the First Amendment of the Constitution established the basis for separation. New Hampshire was the last to give up, specifically on the issue of Catholic emancipation. In 1818-19 the standing order was finally broken in Connecticut.
5. J.M. Bumsted, "Church and State in Maritime Canada, 1749-1807," *C.H.A.R.*, 1967, pp. 41-58. Upper Canada never really implemented the provisions for establishment.
6. R.B. Nye, *The Cultural Life of the New Nation, 1776-1830*, New York, 1960, p. 219. By 1820, the three groups were rising to prominence respectively in Nova Scotia, New Brunswick and Upper Canada.
7. The Protestant Episcopal Church was established in 1783. The Methodist Church became effectively autonomous in 1784 with the election of Thomas Coke and Francis Asbury as its first superintendents. The New York and Philadelphia Presbyterian Synod became independent in 1785.

British counterparts, a relationship that would seriously affect the evolution of their attitudes and hence of their place in society.[8] In both areas, these overt and visible changes were accompanied by a subtle and complex reshaping of the influence exerted by religious institutions and ideas on the development of the climate of opinion.

If these were some of the more remarkable alterations in the North American religious scene, what in greater detail were their distinctive elements and their implications?

From the outset, the religious and political leaders of most of the colonies had assumed that the stability and health of any community depend upon the acceptance of certain common religious beliefs, and that the power of the state can and should be used to support the religious institutions charged with the inculcation of these beliefs. By the mid-eighteenth century, however, this assumption was being undermined philosophically and practically. The rationalists contended that to coerce the individual into the acceptance of theological or moral concepts is inherently wrong. "The care of every man's soul" said Jefferson, "belongs to himself. . . . The magistrate has no power but what the people gave; [they] have not given him the care of souls because they could not . . ."[9] The Pietists argued that true religion is based upon voluntary obedience to God's revealed will, and that such revelation becomes clear only through individual religious experience.[10] The quarrels and persecutions that had arisen in consequence of concerted efforts to repress the exponents of such ideas had brought about a substantial measure of toleration, a growing willingness to reject multiple establishments and to accept the voluntarist principle for all the churches: hence the formulation of Article VI and the First Amendment to the Constitution and the progressive reshaping

8. In 1800 the Methodists in the Maritime Provinces came under the English Wesleyan Conference and would remain within it until 1855. Those in Upper Canada were part of the Methodist Episcopal Church (U.S.A.) until 1828. The Anglican Church secured its autonomy in 1860. On this general theme see J.S. Moir, "The Canadianization of the Protestant Churches," *C.H.A.R.*, 1966, pp. 56-69.

9. From Jefferson's "Notes on Religion," in S.K. Padover ed., *The Complete Jefferson* . . . , New York, 1943, p. 944.

10. Mead, *op. cit.*, p. 29.

of the church-state relationship in the state constitutions.

This formal recognition of religious freedom has properly been hailed as one of the "most profound revolutions . . . in the entire history of the church . . ."[11] What has been overlooked is that neither for rationalist nor pietist did the separation of church and state imply rejection of the social necessity to maintain a common set of religious values in order to ensure "order in government and obedience to the laws."[12] The United States thus was not to be a secular society, but one in which the public welfare may impose limits on religious freedom. The churches in their turn accepted the responsibility of maintaining these essential beliefs and, by implication, the notion that their individual peculiarities have no social relevance. They continued to hold, as well, that the state may legitimately enforce moral prohibitions on behalf of the churches, in order that the "sweet harmony" of a Christian nation may be maintained, a view that prevailed once the genuine rationalists had departed, and which would retain its respectability so long as the evangelical hope of converting the nation endured.[13] Above all, although the churches ultimately surrendered the control of education, this was on condition that the schools taught a diluted form of Protestantism, a task facilitated by the theological developments to which reference will be made later. By this means, more than any other, order and obedience have been upheld.

In striking contrast, the history of the remaining British North American colonies was characterized by muted and rather ambiguous efforts to sort out the relations between church and state. They were not unaware of the massive conflict on this issue in the old colonies; indeed many of the Loyalists were victims of that controversy.[14] But the size and coherence of the Roman Catholic population of Quebec, the close associations between the colonial religious bodies and their parent churches, the continuing determination of the

---

11. W.E. Garrison, as quoted in Mead, *op. cit.*, 18.
12. The phrase was used by President Jefferson in 1808.
13. The words were used by Isaac Backus. See W.G. McLoughlin, *Isaac Backus and the American Pietistic Tradition*, Boston, 1967, p. 150.
14. Bishop Inglis of Nova Scotia and several of his clergy were in this category.

imperial and colonial authorities to regulate and utilize religious forces, and the sharp divisions between the various groups, militated against the ostensibly clear-cut decisions reached in the United States. The concept of religious freedom or the absence of coercion in matters of belief was fully accepted, but sufficient doubt persisted concerning the wisdom and efficacy of this innovation to ensure for some time the continuance of privileged religious groups.[15] These privileges would ultimately be eliminated, but they left a curious legacy: the acceptance of co-operation between the churches and the state, a practice that probably entailed a more assured status for Canadian churches than their American counterparts had. Specifically, the foundations were laid for the peculiarly ambivalent and diverse relationships which developed in education in the nineteenth century between the churches and the provincial governments. More broadly, British North Americans continued to perceive themselves not in rationalist *versus* pietist terms or in secular-religious terms, but as members of a pluralist and religiously-oriented society.

This transformation in the relationship between the churches and the state was accompanied by crucial changes in the theological atmosphere of American Christianity and in the relations between the individual churches. The challenge to orthodoxy was first thrown down by Jonathan Edwards in 1735. Justification by faith alone was to him the "principal hinge" of American Protestantism, but in support of his views he did not cite Scripture but the "remarkable conversions" in his own parish.[16] In so doing, he began the complex process of adapting Calvinism to the spiritual needs and insights of his community, and as did Wesley, he implicitly accepted the notion that the test of religious truth is experience, not Scripture or tradition. The revival spurred by Edwards and his disciples weakened the old order and helped to lay the foundations of the Baptist denomination. The turmoil of

15. For example, financial support was long provided for the churches of England and Scotland and restrictions on the right to solemnize marriage persisted until the 1830's.

16. A. Heimert, *Religion and the American Mind*, Cambridge, 1966, p. 4.

revolution and disestablishment completed the destruction of the old institutional structure. The religious leaders of the new nation were confronted with "a general dereliction of religious principle and practice . . . a visible and prevailing impiety and contempt for the laws and institutions of religion, and an abounding infidelity which in many instances tends to Atheism itself."[17] Moreover, by 1800, the nation was on the verge of a vast and frightening territorial expansion, and with that the "pressing danger of [cultural] fragmentation."[18]

In this new and potentially catastrophic situation, American Protestantism swung inward and westward, cutting for the moment its ties with its British and European roots. Orthodox Calvinism began to relapse into Unitarianism; the Anglicans to minority status. Presbyterians, Baptists, and Methodists launched the second great awakening which set in motion the slow restoration of Protestant ascendancy. Although the evangelical preachers were not as lacking in theological concern as has been supposed, the denominations which they led had certain distinctive characteristics, among them historylessness, revivalism and anti-intellectualism.[19]

The Puritan concept of a fresh beginning in the uncorrupted new world, the pietist experience of conversion, with its early Christian overtones, the rationalist attack on the corruption of pure Christianity by the irrational and the cunning, and the break with the past in the Revolution, formed an appropriate background for the widespread notion that it was possible to go back to the New Testament church as the basis on which all Christians could build. In consequence, all past forms and traditions could be ignored in favour of Biblical literalism and a pragmatic attitude to polity and practice. The churches, as Sidney Mead has said, came to have "the appearance or feeling of freedom possible only to those ignorant of their history."[20]

17. A statement made in 1798 by the Presbyterian General Assembly. Quoted in J.W. Smith and A.L. Jamison eds., *The Shaping of American Religion*, Princeton, 1961, p. 352.

18. *Ibid.*, p. 354. The phrase is Perry Miller's.

19. These are some of the characteristics attributed to denominations by S.E. Mead, who has most clearly described and defined this distinctive aspect of American religious history. See Mead, *op. cit.*, pp. 103-133.

20. *Ibid.*, p. 112.

Among the new techniques, revivalism was pre-eminent. With it came a simplistic approach to doctrinal and moral issues, the tacit assumption that man saves himself, the conviction that "it makes no difference how you get a man to God, provided you get him there," and the rise of the demagogue in place of the pastor and teacher.[21] In this new context American Protestantism forgot the Edwards whose discovery of Locke's *Essay* gave him greater pleasure "than the most greedy miser finds when gathering up handfuls of silver and gold from some newly-discovered treasure," the philosophical apologist and speculative theologian, and rejected the new intellectual currents of the age.[22] Soon "an intellectual clergyman" would be thought "deficient in piety"; society would rate "an eminently pious minister" as "deficient in intellect."[23] With this would come a ready acceptance of the secular ideals of an individualist and acquisitive society.

Here too, the British North American colonies moved along a rather different course. Their spiritual guides were also staggered by the immensity of their missionary task, and they huddled together, especially after 1789, in fear of revolution and infidelity.[24] Many were slow to adapt their practices to the social and political realities of the new settlements. But, these new societies had no rationalist tradition, no Jefferson or Franklin to undermine the orthodox. They were too poor and too fragmented to cut their ties with Britain and they were too divided ethnically and culturally to accept wholeheartedly the teaching of one or more new denominations. Thus by 1815, Presbyterianism was on the way to dominance in Nova Scotia, the Baptists in New Brunswick, and the Methodists in Upper Canada, but in each province this did not entail the disintegration of the Anglican and/or Presbyterian churches. It would be wrong to refer to the nineteenth century as the Methodist phase of Canada's as well as of the United States' history.[25] If the tone of

21. The statement was made by D.L. Moody. Mead, *op. cit.*, p. 124.
22. Smith and Jamison, *op. cit.*, p. 245.
23. Mead, *op. cit.*, p. 129.
24. W.L. Morton ed., *The Shield of Achilles*, Toronto, 1968, pp. 45-49.
25. For example, in 1861 the numbers of Anglicans and Presbyterians in Canada West were not much smaller than the number of Methodists.

Canadian Protestantism was evangelical and often revivalist, it did not lose sight of its past, or pride itself on its newness. The tradition of a learned clergy was not wholly destroyed, and a kind of balance was achieved between history, order, and the practical exigencies of the environment.[26]

Jonathan Edwards' ill-fated vaccination prevented him from carrying out his greatest desire, the writing of the "History of the Work of Redemption," a consideration of "all parts of the grand scheme [of Providence] in their historical order."[27] In this ambition he reflected one of the most powerful currents in American religious history, the belief that God had called its people to the new world to establish "a citty upon a Hill," a godly society whose example would renew the whole Christian world.[28] The sense of participating in this "errand into the wilderness" was not confined to New England, but derived much of its intellectual sustenance from that source.[29] It was reinvigorated and transformed during the Revolution, thereby providing the fundamental substance of American nationalism — the belief that it is America's destiny under God to demonstrate the full potential of government by the people, or as Lincoln put it, to preserve freedom as the "last, best hope of earth."[30]

Behind the noble rhetoric, however, were some remarkably complex intellectual currents. Before and during the Revolution the political crisis was represented as a divine judgment upon a people in covenant with God for their manifold sins and iniquities, wherefore they were called to humiliation and repentance. With this was coupled the assurance that "our cause is so just and good that nothing can prevent our success but only our sins. . . . Providence has designed this continent for to be the asylum of liberty and true religion," and by liberty was meant the whole philosophy of the social compact, inalienable

26. See my article in the *Theological Bulletin*, McMaster Divinity College, Number 3, 1968, pp. 19-35.

27. Smith and Jamison, *op. cit.*, p. 250.

28. The phrase quoted was written by John Winthrop in 1630.

29. "Errand into the Wilderness," the title of one of Perry Miller's works, expresses succinctly the Puritan outlook.

30. Quoted in Mead, *op. cit.*, p. 74.

rights, and the right of revolution.[31] Naturally therefore, President Stiles of Yale could preach in 1783 on the theme "The United States Elevated to Glory and Honor" in which he anticipated the day "when the Lord shall have made his American Israel high above all nations."[32]

The French Revolution would soon reveal the danger of associating the Christian scheme of things with revolution, and would frighten the orthodox into asserting that "the [American] Revolution had not been at all revolutionary, but simply a protest of native piety against foreign impiety."[33] In the new evangelical climate the revolutionary tradition would thus be interpreted conservatively and uncritically. For many, the arrogance of destiny endured, without the moderating influence of Christian humility.

Alan Heimert has argued recently that, within the "black regiment," so eloquent in election and fast day sermons, a real division existed between those who "saw the reality of an order of being other than that walled and hemmed in existence in which a stale institutional religion and bourgeois rationalism were content to dwell, and those who did not."[34] The former were the genuine disciples of Edwards, whose ideas of liberty and union were different from those of the liberals, and whose ideas constituted a radical challenge to the existing order. Liberty, briefly, was the "opportunity to act morally," that is for each man "to regard the good of the whole in all his actions."[35] The motive and the will so to act would be found only in those whose hearts had been touched by the Gospel. Union was essential to secure and preserve liberty, but the basis of union was the communion and community of the faithful. Within that community inequality and party differences would be submerged in the battle for the destruction of tyranny and for universal emancipation. The goal was "a republic of Americans, all *free*, all *equal*, all *united*," an end that could be

31. Quoted in Smith and Jamison, *op. cit.*, p. 347.
32. *Ibid.*, pp. 342-343.
33. Perry Miller in Smith and Jamison, *op. cit.*, p. 350.
34. Here Heimert is using H.R. Niebuhr's words. Heimert, *op. cit.*, p. 10.
35. A paraphrase of Edwards and the words of Isaac Backus respectively. *Ibid.*, pp. 457, 459.

attained only by the perseverance of the saints.[36] The Revolution thus meant that "it does indeed matter how [the goals of the American people] are defined, and that there is more than one spirit in which to pursue them," an insight often obscured in the nineteenth century.[37]

If the new United States conceived itself to be the embodiment of a great human experiment — however ill-defined the nature of that experiment might be — the remaining colonies did not agree on their role or their destiny. Many of the Loyalist clergy and those who joined their ranks from Britain after 1790 believed that Providence looked with special favour on English society and culture. The French Revolution and the War of 1812-14 were interpreted by them as a massive onslaught against the English tradition in which divine intervention assured Britain's triumph; an outcome that would be nullified by the rejection of the Church of England and the separation of church and state.[38] The New Light movement in Nova Scotia partly embodied the belief that as New England had given up its mission the people of Nova Scotia had become "as the Apple of [God's] eye," a group whose function was to further the establishment of God's earthly kingdom, a notion which may have entered into that province's rather ill-defined sense of destiny.[39] The Methodists oscillated between concern for individual regeneration and for English ways; the Presbyterians sought to re-establish the best features of the Scottish order in the New World. The Roman Catholics of Quebec were at least tacitly determined to preserve a French and Catholic civilization in America. By 1815, in effect, British North Americans were committed to a pluralist interpretation of the relationship between their religious, social and political convictions. In a rather groping and ill-defined way they had left room for the emergence of a nationalism tolerant of nonconformity and of a political culture in which religion and politics were not

36. *Ibid.*, p. 550.
37. *Ibid.*, p. 552.
38. Morton, *op. cit.*, pp. 50-59.
39. G. Rawlyk and G. Stewart, "Nova Scotia's Sense of Mission," *Histoire Sociale — Social History*, Vol. 2, 1968, pp. 12-17.

obverse sides of the same coin.

In retrospect, indeed, the revolutionary era stands out as one in which, despite the high level of debate and of concern for the place of the Christian religion in American society, the process of transforming it into an acceptable way of expressing American identity effectively got under way. In consequence the teaching of the churches became progressively more vacuous and the tempo of secularization increased. British North America did not succumb as readily or as wholeheartedly to this trend; hence its churches retained a measure of independence, and secularization proceeded less rapidly than in the United States.

Goldwin French

The Politics of Feminism in the French Enlightenment

Nearly four decades have passed since Mornet conducted his inquiry into the intellectual origins of the French Revolution.[1] Subsequent research into public attitudes during the revolutionary period towards the great charismatic names of Enlightenment thinking has tended to blur rather than clarify the rather precise relationships delineated by Mornet between ideological stimulus and historical phenomena.[2] The general proposition is still an open issue of course, but the debate around the nature and status of women in eighteenth-century France, engendering a formidable corpus of dissident literature, does highlight an example of conspicuous hiatus between the movement of ideas and the movement of events. The feminist dilemma from this point of view underscores the tenuous nature of certain assumptions that are still occasionally put forward with regard to historical processes as well as to the contemporary impact of eighteenth-century liberalism.

Ideals of sexual egalitarianism, voiced in a multiplicity of literary, philosophical and political contexts, seemed on the surface to be a potentially rewarding direction in which to channel reformist energies. The eighteenth century saw fe-

---

1. D. Mornet, *Les Origines intellectuelles de la Révolution française, 1715-1787*, Paris, 1933.

2. Rousseau's *Du Contrat social*, for example, seems to have been little read by the men of 1789. After the initial sensation at the time of publication, inspiring thirteen editions between 1762 and 1763, there was only one new edition between 1763 and 1790. Interest revived only in the post-revolutionary period: by 1796 twenty more editions of the *Contrat* had appeared. See L. Trénard, "La Diffusion du Contrat social (1762-1832)," *Etudes sur le Contrat social de Jean Jacques Rousseau*, Paris, 1964, pp. 425-458; J. Godechot, "Le Contrat social et la Révolution occidentale de 1762 à 1789," *ibid.*, pp. 393-405; H. Peyre, "The Influence of Eighteenth Century Ideas on the French Revolution," *Journal of the History of Ideas*, X, 1949, pp. 63-87; A. Cobban, *Rousseau and the Modern State*, 2nd edition, London, Allen & Unwin, 1964, pp. 20-22; L. Crocker, *Rousseau's Social Contract: An Interpretative Essay*, Cleveland, Case Western Reserve University Press, 1968, p. 116.

minism emerge from its shadowy status as a minority aberration from the Aristotelian-based consensus of opinion into an apparently viable movement. In England and France the ideology of feminism was well orchestrated, and it imparted a distinctive colour to the broader fabric of the period's political thought, not to mention its literary conventions. No longer could the issue of women's rights be kept safely refrigerated within the centuries-long traditional abstractions of theological and metaphysical nicety.

Ever since Aristotle had countered Plato's development of the principle of equality — such as it was in the dialogue between Glaucon and Socrates in the fifth book of the *Republic*, and reaffirmed in the first book of the *Politics* the legitimacy of the state of subordination in which one sex lived in relation to the other, it was clear that much more than a technical collision of philosophical viewpoints was at stake. Any challenge to the rationale of inequality would necessarily represent a challenge to the interpretation of natural law from which society's institutions drew part of their ultimate authority.

A renewed awareness of the radical political element inherent in the problem quickened the pulse of eighteenth-century feminism, and brought into focus the more dazzling corollary: the ephemeral nature of social structures *per se*. What d'Alembert was to describe as "l'esclavage et l'espèce d'avilissement où nous avons mis les femmes"[3] came to be seen as a contingent consequence of positive law and no longer as a necessary fact of natural law. In itself this was nothing new, but the degree to which it permeated the general movement of ideas in eighteenth-century France was new. Scale and momentum gives to eighteenth-century feminism, and indeed to the whole intellectual superstructure of the Enlightenment, much of its characteristic flavour.

Previously liberal trends in this area had made little impact on the view sanctified by that formidable trinity Aristotelian precept, Roman law and Christian ethic, which, together,

3. *Oeuvres philosophiques, historiques et littéraires*, Paris, 1805, V, p. 349.

envisaged the servitude of women as an unalterable and perfectly justifiable part of the nature of things in this world and most probably in the next. The revival of Platonic attitudes during the Renaissance had certainly marked a faint resurgence of respect for the notion of a rationally based egalitarianism.[4] Generally speaking however, dissent on this issue remained the prerogative of eccentrics who could be ridiculed, or of the occasional woman who could be ignored.

It is largely because of their rarity rather than their merit that certain premature luminaries stand out so sharply against the darker conservative firmament of the pre-Enlightenment period. Despite the disappointingly anodyne nature of his arguments, one should perhaps mention Henri-Cornelius Agrippa, who as early as 1509 could publish a work with a title as perverse as *La Supériorité du sexe féminin*. A gradual and inexorable build-up of pressure around feminist preoccupations was however taking place inside and outside literary circles. If the indignant testimony of the jesuit Jean Cordier[5] can be accepted, this coincided in France with a growing expertise on the part of upper and middle class women with the arts of contraception. Statistical evidence indicates, moreover, a decline in population growth[6] during this period, and a correlation has been suggested, at least in part, between this and the increasing concern of women to free themselves from the disadvantages of their biological function.[7] Writing well over a century after Cordier, Auget de Montyon could report in 1778

4. See A. Humphreys, "The 'Rights of Woman' in the Age of Reason: 1. John Dunton to Catherine Macaulay," *Modern Language Review*, XLI, No. 3, 1946, p. 257.

5. In *La Famille saincte*, Paris, 1643. Cordier inveighed against those who would deprive children of the chance of gaining Paradise "en leur refusant entrée au monde," pp. 232-235.

6. See A. Chamoux and C. Dauphin, "La Contraception avant la Révolution française," *Annales, Economies, Sociétés, Civilisations*, XXIV, No. 3, 1969, pp. 662-684. There was of course no question of a decline in population. See Julian Huxley's "A Factor overlooked by the *Philosophes*: The Population Explosion," *Transactions of the First International Congress on the Enlightenment*, II, 1963, pp. 862-863.

7. The argument is vulnerable, but P. Fryer's treatment of this aspect of the growth of the feminist conscience is interesting. See *The Birth-Controllers*, London, Secker and Warburg, 1965, p. 38.

that the use of birth control techniques had percolated down even to peasant women.[8] Between 1771 and 1820 the birth rate in France fell by slightly more than .7 %.[9]

As far as the documentation of the earlier period is concerned, overt feminist protest still remained spasmodic rather than continuous and cumulative. An early radical note had certainly been sounded by Marie le Jars de Gournay, author of two very avant-garde essays: *Egalité des hommes et des femmes* (1622) and *Les Griefs des dames* (1626), both of which were extended and republished in 1634 and again in 1641.[10] An element which was to feature in eighteenth-century feminism was also present in the embryonic feminist world of seventeenth-century France — namely the sympathy that such aspirations and protests found with certain ecclesiastical writers. Jacques Du Bosc's *L'Honneste Femme* (1632) is a well known example, as is François Poulain de la Barre's highly unorthodox *De l'Egalité des deux sexes* (1673), whose circulation benefited a great deal from the scandalous publicity of the author's public renunciation of celibacy, and his abandonment of the priesthood for marriage in a Genevan church. The views expressed by such writers still lacked broad support, but distinguishable patterns of protest were slowly emerging and gaining cogency. This is particularly noticeable in works dealing with questions of education and social training — issues which with birth control and constitutional rights were to become the anchor themes of the feminist polemic as it was to develop in the Enlightenment. However, the need for serious, sustained feminist argument failed to attract the services of a really great name until Fénélon objected to the harmful social and psychological effects of the conditioning given to women through current educational practices. Even with Fénélon, only a small section of his 1687 essay, *Traité de l'éducation des filles*,

---

8. *Recherches et considérations sur la population de la France*, Paris, 1778, II, p. 102.

9. Fryer, *op. cit.*, pp. 37-38.

10. See M. Ilsley, *A Daughter of the Renaissance: Marie le Jars de Gournay. Her Life and Works*, The Hague, Mouton, 1963. For a view of Marie de Gournay as a founder of modern feminism see T. Joran, *Les Féministes avant le féminisme*, Paris, 1910, ch. 6.

is devoted specifically to women, in spite of the title. The Age of the Sun King tended, not surprisingly, to circumscribe its analysis of the society-male-female relationship, and to avoid the more explosive social and political implications.

Those scattered fragments of pre-Enlightenment protest that can be identified however, began to come together in the following century in the work of novelists, playwrights, essayists, *philosophes*, and of course of the women themselves, the new *femmes-hommes* or "hyenas in petticoats" as Walpole called them. Sentimental appeals to the public conscience were now to be supplemented by "hard" argument and research around woman's *condition*, and the legal-political realities which defined and reinforced that condition.[11] The result was that by the 1780's feminism had become well integrated into the broader movements for social change.

In the key areas of jurisprudence and judicial philosophy the work of an Orléans counsellor and respected jurist, Robert Joseph Pothier, remains perhaps the most authoritative and forbidding statement of the position of women before the law. In the defensive elaboration of the situation in his *Traité de la puissance du mari sur la personne et les biens de la femme et des donations entre mari et femme* (1770) Pothier declared the powers of the husband over his wife to consist by natural law in the inalienable right to demand from her all the duties of submission which are due from an inferior to a superior.[12] This in effect was a reiteration of article nine of the *Ordonnance des donations*, passed by the Paris Parlement in 1731, which had virtually deprived women in France of equality before the law, and marked a high water mark in the history of repressive legislation. Pothier, after listing the duties of wives, was still able to reaffirm the justification for submission based on natural law arguments nearly half a century after Montesquieu had re-opened the doubts about the legitimacy of this principle

11. The best detailed survey of the legal structure in France as it affected women is still L. Abensour's *La Femme et le féminisme avant la Révolution*, Paris, 1923.

12. Abensour, *op. cit.*, p. 8.

in the thirty-eighth letter of the *Lettres persanes*.[13] The *arrêt* of the Paris Parlement (February 12, 1731) measures the distance between liberal philosophies and official policies, and it exemplifies the ferocity of the legislation affecting women in a variety of circumstances irrespective of class or economic status. Poverty was, of course, an added disadvantage. Middle class women were reasonably well shielded from the worst indignities, such as those imposed by the laws relating to pregnancy.[14] Pothier's formulations concerning the inviolable rights of men over women were moreover to reappear in the 1804 civil code — a further pointer to the ironic fate that awaited French feminism in the immediate post-revolutionary period.

The edifice of legalised prejudice, together with a public opinion still conditioned to a "tout est au mieux" philosophy of Panglossian proportions, did little however to discourage the upsurge of reformist energy and confidence. This was based, partly at least, upon that endearing faith of the Enlightenment on man's potential ability to rationalize his environment. It was this new found confidence that separated eighteenth-century feminism, in tone at least, from the sporadic outbursts of activity that had preceded it.

Voltaire, in most respects the most influential propagandist of the period, is somewhat ambivalent on the issue. The article *Femme* in the *Dictionnaire philosophique*,[15] for example, has an anthropological rather than sociological emphasis, and contains little trace of feminist sympathies. In the article *Homme* Voltaire saw positive moral advantages accruing to women as a result of their physical and social inferiority (XIX, 382). The sympathetic approach to women's position in the section *Mémoire pour les femmes* in *Adultère* (XVII, 70-72) is more

13. *Oeuvres complètes*, Bibliothèque de la Pléiade, Paris, 1949, I, pp. 185-186. It would seem that with Montesquieu much of the radical egalitarianism of Poulain de la Barre resurfaced. B. Magné suggests convincingly that the source of the thirty-eighth letter in the *Lettres persanes,* usually associated with Fontenelle, was *L'Egalité des deux sexes*. "Une Source de la Lettre persane XXXVIII?," *Revue d'Histoire littéraire de la France*, LXVIII, 1968, pp. 407-414.

14. Abensour, *op. cit.*, pp. 25-26.

15. *Oeuvres complètes*, ed. L. Moland, Paris, 1877-1885, XIX, pp. 95-104. All references in the text are to this edition.

than balanced by his comments on female infidelity in the first part of that article (XVII, 65-70). There are Platonic comments on the political potential of women, at present wasted, in the section dealing with Salic law in the *Essai sur les moeurs* (XII, 14-15), and in the *Dictionnaire* article: *Loi Salique* (XIX, 609-613). A spirited defence of the rights of women to an intellectual life is to be found in the *épître* to Mme du Châtelet prefacing *Alzire* — in which the case for intellectual parity is not quite stated (III, 374-375). Many of Voltaire's comments direct attention to the vulnerability of women in society as a result of their physical disadvantages, and he seems to run close to a regretful acceptance of natural law arguments for the *status quo*. The correspondence, moreover, is very reticent on the point. However, Voltaire, by virtue of his position, gave the whole debate plenty of valuable publicity, even if he added little that was at all original or even sympathetic.

The main political thrust in the second half of the century was to come from Diderot, Holbach and Condorcet. They were supported by a dynamic, now largely forgotten undercurrent of writing. Feminist literature was acquiring status as a modish genre. Even in the rather academic form of essays and treatises, feminist publications were beginning to meet with a remarkable response. A little essay like that of Pierre-Joseph Boudier de Villemert's *L'Ami des femmes, ou la philosophie du beau sexe*, originally published in 1758, could run to six editions within twelve months of publication, and went through three more reprintings in expanded form by 1788. Villemert, another of those strange beasts the clerical feminists, advanced a theory of the complementary nature of the sexes in terms very close to those used by the Saint-Simonians. Equally prominent among those writers who do not occupy centre stage, but whose works were at the time important familiar currency, was Jacques-Philippe de Varennes. Varennes published a robust defence of the egalitarian principle in his 1727 essay *Les Hommes*,[16] insisting somewhat heretically on the equality of perfection in

16. I have only ever seen what purports to be the second edition of this work: *Les Hommes: nouvelle édition revue, corrigée et augmentée par l'auteur*, Paris, Les Frères Barbou, 1727, in -12. xxiv + 301 pp.

the souls of men and women, and explicitly rejecting the traditional confirmations of women's inferiority with regard to natural law and the will of God. Another jesuit Philippe Joseph Caffiaux devoted four *tomes* to the *Défenses du beau sexe*,[17] including, most usefully, a bibliography of contemporary feminist literature. In addition to such tracts, there was a fast growing corpus of works of an ostensibly historical or lexico-graphical nature with strong feminist undertones.[18]

Then there were the more overtly militant brochures from essayists such as Cerfvol,[19] Puisieux,[20] and of course from the women themselves who were far from silent on the issue. Mme Galien's *Apologie des dames appuyée sur l'histoire* (1737), Mme Gacon-Dufour's *Mémoire pour le sexe féminin contre le sexe masculin* (1787) and Mme de Coicy's *Les Femmes comme il convient de les voir* (1787) were in their time all reputable essays on the nature of women, marriage and the role of women in society. They effectively supplemented the more celebrated novels and tracts of such writers as Mme de Lambert, Mme de Graffigny, Mme de Robert, Mme de Roland and Mme d'Argenson and of course Mme de Staël. Between 1734-1736 the aggressive journalism of Mlle Archembault made its mark on the *Mercure de France*, and Mme de Maisonneuve did much to publicise female claims to intellectual respectability in her monthly magazine, the *Journal des Dames*[21] which first ap-

17. *Défenses du beau sexe, ou Mémoires historiques, philosophiques et critiques, pour servir d'apologie aux femmes*, Paris, 1753.

18. Richard de Bury's *Histoire abrégée des philosophes et des femmes célèbres*, Paris, 1773, and Claude-Marie Guyon's *Histoire des Amazones anciennes et modernes*, Paris, 1740, would fall into this category.

19. Author of the *Cri d'une honnête femme qui réclame le divorce*, s.l., 1770, and *La Gamologie, ou de l'éducation des filles destinées au mariage*, Paris, 1772.

20. This is of course Philippe-Florent de Puisieux, author of *La Femme n'est pas inférieure à l'homme, traduit de l'anglois*, Londres, 1750; Abensour refers to this author, but mis-identifies him in his bibliography as Mme de Puisieux, *op. cit.*, p. 471.

21. See E. Sullerot, *Histoire de la presse féminine des origines à 1848*, Paris, Colin, 1966.

In 1788 Mme de Staël published her *Lettres sur les ouvrages et le caractère de Jean Jacques Rousseau*. The second preface appended to this work, some 26 years later, throws an interesting light on the efforts of the leading *femme-auteur* of the period to solve the paradoxical problem of reconciling her feminist preoccupations with her admiration and debt to one of the most forthright of the French anti-feminists. See M. Gutwirth, "Mme de Staël, Rousseau and the Woman Question,"

peared in 1764.

In the novel and the theatre writers continued the exploration of the love relationship, but the theme expanded to take in the victimisation of the female, not simply by men, but by a male-oriented social structure. The psychology of love began to assume in the world of prose fiction and drama uneasy social and political connotations. The novelist, in particular, will present now a picture of empty, fragile relationships in which the female is trapped, vulnerable, an undeserving prisoner of the male and of the system. The literary pattern is exemplified in such works as Crébillon's *Les Egarements du coeur et de l'esprit* (1736-38), and *Lettres Athéniennes* (1771), Duclos's *Les Confessions du Comte de XXX* (1741), Diderot's *La Religieuse* (1760, publ. 1798), and *Supplément au voyage du Bougainville* (1772, publ. 1796). Powerful in impact and implication Laclos's *Les Liaisons dangereuses* (1782) captured in the portrayal of its *héroine malfaisante* the essence of the period's literary treatment of female victimisation and the dehumanising effects of the social game.[22] In an essay written in 1783, a short time after the publication of the *Liaisons*, throwing incidentally an interesting light on the themes of that work, Laclos asserted that there could be no improvement in the position of women until they themselves took the initiative against their male oppressors:

O femmes, approchez et venez m'entendre ... venez apprendre comment, nées compagnes de l'homme, vous êtes devenues son esclave.... Mais si au récit de vos malheurs et de vos pertes, vous rougissez de honte et de colère, si des larmes d'indignation s'échappent de vos yeux, si vous brûlez du noble désir de ressaisir vos avantages, de rentrer dans la plénitude de votre être, ne vous laissez plus abuser par de trompeuses promesses, n'attendez point les secours des hommes auteurs de vos maux: ils n'ont ni la

Publications of the Modern Language Association of America, LXXXVI, 1971, pp. 100-109.

22. See D. Aury, "La Révolte de Mme de Meurteuil," *Les Cahiers de la Pléiade*, XII, 1951, pp. 89-101; R. Kemp, "Autour de Mme de Meurteuil," *Nouvelles littéraires*, April 22, 1948.

volonté, ni la puissance de les finir ... apprenez qu'on ne sorte de l'esclavage que par une grande révolution. Cette révolution est-elle possible? C'est à vous seules à le dire puisqu'elle dépend de votre courage.[23]

In the Republic of Letters at least France seemed to be poised for reformative action during the decade prior to 1789. The mounting tensions were reflected in the work of three writers in particular: Diderot, Holbach and Condorcet. In 1772 Mme Geoffrin's protégé Antoine Léonard Thomas presented a paper to the Académie entitled *Sur Le Caractère, les moeurs et l'esprit des femmes dans les différents siècles.*[24] The blandness of Thomas's comments provoked a sharp review from Diderot, who considered that Thomas "a beaucoup pensé, mais ... n'a pas assez senti."[25] The review in question became a compact, impassioned treatise: *Sur les Femmes.*

Criticising Thomas for his vagueness and lack of radical bite, Diderot moved in, without preamble, on the central, tangible issue of legal prejudice, and deplored a situation in which society was able legally to exploit and perpetuate female subservience through the development of its peculiar social and political institutions:

Le moment qui la délivrera du despotisme de ses parents est arrivé; son imagination s'ouvre à un avenir plein de chimères; son coeur nage dans une joie secrète. Réjouis-toi bien, malheureuse créature; le temps aurait sans cesse affaibli la tyrannie que tu quittes; le temps accroîtra sans cesse la tyrannie sous laquelle tu vas passer. ... Qu'est-ce qu'alors qu'une femme? Négligée de son époux, délaissée de ses enfants, nulle dans la société, la dévotion est son unique et dernière ressource. Dans presque toutes les contrées, la cruauté des lois civiles, s'est réunie contre les femmes à la cruauté de la nature. Elles ont été traitées comme des enfants imbéciles. Nulle sorte de vexations,

23. *Oeuvres complètes*, Paris, Bibliothèque de la Pléiade, 1951, pp. 428-429.
24. This was translated into English in 1781 by Mrs. Kindersley for reasons best known to herself.
25. *Oeuvres complètes*, ed. J. Assézat and M. Tourneux, Paris, 1875-1877, II, p. 251. Volume and page references in the text will be to this edition.

que, chez les peuples policés, l'homme ne puisse exercer contre la femme. (II, 257-258).

Translating issues raised in much of the period's feminist fiction into a commentary on the real situation, Diderot explored the interplay between political structures, social customs and the psychological and physiological nature of women. Again a natural law element begins to intrude, but in Diderot's case it is not allowed to compromise the argument. Diderot is particularly concerned with the damaging propagandist effects of traditional notions of love and *galanterie*,[26] which send women, like the men in Rousseau's state of nature, running to meet their chains: "La seule chose qu'on leur ait apprise, c'est à bien porter la feuille de figuier qu'elles ont reçue de leur première aieule" (II, 260). The deceptions inherent in western notions of love, the harsh legal implications of marriage, the burdens of motherhood and the cruel neglect of old age feature prominently in Diderot's analysis of women's fate in society: "On lui choisit un époux. Elle devient mère. L'état de grossesse est pénible presque pour toutes femmes. C'est dans les douleurs, au péril de leur vie, aux dépens de leurs charmes, et souvent au détriment de leur santé, qu'elles donnent naissance à des enfants.... L'Age avance, la beauté passe ... arrivent les années de l'abandon ..." (II, 257).

The year 1773 saw the appearance of another key feminist document of the decade: Holbach's essay *Des Femmes*, published in the third volume of his *Système social*.[27] Expanding several of the themes discussed briefly in Diderot's essay, Holbach advanced the feminist case at several vital levels. His thesis deployed legal, sociological, moral and psychological comments and data in a pattern of argument that illuminates sharply the political nature of the factors contributing to the subjugation of women and which conditioned them at an early

26. In a letter to Sophie Volland, dated November 22, 1768, Diderot reports a conversation on this very point with his daughter. *Correspondance*, ed. G. Roth, Paris, Editions de minuit, 1962, VIII, no. 513.

27. *Le Système social, ou Principes naturels de la morale et de la politique, avec un examen de l'influence du gouvernement sur les moeurs*, Londres, 1773. Volume and page references in the text will be to this edition.

stage to acceptance of that subjugation: "Par la manière dont en tout pays les femmes sont élevées, on ne paraît se proposer que d'en faire des êtres qui conservent jusqu'au tombeau la frivolité, l'inconstance, les caprices et la déraison de l'enfance. . . . Le gouvernement ne les comptent pour rien dans la société. . . . Dans toutes les contrées de la terre le sort des femmes est d'être tyrannisées" (III, 122). Holbach proceeded to compare the open tyranny practised in so-called uncivilised societies with the equally uncompromising, but camouflaged, tyranny inherent in the European systems. In France, in particular, political and social organisation impelled women, through education, marriage, religious training, sexual convention and legal restraint, to accept passively their secondary role: "L'Européen au fond, malgré la déférence apparente qu'il affecte pour les femmes, les traite-t-il d'une façon plus honorable? En leur refusant une éducation plus sensée . . . en ne leur inspirant que le goût des talents frivoles, ne leur montrons-nous pas un mépris très réel masqué sous les apparences de la déférence et du respect?" (III, 123). Current educational philosophies were for Holbach simply the mirror-image of society's prejudiced view of women's role. If a girl received an education at all, other than that of a "vain and criminally negligent mother," it would probably be in a convent which would send her out into the world armed only with a knowledge of music, dance, posture, the cosmetic arts and of course faith (*ibid.*). If she did not belong to a class fortunate enough to receive even that training, then the situation was worse. Holbach was particularly concerned in his treatise with a phenomenon that had become something of a common-place in English feminist writing of the period, namely prostitution with specific reference to the plight of the working-class girl in an urban environment. With the social effects of industrialisation becoming only too obvious in England, the whole question of class exploitation and economic principles will from now on add another dimension to the feminist problem.

Setting his argument within a broad, but quite specific, political framework, Holbach analyses the processes of moral corruption to which women are purposefully made vulnerable.

At one end of the scale the working-class prostitute is a sacrificial victim to "le vice oppulent." There are no laws to protect her, only pressures to mould her to her role. "Galanterie" has for Holbach aspects which are symptomatic of the malaise of society's institutions: "Quelle idée peut-on former des loix qui laissent sans châtiment des séducteurs aussi cruels que les assassins les plus déterminés?" (*ibid.*). At the other end of the scale, in "respectable" society, marriage itself has contributed, through its inflexibility, to the atmosphere of moral decadence in which infidelity has become the norm, "traitée de bagatelle" (*ibid.*), and adultery and debauchery prevalent. Here Holbach argued the case for divorce as a remedy to the situation: "Une législation assez sensée pour permettre le divorce remédierait en grande partie à la corruption publique" (III, 130). Once more the legal situation stands behind the abuse. As with Diderot the feminist viewpoint is becoming closely linked with wider issues. The social system, with its legal, moral, political, religious and psychological apparatus has succeeded in poisoning at source the citizen's happiness: "L'on voit donc que les usages, les loix, les institutions humaines, loin de chercher à rendre les citoyens plus sages et plus heureux, contribuent très souvent à les rendre insensés et misérables" (III, 131). Holbach, in terms ironically reminiscent of those used by Rousseau in a slightly different context, singled out the arts, in particular the theatre and the novel, as sources of psychological pressure more potent in their conditioning effect than any of the prohibitive legislation still militating against women's freedom (III, 132). Emotionally the theatre has a "funeste effet" on women by appealing to harmful passions; even the plays of France's greatest dramatists conspire to seduce, soften and corrupt the heart and the mind (*ibid.*). Once more the political direction of the argument is made clear:

> Que penser des gouvernements qui non seulement tolèrent mais encore donnent ouvertement leur protection à des amusements, qui sont évidement pour la jeunesse les écoles du vice, des lieux privilégiés, destinés à irriter les passions . . . par là loin de travailler à la réforme des moeurs, ces auteurs, pour la plupart, n'ont fait qu'attiser des

passions nuisibles et alimenter des folies dangereuses,
également contraires au vrai bonheur des femmes et à celui
de la société (III, 132, 134-135).

Like Laclos, Holbach ends his treatise with an exhortation to
action (III, 135-136).

That feminism during the years immediately before the
Revolution was turning into a Trojan horse behind which
proposals aiming at the radical political transformation of
society could be advanced received further confirmation from
the writings of Voltaire's disciple Condorcet. Condorcet's essay,
Sur l'Admission des femmes aux droits de cité[28] (1790), is a
well-known demand on behalf of women for the implementation of full constitutional rights, closely anticipating the
appearance in England of what is perhaps the most celebrated
feminist document of the period — Mary Wollstonecraft's *A
Vindication of the Rights of Women*.[29] As far as France is
concerned Condorcet's *Admission* can be seen quite legitimately
as the climactic point of feminist polemics, marking the final
convergence of the movement with the mainstream of the
period's political iconoclasm. Condorcet pointed up the irony
which had allowed France to have a revolution in the name of
equality "en faveur de trois ou quatre cents hommes qu'un
préjugé absurde en avait privés" (X, 121), but to forget, through
the paralyzing effects of traditional habits of thought, the rights
of twelve million women. To perpetuate a situation in which
women continue to be deprived of their constitutional rights,
observed Condorcet, it would have to be clearly demonstrated
that women were incapable of exercising those rights com-
petently. Condorcet then proceeded in the rest of the
Admission to dismantle point by point the main anti-feminist
positions justifying the exclusion of women from political
affairs (X, 122-126). Prejudice was reducible to one issue: the
public interest ("l'utilité publique"). This, Condorcet insisted,
was merely an argument of convenience, a principle fabricated

28. *Oeuvres complètes*, Paris, 1847-1849, repr. Stuttgart, Frommann Verlag,
1968, X, pp. 121-130. All references in the text will be to this edition.
29. See Humphreys, *op. cit.*, pp. 264-269.

to justify not only woman's continuing subservience to man, but also tyranny in most of its contemporary guises. It was in the name of "utilité" that French commerce and industry were groaning in chains, that the African Negro was enslaved, that the Bastille was full, that books were censored, that torture and secret trials were accepted (X, 126).

The feminist cause with Condorcet was made in effect to encompass the most flagrant aspects of contemporary injustice and cruelty, and as a result the political temperature of the issue rose even higher than with Diderot and Holbach. Answering the "utilité" argument, Condorcet went on to assert that a transformation in women's civil status would not work against the public interest. Women would not necessarily be torn from their domestic duties; on the contrary the fabric of family life would be strengthened once the sense of injustice which women felt had been removed (X, 128). Thus with Condorcet's *Admission* an argument going back at least to Plato comes full circle.

Two years before the publication of the *Admission*, Condorcet had raised the issue of admitting women to full citizenship in the *Lettres d'un bourgeois de Newhaven à un citoyen de Virginie* (1788). In the second of these *Lettres* Condorcet elaborated the general principle which was to preface the more specific proposals of the *Admission*:

Nous voulons une constitution dont les principes soient uniquement fondés sur les droits naturels de l'homme, antérieurs aux institutions sociales. Nous appelons ces droits *naturels*, parce qu'ils dérivent de la nature de l'homme; c'est à dire parce que du moment qu'il existe un être sensible, capable de raisonner et d'avoir des idées morales, il en résulte, par une conséquence évidente, nécessaire, qu'il doit jouir de ces droits, qu'il ne peut en être privé sans injustice. . . . N'est-ce pas en qualité d'êtres sensibles, capables de raison, ayant des idées morales, que les hommes ont des droits? Les femmes doivent donc avoir absolument les mêmes, et cependant jamais, dans aucune constitution appelée libre, les femmes n'ont exercé le droit des citoyens (IX, 14-15).

The principle was reiterated in the 1788 *Essai sur la Constitution et les fonctions des assemblées provinciales* (VIII, 141).

For Condorcet female equality implied an entirely new order of things affecting the full range of society's institutions. It was no longer primarily a moral issue, but a wider constitutional problem relating to the sources of legislative and executive power in the state. Justice for women would involve a basic reappraisal of the mechanics of government administration to enable both sexes to play an active part in political life. Condorcet managed in fact to weld together many of the more explosive ideas of his contemporaries and predecessors into a relatively coherent and practical programme for social change.

Moreover, it was Condorcet who, apart from clarifying the radical political meaning behind the feminist phenomenon, also touched upon the other fundamental principle: the maternal role and the right and necessity to regulate pregnancies. The "maternal role" argument was one of the major weapons in the armoury of the anti-feminists, permitting the invocation of natural law to confirm *de facto* female dependence and the impracticality of egalitarian principles. Most of the eighteenth-century feminists in France conceded the point, but attempt to argue around it — sometimes with considerable intellectual discomfort. Condorcet faced the problem squarely and made some attempt to think through the logical conclusion of the arguments advanced by the opposing group. The issue was mentioned, with differing emphases in both the *Admission* and the *Lettres d'un bourgeois*. In his last and greatest work, the *Esquisse d'un tableau historique des progrès de l'esprit humain* (1795), however, what had appeared to be exclusively a feminine problem and feminist issue was illuminated with a startlingly modern perspective, which took Condorcet well beyond the horizons of his age. Speculating on the possibility of a future in which the prejudices of superstition had ceased to corrupt and degrade men's moral behaviour, he wrote:

> . . . les hommes sauront alors que, s'ils ont des obligations
> à l'égard des êtres qui ne sont pas encore, elles ne
> consistent pas à leur donner l'existence, mais le bonheur;
> elles ont pour objet le bien-être général de l'espèce

humaine ou de la société dans laquelle ils vivent; de la famille à laquelle ils sont attachés, et non la puérile idée de charger la terre d'êtres inutiles et malheureux. Il pourrait donc y avoir une limite à la masse possible des subsistances, et, par conséquent, à la plus grande population possible, sans qu'il en résultât cette destruction prématurée, si contraire à la nature et à la prospérité sociale d'une partie des êtres qui ont reçu la vie (VI, 258).

Such visionary warnings, however, were to have little effect. In the event the efforts of the philosopher-reformers to create an issue of public conscience out of the unhappy position of women were abortive. A climate of opinion sympathetic to the political, social and moral implications of a revolution in the relationship between the sexes, was not really produced. The politics of feminism, in the light of events, turned out to be yet another of those promising little flowers, cultivated carefully in all the best philosophic gardens, which bloomed only to wither in the hostile climate of public opinion. If in France, as Cobban has suggested,[30] the Revolution tended to betray rather than fulfil the aspirations of eighteenth-century liberalism, the betrayal was particularly acute within the melancholy context of women's rights.

After a decade of particularly intense propaganda in favour of equal rights, many thought that with the events of 1789 the cause would be publicly acclaimed. The deputations, petitions and proclamations that went before the Revolutionary Convention from female political organisations and clubs testify to the vigour and confidence with which the feminist viewpoint was now advanced.[31] In 1788 Olympe de Gouges,[32] declared in

30. A. Cobban, "The Enlightenment and the Revolution," *Aspects of the Eighteenth Century*, ed. E. Wasserman, Baltimore, The Johns Hopkins University Press, 1965, pp. 305-315.

31. On the subject of the revolutionary fervour of the "masses féminines" see M. Cerati, *Le Club des citoyennes républicaines révolutionnaires*, Paris, Editions sociales, 1966, pp. 9-14.

32. Her real name was Marie Gouze; she claimed to be the daughter of Le Franc de Pompignan but she was in fact the daughter of a Montauban butcher Pierre Gouze. An incredibly fertile writer, she was, according to Lacour, "une des âmes les plus hautes et les plus généreuses de l'époque." L. Lacour, *Les Origines du féminisme contemporain: Olympes de Gouges, Théroigne de Méricourt, Rose Lacombe*, Paris, 1900.

her *Remarques patriotiques* that her sex was "prêt à secouer le joug d'un esclavage honteux."[33] Together with Théroigne de Méricourt[34] and Etta Palm d'Aelders[35] she went on to found in 1793 the Club des Citoyennes Républicaines Révolutionnaires. In 1791 she issued her *Déclaration des droits de la femme et de la citoyenne,* a fiery brochure of seventeen *articles.* The tenth *article* of that work is an exhortation to the women of Paris to end once and for all the imbalance between the sexes in the sphere of civil rights, and to crown the political revolution with an equally effective moral one: "La femme a le droit de monter sur l'échafaud, elle doit avoir également celui de monter à la tribune." Of the two rights claimed, Olympe was allowed to enjoy only the former. By 1793 the Convention clearly felt that a legion of New Amazons was arising in the streets of Paris. By the end of 1793 the Revolutionary government was moving against the "républicaines révolutionnaires." In October 1793 a deputation of red-bonneted women headed by Claire Lacombe was addressed by Pierre-Gaspard Chaumette, *Procureur de la Commune.* Chaumette, a disciple of Rousseau,[36] was even more uncompromising in his anti-feminism than either Robespierre or Fabre d'Eglantine. Admonishing the demonstration Chaumette pronounced the epitaph upon eighteenth-century feminism in France: "Rappelez-vous l'impudente Olympe de Gouges qui, la première, institua des sociétés de femmes, qui abandonna les soins de son ménage pour se mêler de la République et dont la

33. *Remarques patriotiques, par la citoyenne, auteur de la Lettre au peuple,* Paris, 1788, p. 15.

34. Théroigne de Méricourt was one of the most colourful of the *enragées* to be thrown up by the Revolution. She had a short but spectacular career as a rabble-rouser which came to an end shortly after a speech she gave on March 25, 1792, in which she asserted: "Il est temps que les femmes sortent de la honteuse nullité ou l'ignorance, l'orgueil et l'injustice des hommes les tiennent asservies depuis si longtemps" cit. O. Ernst, *Théroigne de Méricourt, d'après des documents inédits tirés des archives secrètes de la maison d'Autriche,* tr. P. Waechter, Paris, 1935, p. 253.

35. Author of the *Appel aux Françaises sur la régénération des moeurs et la nécessité de l'influence des femmes dans un gouvernement libre,* Paris, 1791.

36. For further information on Chaumette and his advocacy of Rousseau's doctrines see F. Braesch's edition of the *Papiers de Chaumette,* Paris, Société de l'histoire de la Révolution française, 1908, pp. 91-94, and *Annales Révolutionnaires,* Paris, Société des études Robespierristes, 1908, I, pp. 303-305.

tête est tombée sous le fer vengeur des lois."[37] Possibly a blueprint for revolution had been established. For the immediate future, however, not only had poor Olympe's head fallen beneath the "venging blade of the law," but also the hopes and aspirations of a century of feminist activity that had been unprecedented in its volume and intensity: a classic case of Nature refusing to imitate Art.

David Williams

37. Cerati, *op. cit.*, p. 173. For a full treatment of the fateful relationship between the feminist political groups in revolutionary Paris and the political manoeuvrings of J. Roux, "le curé rouge," see L. Abensour, *Problème féministe: un cas d'aspiration collective vers l'égalité,* Paris, 1927, pp. 82-83.

Fray Benito Jerónimo de Feijóo & the Sciences in 18th-Century Spain[1]

Benito Jerónimo de Feijóo's appearance on the Spanish intellectual scene was providential, his impact enormous and his influence long lasting. In 1676, the year of his birth, Spain's circumstances were singularly wretched and showed no signs of improving. Her economy was stagnant, her agriculture neglected, her lower classes burdened by taxes, her government generally incompetent and her monarch, Charles II, the pathetic product of generations of in-breeding. For over a hundred years Spain's intellectual isolation from the rest of Europe had been even more complete than her physical isolation. Since the rise of Protestantism and before, Spanish ecclesiastical authorities had been jealously guarding the purity of the Roman Catholic faith. The Inquisition never dozed and moved swiftly against any whose devotion to the Church seemed less than complete. By the end of the 17th century it exerted a virtual strangle-hold on the country's intellectual life. It warned the faithful that heretics or men of doubtful orthodoxy could offer nothing worth imitating, but it was preaching to the converted in the case of many Spaniards who tended to be disdainful or distrustful by nature of things foreign or things new.[2]

So it was that whilst elsewhere Galileo, Gassendi, Descartes, and Newton were revealing to their fellow men secrets of the natural world, the Spaniard concentrated on theology, Roman law and Aristotle, while his teachers argued over what language the angels spoke, or which might have been greater, the blood

1. I must record at the outset my very great debt of gratitude to Dr. George J. Grinnel of the Department of History, McMaster University, whose assistance with scientific material during the preparation of this study was invaluable. I am very grateful to Dr. Charles Jago of the same department for his many helpful suggestions on matters historical.
2. It is probably significant that the Spanish word for "new thing," *novedad*, also means "mishap" or "accident."

which sprang from the body of Xavier after the lapse of many years, or the milk which flowed from the severed head of Paul.[3] Should the Spaniard have wondered about the heavens, Ptolemy provided him with answers. If he wished to take up medicine, Hippocrates and Galen were the authorities he turned to. He probably knew no other modern language, but if he had a smattering of French, it was almost never sufficient to enable him to translate a book. It was possible for a man to complete his university education without even hearing of mathematics.[4] The new philosophy and the natural sciences were at best scorned in intellectual circles as useless curiosities, or else they were vehemently condemned as the dangerous work of heretics.[5]

It is to Feijóo's credit that he had the courage to be the first to challenge this state of affairs, and that he braved the Inquisition and the venomous malice of his contemporaries to advance the cause of the natural sciences and experimental philosophy in Spain. He joined the Benedictine order at the age of fourteen and developed into an outstanding theologian, receiving the degree of Doctor of Theology from the University of Oviedo in 1709. But his insatiable curiosity led him to read widely in other fields. As a monk he had access to foreign works normally denied to the layman, and so he became familiar with

3. For further details on disputations in Spanish universities, see George M. Addy, *The Enlightenment in the University of Salamanca*, Durham, N.C., Duke University Press, 1966, pp. 69-70.

4. Diego de Torres Villarroel, 1693-1770, who eventually occupied the Chair of Mathematics at the University of Salamanca, tells us in his autobiography that after completing his formal education he began ferreting out unusual books in his father's bookstore. "And I was delighted," he says, "with an indescribable pleasure by a treatise on the sphere by Father Clavius [Christophorus Clavius Bambergensis], which was, I think, the first indication to reach my ears of the existence of mathematics in the world." *Vida*, Madrid, Espasa-Calpe, 1954, p. 51. (The translations throughout are my own.)

Christophorus Clavius' work would seem to be a relic from a more enlightened age, for it had been required reading in 1625 for students of astronomy. See Addy, *op. cit.*, pp. 41-42.

5. In 1700, the University of Seville wrote to the University of Osuna accusing chemists and experimental scientists of being heretics and demanding the suppression of a certain circle or *tertulia* in Seville, which, the University said, supported Cartesian and paraphysical doctrines of Dutch and English origin. See Marcelin Defourneaux, *Pablo de Olavide ou l'Afrancesado, 1725-1803*, Paris, Presses Universitaires de France, 1959, p. 110.

the publications of the French Academy of Sciences, the *Journal de Trévoux*, the works of Galileo, Descartes, Newton, and of the thinker he admired more than any other, Bacon. These explorations of the intellectual world beyond the Pyrenees made the patriotic Feijóo painfully aware of his own country's extreme backwardness. "I weep over Spain's neglect, for Spain's neglect grieves me," he said, thus emerging as the first of a line of Spanish thinkers, extending to Unamuno in the twentieth century, many of whose works have been inspired largely by the anguish of seeing how unfavourably their country compares with foreign nations.

For Feijóo the lonely task of convincing his compatriots of the need for reform began in earnest in 1726 when he published a volume of essays entitled *Teatro crítico universal para el desengaño de errores comunes* (*Universal Critical Theatre for the Correction of Common Errors*). During the next thirteen years seven more volumes appeared with essays covering fields as disparate as medicine, philology, agriculture, the antipathy of the French and Spanish, the glories of Spain, superstitions, Church music, education and the benefits of literary pursuits.[6] The natural sciences, however, were of special concern to Feijóo, for it was here that Spain's backwardness was most evident. He is profoundly distressed to think of the low opinion that foreigners must have of Spanish scholarship:

6. Volume II of the *Teatro crítico* appeared in 1728, Volume III in 1729, Volume IV in 1730, Volumes V and VI in 1733, Volume VII in 1736 and Volume VIII in 1739. I have used the following editions: I, Madrid, Ibarra, 1777; II, Madrid, Herederos de Francisco del Hierro, 1736; III, Madrid, Francisco del Hierro, 1741; IV and V, Madrid, Ortega, 1777; VII, Madrid, Francisco del Hierro, 1746; VIII, Madrid, Imprenta del Supremo Consejo de la Inquisición, 1759. Henceforth I shall use the abbreviation *TCU* when giving references in the text.

In 1730 Feijóo wrote a book entitled *Ilustración apologética* defending the first two volumes of the *Teatro crítico*. I have used a 1769 edition of this work published in Madrid by Ibarra.

The work started in the *Teatro crítico* was continued in a series of five volumes entitled *Cartas eruditas y curiosas* (*Learned and Curious Letters*) which record a small part of Feijóo's vast correspondence. They appeared first in 1742, 1745, 1750, 1753 and 1760 respectively. I have used the following editions: I, Madrid, Real Academia de Derecho Español y Público, 1781; II, Madrid, Imprenta Real de la Gazeta, 1773; III, Madrid, Imprenta Real de la Gazeta, 1774; IV, Madrid, Pedro Marín, 1774; V, Madrid, Imprenta Real de la Gazeta, 1777. Henceforth I shall use the abbreviation *CE* when giving references in the text.

It has often happened that a teacher of ours meets a foreigner who is fairly well versed in physics. The latter touches on a few aspects of physics which are not dealt with here. How shameful for our teacher to have to be silent because he is totally ignorant of physics and perhaps does not even know the meaning of the words the foreigner uses! Or worse still, if the foreigner knows that the Spaniard has the title of Professor of Philosophy, what opinion is he going to form of him and others of his rank? And what panegyrics will he compose about them among his compatriots? (*CE*, IV, 307, *Carta* XXI.)

This acute sensitivity to foreign opinion recurs often among the major writers of Spain's 18th century. In Feijóo it was coupled with an intense desire to be useful to his country and inspired his mighty efforts to stimulate interest in the sciences. "I write mainly for Spain," he says. "And what is more useful for Spain? To write on those faculties in which there are many and very excellent authors? Who would say so? Why take water to the sea? Or to write on those areas in which Spain has almost no authors or information? This can be, and indeed is, very useful."[7] He hopes that people will learn from his writings what kind of instruction Spaniards need under their present circumstances and that "talented people will apply themselves to the cultivation of those areas of literature in which foreigners are so far ahead, and which yield them so many benefits which we lack." (*CE,* III, 378, *Carta* XXXI.)

But precisely why does Spain lag so far behind other countries in the cultivation of the sciences? Feijóo's analysis of the causes is of great interest. He blames six factors for Spain's scientific backwardness. Part of the responsibility lies with the Spaniard's instinctive rejection of anything new. Feijóo recognizes that it is well to be cautious when faced with new inventions or ideas, but he pleads with his readers to examine new things rationally before passing judgment. He warns those who refuse to look for truth anywhere but in the works of Classical and ecclesiastical writers that if they will not accept

7. *Cartas eruditas*, III, 361, *Carta* XXXI.

any recent scientific discovery, they will be denying themselves and Spain the benefits of advances such as Galileo's discovery of Jupiter's four satellites; Huygens' and Cassini's discovery of Saturn's five satellites; they will be excluding Vieta's specious algebra, Nepero's logarithms and Harvey's circulation of the blood. (*CE*, II, 217, *Carta* XVI.)

Another factor contributing to Spain's lack of scientific progress is the commonly held belief that the new philosophers bring out nothing but useless curiosities. Feijóo strongly opposes this opinion. For him the philosophers' quest for knowledge is a divinely inspired urge. "There is no truth whose perception is not useful to the understanding," he says, "because all truths lend themselves to satisfying man's natural thirst for knowledge. This appetite came to man's understanding from the Author of Nature. Is it not a grave insult to God to think that he inspired the soul with an appetite for something useless?" (*CE*, II, 219, *Carta* XVI.)

If scientific curiosity is inspired by God, it cannot pose any threat to the Roman Catholic faith, argues Feijóo, hacking now at a third common prejudice. To exclude new ideas for fear of their possible undesirable influence on religion is to do far more harm than good. To close the door on new doctrines, he says vividly, "is to place the soul in cruel slavery. It is to tie up human reason with a very short chain. It is to put an innocent mind in a cramped prison simply to avoid the remote chance of its going somewhat astray in the future." (*CE*, II, 225, *Carta* XVI.)

Those who denounce the new philosophy as dangerous or useless are motivated more by envy than by religious zeal, Feijóo feels. What such people really hate is not so much the ideas the author expresses but the author himself and the fame his writings bring him. Elsewhere, in a letter addressed to a Minister of Ferdinand VI, Feijóo deals again with the problem of envious attacks on writers:

> I have seen writings where aspersions are cast on a person's birth. I have seen others where the victim's moral defects were published, all quite irrelevant to the subject under discussion. These infamies are seen and tolerated only in Spain. In view of this, is it surprising, Excellent Sir,

that certain people, very capable of enlightening our nation with their writings, should keep their works to themselves, rather than be exposed to such villainous hostility? (*CE*, III, 354-55, *Carta* XXVIII.)

One of the most serious obstacles to the dissemination of scientific knowledge in Spain was the teaching profession itself, many of whose members basked smugly in their belief that they knew everything. "They can scarcely hear the name of Descartes without ridicule and laughter," says Feijóo. "And if one asks them what Descartes said, or what new opinions he offered to the world, they do not know, and have nothing to say in reply..."[8] An irrational fear of Descartes is a sixth factor responsible for Spain's ignorance of the sciences. People mistakenly relate everything to do with modern philosophy to him, and having heard evil reports of the man, assume modern philosophy to be equally diabolical. Although Feijóo differs with Descartes on many points, notably his theory of the indestructibility of matter, he willingly recognizes the Frenchman's "sublime intellect" and "extraordinary subtlety," and praises him as a fine example for other philosophers. He notes, however, that Descartes was inclined to be rash in forming his conclusions. (*CE*, II, 221, *Carta* XVI.)

In his fight to make Spaniards receptive to the natural sciences Feijóo had to campaign constantly against his compatriots' uncritical reliance upon the teachings of Aristotle. He was greatly pleased when a doctor by the name of Martín Martínez published a study entitled *Medicina scéptica,* strongly recommending the value of observation and experimentation in medicine. This work was challenged by another doctor, Bernardo López de Araujo y Azcárraga, in a study entitled *Centinela médico-aristotélica contra scépticos,* a work which claimed to defend Aristotle, though with no success, according to Feijóo. Shortly thereafter, late in 1725, the Benedictine entered the polemic with his *Apología del scepticismo médico escrito por el Rmo. P. M.* Having poured scorn on the

---

8. *Cartas eruditas,* II, p. 216, *Carta* XVI. For other notorious shortcomings of Spanish university teachers at this time see Addy, *op. cit.,* pp. 68-73.

ineffectual López de Araujo, Feijóo presents his own views upon Aristotle. His philosophy tends to be abstract, he says, and consequently more applicable to theological questions. "But to examine nature," Feijóo continues, "I think that mechanical rules are better suited, and that abstract ideas will always be, as they always have been, useless; because as Bacon said in his famous statement: *natura non abstrahenda est, sed secanda.*"[9]

He makes similar points elsewhere. The Aristotelian system is imperfect, he claims, because it deals with abstract ideas and not with the physical nature of things. To illustrate the limitations of Aristotelianism, Feijóo shows how a scholastic philosopher and then a natural scientist approach anatomy. The first notes the various functions of the body. It feeds, therefore it has a nutritive faculty; it grows, therefore it has augmentative virtue, and so on. "This explains nothing about philosophy," retorts Feijóo, "and gets us nowhere so far as religion is concerned." The anatomist studies the organs, the vessels, tubes and other delicately made parts housed inside this "portentous machine," and thus acquires an understanding not only of the human body but also of the "most wise artificer whose infinite skill was capable of making it." (*TCU*, VII, 328-29, Disc. 13.) Feijóo makes the most of every opportunity to show that experimental philosophy, far from blinding us to virtue, in fact increases our love and knowledge of deity. "Oh my God!" he says, "there is no creature which is not a mirror for me to see the reflection of your greatness. But what a remarkable thing, for I see you more imposing the smaller the mirror!" (*TCU*, VII, 330.)

Feijóo was foolishly attacked by Francisco Soto Marne, perhaps the fiercest of his many critics, for despising ancient

9. The edition of the *Apología* I have used is bound immediately after the *Ilustración apologética* in the 1769 edition, and the numbering of its pages runs on consecutively, 191-233. This quotation comes from pp. 214-215.

Martín Martínez became a devotee of Feijóo. He was a doctor of medicine with a special interest in anatomy and rose to be President of the distinguished Royal Society of Seville, the first medical body in Spain. See Gregorio Marañón, *Las ideas biológicas del Padre Feijóo*, 4th edition, Madrid, Espasa-Calpe S.A., 1962.

opinions and of being addicted to modern ones.[10] Feijóo rejects the charge. If he were attracted only by new ideas he would have become a devotee of Newton or Descartes or Gassendi. In fact, says Feijóo:

> I do not consider myself a follower of any of the three. I touch upon Newton occasionally, without showing agreement or disagreement. I speak of the universal system of weight, and the part relating to optics I consider to be very probable. Nowhere in my writings do I show the slightest inclination to Gassendi. And if this is not enough, then I declare him to be somewhat or completely improbable. Descartes I attack as vehemently as possible in several places, not only for being improbable in matters physical but also for being dangerous in places with regard to theology. (*Justa repulsa*, p. 16.)

Feijóo was probably more attracted to Newton than his cautious words here would lead us to believe. In a letter written in 1727 and reproduced by Gregorio Marañón in *Las ideas biológicas del Padre Feijóo* (pp. 39-41) he displays his admiration for Newton and identifies himself as a Newtonian. The *Optics* doubtless appealed to him because of its experimental nature, and he was probably able to accept it without difficulty. The *Principia* with its treatment of gravity was less approachable, and the year 1729 finds Feijóo still puzzled over the reason why objects fall earthwards. "It is not certain what causes heavy objects to fall; it may be some intrinsic faculty of their own, or the attraction of the Earth; therefore it is uncertain whether they would come down if placed at a very great distance." (*Ilustración apologética*, p. 169.)

Feijóo's feelings towards Gassendi are understandable given the latter's association with an Epicurean theory of the universe. Although Gassendi does differ from Epicurus in

---

10. Soto Marne was a Franciscan and author of *Reflexiones crítico-apologéticas sobre las obras del R.P. Maestro Fr. Benito Jerónimo Feijóo*. This work was published in Salamanca in 1748, and its attacks were answered by Feijóo in 1749 in a book entitled *Justa repulsa de inicuas acusaciones*. I have used a 1769 edition of this work, bound, like the *Apología*, with the *Ilustración apologética*, but with pages independently numbered.

concluding that God must have directed the atoms which eventually coalesced to form the world and its original inhabitants, his unmistakably Epicurean leanings would have made Gassendi unacceptable in Spain in the first half of the century.

So far as Copernicus is concerned, Feijóo's attitude is interestingly ambivalent. He can accept his teaching on a scientific level but not on a theological level. In one of his letters Feijóo springs to Copernicus' defence when a correspondent angrily denounces his theory of a motionless sun and rotating earth as "fantasy, delirium and chimera," and says that all who believe it are "deceived, fatuous and mad." All the writer can adduce in support of his claim, however, is the evidence before his eyes. "Oh, how wrong you are!" says Feijóo in reply. He explains that the eyes are deceived in cases such as this. "It is a constant law of optics," he continues, "that for a person on a large body which is moving, the appearance of movement is transferred to another, or other bodies, at some distance away which are still, especially if the movement is uniform . . ." (*CE*, III, 217, *Carta* XX.) There is, in Feijóo's opinion, a great deal to be said in favour of Copernicus. The only obstacle to his fully accepting him is theological.

So far as I am concerned, if only philosophical and mathematical arguments were involved here, I would be the most confirmed Copernican in the world. But the trouble is that having exhausted everything philosophical and mathematical in the subject, there remains against Copernicus an argument far superior to all those that have been brought forth in his favour. Which is it? The one taken from the Authority of the Scriptures, in various parts of which it is expressly stated that the Earth is immobile and the sun rotates around it.[11]

Even for someone of Feijóo's open mind Copernicus was strong medicine in Spain in the first half of the 18th century. To accept his theory, it was thought, would incur the heresy of

---

11. *Cartas eruditas*, III, pp. 228-29. Feijóo refers his reader to Genesis 25, Joshua 10, Kings 20, Psalm 18, and elsewhere.

doubting that Joshua had made the sun to stand still upon Gibeon or that Isaiah had brought the sun's shadow back ten degrees. Other Spaniards found Copernicus even more difficult to accept at that time. Jean Sarrailh mentions the geographer, Ramón Cansino, writing around the middle of the century, who opposed the Copernican system on the grounds that we can see the sun, moon and stars moving, and that the Holy Scriptures oppose it as well as most mathematicians and philosophers. Sarrailh mentions also the enlightened Andrés Piquer, writing in 1747, for whom Copernicus was unacceptable mainly for religious reasons.[12]

Feijóo therefore rejects Copernicus in the long run, and for Ptolemy he has only scorn. He conveniently sums up his astronomical loyalties when he says:

> We must confess that the common system, or the Ptolemaic, is absolutely indefensible, and it only prevails in Spain thanks to the great ignorance in our schools on astronomical matters; but this system may be abandoned along with the Copernican, as we embrace that of Tycho Brahe, in which heavenly phenomena are given considerable explanation. (*CE*, III, 229, *Carta* XX.)

Indeed Tycho Brahe came to the rescue of the pious with a theory of the universe which was new but which did not involve any compromise of their Catholic conscience. For Tycho Brahe the Earth was stationary and it was the sun, along with the moon which rotated around the Earth, whilst the stars and planets rotated around the sun.

Feijóo appears, therefore, not as the advocate of a particular school of scientific thought, and certainly not as an original scientific thinker, but as a scholar and writer whose goal is to shake his readers out of their intellectual stupor, to foster

12. Jean Sarrailh, *L'Espagne éclairée de la seconde moitié du XVIIIe siècle*, Paris, Imprimerie Nationale, 1954, p. 491. Piquer was an outstanding physician and the author of a work entitled *Lógica moderna o arte de hallar la verdad y perfeccionar la razón* (*Modern Logic or art of finding truth and perfecting reason*), Valencia, J. García, 1747. The fact that Copernicus had appeared in the curriculum of the University of Salamanca as early as 1561 and yet was meeting stiff opposition nearly two hundred years later is surely a symptom of Spain's academic decline.

among them a more rational attitude towards new ideas and to make them more receptive to experimental science. He militates constantly against intellectual rigidity.

I wish there could be some moderation in that blind veneration for antiquity, so dominant in some, that they look upon the ancients as gods and upon modern men as beasts, and upon neither as men (as they should). But there is even more need to wipe out the indiscreet love of new things which predominates in others . . . The former obstinately reject, the latter blindly embrace whatever the modern thinkers say, and both extremes, as the Lord Chancellor of England noted, are great obstacles to the progress of the sciences. (*Apología del scepticismo médico*, pp. 216-217.)

Feijóo's task was extraordinarily difficult, for he not only had to teach but also to persuade his readers that what he had to teach was useful and desirable. His efforts met often with apathy or crude hostility, and there must have been many moments of great discouragement. In 1742, for example, he penned the following melancholy lines: "For fifteen years I have been continually declaiming against the fatuous credulity which prevails in the world, and I think that the world, with the exception of a few individuals, so far as this part is concerned, is as it was. All hear my cries, and almost all, it seems, are deaf to them." (*CE*, I, 342, *Carta* XXXV.)

It is safe to say that almost every literate Spaniard had heard Feijóo's cries by that time. His works enjoyed a popularity equalled before only by *Don Quijote*. By 1732 there had been four editions of the first volume of the *Teatro crítico* in six years, three editions of the second volume in four years, three editions of the third volume in three years, and two editions in two years of the *Ilustración apologética*. A second edition of the fourth volume of the *Teatro* was imminent. Each edition produced approximately two thousand volumes. By 1750 he had been translated in whole or in part into Italian, French, Portuguese and English, and by 1786 his works had run to fifteen Spanish editions.[13] If Feijóo felt in 1742 that his message was falling on stoney ground, he must have been much comforted when six years later Ferdinand VI made him Royal Counsellor and in 1750 forbade any further attacks on him. There was probably little outward evidence in Spain of the enlightenment he had to offer, but there was abundant evidence of the impact he was making on men's minds. Every post brought him huge quantities of mail from correspondents seeking information on medicine, theology, the sciences, and any of the many topics he dealt with. In the Introduction to the *Ilustración apologética* he complains that often his correspondence alone takes up two days of each week (p. XXXI). In a letter written in 1750 he apologizes for being brief, but is "snowed under by mail" (*"sofocadísimo de cartas"*).[14]

The appearance in Spain of certain medical and scientific institutions coincided with the period of Feijóo's greatest productivity. It is true that the Royal Society of Seville was inaugurated in 1697, but it was not until Feijóo's admirer, Martín Martínez, became its President that it distinguished itself. In 1733, seven years after the appearance of the first volume of the *Teatro crítico*, the Madrid Academy of Medicine was founded. Feijóo must have read with great pleasure the fiftieth article of the Academy's statutes which said: "The primary goal and general idea of the Academy will be to make manifest the truths and beneficial maxims of Medicine and Surgery by means of Observation and Experience." (Marañón, p. 265.)

During Feijóo's lifetime it must have been fairly common for enlightened men to meet and discuss his works and problems of national concern. In 1764 these groups began to acquire greater formality and permanence as Spain's *Sociedades Económicas de Amigos del País* (Economic Societies of Friends of the Country) started to spring up. The first of these was

---

13. For fuller details on the chronology and editions of Feijóo's works, see the introduction by Vicente de la Fuente to the *Obras escogidas* of Feijóo, Vol. I, *Biblioteca de Autores Españoles*, Vol. 56, Madrid, 1952, especially pp. IX-XII and XXXI-XXXIII.

14. See Gregorio Marañón, *Las ideas biológicas del Padre Feijóo*, p. 18.

formed in the Basque Country and was followed quite soon by other Societies in Seville, Madrid, Zaragoza and elsewhere. These Societies, of which there were over seventy by the end of the century, aimed to foster in Spain all those areas of endeavour which would most benefit the country. They set up libraries and schools and sought ways to improve Spain's agriculture, industry and science. Although Feijóo did not live to see any of them in operation, their complete conformity to his ideals leads one to believe not unreasonably that his influence must have been a powerful factor in their development.

The scientific spirit, the desire to observe and to learn was spreading in Spain thanks in part to Feijóo and his followers, but there was still a discouraging amount of resistance to overcome. The General Plan of Studies sent by the Royal and Supreme Council of Castile to the University of Salamanca in 1772 declares on page twelve the unacceptability of Descartes, Gassendi and Newton, for their teachings do not conform to those of Aristotle.[15] The teaching profession seems to have been still generally as arrogant in the second half of the century as it was when Feijóo had attacked it in 1745. José de Cadalso, writing in the 1770's describes what for him is a typical teacher. "Imagine first that you see a very dry, tall man, smelling of tobacco, heavy-laden with spectacles, quite incapable of bowing his head or of greeting a living soul . . ." Talk to this man of any interests of yours which differ from his, says Cadalso, and you may expect answers such as:

"Modern physics is a puppet show. I have seen those things they call experimental physics machines: I repeat, a puppet show, water that goes up, fire that comes down, threads, wires, boxes, nothing but a children's plaything!" If you stress that what he calls a puppet show is what all nations owe their progress to . . . for certain provinces would be under water without use of the dikes and machines built by the good principles of this science; if you tell him that every mechanical art needs physics in

15. See Sarrailh, *op. cit.*, p. 482.

order to subsist and advance; if you tell him in a word, that in the whole cultured universe men pay great heed to this science and to its teachers, he will call you a heretic.[16]

Influential figures continued to deplore the study of science, maintaining it to be incapable of instilling virtue. Ignacio Luzán, addressing the Barcelona Academy of Bellas Letras in 1752, had lumped all the sciences under the heading of mathematics and said: "What shall I say of mathematics which today walks so proudly with its inventions, its machines and its investigations . . . . Can these sciences pride themselves on making us happy with such vaunted discoveries?"[17] Thirty-five years later Juan Pablo Forner published some lengthy and highly unreadable poems entitled *Discursos filosóficos sobre el hombre (Philosophical Discourses on Man)*, where he expresses the opinion that the pursuit of scientific knowledge is directly opposed to the pursuit of virtue. "The brilliance of the mantle of light spreading from the greatest to the lesser orbs does not illumine virtue."[18] His conclusion is that science corrupts man.

But fortunately there were figures just as influential if not more so who continued to uphold Feijóo's principles. For Jovellanos, as for Feijóo, the study of science and the contemplation of the universe have a spiritualizing effect. "Oh, how God's beneficence shines upon [the globe]!" says Jovellanos. "Wherever you turn your eyes you will find the imprint of his omnipotence and goodness."

16. *Cartas marruecas (Moroccan Letters)*, ed. Lucien Dupuis and Nigel Glendinning, London, Támesis Books Ltd., 1966, pp. 174-75. José de Cadalso, 1741-1782, was one of the most important writers of 18th-century Spain. The *Cartas marruecas* are for the most part a stern criticism of contemporary Spain in which Cadalso protests against the frivolity and growing effeminacy of the country's leaders and proclaims the virtues of patriotism and stoicism.

17. Luzán, 1702-1754, was born in Zaragoza and received a classical education in Italy. On returning to Spain he was horrified at the state of Spanish theatre which did not always observe the Aristotelian rules. He is remembered chiefly for his *Poética*, published in 1737, which influenced subsequent neo-classical authors.

I have taken this quotation from the Spanish translation of Sarrailh's work, *La España ilustrada de la segunda mitad del siglo XVIII*, Mexico — Buenos Aires, Fondo de Cultura Económica, 1957, pp. 479-80.

18. *Biblioteca de Autores Españoles*, Vol. 63, 357a. Forner, 1756-1797, was a secondary figure in 18th-century Spanish letters. He is at his best when engaged in literary polemic. His most interesting legacy is his *Exequias de la lengua castellana (Funeral Rites of the Castilian Language)*.

He continues in an equally Feijoonian vein:

And this is how the simple observation of nature will lead you to higher studies of natural philosophy; because I would have you know that your mind [espíritus] will never be satisfied with the counting and classification of beings, but will crave mainly to know their properties. Man cannot yearn for them without yearning for close acquaintance with them; inherent in his being is an insatiable curiosity with which he was inspired for a purpose, namely to raise him to the contemplation of the universe, and this curiosity carries him in pursuit of the great system of causation which he imagines and discovers all about him.[19]

In exile in Italy the remarkable Jesuit, Father Juan Andrés, wrote:

Certainly Galileo, Cassini, Descartes, Leibnitz, Newton, Boerhave, Morgagni, Haller, Linneus and so many other great, and if you like, supernatural men honour humanity . . . and the vast supply of so many machines and so many surgical, anatomical, chemical, physical and astronomical instruments manifested in these two centuries; and the continuous and uninterrupted series of many and so resounding discoveries made these days in all the sciences, prove a vigour and a fertility of the human spirit, which in some manner raise it to partake of the divine spirit.[20]

19. *Biblioteca de Autores Españoles*, Vol. 46, p. 338a-b. This is from an address entitled *Sobre el estudio de las ciencias naturales* delivered to the Instituto Asturiano in 1799.

Gaspar Melchor de Jovellanos (1744-1811) was one of the most important figures of 18th-century Spain. Born of an aristocratic Asturian family, he studied in Madrid where his outstanding talents attracted attention. He was given a governmental job in Seville where he came into contact with a circle of enlightened people. He became an energetic reformer and rose to great prominence in the Government. Godoy made him Minister of Grace and Justice in 1797. One of his most significant achievements was the creation of the Instituto Asturiano in 1794 where the study of the natural sciences was given every encouragement.

20. *Origen, progresos y estado actual de toda la literatura*, VII, pp. 26-27, quoted by Julián Marías in *La España posible en tiempo de Carlos III*, Madrid, Sociedad de Estudios y Publicaciones, 1963, p. 118. Father Andrés' work was originally written in Italian. Its ten volumes were translated into Spanish by D. Carlos Andrés and appeared in Madrid between 1784 and 1806.

Father Andrés' good sense and tolerance are very reminiscent of Feijóo's. He was able to admire not only Descartes and Newton but Voltaire and Rousseau as well, for he insisted on isolating their writings from their attitude towards religion. ". . . if erudition and wit can be separated from irreligion, and can be joined to piety, as indeed we often see happen, I do not understand why one cannot, or rather should not, desire Voltaire's fine taste, Rousseau's eloquence and Fréret's erudition over the mediocre talents of a great many of their opponents." (Marías, p. 110.)

The last decades of the eighteenth century proved to be far more congenial for the progressive thinker than the first decades had been, when Feijóo courageously took up his pen. The soil he had helped to loosen bore the fruit of the seeds he sowed. The Economic Societies flourished, scientific and medical institutes were set up, the power of the Inquisition waned, Spaniards began to travel and to read foreign books, foreigners came to Spain in growing numbers and although no Buffons or Newtons appeared, an influential number of aristocrats showed a keen interest in the natural sciences. Although Spain still lagged far behind France and England in scientific progress, these last years were a time when the patriotic reformer could look into the future with confidence, a luxury which Feijóo had seldom been able to enjoy. Acutely aware of the distance Spain has yet to travel in order to catch up with other countries, Cadalso none the less looks forward eagerly to the day when foreign academies will no longer have cause to despise Spain.

Let us work at the positive sciences, so that foreigners shall not call us barbarians; let our young people make the progress they can; let them give the public works on useful matters, let them leave the elderly to die as they have lived, and when those who are now youthful reach a mature age, they will be able to teach publicly what they now learn in secret. Within twenty years Spain's entire scientific system will have changed imperceptibly, without commotion, and then foreign academies will see if they have cause to treat us with disdain. If our scholars are somewhat slow in catching up with theirs, they will have this excuse to give them: Gentlemen, when we were young, we had teachers who said: *My sons, we are going to teach you everything there is to know in the world; be careful not to take other lessons, because from them you will learn nothing but frivolous, useless, contemptible and perhaps harmful things.* We had no wish to spend time on anything save that which could give useful and sure knowledge, and so we applied ourselves to what we heard. Gradually we began to hear other voices and to read other books, which may have alarmed us at first, but which we came to like. We started to read them assiduously, and since we saw that they contained a thousand truths in no way opposed to religion or to the fatherland ... we gradually found other uses for our various scholastic tomes and notebooks, until not one was left. Some time has passed since then during which we have caught up with you, although you had almost a century and a half's lead. Disregard everything I have said, and let us start writing the date as from today, supposing that the Peninsula sank beneath the waves in the middle of the seventeenth century and that it has emerged from the waves at the end of the eighteenth. (*Cartas marruecas*, p. 176.)

For today's reader there is pathos in Cadalso's words, for of course his optimistic predictions did not come to pass.[21] The intellectual activity of Charles III's reign lost much of its

---

21. Julián Marías, p. 152, quotes the following words written in 1788 and probably revised the following year:

Blissful ignorance ours if it has brought us no other ills save the lack of a few works such as our Religion condemns, and kindly the barrier which contains the Spaniards' freedom of understanding so they shall not run along the precipices of impiety ...

Let our bold scholars study, therefore, *the progress of reason in all ages and nations, and they will find the horrible monsters* it has produced among the most cultured and civilized nations, and they will see what good grounds Spain has for trying to keep it in check ...

Marías believes the author to have been a priest possibly working directly for the Inquisition. The passage appeared in an article entitled "La intolerancia civil" and was published in a periodical known as *Espíritu de los mejores diarios*, April 6, 1789, pp. 1061-62.

momentum under Charles IV. The French Revolution spread panic through Spanish governmental and intellectual circles. After the chaos of the Napoleonic invasion and the Peninsular War it seemed briefly that a new age of progressive liberalism was about to dawn upon Spain. But Charles IV's son, Ferdinand, returning in 1814 as Ferdinand VII, brought with him all of his ancestors' despotism and none of their benevolence. Earlier promises were broken, Liberals were persecuted, the Inquisition was restored and for the last two years of Ferdinand's reign the universities were obliged to close down.

But Cadalso's words give us some idea of the extent of the intellectual revolution which took place in Spain in the eighteenth century. In 1726 Feijóo was virtually alone, looking beyond the Pyrenees at an enlightened Europe and striving to admit some of this enlightenment into Spain. He was one of the very few Spaniards tolerant enough and perceptive enough to recognize that heretics could have something useful to teach those who were loyal to Rome. Feijóo's was the loudest of the "other voices," as Cadalso puts it, which were heard in the land advocating reform and a degree of Europeanization. By the end of the century there was a solid core of writers and intellectuals who, whilst remaining intensely patriotic, saw clearly that the only hope for Spain was to retain what was best in the country's heritage and to become better integrated into the mainstream of European thought.[22] They saw that if their nation was to improve its lot, it would have to pursue the sciences, economics and all branches of useful knowledge with

22. El Conde de Campomanes, one of Spain's most important thinkers of the 18th century, wrote in 1776:

We should imitate whatever each nation does best: in this way, merely copying for the time being their advances and adapting them to our uses, retaining whatever is good of our own, we shall soon catch up with other nations, becoming meek in order to adopt what we do not know, or cannot do so well as the foreigner. (Marías, pp. 82-83.)

In addition to Cadalso, Jovellanos, Father Andrés and Campomanes, we might mention in this regard Juan Sempere y Guarinos, writing c. 1785; El Duque de Almodóvar, writing c. 1780 as "D. Francisco María de Silva"; Pablo de Olavide, writing and active c. 1770; Tomás de Iriarte, writing c. 1780; "Pedro Fernández," writing c. 1773 (see Marías, pp. 169-218); Leandro Fernández de Moratín, writing c. 1800; Meléndez Valdés, writing c. 1790.

the same determination as other countries had done. In this radical shift from scholastic isolationism to enlightened internationalism, the efforts of Feijóo played a very important part.

John Browning

"An Original Champion of Enlightenment": M. V. Lomonosov & Russian Education in the 18th Century

In the intellectual history of eighteenth-century Russia no name now stands higher than that of Michael V. Lomonosov. Writing some seventy years after Lomonosov's death in 1765, Alexander Pushkin stated the basis of this pre-eminence in a sentence which subsequent historiographical vicissitudes in Russia have failed significantly to alter: "between Peter I and Catherine II Lomonosov was the original champion of enlightenment [in the Russian Empire]. He founded our first university, rather he himself was our first university."[1] The last half of Pushkin's judgment provides the key to Lomonosov's extraordinary hold upon so many of his nineteenth- and twentieth-century countrymen. Simultaneously physicist, chemist, poet, historian — to name only his major concerns — he stands for later Russians as a heroic figure in their country's "Dark Era," the depressingly obscurantist middle decades of the eighteenth century. Twentieth-century Russians have carried Pushkin's assessment to further rhetorical heights. To the literary historian Prince Mirsky, Lomonosov is simply "the father of modern Russian civilization,"[2] while from the opposite end of the ideological spectrum comes the voice of *Pravda* greeting the "talented son of the great Russian people, whose legacy has made a precious contribution to Russian and world culture."[3]

Yet world culture, through the medium of its non-Russian historians, has been slow to acknowledge this debt or even the

---

1. A.S. Pushkin, "Stati i Zametki: Puteshestvie iz Moskvy v Peterburg" [sic], *Polnoe Sobranie Sochinenii*, Moscow, 1949, XI, p. 249.
2. D. S. Mirsky, *A History of Russian Literature from its Beginnings to 1900*, New York, 1958, p. 47.
3. *Pravda*, November 18, 1936, cited in B. Menshutkin, *Russia's Lomonosov*, trans. J. E. Thal and E. J. Webster, Princeton, 1952, p. 3.

value of the contribution. Inevitably perhaps, Lomonosov the poet and historian has been left largely to Russians to judge, but the scientist and Pushkin's "original champion of enlightenment" has made a scarcely greater impact outside his native country. A recent Anglo-French anthology on the history of modern science places him literally as a mis-spelt footnote to the greater glories of contemporary Englishmen, Frenchmen and Germans. The editor admits that familiarity with Lomonosov's ideas would have given eighteenth-century chemistry "a tremendous impetus" but "unfortunately he wrote in Russian" — which closes the matter.[4] In fact Lomonosov wrote as often in Latin, a tongue not unknown to scientists elsewhere than Russia, but it is the widespread attitude behind this bland dismissal, rather than the words themselves, which subsequent Russian intellectuals have found so infuriating.[5] They see in it a comfortable Western assurance that no Russian of the eighteenth century and few since have had much of value to offer intellectual Europe and that the pattern of Russian intellectual effort at least until recent years has been to accept gratefully and uncritically whatever more talented foreigners might throw their way.[6] The Russian response to a challenge in these terms usually begins with the name of Lomonosov: does he merit this confidence? What were the values that he defended which brought Pushkin's praise and what relationship did these have to the dominant cultural values of the Russia and Europe of his day?

Lomonosov was born the son of a free peasant in 1711. His early years were thus those of Russia's "great metamorphosis": the pell-mell upheaval by Peter the Great of all national

4. R. Taton ed., *History of Science: The Beginnings of Modern Science,* trans. A. J. Pomerans, New York, 1963, p. 499.

5. For example Ilya Ehrenburg's reaction to Georges Bidault's sneer at "a certain Lomonosov" as recorded in his memoirs, *Post-War Years, 1945-1954,* trans. T. Shebunina, New York, 1967, p. 110. For a brief but balanced Western academic view of Lomonosov and his intellectual relationship to his age, see Valerie A. Tumins, "Enlightenment and Mysticism in Eighteenth Century Russia," *Studies on Voltaire and the Eighteenth Century,* LVIII, Geneva, 1967, pp. 1673-77.

6. This assurance was well illustrated in the period of the post Sputnik panic by the appearance of a study of this very question: Werner Keller, *East Minus West Equals Zero: Russia's Debt to the Western World, 862-1962,* New York, 1962. The title explains the thesis.

institutions and the forcing of a Russian elite through the schoolroom of technical, secular instruction. Lomonosov was himself a graduate of that schoolroom and he acquired in it the same avid curiosity in the natural and physical sciences which so fascinated Peter. The few Russian youths who shared that taste were singled out for special attention. In 1736 a small group, including Lomonosov, was dispatched under the auspices of Peter's Academy of Sciences to the Universities of Freiberg and Marburg. Lomonosov spent four and a half years in Germany and while at Marburg attracted the favourable attention of the physicist and mathematician Christian Wolff, an influential figure of the contemporary German Enlightenment[7] and one for whom Lomonosov felt a life long respect and affection.[8] Wolff's comments on his Russian student afford us an early glimpse of Lomonosov's versatility. Within a few months of his arrival at Marburg, he was already proficient "in drawing, mechanics and natural history," and would soon be embarking on "experimental physics and mathematics."[9] He was also trying his hand at poetry. In 1739 he sent from Freiberg an elegant congratulatory ode addressed to the Empress Anne in celebration of a recent triumph of Russian arms over the Turks. Any eighteenth-century Lord Snow would have rejoiced at the budding poet and scientist who returned to St. Petersburg in 1741, to set about justifying in both cultures Wolff's prediction that his pupil would bring great benefit to his Russian fatherland.[10]

For the next twenty-four years Lomonosov produced a steady flow of poems, essays, notes on scientific experiments and natural phenomena to a degree which has enabled Russians of a later age to compare him favourably to Leonardo da Vinci.[11] At least in terms of mass and scope the comparison is not inappropriate; a twentieth-century bibliography of Lomo-

7. W. J. Bossenbrook, *The German Mind,* Detroit, 1961, p. 198; L. Krieger, *Kings and Philosophers, 1689-1789,* New York, 1970, pp. 156, 157.

8. Menshutkin, *op. cit.,* p. 28.

9. A. Morozov, *Mikhail Vasilievich Lomonosov, 1711-1765,* Leningrad, 1952, pp. 228-229.

10. P. Pekarskii, *Istoriia Imperatorskoi Akademii Nauk v Peterburge,* St. Petersburg, 1873, II, p. 294; Menshutkin, *op. cit.,* p. 31.

11. A. Vucinich, *Science in Russian Culture,* Stanford, 1963, p. 113.

nosov's output devotes two hundred pages of close print to list his contributions to literature, science and the fine arts.[12] From all this two features emerge most clearly: an insatiable curiosity about the wonders of the physical world and a profound belief in science as an impulse to human progress. "What can be found," he asks rhetorically, "that is nobler, more useful, more diverting, more indisputably necessary in human affairs" than science?[13] These are not the tones of Lomonosov alone. His versatility of interests was his own, but his conviction that all things exist in the world to be used for man's benefit and that the mind enlightened by science must work to that end in the interests of human happiness shows how great was his indebtedness to the years at Marburg under Wolff's guidance.[14] Science was knowledge, its application to human affairs would provide the Russian people with the keys to its future progress. This must be the function of education: without question Lomonosov agreed with Wolff and Leibnitz that the first requisite of a truly enlightened people was receptivity to the benefits of scientific knowledge.[15] His return to St. Petersburg placed him squarely before the very different reality of mid-eighteenth-century Russian education.

Russian education in 1741 was the result of fifteen years of tampering with the legacy bequeathed by Peter I. Education for Peter had mirrored his own intellectual bent: practical, secular, technical, geared to the need to transform Russia along the lines he had judged imperative for her further progress. His instruments to that end were his "fledglings," the young (and sometimes not so young) aristocrats tied in service to the Petrine state. With service came education; as Mark Raeff aptly observes of Peter's whole approach: the obligation to serve implied the obligation to be educated.[16] Positive incentives,

12. G. S. Kuntsevich comp., *Bibliografiia izdanii sochinenii M.V. Lomonosova na russkom iazyke,* Petrograd, 1918.

13. Morozov, *op. cit.,* p. 651.

14. Bossenbrook, *op. cit.,* pp. 198, 199.

15. Peter I solicited Leibnitz' opinions on his planned Academy of Sciences and received a lengthy explanation of Leibnitz' thoughts on the function of such an institution in Russia, Pekarskii, I, p. xxi.

16. M. Raeff, *Origins of the Russian Intelligentsia: The Eighteenth Century Nobility,* New York, 1966, p. 131.

typical of Peter, played their necessary part. A nobleman who failed to pass examinations in basic subjects, mathematics in particular, was not permitted to marry and was regarded by the government as a permanent minor, regardless of his biological age.[17] The autocratic state compelling education in the interests of technical progress, hence national enlightenment, constituted the essence of Peter's concept of government, even though the results in his lifetime hardly measured up to his expectations. The most tangible expression of these expectations was the Academy of Sciences in St. Petersburg and its two attached institutions: the Academic University and the Gymnasium or preparatory school. Leibnitz and Wolff had both strongly encouraged Peter to found an academy of this nature and the Tsar himself acknowledged Russia's need of institutions "where young people could begin to study and afterward assimilate the higher level of the sciences."[18] The educational hierarchy thus called into being would, hopefully, begin the process of bringing scientific enlightenment to the nation, indispensible to its welfare. This Petrine emphasis exactly reflected Lomonosov's own ideas and accounts for his deep veneration of Russia's first Emperor: "to defend the work of Peter the Great" became a stated purpose of his public and private activity.[19]

By the time Lomonosov returned to Russia the work of Peter the Great on behalf of education urgently needed defending. Inside the Academy, as outside, Peter had left an enormous task. Its complexity was evident at the Academy's first meeting a few months after Peter's death. No Russian scholars were present when members discussed in Latin the respective merits of Newton and Descartes. Of course the encouragement of native talent was and remained a vital part of the Academy's function, one from which Lomonosov had himself benefited. But that was a long range prospect; in the meantime foreign scholars dominated the Academy's early sessions. Figures such

17. *Ibid.*, p. 132.

18. P. Alston, *Education and the State in Tsarist Russia,* Stanford, 1969, p. 7; K. V. Ostrovitianov ed., *Istoriia Akademii Nauk SSSR*, Moscow/Leningrad, 1958, I (1724-1803), p. 430.

19. J. M. Letiche ed., *A History of Russian Economic Thought,* Berkeley, 1964, p. 373.

as the mathematicians Leonhard Euler, the brothers Nicholas and Daniel Bernoulli, the chemist J. F. Gmelin gave Peter's institution a European reputation before, paradoxically, it had made any name for itself in Russia.[20] The picture was bleakest for the Academic University. In 1731 not a single student remained enrolled and government attempts to induce seminarians to enter had no appreciable effect. The University suspended operations in 1753.[21]

The reasons for this unpromising situation did not lie only in the weakness of a secular, technical tradition in Russian education. They stemmed even more from the nature of the Petrine state itself. Peter's mobilization of a privileged gentry class bound in service to the state indeed made that class dependent on the autocrat for advancement; equally it made the autocracy dependent on the support and co-operation of the serf-owning element of Russian society. This Peter might successfully command. He could order squads of young aristocrats abroad to learn navigation, gunnery, geometry and other hatefully un-Russian subjects. But those who followed him on the throne could not hope to duplicate his tactics. Peter's decree of 1722, leaving the throne at the personal disposal of the incumbent, introduced an element of chance into the post-Petrine succession from which the gentry, in particular the King-maker clique of Guards officers in the capital were quick to profit. Each change of ruler between 1725 and 1762 brought increasing gentry pressure to rid itself as a class of the more distasteful features of state service; high on the list stood the need to submit to unpleasant academic curricula. Within two decades of Peter's death this ambition was within sight of realization. The mathematics school in Moscow, founded by Peter, was closed and the Slavic-Greek-Latin Academy, where Lomonosov had studied, was turned into a theological seminary.[22] Military schools remained but even they were shaped in accordance with the prevailing social trend. Thanks to the Empress Anne, young noblemen aspiring to

20. Ostrovitianov, *op. cit.*, I, p. 152; Vucinich, *op. cit.*, p. 78.
21. Alston, *op. cit.*, p. 7.
22. *Ibid.*, p. 8.

commissions in the pampered Guards Regiments were relieved in 1731 of the requirement to pass through the lower ranks of the St. Petersburg Military Academy and they had the added satisfaction of seeing students from non-aristocratic backgrounds excluded from their midst.[23] In sum, by Anne's death in 1740, her uncle's aim that the gentry should be inculcated "with an education in citizenship and economics" seemed as remote from fulfillment as possible.[24] Ten years later the situation was such that practically no opportunity existed in Russia of acquiring a higher education along the lines conceived by Peter in institutions designed for that purpose. All such establishments were dying or dead and no one seemed interested in reviving them.[25]

In the face of government uninterest the responsibility of educating Russian gentry youth fell upon non-Russian shoulders. The middle decades of the eighteenth century were in Russian education the great age of the *petit-maître*, Russians raised by foreign adventurers attracted to the Empire by the voracious appetite of the Russian aristocracy for the subject it found most congenial: the latest cultural fashions of Western Europe. The more disreputable of these foreign amateurs found their pupils an easy prey. How great, for example, must have been the gratification in one gentry household on hearing from their newly acquired "monsieur" (unknown to them an ex-galley slave) that the fleur-de-lys branded on his shoulder designated his close relationship to the Bourbon family. Probably less enthusiastic was the *petit-maître* who reportedly discovered after some years of instruction that his French thus painfully learned was in fact Finnish, his teacher's only known tongue.[26] Unsurprisingly, entire generations of young Russian landowners grew up strangers to their own national traditions, history and, not infrequently, language. In 1805 the great-nephew of one of Lomonosov's Court patrons Count M. I.

23. Raeff, *op. cit.*, p. 68.
24. V. O. Kliuchevskii, *Sochineniia*, V, "Kurs Russkoi Istorii," Part 5, Moscow, 1958, p. 166.
25. G. Makogonenko, *Nikolai Novikov i Russkoe Prosveshchenie XVIII veka*, Moscow/Leningrad, 1951, p. 33.
26. E. Haumant, *La Culture Française en Russie*, Paris, 1913, pp. 86-87.

Vorontsov remarked of his family's upbringing, which was also that of his class:

> It can be said that Russia is the only country where knowledge of the native language and all matters relating to our own country are scorned. Those who in Moscow and St. Petersburg consider themselves enlightened make every effort that their children should know French, surround them with foreigners, give them dancing and music teachers who know not one word of Russian. This splendid education . . . leads to a total ignorance of one's own country, to indifference, perhaps even to scorn for [Russia] and to a devotion to everything relating to other countries and customs, especially France.[27]

At the onset of the seventeen-forties Lomonosov confronted a combination of aristocratic indolence, a dearth of native talent, governmental inertia and an uncritical worship from his prospective pupils of non-Russian styles and culture. These deficiencies he neither could nor would deny. He retained nonetheless a fundamental confidence in the abilities of his countrymen to follow the Petrine model if only their potential were given the same opportunities for expression as his had enjoyed. The political omens seemed especially favourable. Four months after Lomonosov's return to St. Petersburg a sudden palace coup placed Peter the Great's daughter Elizabeth on the Russian throne.

The new Empress owed her throne to the fortuitous combination of two factors: her parentage and court revulsion against the German favourites of previous reigns. Her accession did nothing to lessen aristocratic Gallomania – rather the contrary – but it did encourage those, like Lomonosov, who looked for an immediate revival of the Petrine spirit in the government of Russia. Lomonosov at once addressed Elizabeth in a series of eulogistic odes whose underlying hope is that the promise of the father might be gloriously fulfilled by the daughter. These struck a responsive chord and Elizabeth showed herself ready to protect their author from the attacks of his

---

27. *Arkhiv Vorontsova*, V, p. 12, cited in Makogonenko, *op. cit.*, p. 34.

German colleagues in the Academy of Sciences.[28] More important, she grasped the value of the Academy as an instrument to
assist the government in its various administrative and technical
problems. Her formal recognition of this role was the Academy's new charter of 1747, increasing its financial support
from the state, but subjecting it more firmly to the supervision
of the bureaucracy. Although Lomonosov was displeased at the
manner in which the charter had been drawn up and worked for
its further revision, his reservations did not in any way diminish
his expectations of Imperial benevolence toward the cause he
was promoting: the Petrine state working for progress through
national enlightenment.[29] His ode of 1747 clearly showed his
encouragement at Elizabeth's interest in her parents' Academy
and he calls upon Russian youth to respond: "to show by their
own intellects that the Russian land too can produce its Platos
and Newtons."[30] Two years later the unofficial court laureate
had his opportunity to make a public debut as Russia's chief
spokesman for the Petrine pattern of enlightenment. In 1749
the Academy of Sciences decided to revive a discarded custom
of a public session devoted to an oration on a chosen subject.
Since the date fell upon the anniversary of Elizabeth's accession
the subject posed no problems, but the arguments within the
Academy as to who should deliver the speech present a telling
commentary on the condition of Russia's intellectual elite of
the day. Lomonosov's biographer informs us that one academician was unsuitable "on account of his physique, the voice of a
second was too weak, a third knew no Russian, a fourth was
engaged on an unpleasant lawsuit, a fifth had a mistress of low
origin."[31] That left Lomonosov who duly appeared on November 25 with his customary ode to the sovereign. Its extrava-
gently patriotic eulogies were a clear overture for the Empress'
favour from a man who had already identified himself as an

28. Lomonosov was briefly arrested in 1743 as the result of a feud within the
Academy. He was fully pardoned by Elizabeth. Menshutkin, op. cit., pp. 39-40.
29. Ostrovitianov, op. cit., I, pp. 158-159.
30. "Oda na den' vosshestviia na vserossiisskii prestol eia velichestva Gosudaryni
Imperatritsy Elisabety Petrovny 1747 goda," M. V. Lomonosov, Sochineniia, ed. A.
A. Morozov, p. 86.
31. Menshutkin, op. cit., pp. 73-74.

admirer of her father's work, particularly of Peter's belief in science as an essential condition for the introduction "of just laws, efficient courts and honest mores."[32]

Apart from her likely receptivity to an appeal of this nature, Elizabeth had other, more personal reasons to favour a vigorous approach to the issue of Russian enlightenment. Shortly after Lomonosov's address, his principal court patron Count I. I. Shuvalov became the Empress' lover. As such, Shuvalov was able to channel his protegé's ideas backed by his own enthusiastic support, directly to the autocrat, bypassing the inevitable obstructions of the Tsarist bureaucracy. This was a crucial advantage to Lomonosov's cause. While not even the most charitable historian can term Elizabeth truly enlightened or even for that matter educated, as her father's daughter she proved extremely sensitive to any implication that the Tsar-Reformer's progressive work might be imperilled. Vulnerability on that score prompted her major — one might better say single — act in the Petrine spirit of enlightenment: the establishment of a new university in Moscow, the forerunner of all others subsequently founded in Russia, inspired by Lomonosov and, since 1940, bearing his name.

Though sympathetic to Peter's achievement, Lomonosov accepted fully the need of an institution of higher learning away from Peter's capital. The Petersburg Academic University had quite failed to live up to the hopes of its founder that it would become the nursery of an administrative and technical elite. Shortly before its demise in 1753 Lomonosov could see no similarity to any university known to him in the St. Petersburg establishment.[33] Neither was the summit of Peter's educational creation, the Academy of Sciences, yet producing Russians of sufficient numbers and calibre to stand beside the foreign talent in its midst. After thirty years of existence it was perhaps unrealistic to have expected otherwise, doubly so given the dominance of German favourites at court between Peter's death

32. G. A. Gukovskii, *Russkaia Literatura XVIII veka*, Moscow, 1939, p. 110; V. V. Sipovskii, *Literaturnaia Deiatel'nost' Lomonosova*, St. Petersburg, 1911, p. 19, cited in Vucinich, *op. cit.*, p. 112.

33. Kliuchevskii, *op. cit.*, V, p. 165.

and the accession of his daughter. The anti-German reaction under Elizabeth contributed to the sudden return to Berlin in 1741 of Leonhard Euler, bearing with him horrifying tales of Russian barbarism to relate to the Prussian court.[34] Expatriate members continued nevertheless to lord it over their Russian colleagues. The Germans at the Academy's highest level saw no reason this should end, one remarking in justification that the institution had no need of ten Lomonosovs when one was already a burden.[35] In some senses then, both personal and public, Peter's window on the west was working too well, a retrenchment in the landlocked capital of Moscovite Russia promised possibilities of a new start for Russian education.

It is therefore appropriate to see in the project for a new university evidence of a nationalist desire, embodied at court by Shuvalov and in the Academy by Lomonosov, to breathe new life into Russian higher education, as the source of the scientifically enlightened mind on which Russia's future would depend. Equally, it held out the promise of lessening, if not ending, the degrading spectacle of young Russians acquiring their "education" at the hands of obscure foreign parvenus. The Empress concentrated her attention on this aspect. As far as she was concerned, the new university's first priority must be to protect gentry youth from frittering away their lives "in the company of lackeys, barbers and other such tradesmen."[36] Lomonosov's ambition was more lofty and national. To him the "honor of the Russian people" required that native talent be given a chance to demonstrate "its ability and skill in the sciences," so that the nation might benefit from the efforts of its own sons "in the consideration of all advanced knowledge."[37] That day perhaps lay far off, but its remoteness did not mean it was hopeless even to begin. In fact the reverse: "we must use what we can get, in time the edifice will be built" summed up Lomonosov's attitude.[38]

---

34. This did not stop his returning twenty years later on the pressing invitation of Catherine the Great. Vucinich, *op. cit.*, p. 97.
35. Pekarskii, *op. cit.*, II, p. xlviii.
36. Morozov, *Mikhail Vasilievich Lomonosov*, p. 652.
37. Pekarskii, *op. cit.*, I, p. 847.
38. Morozov, *op. cit.*, p. 653.

Given the political realities of eighteenth-century Russia Lomonosov could not claim sole credit for beginning the construction of his edifice. Alone, the academician and laureate would have made little impression; the combination with Shuvalov was enough to win over a naturally indolent ruler to his side. The same realities ensured that the Imperial favourite would overshadow the peasant-born scientist throughout the various planning stages; in due course Shuvalov was named the university's first curator. In one respect that would prove of incalculable significance for the future, however, the university's organization was decisively influenced by the non-aristocrat of the pair. From the start Lomonosov urged that Moscow University must not draw its students exclusively from the privileged gentry elite of the nation. Russia's needs were too great to be met from that source alone. Sons of all classes should, he felt, be eligible for admission, even serfs with their owners' permission. Shuvalov, himself very much the product of that elite, at first was cool toward the idea and even Elizabeth may have had reservations.[39] After all, she, along with every other eighteenth-century autocrat after Peter had constantly to remember that aristocratic support had put her on her throne and aristocratic hostility could as easily remove her from it. Still, the encouragement of talent outside of noble ranks had been a feature of her father's policies and not even she could maintain that her government was distinguished for its intellectual capacities. Indeed, if her niece, the future Catherine the Great is to be believed, none at Elizabeth's court ever spoke of art and science because everyone was so ignorant: "it is very likely that half of the company could barely read and I am not certain that one-third could write."[40] Lomonosov's idea was allowed to carry the day with some modification. As Peter had done in his Academic University, Lomonosov set up preparatory schools (gymnasia) to train incoming students for university life. One of the two gymnasia was reserved for youths of

---

39. *Ibid.,* pp. 655-657 where Shuvalov's resistance is probably exaggerated. Also S. Shevyrev, *Istoriia Imperatorskogo Moskovskogo Universiteta,* Moscow, 1855, p. 11.

40. Quoted in M. Florinsky, *Russia, A History and An Interpretation,* New York, 1961, I, p. 691.

noble family. There they were offered, as befitted their pre-eminence in eighteenth-century Russia, the richer choice of subjects: Russian, mathematics, philosophy, foreign languages. Their social inferiors, the "men of various ranks" were enrolled in the second gymnasium where their choice of curriculum was limited to the fine arts, singing and "technical" subjects: architecture, drawing and the like.[41] These inhibitions were unavoidable sacrifices to the facts of eighteenth-century Russian society. Lomonosov was confident nonetheless that the gymnasia would serve, in his own metaphor, "to supply the seeds to be scattered on the ploughed fields" of the new university and its three faculties of law, philosophy and medicine.[42] The way was clear for Elizabeth's manifesto of January 12, 1755, formally inaugurating the institution. In words which any eighteenth-century devotee of enlightened principles could safely applaud her statement proclaimed: "Since every good comes from the enlightened mind and since the enlightened mind uproots evil, it is vitally necessary to spread in our Empire all useful knowledge obtainable by means of the appropriate sciences."[43]

Unfortunately these brave words were not to be matched by any real fulfillment in the years that followed. Executive fiat could change none of the realities of the contemporary Russian cultural scene, for example its dominance by foreigners. German academics manned all but two of the university's first twelve teaching positions in a manner analogous to their role in the Academy of Sciences. The main obstacle encountered was also familiar: how were the *petit-maîtres* to be induced to abandon their easygoing ways in favour of the more rigorous training envisaged in the new establishment? The government did what it could. Its promise of quicker promotion in the civil and military hierarchies of the Table of Ranks encouraged some of the most aristocratic families in the land to ship their sons off to the old capital for the university's opening session. Two

41. Paul Dukes, *Catherine the Great and the Russian Nobility*, Cambridge, 1967, p. 27; Shevyrev, *op. cit.*, p. 13.

42. *Ibid.*; P. N. Polevoi, *Istoriia Russkoi Slovesnosti*, St. Petersburg, 1900, I, p. 531.

43. Shevyrev, *op. cit.*, p. 10.

years later came an added attraction to the gentry, when most graduates from the second gymnasium began to be sidetracked from the University into a newly founded Academy of Arts. There they could develop skills that would not challenge the aristocracy's stranglehold on eighteenth-century government and administration.[44]

The short term result of all these efforts hardly seemed to justify their having been made. Actual want afflicted all students regardless of their social origin. In October 1758 a notice to the university authorities reported the absence from classes of nine gentry students and six of other ranks "for lack of shoes."[45] By 1765 only one student remained in the law faculty, one in the medical. In the entire thirty-five year reign of Catherine II only one student graduated successfully from Russia's single medical school.[46] Virtually all that can be claimed for Moscow University in the eighteenth century is that, like the Abbé Siéyès, it survived into the nineteenth. In retrospect this proved sufficient, but from the vantage point of the seventeen sixties it was hard to be optimistic about the university's prospects. Lomonosov himself died pessimistic about the future of his brainchild and bitterly disappointed that it had made no apparent dent in his country's intellectual dependence on foreigners and foreign styles.[47]

Disappointment in the slowness of his "ploughed field" to return a bountiful harvest did not lessen Lomonosov's belief in his correct diagnosis of Russia's malady or in his prescription for it. Backwardness and ignorance would yield to the irresistible advance of science, with the autocracy, as under Peter the Great, presiding and setting the pace. To Lomonosov this was part of the monarchy's essential function. His constant hymns of praise between 1739 and 1765 directed at the occupant of the throne need not be regarded as a mere ritualistic gesture on the part of the court poet. They are

44. Ibid., pp. 22, 39.
45. Morozov, op. cit., p. 658.
46. Shevyrev, op. cit., p. 255. Kliuchevskii denies that even one student graduated, (op. cit., p. 166), but the official history of Moscow University is clear on the point. See also Entsiklopedicheskii Slovar', III, p. 106, the article on F. Barsuk-Moiseev.
47. Shevyrev, op. cit., pp. 5-6. For the poet Fonvizin's unflattering portrait of the university at the same time see ibid., pp. 64-66.

reminders to Peter's heirs, phrased in the most flattering terms, that their first duty lay in fulfilling the substance of Peter's legacy, as Lomonosov saw it. The main thrust of his appeal was toward Elizabeth, Peter's daughter and therefore, so it might be supposed, most committed to the defence of the Petrine tradition. Whenever she acted in this pattern, in the Academy or the new University, Lomonosov's insistence on the continuity of the Petrine enlightenment became particularly lyrical. On the day of Moscow University's opening session he delivered before a gala reunion of the Academy a prolonged address in favour of his hero-Emperor. The portrait drawn could not have been more fulsome and he invited Peter's immortal shade to view with satisfaction the splendid future now before Russia: "your daughter rules, your grandson is the heir; we, by you raised, strengthened, enlightened, embellished; by her, liberated, inspired, enriched . . ."[48]

Lomonosov's view of Peter and the Petrine state is inseparable from his image of contemporary Russian society. In that society Lomonosov was without doubt the most articulate defender of the virtues of enlightened absolutism. An idealized Peter was held up to his successors, even though their personal qualifications or political conditions scarcely permitted them to act with the same vigour as their great predecessor. Anne, the first recipient of Lomonosov's eulogies, is generally regarded as the most degraded of Peter's heirs; her successor, praised by Lomonosov for his generosity and future deeds of heroism was, at the time of writing, six months old.[49] The actual identity of the autocrat thus seems largely irrelevant, it is an ideal monarch or rather a reincarnation of the ideal Petrine original that Lomonosov was seeking. Conversely, his appeal as spokesman for Peter's legacy was greatest to those eighteenth-century rulers who tried most energetically to cast themselves in Peter's mould. Elizabeth showed this, so too in her way did Catherine II. Her unexpected arrival in power at first boded no good for

48. "Slovo pokhval'noe Petru Velikomu 26 aprelia 1755 goda," M. V. Lomonosova, *Sochineniia,* ed. A. A. Morozov, p. 457.

49. Gukovskii, *op. cit.*, p. 101; *Sochineniia M. V. Lomonosova*, ed. S. I. Vavilov, I, pp. 24-20, "Pervie Trofei Ioanna III Antonovicha," "Oda na rozhdenie Ioanna III Antonovicha."

Lomonosov. His two court patrons, Counts Shuvalov and Vorontsov, were obliged to go abroad as too deeply identified with Catherine's two immediate predecessors; their protegé shared briefly in their disgrace. His unhappy prospects drew from his pen an appeal to the Empress couched in terms that were a mixture of abasement and flattery, flattery not of the recipient, but of the sender. "Various academies and great men," he wrote, "have testified that I have brought with my science great fame to the fatherland throughout all the enlightened world . . ." Whether or not convinced by his tone, Catherine relented to the extent of restoring his income and bureaucratic rank and visited his studio to admire a mosaic he had created depicting Peter's triumph over the Swedes at Poltava.[50] Had Lomonosov lived longer it seems likely that Catherine's further policies would have elicited from him outbursts even more ecstatic than those he had showered on her aunt. She too announced ambitious plans for the regeneration of Russian education, but like so much else in her Russia ambitious plans failed to make the jump to material reality. Her efforts as ruler eventually concentrated within the areas of war and diplomacy which traditionally promised the eighteenth-century Russian autocrat the most spectacular returns at the least political cost.[51]

Was Lomonosov's estimate of his worth justified by contemporary European standards? Outside of Russia it is true that his work did win him a degree of recognition in his lifetime. He was elected an honourary member of the Swedish Academy in 1760 and of the Bologna Academy four years later.[52] But these were hardly at the summit of enlightened Europe, there he remained an unknown figure. Least of all did the *Encyclopédiste* pacesetters of the century's middle decades acknowledge Lomonosov as one of themselves, always assuming the improbable hypothesis that they had heard his name. The fault here lay less in Lomonosov the poet and scientist than in

50. Polevoi, *op. cit.*, p. 531. *Russkii Biograficheskii Slovar'*, X, p. 608.
51. For Catherine's projects of education reform see Dukes, *op. cit.*, pp. 189-193.
52. Morozov, *Mikhail Vasilievich Lomonosov*, pp. 840-841. He owed his election to the Bologna Academy to Count Vorontosov's influence, Vucinich, *op. cit.*, p. 114.

Lomonosov the Russian. Prior to the mid-sixties, no light came from the East and none was expected. When its rays were at length acknowledged, it was not a Russian who garnered the tributes of the Republic of Letters but Diderot's German born patron "with the mind of Brutus in the body of Cleopatra."[53] In Catherinian Russia, even more than in Elizabethan, the path to enlightenment for young Russians was that blazed by the philosophes, in particular Voltaire. The limitless gentry mania for the sage of Ferney amused the visiting Casanova, who noted that when young gentry sprigs had read all Voltaire's works "they thought themselves as wise as their master."[54] Form, not content, was what mattered to the *petit-maître* of the fifties and sixties. If he wished to attract the attention of those who decreed intellectual fashions, he must pay court in the approved manner together with every other European suitor. Shuvalov's nephew, A. P. Shuvalov, was a case in point. In 1765 he made his way westward to present Voltaire with a short ode in impeccable French on the death of Lomonosov, recommending the latter's virtues and fame to the Master's notice. The verse, if ever received, appears to have made no impression.[55] This would not have disturbed its subject. Lomonosov's opinion of the author of *Histoire de l'Empire de Russie sous Pierre le Grand* was in any case not high,[56] and when this was added to his interests and nationality his invisibility from Paris was not surprising. His central theme of the enlightened ruler sponsoring an enlightened people was one which, to judge from their later ecstacies over Catherine, both Diderot and Voltaire could endorse as appropriate to the circumstances of her Empire. But hers remained the only significant voice audible to them from Russia.

53. Haumant, *op. cit.*, p. 133.

54. A. Machen ed. and trans., *Memoirs of Jacques Casanova*, V, "In London and Moscow," New York, 1959, p. 537.

55. P. N. Berkov, *Lomonosov i Literaturnaia Polemika ego Vremeni, 1750-1765*, Moscow/Leningrad, 1936, pp. 277-280.

56. Lomonosov had been asked by Shuvalov to supply Voltaire with literary and archival materials for his biography of Peter. Lomonosov was very critical of the use, or lack of it, made of these materials; the book itself was not highly thought of in official and literate Russia. Menshutkin, *op. cit.*, p. 161; Haumant, *op. cit.*, p. 110. He also commented unfavourably on Voltaire's religious views, his "half-clever wit and abusive praise." Pekarskii, *op. cit.*, I, p. 504.

Lomonosov's Russian contemporaries did not treat him with markedly. greater favour. By his death, many educated Russians regarded his poetry as old-fashioned, his literary work, his activity in the Academy of Sciences and his efforts on behalf of an enlightened approach to education were ignored or unknown.[57] One prominent exception to this indifference was Alexander Radishchev, "the father of the Russian intelligentsia" and unsparing critic of the reality behind the Petersburg facade of Russian eighteenth-century society. In his famous *Journey from St. Petersburg to Moscow* Radishchev related his emotional reaction over Lomonosov's grave. Here lay the "creator of Russian letters," the discoverer of Nature's secrets, a poet, historian, rhetorician, and scientist worthy of the highest respect. "Nature, behold thy triumph! Eager curiosity . . . strives after the knowledge of things, and the heart flaming with ambition cannot brook the fetters that would hold it captive." Lomonosov was such a man; significantly Radishchev's only reservations about his hero concern his role as the defender of enlightened autocracy: "I do not envy you because, following the common custom of flattering kings . . . you praised Elizabeth in fulsome verse . . ."[58] Radishchev was kind; unlike him, Lomonosov had confined his social criticism to safe areas or cautious expression. A widely circulated "Hymn to the Beard" of 1757 satirised religious ignorance and predictably aroused the fury. of the Orthodox hierarchy. Its cries for vengeance went unheeded, to have paid attention would not have seemed right to the daughter of the man who had reduced the Russian church to the status of a bureaucratic department. Lomonosov's private works were only marginally more adventurous. An essay "On the Use of Glass" eloquently defended the thesis that science must develop free of superstition; this was hardly a revolutionary thought at the time it was advanced in 1752. The man who saw science and religion as "daughters of the Divine parent" was a dangerous ideological subversive only to the watchdogs of the Holy Synod.[59] More serious was

57. Berkov, *op. cit.*, p. 273.
58. A. N. Radishchev, *Journey from St. Petersburg to Moscow*, trans. Leo Wiener, ed. R. P. Thaler, Cambridge, Mass., 1958, pp. 222-237.
59. M. V. Lomonosov, *Sochineniia*, ed. A. A. Morozov, pp. 237-246. "Pis'mo o

Lomonosov's failure to consider the evil of serfdom, Radishchev's "grim monster, hundred mouthed and bellowing," which even Catherine was to admit two years after Lomonosov's death to be a prime cause of Russian backwardness and poverty.[60] Of course the ruler may admit what the prudent subject cannot and it is true that in his essay to Shuvalov of 1761, "On the Preservation and Increase of the Russian people," Lomonosov wrote of the far from ideal conditions of the Russian countryside. His proposals for improvement mirrored his belief in the autocracy, which should encourage the founding of new cities, suppress rural banditry, regulate peasant and priestly marriages. The text was unknown to the younger generation of educated Russians but they would not have been impressed even had they read it. Its remedies were pallid when compared to those being discussed and tried in the West.[61]

By Catherine's death in 1796 the two basic conditions of Russian cultural life that Lomonosov had failed to overcome still effectively prevented the implementation of his approach to Russian education. Literate Russia continued to worship at the shrines of Western Europe, while the autocracy remained disinclined to follow up the initial promises made on behalf of Russian enlightenment at the founding of Moscow University. The occasional newspaper lament at persistent intellectual subservience to France was without effect.[62] It took the military and diplomatic shocks of the two decades after Catherine to bring the first real change. By 1805 conservative gentry opinion was visibly hardening against France, no longer the source of all earthly delights, though to be sure, as Tolstoi's epitomes show in the opening lines of *War and Peace*, this hostility itself could still be expressed in French. More representative of the spirit of rising cultural nationalism was the

Pol'ze Stekla," pp. 253-255, "Gimn Borode." G. V. Plekhanov, *Literatura i Estetika*, Moscow, 1958, II, pp. 19-25, cited by Vucinich, *op. cit.*, p. 401.

60. Dukes, *op. cit.*, pp. 87-88; Radishchev, *op. cit.*, p. iii.

61. M. V. Lomonosov, *Sochineniia*, ed. A. A. Morozov, pp. 466-479, "O Sokhranenii i Razmnozhenii Rossiisskogo Naroda." Lomonosov's reticence on serfdom is embarrassing to his Soviet apologists, one of whom blames it on "the weak aspects of his world view." M. T. Beliavskii, *Krestianskii Vopros v Rossii nakanune vosstaniia E. I. Pugacheva*, Moscow, 1965, p. 59.

62. Shevyrev, *op. cit.*, p. 261.

historian Nicholas Karamzin, himself educated at the University of Moscow and widely travelled in the West. In 1803 he noted with pleasure the determination of Alexander I to champion the cause of Russian national enlightenment, as evidenced by a new ministry of that name and schemes for new universities. Loyal Russians must respond to their young Emperor's initiative; in Karamzin's view "we shall not be fulfilling our patriotic duty . . . if we still send our young people to study in foreign lands [subjects] which are taught in our universities."[63] Three new institutions in St. Petersburg, Kharkov and Kazan eventually emerged to redeem the Imperial promise. Their model was Moscow, to Karamzin the first in stature among all Russia's establishments of higher learning. An account of the university in 1811 seemed to justify his pride and Lomonosov's earlier hopes: it was seen at last to be a genuinely Russian institution, relying on Russians and no longer obliged to turn to foreigners for the job of educating Russian youth.[64] Naturally, this cultural emancipation took some time to filter downwards; eleven years later one could still read in the situations wanted column of a Moscow newspaper notices such as the following: "a dog keeper, German born, seeks position in kennel or as tutor."[65] Nonetheless, the Russian occupation of Paris dealt a mortal blow to the era of the *petit-maître* and to the uncritical acceptance of foreign ways which had distinguished him since Lomonosov's day. Russian education would still meet many obstacles but the prospect of a larger harvest from Russia's several "ploughed fields" was now in sight.

A distinct national self-confidence was the most important legacy to intellectual Russia of the Napoleonic War. Karamzin gave early voice to this, thirty years later Pushkin chose the same theme in directing attention to the one native voice of eighteenth-century Russia that had called for the nation to stand on its own feet and had shown how this might be done:

63. *Ibid.*, p. 335.
64. The "Russianness" of even Moscow University was still far from complete. Throughout the Napoleonic Wars German scholars were still being recruited for positions at the institution. *Ibid.*, p. 341.
65. Moskovskie Vedomosti, no. 72, 1822, quoted in Henri Troyat, *Pushkin*, trans. Nancy Amphoux, Garden City, N. Y., 1970, p. 4.

"with what warmth he speaks of the sciences, of enlightenment" wrote Pushkin approvingly of Lomonosov.[66] His praise
for the champion of science and enlightenment, rather than for
the poet and historian, mark a clear break in the view held of
Lomonosov by Russian posterity. His attitude to the needs of
Russian society — national, rational, scientific — appealed to the
nineteenth- and twentieth-century intelligentsia far more than
to his own generation and help to account for the fact that in
death Lomonosov has become much larger to educated Russians
than he ever was in life. In his own time he stood for a pattern
of enlightenment that was basically at variance with contemporary social and political tastes. There is a striking reflection of
this in a story related by the last French ambassador to Imperial
Russia, Maurice Paléologue, a few weeks before the monarchy
collapsed. According to Paléologue's anecdote, the governor of
Moscow once complained to Catherine II about the indifference
of the Russian people toward education. The Empire's first
pupil of the Enlightenment at once replied that this was hardly
a matter for regret: if that indifference should ever change
"neither you nor I will remain where we are."[67] Lomonosov had
tried to combat that indifference, though he was certainly no
revolutionary by the standards of 1789, let alone 1917. Nor
would the defender of enlightened absolutism have understood
how, within a century after his death, his cherished university
could have become so much the fountainhead of opposition to
the existing order that Nicholas I might justifiably point to the
building with the comment "voilà l'ennemi." Lomonosov
contributed to that process nonetheless by the values he had
held and propagated throughout his adult life. The scientifically
enlightened mind dedicated to progress, of which he was the
unique embodiment in eighteenth-century Russia, cannot rest
content with considering the marvels of the physical world.
Neither Catherine II nor her grandson ever forgot that such a
mind will, if given the chance, go beyond to examine the
society which lives in that world and, ultimately, the institu-

66. A. S. Pushkin, *Polnoe Sobranie Sochinenii*, XI, p. 249.
67. Maurice Paléologue, *An Ambassador's Memoirs*, trans. F. A. Holt, New
York, 1923, III, p. 37.

tions which govern it. Because he had insisted on the need to provide Russians with that chance, if not to that end, and because he did his utmost to see that at least the beginning steps toward it were taken, Lomonosov and his cause have deserved the judgments of Pushkin and Nicholas I alike. In this sense, the rebaptism in 1940 of his particular "ploughed field" was overdue recognition to the man who was, and not to Pushkin alone, truly "our first university."

Robert Johnston

Plate 1. Raphael, *Paul Preaching at Athens.*

Plate 2. Hogarth, *Paul before Felix*.

Plate 3. Hogarth, *Paul before Felix Burlesqued.*

Plate 4. Hogarth, *A Harlot's Progress*, Plate 6.

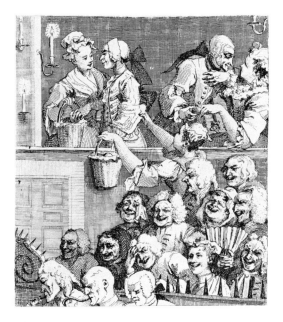

Plate 5. Hogarth, *A Laughing Audience*.

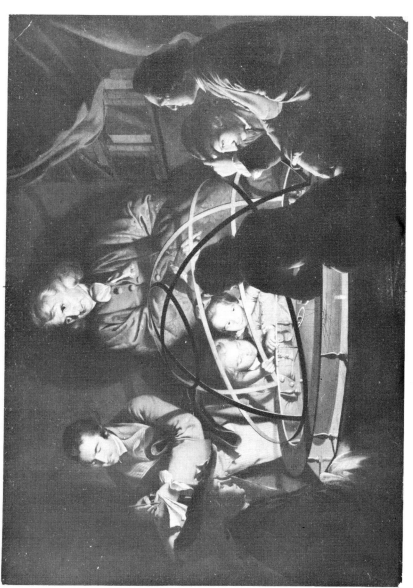

Plate 6. J. Wright of Derby, *A Philosopher giving a Lecture on the Orrery.*

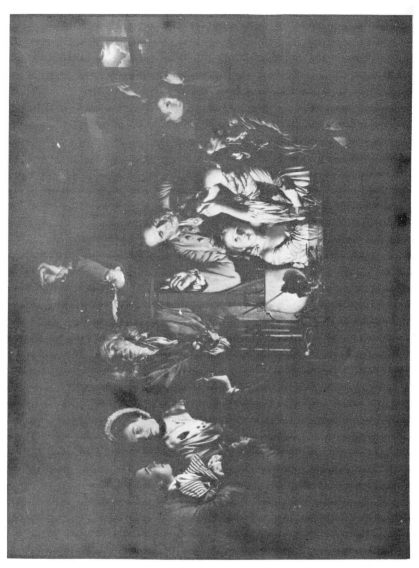

Plate 7. J. Wright of Derby, *An Experiment on a Bird in an Airpump.*

Plate 8. J. Wright of Derby, *An Academy by Lamplight*.

Plate 9. B. West, *Death of General Wolfe.*

Plate 11. J. Barry, *Portrait of Edmund Burke and the Artist in the Character of Ulysses and his Companions escaping from the Cave of Polyphemus.*

Plate 10. J. Reynolds, *Lady Charlotte Spencer.*

Plate 12. R. Wilson, *Cader Idris: Llyn-y-Cau.*

Plate 13. G. Barret, *Powerscourt Waterfall.*

Plate 14. G. Barret (and S. Gilpin), *Llanberis Lake, North Wales.*

Plate 15. J. Wright of Derby, *Vesuvius in Eruption*.

Plate 16. W. Marlowe, *Lake Geneva*.

Plate 17. W. Hodges, *A Crater in the Pacific*.

Plate 18. W. Hodges, *The Monuments of Easter Island*.

Plate 19. J. Webber, *Poedooa*.

Plate 20. J. Reynolds, *Omai*.

Plate 21. J. Reynolds, *Wang-y-Tong*.

Plate 22. G. Stubbs, *Kangaroo*.

Plate 23. G. Stubbs, *A Tiger*.

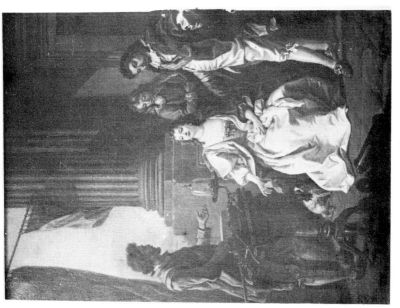

Plate 25.   C.A.P. Van Loo, *Experiment on a Bird in an Airpump.*

Plate 24.   G. Stubbs, *Lion Attacking a Horse.*

Plate 26. B. West, *Death of Epaminondas*.

Plate 27. B. West, *Death of the Chevalier Bayard*.

Plate 28. J. Barry, *Death of Adonis.*

Plate 29. R. Wilson. *Celadon and Amelia.*

Plate 30. W. Williams, *Celadon and Amelia.*

Plate 31. G. Romney, *King Lear in the Tempest*.

Plate 32. J. Runciman, *King Lear in the Storm*.

Plate 34. J. Barry, *Philoctetes*.

Plate 33. A. Runciman, *Fingal Engaging the Spirit of Loda*.

Plate 35. B. West, *Cave of Despair.*

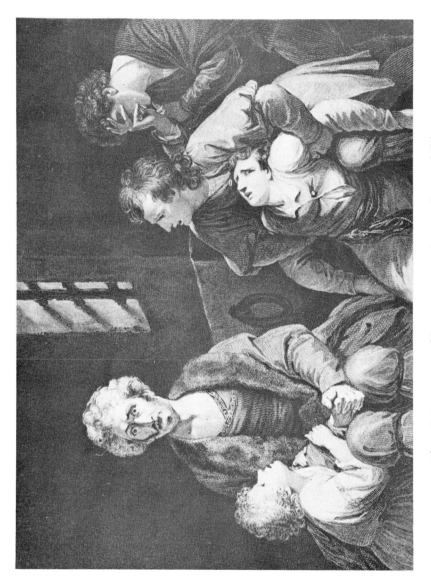

Plate 36. J. Reynolds, *Count Ugolino and His Children.*

Plate 37. H. Fuseli, *The Dream of Prince Arthur.*

Plate 39. J. Mortimer, *Sextus the Son of Pompey Applying to Erictho to Know the Fate of the Battle of Pharsalia.*

Plate 38. B. West, *Saul and the Witch of Endor.*

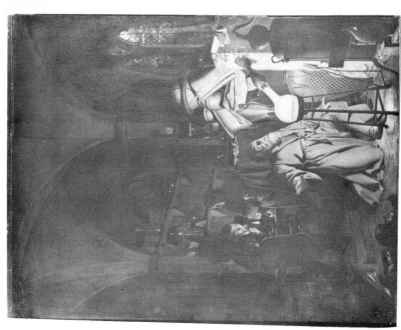

Plate 40. J. Wright of Derby, *The Alchemist*.

Plate 41. J. Reynolds, *Recovery from Sickness (an Allegory)*.

Plate 42. J. Wright of Derby, *The Old Man and Death.*

Plate 43. John Singleton Copley, *Watson and the Shark*.

Plate 44. J. Mortimer, *Death on a Pale Horse*.

Plate 45. T. Jones, *The Bard.*

Plate 46. J. Ward, *Gordale Scar.*

Plate 47. Portrait of Chin Nung.

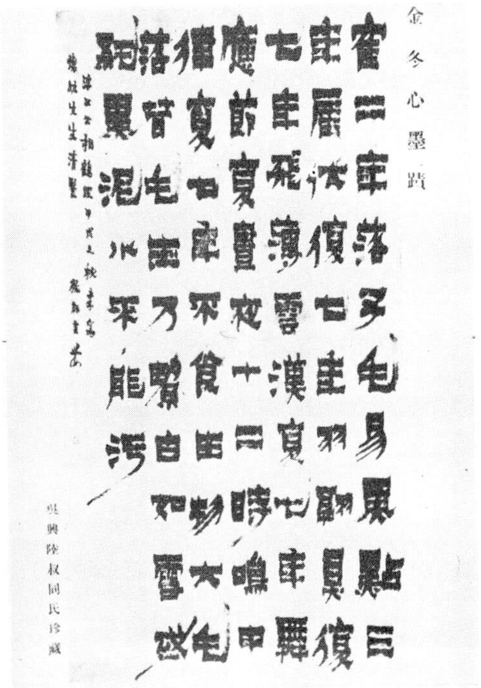

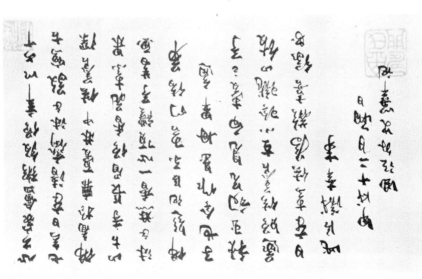

Plate 48. A typical example of Chin Nung's calligraphy:
Li Shu style.

Plate 49. A typical example of Chin Nung's calligraphy:
Hsing Shu style.

空山極寂闊自足斷緣想況此山中人智識已超朗
兀立志朝膽留定非免殆豈惟人班知異類赤欽仰乃
知象教力集用眼裟翅唯：世上人撥：向塵細叩左弄
無言何由剗次廣
乾隆丁卯三月十有六日杭郡金農畫記

Plate 50. Bodhidarma crossing
the river on a branch.

Plate 51. Portrait of a
monk.

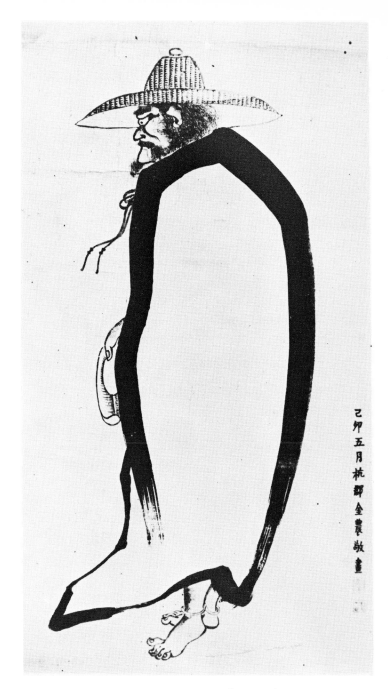

己卯五月杭郡金農敬畫

Plate 52. Portrait of a monk.

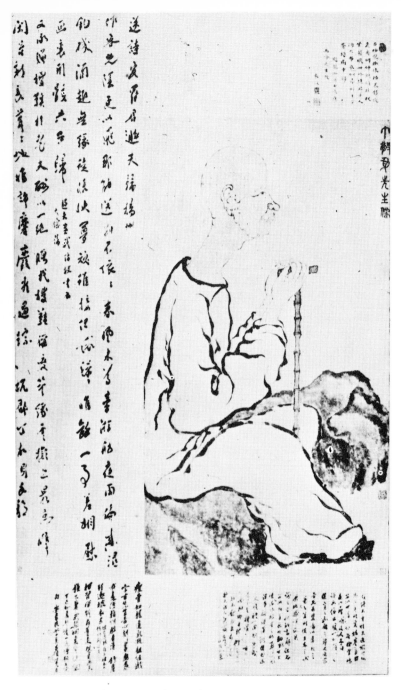

Plate 53. The seal carver Ting Ching.

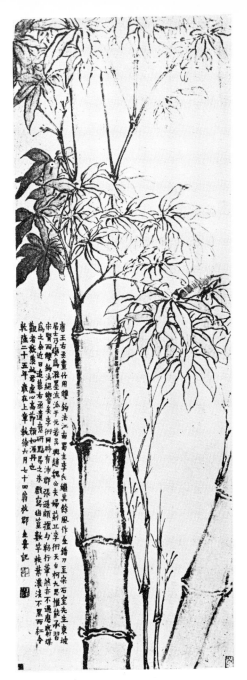

Plate 54. Bamboo.

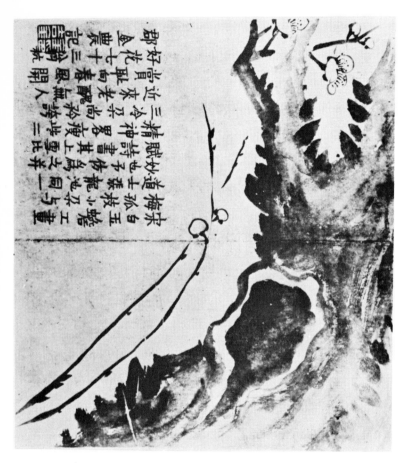

Plate 55. Plum blossom and old tree trunk.

禿筆梛骅骝韋侯畫馬之妙也其紅鬃覆背圖一軸乾隆元年見之
京師王侍郎宅曾題詩左方侍郎遊後此畫為厮養卒竊去
歸之内城賣漿家矣今粘豪追想其意所謂頭一點尾一抹者
乃於素縑中摹得之每逢上巳浣幕之日亦無有斜陽芳草香
韓幹遠之感也　　乾隆二十五年四月百二硯田富翁金農畫記

Plate 56. Old horse.

Plate 57. Buffalo and sleeping man.

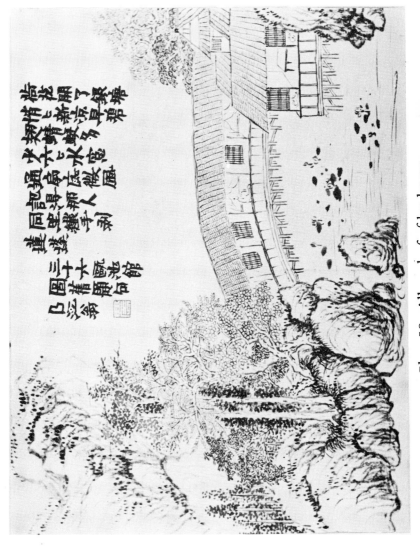

Plate 58. Album leaf of landscape.

Plate 59. Chin Nung at the age of seventy-five.

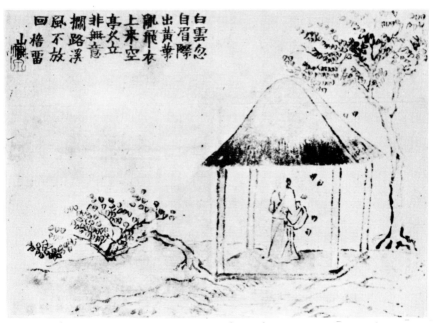

Plate 60. Autumn: Man standing alone in empty pavilion.